# Bigg's Cost and Management Accounts

Volume One
Cost Accounts

# Bigg's Cost and Management Accounts

### 10th EDITION

### Volume One
## COST ACCOUNTS

## J. WALD, A.C.M.A.
*Head of Management Studies*
*H. Foulks Lynch and Co. Ltd.*

## MACDONALD AND EVANS

MACDONALD & EVANS LTD.
Estover, Plymouth PL6 7PZ

*First published as* "Cost Accounts" *1932*
*Second edition 1934*
*Third edition 1935*
*Fourth edition 1937*
*Fifth edition 1939*
*Reprinted 1941, 1944, 1945 (twice), 1946, 1947 (twice), 1948*
*Sixth edition 1950*
*Reprinted 1950, 1951, 1952, 1953, 1954, 1955, 1956*
*Seventh edition 1957*
*Reprinted 1959, 1960, 1961*
*Eighth edition 1963*
*Reprinted 1964, 1965, 1966, (with amendments) 1967, 1969, 1970*
*Ninth edition 1972*
*Reprinted 1973, 1974, 1975, 1976*
*Tenth edition (in two volumes) 1978*

ISBN 0 7121 0263 9

©

MACDONALD AND EVANS LIMITED
1978

*Printed in Great Britain by Richard Clay (The Chaucer Press), Ltd.,*
*Bungay, Suffolk*

# Preface to the Tenth Edition

In recent years, several important developments have occured in the fields of cost accounting and management accounting, especially in relation to the examinations set by the major professional bodies. The substantial revision contained in this edition is an attempt to reflect those developments so that the needs of students are more precisely accommodated.

The major change lies in the scope of subject matter covered. It has become apparent that it is impractical to attempt to cover, in a single volume, the wide range of topics now included in cost accounting and management accounting examinations; the tenth edition is designed to prepare students for cost accounting at Foundation level or at early Professional stage. To meet the objective, coverage of certain subjects has been expanded while others have been condensed or deferred to a later volume. Self-study tests, together with outline solutions, further reflect the intention to improve the book's usefulness as an aid to study.

The revision also incorporates the clearer definition of principles and techniques embodied in *Terminology of Management and Financial Accountancy* published by the Institute of Cost and Management Accountants. My thanks are due to the Council of the Institute for permission to reproduce extracts from that publication.

Finally, I would like to express a personal view as one who has worked in industry and commerce before moving to the academic field. In my experience, many problems which arise in the day-to-day operation of a cost accounting system involve a compromise between the ideal and the practicable. When attempting to solve such problems, a return to basic principles can often help and an accountant or administrator in business may be well advised to keep abreast of any conceptual developments, even when the subject is one which is well established and has clearly defined principles.

*October* 1977                                                    J.W.

# Contents

# List of Illustrations

# CHAPTER 1

# The Role of Cost Accounting

## THE NEED FOR ACCOUNTING

In all the varied fields of human activity we try to make the best use of the limited resources that are available to us. The intention is to obtain the greatest output from a given input and in measuring this we may state how efficiently the input has been used. The quest for improvements in efficiency is characteristic of a materialistic society but it is not confined to industry and commerce. The aim to get value for money and increase our material standard of living would appear to be an essential part of our daily lives.

While the measurement of efficiency may be done in quantitative terms, e.g. a number of kilograms of wheat from a hectare of ground, it is normally essential to express inputs and outputs in terms of money—this is the common denominator of the resources we use. Thus the cost of inputs is measured against the value of the output, value being expressed as perhaps the price a person may be willing to pay, or the cost of an alternative equivalent item. By recording monetary values the accountant can measure the results of industrial and commercial activities and convey information to those persons who can direct the activities. The success of a business depends to a large extent upon an adequate measurement of its activities because, once the critical areas have been thrown into relief, the managers are able to bring their concentrated efforts and expertise to bear upon them.

The focus of accounting has developed over the years from recording movements in cash and transactions with third parties to the provision of financial data; data to help management plan future activities; data to measure how efficiently activities are being managed; and data to assist in solving problems as they arise.

The accounting function embraces financial accounting, cost accounting and management accounting. Cost accounting may be described as making available cost data by means of operating a cost recording system. Management accounting uses cost and financial data to advise management in planning and controlling the enterprise.

It is beyond the scope of this book to consider all aspects of management accounting, but the management accountant uses cost data and therefore there will be an overlap. The reader should note that it is vital for the management accountant to be familiar with costing systems because, if there are any shortcomings in the cost data he uses, much of his work will be meaningless and, sometimes, positively harmful. Both cost and financial data are tools for the management accountant and their limitations must be appreciated before they can be properly used.

## FINANCIAL AND COST ACCOUNTING

The financial accountant is largely concerned with transactions between an undertaking and those with whom it is in contractual relationship, i.e. with suppliers, customers, employees and others to or from whom money is ultimately paid or received. In recording these transactions, references in cases of difficulty may be made to company law, case decisions, the recommendations of the accountancy bodies and to the rules of sound professional practice. He is concerned with the ascertainment of the profit of the business as a whole, i.e. with reporting on past events by means of accounts. Annual accounts are prepared for presentation to the shareholders and the Inland Revenue and there are many signposts to guide the financial accountant in the presentation of the figures.

The cost accountant will draw on information provided by the financial accounting system but he will also need to obtain much more detail of the internal workings of the business. He will use data in monetary and non-monetary forms, e.g. hours worked, quantity of materials used, products manufactured, machine running hours, idle time, etc. He is concerned with finding the actual cost of products, operations and departments, often comparing this with an estimated or ideal cost.

## THE COST ACCOUNTING SERVICE

Some of the work of the cost accountant will be directed towards evaluating stocks and work-in-progress for the financial accounts. Also, he may be responsible for supplying estimating and pricing departments with cost information in order that estimates and selling prices may reflect costs incurred. Those aspects of his work, however, are overshadowed by the important function of maintaining an information service to provide cost data for management.

*EXAMPLE*

A chocolate manufacturer finds that his net profit for the past two years and his estimated profit for the current year (based on ten months actual and two months estimated) is showing a decline:

|  | Year 1 | Year 2 | Year 3 |
|---|---|---|---|
|  | £'000 | £'000 | £'000 |
| Sales | 1,000 | 1,200 | 1,500 |
| Costs | 800 | 1,050 | 1,450 |
| Profit | 200 | 150 | 50 |

After investigation the cost accountant supplies the following data:

| | | | |
|---|---|---|---|
| Sales units ('000s) | 10,000 | 15,000 | 20,000 |
| Average price (£) | 0.10 | 0.08 | 0.075 |
| Cocoa used ('000s kg) | 2,600 | 4,000 | 7,000 |
| Sugar used ('000s kg) | 1,000 | 1,600 | 2,800 |
| Labour hours paid ('000s) | 200 | 300 | 550 |
| Idle hours ('000s) | 10 | 20 | 80 |

|  | £'000 | £'000 | £'000 |
|---|---|---|---|
| Cocoa | 250 | 390 | 510 |
| Sugar | 150 | 80 | 120 |
| Other ingredients | 50 | 75 | 130 |
| Wrapping paper | 50 | 90 | 105 |
| Labour | 100 | 160 | 250 |
| Salaries | 75 | 80 | 85 |
| Office costs | 60 | 65 | 70 |
| Selling and distribution | 50 | 80 | 125 |
| Overtime and shift premium | 5 | 10 | 30 |
| Sundries | 10 | 20 | 25 |
|  | 800 | 1,050 | 1,450 |

The analysis reveals many fluctuations that require explanation. The unit sales price has declined while more ingredients have been used than are warranted by the output in terms of sales units. The increase in idle time and shift and overtime premium is another unwelcome feature. The whole statement seems to indicate a history of inadequate planning and control. The reader will appreciate that the investigation has merely brought to light past weaknesses. It is now the responsibility of the manufacturer to take appropriate action to reverse the unprofitable trends. Thus, formal plans, budgets and standards must be established which will form the basis for planning future activity and provide a yardstick against which performance may be measured.

This aspect of planning and control assumes increasing importance as businesses grow in size and complexity. The proprietor of a small business, aided by common sense or intuition, can usually gauge the efficiency of his business. He is near enough to each section to form accurate judgments and to act quickly in order to correct anything he considers to be unsatisfactory. As a business grows, however, the proprietor tends to become more and more remote from the factory floor as problems of policy increasingly claim his attention. He is therefore compelled to delegate much of his authority and at the same time, to control his executives to ensure that each is performing efficiently and within the general policy which he has established. He finds it necessary to look for quantitative interpretations of performance, where previously his eye told him all he wanted to know, and it is at this point that the cost accountant comes to his assistance. The ways in which this assistance is given forms much of the subject matter of this book. At this stage it is sufficient to emphasise that the cost accountant deals not only with cost ascertainment but also with current results compared with plans, and the analysis of any variations.

Much has been written by management experts on the subject of the management control process and emphasis has been given to the significance of planning as being the most important aspect of management control. Cost accounting will serve in this field in a variety of ways, both in formal long-term planning and also in day-to-day decision-making. As a guide to the ways in which cost accounting will be called upon to help management the following questions are typical of the type of problem confronting the cost accountant:

1. Should an attempt be made to sell more products, or is the factory, warehouse or shop already operating to capacity?

2. If the manufacture or sale of product A were discontinued and efforts made to increase those of product B, what would be the effect on net profit?

3. If an order or contract is accepted, is the price obtainable sufficient to show a profit?

4. Why is it that the financial accounts for last year showed such a small profit, despite the fact that the output of product A was increased substantially?

5. If a machine is purchased (as recommended by the works engineer) to carry out a job at present done by hand, what effect will this have on profits?

6. Wage-rates have increased by 15p per hour; should selling prices be increased and, if so, by how much?

The ordinary financial accounts of the business will not help to answer these questions, and there is no reason why they should, as they are prepared for a totally different purpose, viz. to show the proprietors the overall trading result for a period and the financial position of the business at the date of the Balance Sheet. In any case, the financial accounts are probably prepared only at yearly or half-yearly intervals and, frequently, at some considerable time after the end of the period to which they relate, so that they are historical rather than topical. On the other hand, a system of cost accounts must provide management with prompt and accurate information as to the cost of a certain section (e.g. a particular job or contract, or a particular department or service) and details of how the cost has been arrived at.

## COST ACCOUNTING SYSTEMS

Without an effective system of cost accounts it is doubtful whether a business of any size can survive in the intensely competitive conditions of today, but it must be emphasised that no two businesses are alike, even in the same industry, so that no ready-made system of cost accounts can be provided to suit each and every business. The underlying principles, conventions and objects of all costing systems are the same, but the application of those principles and the methods by which the objects are to be achieved must vary with circumstances. This does not mean, however, that the processes and procedures of a business must remain unaffected by the introduction of a system of cost accounts. The preliminary investigation which must be made before a system is installed will often disclose weaknesses and inefficiencies, and, if the costing records are to be accurate, a system of materials, wages and production control is essential. Assuming that the organisation is reasonably satisfactory, the system of costing should be practical, i.e. it must be designed to suit the business. There must be no attempt to make the business suit the system.

Furthermore, the cost of the costing system must be considered in relation to the size of the business and the benefits to be obtained. The system must not be over-elaborate, but in considering its cost, the savings which should accrue through the control of materials, labour and production which the system affords should be borne in mind. In particular, careful consideration should be given to the following matters:

### Requirements of the management
Cost accounting is part of the overall management information service and care must be taken to ensure that there is no duplication by reporting the same matter in a different way. Further, only information which is relevant in the context of helping management to manage the business should be reported upon.

### Factory layout and production sequence
The cost accounting system must have regard to the points at which work has begun and finished and where the finished product of one section becomes the input to the next section. Further, the incidence

of scrapped work and the point at which it is normally recognised will be important. The costing system will also need to reflect the location and purpose of items of plant and machinery.

### Control exercised over production
The costing data must identify specific areas of control so that each foreman or manager may take action on the information relevant to his activity. By merely showing the total expenses of a whole department the cost accountant is not helping the manager to direct his attention to trouble spots.

### Nature of the raw materials used
It is inherent in the nature of some materials that a high degree of waste will occur, e.g. finely powdered chemicals, evaporable solvents, etc. With materials used in bulk it may be difficult to measure the usage accurately. These matters will affect the system adopted for recording issue of material.

### Deployment of workers
Workers may be employed to work as individuals or as a team, in doing simple repetitive work or in highly skilled work, at a single work station or moving round the factory, or even moving from place to place outside the factory. The method of remuneration and the analysis of time worked will be influenced by these factors.

### Key personnel and the office staff
Much of the cost data will originate from the factory level, figures and codes being recorded by clerical and non-clerical workers. Managers and foremen will be responsible for seeing this is done adequately and it is they who will ultimately use reports and statistics prepared from this data. The scheme must be seen as an aid and not a burden, otherwise their lack of co-operation may wreck the system. Simplicity will be the keynote of a successful scheme.

### Relative size of the cost items
There is no useful purpose in going to great length to analyse items of insignificant value. For example, the total cost of stationery is normally a sufficient heading on an expense report without considering the values of paper, pens, rubber bands, paper clips, etc., separately.

### Need for uniformity
A business that belongs to a trade association will normally follow its association's recommendations on cost accounting principles in order to facilitate comparison of its own cost data with averages produced for the industry. In addition, if a business is in association

with others, e.g. through a holding company, there are advantages in adopting common cost accounting practices.

## Practical considerations

The technical staff must be consulted and due weight given to their views and suggestions when framing the system. It is usually wiser to make haste slowly and to gain the co-operation, stage by stage, of all concerned, rather than to thrust a complete system of costing upon a business whose staff are not ready for it and who may, in fact, be hostile to it. A system of costing must be an investment and must produce benefits commensurate with the expenditure in time and money incurred in running it. Although theory may demand a certain procedure, if it is found in practice that this is inexpedient or unduly expensive it must, for the time being at any rate, be discarded in favour of something more practicable. The system should be flexible and capable of adaptation to changing conditions. It should be basically logical and simple, so that it does not fall to pieces if one or more of the costing staff leave the service of the business or are promoted. Every system requires periodical and skilled scrutiny to avoid the danger of obsolescence due to changes and developments in the business.

# PRINCIPLES OF COST ACCOUNTING

## Cost units

The Trading and Profit and Loss Accounts in the financial books of a business are designed to disclose the financial results as a whole and in respect of a definite period. The principal items of expenditure and income are usually shown in the accounts under headings which will describe the nature of the cost or revenue. Some accountants will analyse expenditure to such an extent that every type of expense is shown under a separate caption in the accounts; others are content to employ only a few main headings sufficient to give a general indication of the items included. However detailed the accounts may be, they reveal merely the net result of the collective activities of the business. Expenditure in total is set against total turnover or income, but no detailed information is afforded to the exact manner in which the net profit or loss has been made.

It will be appreciated that the total turnover may comprise many varied products, services, jobs or contracts, some of which may be profitable, while others are being conducted at a loss. Considerable benefit therefore will be derived from accounts which disclose the separate result of each activity, and at the same time reveal in detail how such a result has been achieved.

The extent to which the analysis of expenditure should be carried out will depend upon the nature of the business and the degree of accuracy desired. Expenditure will ultimately be charged to "cost units", which are defined by the Institute of Cost and Management Accountants as follows:

> *Cost unit.* A quantitative unit of product or service, in relation to which costs are ascertained.

The cost unit must not be confused with the cost centre, which is usually an intermediate point to which expenditure can be charged for later distribution, if necessary, between cost units.

The cost units and centres should be those most natural to the business and which are readily understood and accepted by all concerned. Thus, a building contractor will allocate expenditure to each individual contract; a brewer will wish to ascertain the cost of a barrel of beer; a quarry, the cost per tonne of stone raised; a brickmaker, the cost per 1,000 bricks. For the last three businesses it will also be desirable to ascertain the cost per unit of each of the various processes through which the beer, stone or bricks pass before they are rendered saleable.

## Cost centres

To facilitate the charging of costs to cost units, it is invariably necessary to divide the business into logical parts which can be conveniently used to accumulate costs for subsequent distribution.

In addition, this separation will permit the cost of identifiable activities and departments to be disclosed and will assist in relating costs to individual responsibility.

Such sections of the business are termed "cost centres". The following definitions have been given by the Institute of Cost and Management Accountants:

> *Cost centre.* A location, person or item of equipment (or group of these) in respect of which costs may be ascertained and related to cost units.
>
> *Process cost centre.* A cost centre in which a specific process or a continuous sequence of operations is carried out.
>
> *Production cost centre.* A cost centre in which production is carried on.
>
> *Service cost centre.* A cost centre for the provision of a service or services to other cost centres.
>
> NOTE: This term does not usually apply when the output of an organisation is a service, rather than goods.

## Direct and indirect costs

Before attempting to charge costs to cost centres or cost units it is important to consider why costs are incurred. Whereas in the

Trading and Profit and Loss Accounts costs are classified by nature, it is important in cost accounting to regard them from a different viewpoint.

Direct costs are those which are incurred for, and may be conveniently identified with, a particular cost centre or cost unit. A steel forging will be a direct (materials) cost as regards the finished product, and a time clerk's wages are a direct (wages) cost for a particular department.

Indirect costs are those which are incurred for the benefit of a number of cost centres or cost units and therefore cannot be conveniently identified with a particular cost centre or cost unit. Rates paid to a local authority is an example of an expense which benefits a number of cost centres, and the time clerk's wages referred to above would be an example of an indirect (wages) cost of the units produced by his department.

A cost that is direct for a cost centre may be indirect as regards the cost unit produced by that cost centre.

*EXAMPLE*

The following annual costs are incurred by a manufacturing company in which there are two production centres of equal area:

| | |
|---|---|
| Indirect costs, e.g. rates | £400 |
| Cost centre costs, e.g.: | |
| Time clerks: Cost centre 1 | £500 |
| Cost centre 2 | £600 |

Raw material (steel forging) = £2 per unit
Production wages = £1 per unit

The production costs would be calculated as follows:

| | *Cost centre 1* | *Cost centre 2* |
|---|---|---|
| Indirect costs (shared on area basis) | £200 | £200 |
| Cost centre costs | 500 | 600 |
| | £700 | £800 |
| Production | 700 units | 400 units |
| Indirect cost per unit | £1 | £2 |
| Direct wages cost | 1 | 1 |
| Direct material cost | 2 | 2 |
| Production cost | £4 | £5 |

The total costs incurred in cost centre 1 are £2,800, i.e. £4 × 700 units, and of these £2,100 represents the direct cost of production (direct wages and direct materials) and £700 represents costs which are shared by each unit produced in cost centre 1. However, of the

£700 indirect costs, £200 represents a sharing of total indirect factory costs. In normal cost accounting language we may say the direct costs can be allotted or *allocated* wholly to cost centres or units whereas indirect costs are *apportioned* over cost centres or units.

The reader will note that in cost centre 2 the indirect part of unit costs represents 40 per cent of production cost, and that this has been arrived at by a series of arbitrary calculations; firstly, the apportionment of a share of indirect costs to cost centre 2 and secondly, by averaging the cost centre costs of £800 over production of 400 units. It is impossible to say whether each unit produced by cost centre 2 actually cost £5, but it is the closest to an actual cost that can be obtained. This illustrates the cost accountants' problem of apportioning indirect costs to cost centres and units in order to reflect (as accurately as is warranted by the size of the figure) the proportion by which the cost unit has benefited. Thus the cost accountant will seek to treat most items of cost as direct so that by identifying each item at an early stage with a cost unit he does not have to use averaging methods. However, he must be realistic in his work and for convenience will treat insignificant items as indirect so that the analysis work is reduced. For instance, nails and washers used in production will be treated as indirect costs although with some effort each nail could perhaps be identified with the finished product.

It will be appreciated that the nature of the business and the cost unit chosen will determine which are direct and which are indirect expenses. For example, the hire of a mobile crane for use by a contractor at a site would be regarded as a direct expense to the cost unit, i.e. the contract, but if the crane is used as part of the services of a factory, the hire would be regarded as an indirect expense, because it would probably benefit more than one cost unit, and it might not be convenient or possible to allocate the hire charge to individual cost units with any degree of accuracy.

**Cost classification**
It is common practice to collect costs under suitable headings in the cost and financial accounts and the headings will clearly be chosen to suit the type of business. In a manufacturing organisation, the following headings are often used:

> Production cost      General administration cost
> Marketing cost        Research cost
> Development cost

The above represents classification by major function. It will be apparent that costs can be further classified by sub-function, e.g. marketing costs by selling, publicity and distribution, by nature (subjective classification) and by cost centre (objective classification).

The value of such classifications is that where comparisons are made between businesses or between accounting periods, at least like will be compared with like. Clearly, for detailed cost investigations initiated to provide information on specific matters, these headings may not be helpful.

It may be useful at this stage to consider a typical cost estimate for a job to be manufactured and delivered to a customer:

| | |
|---|---:|
| Direct production materials: 2 kg of X | £1.50 |
| Direct production wages: 4 hours at £1.50 per hour | 6.00 |
| Direct production expenses: special finishing process by sub-contractor | 3.00 |
| | |
| PRIME COST | 10.50 |
| Indirect factory costs (apportionment) | 4.50 |
| | |
| PRODUCTION COST | 15.00 |
| Direct selling costs: salesman's commission | 0.30 |
| Indirect selling costs (apportionment) | 2.40 |
| Direct distribution costs: freight and insurance | 1.80 |
| Indirect distribution costs (apportionment) | 1.50 |
| Indirect administration costs (apportionment) | 3.00 |
| | |
| TOTAL COST | 24.00 |
| Profit | 6.00 |
| | |
| SELLING PRICE | £30.00 |

Production cost comprises:

Direct production materials ⎫
Direct production wages     ⎬ Prime cost.
Direct production expenses  ⎭

*plus* Indirect factory costs comprising direct and indirect cost centre costs (as previously described).

It should be noted that prime cost specifically excludes direct non-manufacturing costs, e.g. commission to a salesman, or a freight charge incurred wholly for a particular cost unit.

In cost accounting language, all indirect costs are termed "overhead" so that, for instance, indirect factory costs are called factory overhead.

## Fixed and variable costs

The cost accounting system has been presented so far as a formal system of analysing cost data between cost centres and units and distinguishing direct from indirect costs. The purpose is to identify costs with the cost centres or units for which they are incurred and thus help in cost control, evaluating stocks and price fixing. However, in planning future activities and making day-to-day decisions involving a choice between alternatives, the question that often needs to be asked is not "who benefits from a cost?" but "how is this cost incurred?" In the previous example, if an order was received for 1,000 units the buyer might expect a substantial reduction in price by way of a quantity discount. Management will expect the cost accountant to give advice on this matter, and he will need to have detailed knowledge of the relationship between cost levels and the volume of output. There will be those costs which remain unaffected by changes in output; rent, for example, will not increase when the factory is working overtime to produce more units. Other costs will tend to be directly affected by changes in volume—the material cost, for example. Many costs (semi-variable) will tend to rise with volume increases but not in direct proportion.

The analysis of costs in relation to changes in activity is crucial to management control and decision-making, and is dealt with at length in Chapter 12.

**Integration of cost and financial accounts**
Enough has been written to indicate that there is no one cost accounting system which will suit every business. A flexible approach is essential and one must not be afraid of adopting expedient measures. However, although the cost accountant will be prepared at times to sacrifice 100 per cent accuracy in the interests of timing and relevance of information, the formal system of cost accounts must agree with the financial accounts as essentially they are dealing with the same basic data. Cost accounting in terms of double-entry systems is dealt with in Chapter 13.

## BASIC COSTING METHODS

Most firms, industrial and commercial, can be grouped together according to type, e.g. mining, agriculture, building, manufacturing, transport, catering, insurance, banking, wholesaling, retailing, etc. All the firms in a group will be involved in similar work processes having similar production and control problems and, therefore, principles have developed which the cost accountant may use in formulating a system of cost accounting for a particular business.

Industry can be grouped into two basic types: those firms which manufacture identical products, e.g. gas, electricity, bread, bricks, etc., and those which manufacture related but different products, e.g. made-to-measure suits, special purpose machines, etc. There are many firms that fall between the two types—where batches of identical products or slight variations of the basic products are made. Consequently, there are two basic costing methods, specific order costing and operation costing.

## Specific order costing

This method is applicable where the work consists of separate contracts, jobs or batches, each of which is authorised by a specific order or contract (I.C.M.A.). In a jobbing business, work moving through the factory can be clearly identified. Normally, raw material is issued at the beginning and is physically transported from one department to another, operations being performed which gradually convert the material into the finished product. The identifiable direct costs are charged to the order and also a share of the indirect costs of each department. This may be shown graphically, *see* Fig. 1.

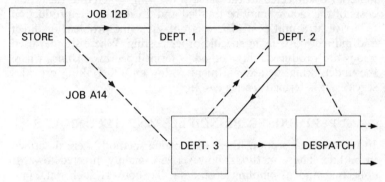

FIG. 1.—*Flow of work in a jobbing business.*

The material for Job 12B in Fig 1 is processed in departments 1, 2 and 3, whereas Job A14 only requires processing in department 3 and then 2.

Sometimes the nature of the work requires the operations to be performed outside the factory, and each order is of a relatively long duration, e.g. housebuilding and central heating installation. The principles of job costing apply, but there will be certain distinguishing features. Costing for construction contracts is termed contract costing.

It is in the interests of production management to obtain, where possible, long runs on machines. This reduces set-up costs and makes better use of factory capacity. There is, therefore, emphasis on standardising products and even where this is difficult it is often found possible to standardise the component parts. This leads to batch costing, where a batch of identical components is treated as a job and costed as such. The total cost of the completed batch is averaged over the number of components.

## Operation costing

Operation costing is the basic costing method applicable where standardised goods or services result from a sequence of repetitive and more or less continuous operations or processes to which costs are charged before being averaged over the units produced during the period (I.C.M.A.). Graphically, it may be shown as in Fig. 2.

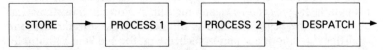

FIG. 2.—*Flow of work in a processing business.*

The reader should compare this diagram with Fig. 1. All the material is subjected to the same processing. Therefore the whole costs of the factory may be totalled and divided by the production to arrive at a unit cost. There is not the same problem of direct and indirect costs as in specific order costing. Where standardised goods are produced, the method is termed *process costing*; where the undertaking, or a department within an undertaking provides services, it is termed *service costing*.

## SUPERIMPOSED PRINCIPLES AND TECHNIQUES

In the previous section, the basic costing methods were described in outline. Those methods, however, are mainly directed towards collecting and assembling cost data. To convert such data into meaningful management information, certain established principles and techniques are available; principles and techniques devised to suit the purpose for which the information is required.

Most of this book is concerned with explaining the purposes and applications of the principles and techniques and as the reader enlarges his understanding, he will develop a critical awareness of their limitations and benefits. Meanwhile, a general understanding of the meaning of the terms used will suffice. For that purpose, the definitions recommended by the I.C.M.A. are ideal.

*Absorption costing.* A principle whereby fixed as well as variable costs are allotted to cost units. The term may be applied where (*a*) production costs only, or (*b*) costs of all functions are so allotted.

*Marginal costing.* A principle whereby marginal costs of cost units are ascertained. Only variable costs are charged to cost units, the fixed costs attributable to a relevant period being written off in full against the contribution for that period.

NOTE: It is recommended that the term be applied only where the *routine* system incorporates the marginal principle.

*Actual cost ascertainment.* A principle whereby costs of cost centres and cost units are ascertained which, subject to certain approximations, are deemed to represent actual costs. (The term "historical costing" is often used to describe this concept but is not recommended because the word "historical" may equally be applied to other concepts, e.g. statements of variances related to past events.)

*Variance accounting.* A technique whereby the planned activities of an undertaking are expressed in budgets, standard costs, standard selling prices and standard profit margins, and the differences between these and the comparable actual results are accounted for. Management is periodically presented with an analysis of differences by causes and responsibility centres, such analysis usually commencing with the operating profit variance. The technique also includes the establishment of a suitable arrangement of accounts in the principal ledger.

*Standard costing.* The preparation of standard costs of products and services.

*Budgetary control.* The establishment of budgets relating the responsibilities of executives to the requirements of a policy, and the continuous comparison of actual with budgeted results, either to secure by individual action the objective of that policy or to provide a basis for its revision.

NOTE: The term *variance accounting* is more appropriate where planned performances are expressed in standard costs per unit of product or service as well as in budgets, all being used in comparisons with actual results.

*Variance analysis.* That part of variance accounting which relates to the analysis into constituent parts of variances between planned and actual performance.

*Differential costing.* A technique used in the preparation of *ad hoc* information in which only cost and income differences between alternative courses of action are taken into consideration.

*Incremental costing.* A technique used in the preparation of *ad hoc* information where consideration is given to a range of graduated changes in the level or nature of activity. The additional costs and revenues likely to result from each degree of change are presented.

*Uniform costing.* The use by several undertakings of the same costing systems, i.e. the same basic costing methods and super-imposed principles and techniques.

## PURPOSES OF COST ACCOUNTING

Before moving into the next few chapters concerned with obtaining data and applying it usefully, it may be helpful at this point to summarise the purposes of cost accounting because these must be kept constantly in mind. The list cannot be exhaustive as each business will doubtless find other advantages which are secured by its own system.

1. To disclose profitable and unprofitable activities so that steps can be taken to eliminate or reduce those from which little or no benefit is obtained, or to change the method of production or incidence of cost in order to render such activities more profitable.

2. To analyse the various items of expense incurred so that wastage can be traced and economies effected.

3. To provide data for comparison of costs.

4. To provide information upon which estimates and tenders may be based. Prices may be adjusted to meet market conditions, so as to ensure that no orders are lost through prices which are either too high or too low to be remunerative. These matters are of vital importance in obtaining orders in competitive markets.

5. To indicate the exact cause of a decrease or an increase in profit or loss shown by the financial accounts.

6. To provide the cost information necessary for realistic stock valuations.

### SELF-STUDY TEST No. 1

*The Role of Cost Accounting*

(*Refer to the Appendix on p. 339 for outline solutions.*)

1. Accounting data is provided to assist in three main management activities. Describe the activities and give an example of the kind of data which would be provided for each activity.

2. List the major factors to be considered and analysed before a costing system is introduced.

3. Define "cost unit" and "cost centre"; give an example of each.

4. Explain why the separation of direct and indirect costs is important in cost accounting.

5. (*a*) Costs in a manufacturing organisation are usually classified by major function. Name the major functions.

(*b*) Give an example of:

(*i*) a subjective cost classification and

(*ii*) an objective classification within each major function.

6. Cost behaviour involves classifying costs in relation to the way they are affected by changes in the volume of activity; name the three behavioural classifications and give an example of each.

7. Name the basic costing methods and give an example of a type of business relevant to each method.

8. Show your understanding of the term "Variance Accounting" by describing what you consider to be the essential elements of such a system.

CHAPTER 2

# The Nature of Manufacturing Business

## A DYNAMIC UNIT

Within every business engaged in the manufacture and sale of products there is constant activity. Like a living organism it comprises many interdependent parts in which people are contributing towards changing the form of raw materials in order to supply customers with a desirable product, the overall object being to make a profit and continue in existence. The actual parts which can be clearly distinguished in the business will depend on its size and nature, but it is normally possible to identify the following major functions:

1. Administration.
2. Manufacturing.
3. Marketing.
4. Research and development.

It will be useful to refer to the organisation chart (Fig. 3) when considering the activities of the four parts.

## ADMINISTRATION

There are various aspects of administration, and it will be useful to study these briefly. Firstly, it is here that ultimate power and authority rests. The policy of the business is formulated and commands given to ensure that the objectives of the policy are achieved. Authority is embodied in a Board of Directors in the case of a company, from which it is delegated to a managing director, who in turn delegates to various executives.

Closely linked with the policy aspects of administration is the planning activity. Some larger companies have set up planning departments whose responsibility is to predict how the company can profitably exist in the future, with known changes in all factors affecting the business. Predictions are compared with basic objectives, and decisions taken to overcome obstacles preventing the objectives being realised.

A third aspect of administration is the management information service, which comprises secretarial, accounting and data processing

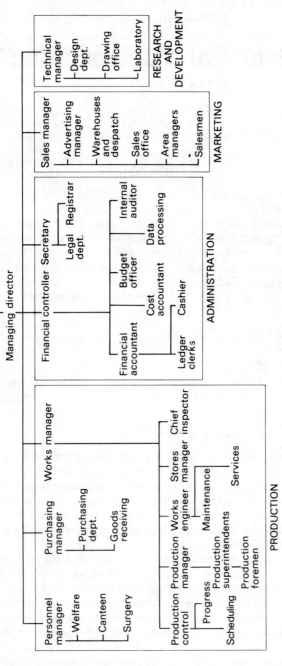

FIG. 3.—*Chart of a typical management structure.*

The above chart is not an attempt to state how formal links should always be arranged. The personnel and purchasing managers may sometimes report to the works manager, and data processing will occasionally come under a management information manager reporting direct to the managing director. The nature and size of the business and the personalities involved will have a considerable influence on the structure adopted. For example, a company engaged in a highly competitive business may well need a marketing executive supported by sales, publicity and distribution managers. Whilst senior executives have been identified with their specialist functions, they will also have an important role in policy making.

functions and also provides information in other areas, e.g. for marketing and production. The relationship of this final part of administration to planning and policy making will be apparent: they cannot function without reliable and comprehensive information.

# MANUFACTURING

Manufacturing is concerned with converting raw material into saleable products and involves production control and the departments which provide services as well as the workshops and processing centres themselves.

## Production centres
The production centres or workshops will be arranged according to the type of production and machines used, and each centre will come under the supervision of a foreman who reports to a production superintendent, who in turn reports to the production manager.

## Production control
The production control department is responsible to the production manager for seeing that the planned programme of work is carried out. Therefore it controls all activities directly concerned with manufacture. Detailed scheduling is required to ascertain material, labour and equipment requirements, and the production controllers must ensure that everything is available to begin production at a certain time in order that production facilities are fully utilised. The work programme is rarely a static instruction to manufacture the same number of products week after week. Where this is so, production control problems are few and may only arise when there are shortages of material or machine breakdowns. In most businesses, the work programme is determined by demand and therefore the production control department is concerned with analysing customer requirements in order to provide detailed schedules of material, machines, tools, etc., required for production. As products are completed or scrapped, and new orders come into the business, the work programme changes. Where the product comprises many hundreds or thousands of parts, e.g. an aircraft, the complexity of scheduling all requirements is such as to require the aid of computers. The preparations for production may be shown graphically as in Fig. 4.

It is the job of the progress clerks to keep records of production data and quantities to see that scheduled delivery dates are met. The clerks have no authority to switch production to more urgent work, but must bring information to the attention of the production supervisor who will then decide what action is to be taken.

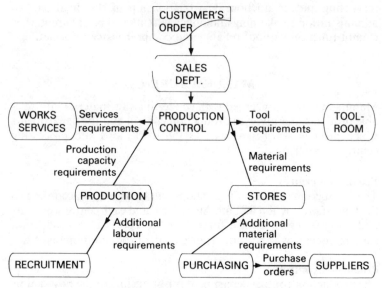

FIG. 4.—*Preparing for production.*

## Materials

The procedures for recording movements of material are dealt with in the next chapter, as they are complementary to the costing system. It is sufficient here to consider the chief functions involved, which are purchasing, storekeeping and inspection.

PURCHASING

This department has the responsibility of ensuring that the necessary supplies are purchased at an acceptable price, and that they are ready when required. The purchasing manager must keep adequate records to be aware of the reliability of suppliers to keep to delivery times, prices and quality, and he should always be seeking alternative sources of supply. So far as possible, all purchases should be made by the purchasing department, as this avoids duplication of work and difficulties over authorising purchase invoices.

STOREKEEPING

The duties of the storekeeper include the following:

1. Maintaining the stores in an orderly and tidy manner, preventing waste and deterioration by using suitable storage facilities, viz. correct bins, racks and other receptacles and, especially, accommodating perishable materials in such a manner that those longest in stock can be used first.

2. Accepting materials after ascertaining that they are in accordance with what has been ordered.

3. Recording receipts and issues so as to maintain a running total of each item in the stores.

4. Preventing the entry into the store of unauthorised persons and supplying goods only to those who have proper authority.

5. Advising the purchasing department when the stock of a material approaches the minimum or re-order level.

INSPECTION

The inspector is responsible for ensuring that materials purchased from suppliers are of the standard specified in the purchase order. He is also responsible for ensuring that finished and semi-finished products manufactured by the production centres are in accordance with inspection standards laid down by the technical departments or specified by the customer. Records will be kept of materials and work rejected.

## Labour

The personnel and welfare functions in most businesses tend to include both works and office employees and therefore often come directly under the managing director. In providing operators for the factory, the personnel manager will be guided by the production manager's advice on future requirements. Details of transfer requests and surplus operatives will be advised to him, so that the personnel manager is sometimes able to switch employees between departments to obviate recruiting additional labour.

## Services

Each business will have services peculiar to its production process. They may include space heating, steam, maintenance, compressed air, electricity, tools, drawings, etc. Not all of these activities will come under the same manager. Maintenance workers may report to the works engineer, whereas the drawing office will be controlled by the technical manager. However, the provision of the service must be controlled by the production schedule so that, for example, maintenance workers are available to service plant at times when it is not being used for production.

# MARKETING

The marketing function is usually deemed to include the activities connected with selling, publicising and distributing the product. Selling involves the practical task of obtaining orders and normally necessitates a sales force of representatives plus an office staff. Publicity embraces all forms of advertising and sales promotion.

Distribution is the sequence of operations from packing the product for despatch to ensuring that it safely reaches the customer.

## RESEARCH AND DEVELOPMENT

Research covers the activity of broadening knowledge about materials, etc., of searching for new ways to improve existing products, materials and by-products, and of improving production methods.

Development takes over from research once a new product or an improvement to an existing product has been authorised, and is responsible for detailing technical specifications, production methods, material requirements, etc., so that production can commence.

## THE COST ACCOUNTANT AND THE ORGANISATION

The cost accountant must make himself fully conversant with the areas within the business where the major items of cost are incurred. His attention will often be focused on these areas in seeking to help management to control and reduce costs and, as the custodian of cost information, he is responsible for guiding management in those areas where their concentrated activity will be most rewarding. No cost accountant should be content merely to record figures; as a member of the middle management team he must make the influence of his function felt within the business.

Part of the cost accountant's duties is to devise systems for recording costs, and the next few chapters deal with the systems for recording the three elements of cost, namely materials, wages and expenses.

# CHAPTER 3

# Materials

## PURCHASING AND STORES ROUTINE

Figure 5 illustrates the basic flow of materials and the documents used, but it is not intended to be exhaustive nor to apply to every business.

## ORIGINATING A PURCHASE

### The cost of purchasing

The purchasing procedure outlined in this chapter will be seen to involve a great deal of time and documents, and is therefore costly. Requisitions are placed on the purchasing department, enquiries sent to suppliers, quotations obtained and orders placed; then deliveries are received and recorded, and finally invoices are received, checked and paid. It is, therefore, important to consider how this routine can be simplified, or at least confined to purchases of significant value. The benefit of the purchasing procedure is in exercising control over the purchase orders and in obtaining the goods and services at the right time, quantity, quality and cost.

This is but one part of the problem of relating the degree of control exercised over various aspects of business activity to the costs which would be incurred if the control were relaxed. In this connection, items of small value could perhaps be obtained by simpler methods, e.g. purchased out of petty cash.

With this note of warning the detailed procedure will now be described.

### The purchase requisition

The purchasing manager must obtain the proper authority before placing orders on suppliers. The means of doing this is the Purchase Requisition (Fig. 6) which instructs the purchasing manager to purchase specific materials, to be delivered at a specific time and place.

Requisitions will normally be received from:

1. The storekeeper, in respect of standard materials, the stock of which is approaching the re-order level.

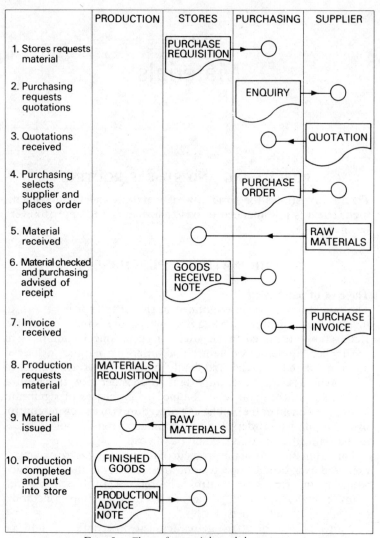

FIG. 5.—*Flow of materials and documents.*

NOTES

1. When non-stock items of materials are received and cleared by the goods-receiving storekeeper they will be sent to the department requesting them. Only the movement of stock materials has been shown in the above chart.

2. After production the work will go either to a finished parts store or to the despatch department for packing and despatch to the customer. This latter movement has not been shown.

3. The route of the top copy only of all documents has been shown. Other copies would be circulated in order to update records and/or general action in the various departments. The flow of documents to provide accounting entries is shown later.

2. The production control department for non-standard materials required for production.

3. The plant engineer for special maintenance or capital expenditure requirements.

4. A departmental head for small supplies, office sundries, ambulance room requirements, etc.

**P.Q.R. CO. LTD.**
**PURCHASE REQUISITION**

Date:................................ 19......          Serial No.:..............................................

Purpose*: stock purchase/special production material/consumables/

small equipment/major equipment (budget approval No.:..........)

*Delete whatever does not apply.

| Quantity and units | Description | Material code | Job or dept. code | Delivery required | | Purchase order | | |
|---|---|---|---|---|---|---|---|---|
| | | | | Date | Place | No. | Date | Supplier |
| | | | | | | | | |

Originating dept.:....................................................          Authorisations:................................

FIG. 6.—*Purchase requisition.*

### NOTES

1. Although the above ruling would be suitable for most kinds of purchases it is often better to use a separate purchase requisition for stock replacements. The stock control department would keep a master file of purchase requisitions, one for each item of stock. Each would permanently record the full purchase specification with details of previous orders and deliveries. This saves a great deal of time in writing out requisitions and in investigating previous suppliers' performances. There is also less danger of errors in copying out detailed specifications and codes. When stock is required the appropriate requisition is withdrawn from file and the requirements entered, i.e. quantity and date. With careful design it is sometimes possible to produce the stock purchase order by photographing the purchase requisition.

2. The details noted against "Purpose" on the purchase requisition will serve to indicate the codes required in the appropriate columns: stock items would require a material code, special production materials a job code, and consumables and small equipment a department code. Major equipment needs a reference to an approval by the budget committee.

3. Details of the purchase order are entered by the purchasing department when the order is placed.

4. A copy of the purchase requisition will be retained by the originating department except when a permanent stock requisition is used, in which case a note is made on the stock record.

**The purchase order**

The purchasing department must place orders with those suppliers who will provide the necessary goods at competitive prices. The purchasing clerks will probably be aware of the performance of the various competing suppliers, but often with new or special materials it is necessary to obtain quotations in order to obtain the cheapest price. Enquiries are therefore sent to suppliers giving details of the requirement and requesting details of available materials, prices, terms and delivery, etc. Quotations received will then be compared and if necessary, after consulting the originating department, an acceptable supplier is selected. This being done, a purchase order (Fig. 7) is prepared and sent to the supplier. With low-value purchases or re-orders, a purchase order would be placed directly with known suppliers to avoid the cost and delay of obtaining quotations.

| | | | | | |
|---|---|---|---|---|---|

P.Q.R. CO. LTD.
PURCHASE ORDER

Serial No.:...........................................

To: .............................................................    Date:..................................................

............................................................    Purchase Order No.:......................

............................................................    P.R. No.:............................................

Please supply, in accordance with the attached conditions of purchase:

| Quantity | Description | Code | Delivery Date | Price | Per |
|---|---|---|---|---|---|
| | | | | | |

Your quotation.........................................................

To be delivered, carriage paid, to:......................................    Terms 2½% Monthly account

Please quote our Purchase Order number on all correspondence, advice notes and invoices, and acknowledge this order.

For P.Q.R. Co. Ltd.

............................................................

Chief Buyer

FIG. 7.—*Purchase order.*

NOTES

1. P.R. No. is the purchase requisition number, which is useful for internal communications with the originating departments.

2. Conditions of purchase are often printed on the reverse side of the order and refer to the terms under which the purchase order becomes a contract between the company and the supplier.

The number and routing of the copies of the purchase order will vary with each business, but the following distribution is normally found essential:

1. To the supplier.
2. To the department originating the purchase requisition.
3. To the goods inwards department as advance warning to expect the goods.
4. Retained in the purchasing department as a permanent record on which deliveries and invoices may be recorded.

The purchasing manager normally confines his activities to purchasing materials that are not subject to speculative dealing. Where the business uses commodities such as cocoa, copper, rubber, etc., the task of purchasing supplies may be undertaken at director level, and specialist advice obtained on future price movements in the commodity markets.

Some businesses may enter into long-term contracts for the supply of materials in order to (a) guarantee a constant source of supply, (b) obtain a competitive price and (c) reduce the stock levels by obtaining the suppliers agreement to deliver at short notice. The contract will be drawn up, say, for a year, for a total quantity of material which can be altered with reasonable notice. Periodic withdrawals against the contract will be made by raising a purchase order. Alternatively, the contract may specify the periodic deliveries and no order is then required. It is important, however, to maintain a record of materials delivered under the contract and for this purpose a purchase contract register is kept (Fig. 8).

## P.Q.R. CO. LTD.
## PURCHASE CONTRACT REGISTER

Supplier:.................................................    Contract No.:.................................................

Material:.................................................    Contract date:.................................................

Quantity:.................................................    Price:.................................................

Deliveries to commence:.................................................    Period:.................................................

| Orders | | | Deliveries | | | | |
|---|---|---|---|---|---|---|---|
| Date | Quantity | Balance to order | Date | Quantity | Invoice value £ | Invoice ref. | Balance to deliver |
|  |  |  |  |  |  |  |  |

FIG. 8.—*Purchase contract register.*

## RECEIPT OF GOODS

It is usual to set up a receiving, or goods inwards department at the entrance to the factory, to which all carriers of goods must report. If the factory possesses its own sidings or wharf it may be necessary to have more than one receiving office so that goods arriving by rail, water or road can be conveniently controlled. Suppliers usually send an advice note either with the goods or by post, and these should be passed to the appropriate receiving office so that the necessary arrangements for unloading and storing the goods can be made in good time. The receiving office should already possess a copy of the order, and this should assist the receiving clerk to decide upon the disposal of the goods.

On receipt of the goods they should be checked either by inspecting, weighing or counting the goods themselves (if their nature makes this possible), and the carrier's way-bill or copy delivery note should be signed. If there is manifest damage or shortage the fact should be noted on the carrier's copy, or the goods should be signed for "Unexamined".

Particulars of the goods should then be entered on a Goods Received Note (Fig. 9) which, depending upon the size and complexity of the firm, should be prepared with additional copies for distribution as follows:

1. To the purchasing department to update purchase records.
2. To the department originating the purchase requisition, with the goods themselves. In the case of material for stock, receipt of the material would be entered on the stock record.
3. Retained for reference in the goods inwards department.

The goods received note will indicate to the purchasing clerk whether the goods delivered are in accordance with the purchase order. Where this is not so the supplier is informed by a formal communication and is asked to give instructions for disposal of the unwanted items. If the whole consignment has been invoiced, it is customary to send a debit note to the supplier for the value of the rejected items plus carriage incurred in returning them. The supplier may accept this debit note as an adjustment to the invoice, or he may prefer to raise his own credit note and send it to the purchasing department, who may then use it as an accounting document in place of their original debit note.

## APPROVAL OF PURCHASE INVOICES

Normally, clerks who check purchase invoices are responsible to the purchasing manager. This is because the clerks need information

```
┌─────────────────────────────────────────────────────────────────────┐
│                         P.Q.R. CO. LTD.                               │
│                      GOODS RECEIVED NOTE                               │
│  Supplier:..............................................   Serial No............................................  │
│         ..............................................   Date issued:..................................  │
│  Carrier:...............................................  Purchase Order No.......................  │
│  Date of delivery:.............................   Advice Note No..............................  │
├──────────────┬────────────┬──────────┬────────────┬───────────────┤
│  Description  │    Code    │ Quantity │  Packages  │ Gross weight  │
│              │            │          │            │               │
│              │            │          │            │               │
├──────────────┴────────────┴──────────┼────────────┴───────────────┤
│           INSPECTION REPORT            │                            │
├──────────────┬────────────┬──────────┤ Received by:................ │
│Quantity passed│Quantity rejected│ Remarks │                       │
│              │            │          │ Required by:................ │
│              │            │          ├────────────────────────────┤
│              │            │          │ Accepted by:................ │
│ Inspector:............  Date:........ │ Date:...................... │
└──────────────────────────────────────┴────────────────────────────┘
```

FIG. 9.—*Goods received note.*

NOTES

1. If the quantity received differs from the quantity advised, this fact should be noted in the quantity column.

2. The code of the goods shown on the purchase order copy may be sufficient indication of who requires the goods, but if not the purchase clerk should note this on the copy sent to the goods inward department.

on orders, deliveries and rejections, and the manager verifies the prices charged, approving any price increases before the invoice is paid.

It is sometimes the practice for a purchase ledger clerk to number invoices consecutively and enter brief details into an invoice register. Where invoices are sent to various departments for approval, the invoice register is the means of ensuring that they do not go astray. Each invoice is impressed with a rubber stamp which contains boxes for recording the register number, the initials of each individual who has a part in checking the invoice and details of the account to be charged. The invoice is checked against the goods received note and purchase order copy to ensure that the quantity, price, carriage, packing and discounts have been charged correctly. Invoice details will be noted on the purchase order copy at the same time. Extensions and additions are then checked and, when they have been agreed and signed for, the invoice is returned to the purchase ledger clerk for entry in the accounts and payment.

Here again an area arises where the cost of detailed checking may be greater than the savings that can be expected as a result of the checking. Many companies, therefore, adopt the practice of not checking purchase invoices below a small value—say £10. It is advisable, however, for occasional spot checks to be made to make sure that nobody is systematically defrauding the company.

## RESPONSIBILITY FOR STORES

The total value of stocks and work-in-progress may comprise a great variety of items, e.g. raw materials, part-finished components, finished products, work-in-progress, consumable materials, tools, maintenance spares, etc., and not all of these are the responsibility of the stores manager. Responsibility can only be given where there is also authority over receipts, issues and storage conditions generally. For this reason, managers other than the stores manager are occasionally made responsible for specific stocks such as the tools' or maintenance equipment. Finished-goods stores and warehouses are frequently found under the control of the distribution manager. The basic principles of stock control and storekeeping apply in all stores areas and for simplicity the raw materials and part-finished components which are generally made the responsibility of the stores manager will be considered in detail.

The cost of materials is one of the largest elements of cost; *but no reliance can be placed on the accuracy of costing records if the conditions under which materials are stored are not under strict control.* Losses from damage, deterioration and pilferage may be considerable unless proper storage conditions are provided. The stores department must, therefore, be properly organised and equipped for the handling of raw materials. It should be in a position which is readily accessible from any part of the factory and as near to the road, railway siding or wharf as is possible in order that the minimum of expense is incurred in unloading. In this way, delay and unnecessary movement of materials may be avoided. It is particularly important that bulky and heavy stores should be stored as close as possible to the department requiring them. It should be noted that handling materials and components adds to their cost without adding to their value.

Efficient and inexpensive systems of materials handling apply to movements within the stores as well as outside. Racks and bins must be arranged for easy access and as floor space will often be at a premium, full use will need to be made of the height within the stores. Specialised equipment must be obtained for stacking and attention given to the strength of boxes and containers so that lower levels are not damaged. At the same time the stores manager must ensure a good turnover of stock, i.e. he must not allow the situation where stock is left at the bottom of a stack and deteriorates. Systematic issuing of the oldest stock first is one of the fundamentals of good storekeeping. Movable racks on rails are being used in many stores with advantage, but are not always suitable for items which are used frequently. The storage and handling methods and equipment must suit the needs of the materials and manufacturing methods, and for this reason large firms employ material handling specialists to study their particular requirements.

## CENTRALISED OR DECENTRALISED STORES

In a large factory it may be convenient to have subsidiary stores situated within productive departments to maintain stocks of materials required by the department. Supplies will be obtained from the main stores, and those in charge of the subsidiary stores must account for these to the chief storekeeper. Before a decision is reached to set up subsidiary stores all the factors should be carefully weighed.

The following advantages may obtain from centralising the stores:

1. Purchase orders can be made out for the total requirements of the firm and the larger order may result in cost savings.

2. The total stock level is reduced because, with many small stocks, the total buffer stock is much higher. The central store, therefore, results in less:

(a) capital invested in stocks;
(b) space taken up;
(c) danger of obsolescence and deterioration;
(d) time taken in checking stock balances.

3. Fewer stock records, i.e. only one record per individual item. Consequently, administration costs of stock recording will be less.

4. More effective control through greater opportunity for using specialised skills and equipment.

However, there are possible disadvantages:

1. More frequent movements of small quantities of materials, which will increase costs and cause production control problems.

2. Administration may prove too complicated in a very large store.

3. Specialised technical knowledge, available in production departments, may help efficient storekeeping. A wide range of such knowledge is unlikely to be available in a central store.

Some of the disadvantages of a decentralised store can be overcome by introducing an imprest system of control. By this method the sub-stores have an agreed stock level and all requisitions for a given period, representing issues from the sub-stores, are passed to the main store which reimburses the sub-store thus restoring stocks to their original levels. This system can result in considerable administrative savings as only one central set of stock records is necessary and there is only one source of purchase requisitions for re-ordering material.

## CONTROL OF STOCK LEVELS

Stocks of materials and products are necessary for a variety of reasons. Even if the factory is situated close to a source of supply it is normally impossible to guarantee a constant flow of raw materials, but adequate stocks will ensure that production does not come to a standstill as a result of delay in delivery. Machinery takes time to be set up for production and consequently it is costly to manufacture in small quantities. Moreover, customer demand may fluctuate from week to week. Long runs of standard products are therefore made and finished-goods stores house the products until customers take delivery. Clearly, the ensuing problems are (*a*) what materials are required to be kept in store, and (*b*) what is an adequate stock level?

The decision concerning which materials should be kept in stock must be based on the particular circumstances of the business. If the customer always gives sufficient notice when ordering, i.e. he is willing to accept long delivery times, material may be purchased as and when required. Special materials for which there is no regular demand are not usually stocked. Normally, standard materials that are frequently required will be kept in stock, and the cost accountant should ensure that any slow- or non-moving items are investigated with a view to their being classified as non-stock items. In a manufacturing company, material is sometimes processed to a semi-finished state and then put into store. This practice may ease difficulties in production scheduling or improve on delivery times. Advantages must be carefully weighed against costs incurred, however, because the total quantity of material held will probably increase and the inclusion of processing costs will result in a substantial increase in the value of stock.

Sometimes the problem of stock levels is automatically solved through restrictions on storage space, shortage of funds, etc., but it is usually a matter of balancing demands from production and sales management for substantial stocks with the demands for low stocks from financial management. The former are concerned with the risks of holding up production and turning away prospective customers, and the latter with costs. Modern stock and inventory practice takes account of both risk and cost in using statistical and operational research techniques.

While this is not the place to discuss such techniques, the opportunity is taken to stress that the cost accountant should appreciate the contribution of the mathematical sciences in helping to solve many fundamental management problems. He will need to provide cost data and may be able to advise on the relevance of the data to particular situations.

The cost of holding stocks includes:

    employment of storekeepers and record clerks;
    provision of storage space with adequate security;
    provision of equipment—bins, racks and handling equipment;
    paperwork—records, requisitions, files, etc.;
    insurance of stocks;
    deterioration and obsolescence;
    interest on capital;
    adverse fluctuations in market prices.

Keeping stocks as low as possible will minimise stock-holding costs but may cause other costs to rise as a direct result. If stocks are kept low, the number of replenishment orders will automatically rise and the order quantity fall as shown in Fig. 10. We have already seen the volume of paper work that is generated by a purchase requisition—enquiries, quotations, orders, advice notes, goods received notes, invoices, cheques, daybooks, etc.—which can be extremely costly. Coupled with this, the supplier may charge higher prices for small-order quantities.

The alternative is to have high stock levels as shown in Fig. 11, which will result in higher stock-holding costs.

A similar situation arises when manufacturing for stock where the cost of scheduling work and setting up machines will increase with the number of orders put through the factory. Also, though difficult to quantify, sales lost through having insufficient stocks causes a loss in revenue and, possibly, goodwill. It is, therefore, theoretically possible to calculate the total costs incurred in issuing

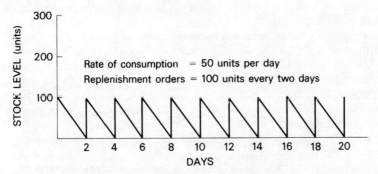

FIG. 10.—*Pattern of stock movements with low stock levels.*

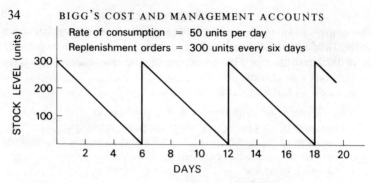

Fig. 11.—*Pattern of stock movements with high stock levels.*

replenishment orders in various quantities and select as the ideal
the least costly. This can be seen graphically in Fig. 12.

Cost is one aspect of deciding upon stock levels. Risk or uncertainty is another. Uncertainty in the pattern of demand and in
delivery promises made by suppliers means that to be absolutely sure
of never running out of stock, management might decide to adopt
a policy of high stock levels. However, risk and uncertainty can be
measured statistically and, by analysing past stock movements, it
is possible to relate a given stock level with a degree of risk, e.g.
by maintaining a buffer stock of, say, 100 units, the risk of running
out of stock may be about one in one hundred which is equivalent
to one week in every two years. By adding the normal consumption
during the re-order period to the buffer stock, the re-order stock
level can be found. (The re-order period, or lead time, is the time
taken to obtain replenishments, i.e. from recognising when additional
stock is required to the delivery into stores.)

Even where a statistical method is not employed, common-sense
approaches will yield adequate results in keeping stock levels to a

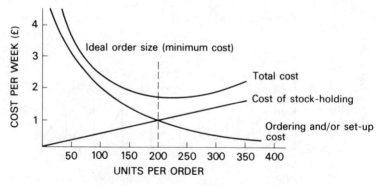

Fig. 12.—*Ordering and stock-holding costs.*

reasonable level compatible with providing a good service. One such approach is as follows:

|  | Maximum | Average | Minimum |
|---|---|---|---|
| Stock out-flow per day | 75 units | 50 units | 25 units |
| Re-order period (lead time) | 5 days | 2 days | 1 day |
| Ideal order size = 125 units | | | |

The re-order level must be sufficient to cover the maximum possible consumption of stock during the re-order period, i.e. $75 \times 5 = 375$ units. With a normal consumption of 100 units $(50 \times 2)$, the buffer stock is, therefore, the difference, i.e. 275 units. It follows that the maximum stock would not be greater than the re-order level plus the re-order quantity less the minimum consumption during the shortest re-order period, i.e. $375 + 125 - (25 \times 1) = 475$ units.

Summarising then, we have:

| Maximum stock | 475 |
|---|---|
| Re-order level | 375 |
| Buffer stock or minimum stock | 275 |

The significance of the minimum or buffer stock is that it may be advisable to contact the supplier when stocks have fallen to this level to ensure that delivery promises will be met.

The maximum level acts as a control indicator for management. If the maximum stock is exceeded, then either the consumption and/or lead time has changed or the established re-ordering level/quantity has not been adhered to.

A practical approach in applying the re-ordering procedure is advisable as apparent stock levels can be affected by the time period between stock reviews and also by the time lag between when a physical movement of stock occurs and when that movement is recorded. An illustration of the re-ordering procedure is as follows:

| End of day | Stock movement | Qty. | Stock balance | Stock replenishments |
|---|---|---|---|---|
| | Commencement | | 375 | Purchase order No. 1 |
| 1 | Issue | 25 | 350 | |
| 2 | Receive Order No. 1 | 125 | 475 | |
| 2 | Issue | 50 | 425 | |
| 3 | Issue | 50 | 375 | Purchase order No. 2 |
| 4 | Issue | 50 | 325 | |
| 5 | Issue | 50 | 275 | |
| 5 | Receive Order No. 2 | 125 | 400 | Purchase order No. 3 |
| 6 | Issue | 75 | 325 | |
| 7 | Issue | 75 | 250 | Purchase order No. 4 |

| End of day | Stock movement | Qty. | Stock balance | Stock replenishments |
|---|---|---|---|---|
| 8 | Issue | 75 | 175 | Purchase order No. 5 |
| 9 | Issue | 75 | 100 | |
| 10 | Issue | 75 | 25 | |
| 10 | Receive Order No. 3 | 125 | 150 | |
| 11 | Issue | 75 | 75 | |
| 12 | Issue | 75 | NIL | |
| 12 | Receive Order No. 4 | 125 | 125 | |
| 13 | Issue | 75 | 50 | |
| 13 | Receive Order No. 5 | 125 | 175 | |

NOTES: 1. Although the re-order level has not been reached at day 5, a new order is issued because by the end of day 6 when the new stock level is recorded, it may be found to be well below the re-order level. In this case the maximum consumption during the re-order period (375 units) could exhaust the stock.

2. On day 7 the effective stock is the physical balance plus the stock on order, i.e. $250 + 125 = 375$. This being the re-order level, a new order is placed.

3. Between days 8 and 9 the effective stock is the two purchase orders outstanding (250 units) plus the physical balance, i.e. between 425 and 350 units. A new order is therefore necessary.

The person who raises a purchase requisition may be either the storekeeper or the records clerk. It is possible, for example, to establish simple arrangements in the store so that a reserve of stock, representing the re-order level, is kept in a special place or is designated in some way. This is sometimes known as the two-bin system. When the storekeeper finds that his stock has been reduced to this reserve, he issues a purchase requisition. However, this method is not always practicable, e.g. where it is difficult to measure the stock or where stocks are decentralised. The normal practice is to maintain a record of all movements of stock in a stores record office.

## STORES RECORDS

The essential records of any stock system are firstly the documents required to authorise and control material movements into or out of the stores; these are the goods received note, materials requisition and materials returned note. Secondly, a central record is required on which movements are entered so that the balance at any time is known; this is known as the perpetual inventory record because the recorded stock balances are perpetually updated to take account of what is actually happening in the store.

The actual records used and their format will differ from business to business. Small businesses may find it expedient merely to record issues of materials for costing purposes and not to maintain a perpetual inventory record.

In a small store it may not be difficult to keep adequate control of stock levels by visual inspection of physical quantities. In larger firms, however, this method may not be practicable and often two records are kept—a bin card located in the store, perhaps clipped to a rack or bin, and also a ledger card kept by stores record clerks who may be housed in an office adjacent to the store or in a separate building. The ledger card is so called because it is a subsidiary account within the stock ledger.

### Stores ledger card

This document is the key to stock control, as it is the basic record used in procedures designed to maintain optimum stock levels. In addition, it provides the detail necessary to ascertain accurate stock values and to check physical stocks.

For stock control to be efficient, there must be a minimum delay between the time when the material is withdrawn from store and the time when the movement is recorded. The illustration of a typical series of stock movements implied that, to apply a re-ordering routine successfully, note must be taken both of the existing stock balance and the amount of stock on order. For this reason a column may be included on the record headed "free balance", which is the sum of these two figures. Where the pattern of demand has been studied carefully and figures extracted of average, maximum and minimum demand, etc., as already shown, then the ruling as in Fig. 13 will be found sufficient.

However, there are instances where the pattern of demand is not easily determined, e.g. new materials, or where it is erratic. For such

---

**P.Q.R. CO. LTD.**
**STORES LEDGER CARD**

Description:............. Unit:...................... Location:.................... Code:..........................

Maximum:................. Minimum:............. Reorder level:.......... Reorder quantity:........

| Receipts | | | Issues | | | | On order | | | Free balance (3+4) |
|------|------|---------------|------|------|---------------|----------------------|------|------|------------------------------|----------------------|
| Date | Ref. | Quantity 1 | Date | Ref. | Quantity 2 | Physical balance 3 | Date | Ref. | Cumulative quantity 4 | 5 |
| | | | | | | | | | | |
| | | | | | | | | | | |
| | | | | | | | | | | |
| | | | | | | | | | | |
| | | | | | | | | | | |

FIG. 13.—*Stores ledger card*

materials, as soon as an order is received from a customer detailed material requirements are sent to the stores records office and stock is reserved against those orders so that the material is available when it is required for production. Thus, the free stock is reduced by the amount reserved. When the free stock falls below the re-order level, then a purchase requisition is sent to the purchasing department. The danger of this system is that where the material is not required until some time ahead, stock balances will increase. For this reason, requests for additional material should be carefully vetted by an experienced stock control clerk. The reserving procedure is best confined to stock critical to production or significant in terms of value. Items such as nuts, bolts, screws and washers, etc., are unlikely to require such elaborate procedures. The ruling of a stores ledger card used in the reserving procedure may be as in Fig. 14.

---

### P.Q.R. CO. LTD.
### STORES LEDGER CARD

Description:....................................................

Code:........................ Unit:............................. Location:................................................................

Maximum:.............. Minimum:.................... Reorder level:............ Reorder quantity:......

| Receipts | | | Issues | | | Physical balance 3 | Reserved | | | Ordered | | | Free balance (3−4+5) 6 |
|---|---|---|---|---|---|---|---|---|---|---|---|---|---|
| Date | Ref. | Quantity 1 | Date | Ref. | Quantity 2 | | Date | Ref. | Cumul. quantity 4 | Date | Ref. | Cumul. quantity 5 | |
| | | | | | | | | | | | | | |
| | | | | | | | | | | | | | |
| | | | | | | | | | | | | | |
| | | | | | | | | | | | | | |
| | | | | | | | | | | | | | |

FIG. 14.—*Stores ledger card used in reserving procedure.*

The free balance will equal the physical balance plus the amount on order, less the amount reserved. When issues are recorded, if they have been previously reserved, the quantity should be deducted from both the physical balance and reserves, leaving the free balance the same. Clearly, if the material has not been reserved, both the free balance and the physical balance will be reduced.

Although the word ledger suggests that monetary values are being recorded this may not always be so. Where a fixed or standard price is used, there is little advantage in recording values as well as quantities. The total value of a stock item can be found by multiplying the quantity by the price, reconciled with the stock account in the financial books. Occasionally, a perpetual inventory record showing just quantities is kept as well as a stores ledger record showing values.

## Bin card

The bin card would not contain detailed information of material reserved and ordered, but is a simple record of actual material movements. Where the stock control clerk is responsible for re-ordering material, it may be the responsibility of the storekeeper to advise him when stock reaches the minimum level to ensure that there is no danger of stock being exhausted because of error in the stock records office. A typical bin-card ruling is shown in Fig. 15.

**P.Q.R. CO. LTD.**
**BIN CARD**

Description:.................................    Bin No.:.................................
Stores Ledger No.:.....................    Code No.:.................................
Minimum level:...........................    Unit:.................................

| Date | Received | | Issued | | Balance | |
|------|------|----------|------|----------|----------|-------|
| | Ref. | Quantity | Ref. | Quantity | Quantity | Check |
| | | | | | | |
| | | | | | | |
| | | | | | | |
| | | | | | | |

FIG. 15.—*Bin card.*

It is often contended that the bin card is an unnecessary duplication of work. That it is a duplication of work is undoubted, but the necessity for it will depend on the proximity of the stores records office to the store, and the accuracy and speed with which stock control records are updated.

## Goods received notes

In the early part of the chapter, reference was made to goods received notes for recording deliveries from suppliers. These notes are recorded on the bin card and passed to the stock control office. A similar document is required when components are produced within the factory and put into store. The document will record the production order code and the cost as a basis for the accounting entry, i.e. debit stock account, credit work-in-progress account.

## Materials requisition

It is clearly important for a business to ensure that materials are only withdrawn from store after proper authority has been given. This is achieved in various ways. When a production foreman is asked to produce certain products, he calculates his material requirements and signs a requisition authorising their withdrawal from store. Where the product is of a standard nature the production-planning department may detail the exact quantities required by reference to plans and drawings but the foreman's signature is still required as he is to be held accountable for the use made of the materials. The materials requisition is handed to the storekeeper as a receipt for the materials withdrawn. The storekeeper enters the details on the bin card and then passes the requisition to the stock control office. If the requisition is prepared in advance by the production-planning department, it will probably indicate the material codes as well as the production order numbers to be charged. It is the responsibility of the storekeeper to see that the requisition is properly authorised and that it indicates the correct material and order codes. This is important for pricing and posting the requisition at a later stage. It will be observed that the materials requisition is a kind of internal bill or invoice, the effect of which is to credit the stock account and debit the appropriate job or cost centre account and that its purpose is completely different to that of a purchase requisition.

| | | | | Cost Office only | | | | |
|---|---|---|---|---|---|---|---|---|
| Code No. | Description | | Quantity or Weight | Rate | Unit | £ | p | Stores ledger |
| | | | | | | | | |
| | | | | | | | | |
| | | | | | | | | |
| | | | | | | | | |
| | | | | | | | | |
| | | | | Job No. | | | | |

P.Q.R. CO. LTD.
MATERIALS REQUISITION    Serial No..........................
Charge Job No.................................    Date:..............................

| Authorised by: | Storekeeper: | Prices entered by: |
|---|---|---|
| Received by: | Bin card entered: | Calculations checked: |

FIG. 16.—*Materials requisition.*

An example of a materials requisition is given in Fig. 16.

**Materials returned note**

Where some materials issued for production are subsequently found to be in excess of requirements, they are returned to store and a document similar in ruling to a materials requisition is used to record the movement. The form is normally in a different colour, often red.

**Transfer of materials**

Occasionally, material issued for one job is subsequently used on another, more urgent, job. It is obviously essential that a record is made of this in order to transfer costs from the original job to the new job. This can be done by issuing a materials returned note on the original job number and a requisition for the new job number. This method has the advantage that the transfer is noted in the stock records. However, a special document can be used called a materials transfer note (Fig. 17).

| P.Q.R. CO. LTD. MATERIALS TRANSFER NOTE | | | | | |
|---|---|---|---|---|---|
| Serial No...................... | | | | | |
| Date:.............................. | | | | | |
| The following material has been transferred | | | | | |
| from Job No.............................................................. to Job No........................................... | | | | | |

| Code | Description | Quantity | COST OFFICE | | |
|---|---|---|---|---|---|
| | | | Rate £ | Unit | Value £ |
| Authorised | Delivered | Received | Priced | | |

FIG. 17.—*Materials transfer note.*

## STOCK-TAKING AND PERPETUAL INVENTORY

The Balance Sheet prepared at the end of the accounting year contains a valuation of all stocks and work-in-progress. The work involved in obtaining a valuation is substantial and costly, and businesses using the perpetual inventory system find that they are able to make considerable savings.

It is an essential feature of the perpetual inventory method that items of stock are checked periodically, normally at least once or twice each year. Unless the stock checks reveal an unacceptable number of discrepancies, it may be assumed that the stock records are in agreement with physical stocks, which is vital if the control procedure is to function properly. The check is done by staff who are unconnected with stores work, but are responsible to the chief accountant or the internal auditor.

Secrecy should be maintained concerning the stocks to be checked each day so that there is an element of surprise.

Intelligent storekeeping will enable the actual stock to be compared frequently with the book stock, even in those cases where it is physically impossible to measure or weigh it. For example, it may be possible to use up a particular coal bunker entirely and at that point to ascertain the book stock shown by the account for that particular bunker; any remaining balance must of course be written off. The stock count is compared with the balances shown on the bin card and stores ledger card, and it is obviously important that all movements of stock up to the time of check have been recorded.

It is inevitable that differences between physical stocks and those shown by the stores ledger will arise when the following factors operate:

1. Evaporation.
2. Absorption of moisture.
3. Temperature changes affecting the volume of stock.
4. Unavoidable approximation of quantities issued.
5. Deterioration of quality in store, e.g. through rust.
6. Impossibility of breaking bulk or cutting up without loss.

Appropriate adjustments in the price of issues may be made to allow for these factors, but it is one of the purposes of stores accounts to control and, if possible, avoid losses. Avoidable losses may be caused by the following:

1. Pilferage.
2. Unsuitable storage, which allows the materials to be contaminated.
3. Careless handling.
4. Using up later purchases first, so that earlier purchases suffer unnecessary deterioration.
5. Careless measurement of issues.
6. Incorrect allowances for the factors set out above.

All such differences should be transferred at full cost, inclusive of normal wastage, to a Difference on Stores Account pending investigation and the closest enquiries made into significant discrepancies. The investigation should establish the cause of the discrepancy and so indicate the lines of remedial action. The cost of avoidable stock differences should be charged direct to Costing Profit and Loss Account; where the differences are substantial a senior executive's authority must be obtained first. If discrepancies are slight, the balances shown on the stock record may be relied upon for the end-of-year valuation.

If it is impossible to maintain a regular staff of checkers throughout the year, then if will be advantageous to check the whole stock, say one month before the year end, adjust the recorded balances where necessary, and take the year-end balances from the updated record cards. This means that the whole exercise can be done without undue haste and there is time to hold inquests on discrepancies without delaying the production of the annual accounts.

## CONTROL OF INVESTMENT IN STOCK

There are few businesses that can boast a surplus of liquid capital and most businesses need to take great care to remain solvent. It is clearly important therefore to keep stocks to a minimum. Various aspects of the problem have already been dealt with, but it is convenient here to stress the continuous review that must be made of stock levels. The pattern of business is rarely static and all too often the accountant finds excess stocks being carried due to an over-optimistic sales forecast, a desire for large trade discounts or perhaps a fall in demand. It may of course be due to the fact that maximum and minimum levels were not related to demand or were not referred to.

In order to guard against this sort of thing happening, it is advisable to select for particular appraisal the stocks which represent a substantial proportion of the stock value. Often 80 per cent of the value will be accounted for by just 20 per cent of the stock items. Regular information should be given to the stores manager concerning the consumption of stock in past months in order to ensure that maximum, minimum and re-order levels are adequate and not excessive.

The periodic accounting reports should contain information on the stock turnover ratios for groups of stock, i.e. relating stock levels to past demand or, where available, forecast demand. In addition, when stock lists are prepared, stock should be classified into fast-, slow- and non-moving categories. The slow- and non-moving groups should be investigated with a view to their disposal.

Finally, it is necessary to mention adequate classification and coding of stock items. Many larger companies find that new stock items are added to the inventory each year and yet some of the items are not so very different from existing stock. This is not always appreciated at the time because the items are required for different purposes and may have different descriptions. However, when the items are properly classified these similarities become apparent and it is not difficult to alter the design of the product slightly and thus standardise on the components. The next section will cover this matter in greater depth.

## STOCK CLASSIFICATION AND CODING

In a small business using a few items of material it may be sufficient to use accepted terminology, e.g. 150 mm × 50 mm Soft Copper Strip, 225 g White Lined Strawboard 80 cm × 100 cm. However, when the firm grows or is allied to other similar businesses it is quite likely that some of the many people dealing with stock materials will use different descriptions for the same article. A product used when metal pipes, etc., are joined together may be referred to as a seal, a ring, an "O" ring, a gasket or a joint. It is possible that the same article may be purchased under different descriptions and held in various stores throughout the business. A major British group of companies, after an investigation of their engineering maintenance stores of 500,000 different items, found that by classifying each item according to certain characteristics, e.g. shape, dimensions, etc., and coding according to those characteristics, they were able to reduce the inventory by 20 to 33 per cent, because identical items were revealed.

If stock items are given a scientific classification code, a complete catalogue can be assembled so that when a part is required it is possible to determine very quickly if it is in stock. The stock records themselves will then indicate the exact stores location. The British Standards Institution has done a great deal of work in establishing standards for materials and products, and when a standard specification number is quoted both customer and supplier know exactly what is being referred to. These specification codes may be used within the materials coding structure of a firm.

Even where it is not possible to develop a sophisticated coding system, one arranged on logical lines will be of great benefit to a business in avoiding errors in ordering, issuing and pricing, etc. The code should appear on all documents relating to the movement and use of material, and should be marked against the appropriate bins and racks.

The material code is but one aspect of a complete coding structure within a business and this subject is dealt with more fully in Chapter 13.

An illustration of a material coding structure is as follows:

*EXAMPLE*

Approval has been given for the following item to be kept in stock and you are requested to issue a material code:

*400 mm Steel nail with flat top head, for Maintenance Department.* The code structure consists of seven digits and the code is found by reference to a coding manual. The first two digits cover the material comprising the item, the first deals with the basic material type:

1. Wood
2. Metal
3. Rubber, plastics and synthetics
4. Glass
5. Building materials

6. Paper and card
7. Chemicals
8. Composite materials
9. Miscellaneous

The first digit is therefore "2". The second digit shows the actual material specification. Thus for metal the following details apply:

1. Mild steel
2. Stainless steel
3. Toughened steel
4. Brass
5. Copper

6. Bronze
7. Cast iron
8. Aluminium
9. Miscellaneous

The coding clerk therefore needs to know which kind of steel is used in the nail. It is assumed that mild steel applies, giving a code 1 for the second digit. Note that if the first digit had been "6"—for paper and card, another page in the manual would have been referred to, giving further details for the second digit, e.g. art paper, tissue paper, greaseproof paper, blotting paper, corrugated card, etc.

The third digit is used to indicate the basic physical characteristics of the material:

1. Bars (flat, round, oval, hexagonal, etc.)
2. Sheets
3. Tubes
4. Strips and wire

5. Powder and granules
6. Liquids
7. Gases
8. Irregular solids
9. Miscellaneous

The third digit would therefore be "9". A fourth digit is used to denote the basic purpose of the material and will help the stock controller to locate the material:

1. Raw materials for foundry (ores and chemicals, etc.)
2. Raw materials for fabrication (sheets, bars, etc.)
3. Components for assembly
4. Sub-assembly/final assembly

5. Miscellaneous maintenance components
6. Office requisites
7. Containers
8. Food and drink
9. Miscellaneous

The fourth digit is therefore "5". The fifth digit is allocated to specify the physical characteristics in greater detail. Maintenance items would be classified accordingly:

1. Pins and nails
2. Screws
3. Bolts
4. Nuts
5. Washers

6. Springs
7. Electrical fittings
8. Tools
9. Miscellaneous

The fifth digit would therefore be "1". The remaining two digits would be allocated sequentially, i.e. a full list of allocated codes would be maintained and the next free code will be given to this new item.

The final code could therefore be 2195146 and may be written as 2195–146 to aid the memory.

## MATERIAL COST PRICES

The cost of materials purchased will be debited to the stock account but there may be a number of adjustments to the original purchase price and these need to be considered.

### Trade discount

This is a reduction in price given by a supplier to a retailer who is going to re-sell the material. It is given to cover the expenses and profit of the retailer who is providing a service to help the original supplier to distribute his goods. Trade discount is deducted from the purchase price in arriving at the material cost price.

### Quantity discount

This is a reduction in price given by a supplier to all large users of his products. The discount often varies according to the size of the order and is deducted from the purchase price in arriving at the material cost price.

### Cash discount

This arises after the material has been invoiced and is offered by the supplier to his customer provided payment is made within a stipulated time, e.g. 5 per cent for payment within 10 days, $2\frac{1}{2}$ per cent within 30 days. The treatment of the discount is subject to some debate among cost accountants but it is usually treated as additional income, leaving the material cost price as the gross purchase price.

### Transport charges

As a general rule, all transport charges incurred in bringing the material to the factory should be included in the material cost price. These will include sea, land and air freight, insurance, duties, dock charges, etc. There may be instances where these costs are small, the invoices are received late, and the total would have to be apportioned over a number of stock items which were included in the consignment. It is expedient to treat such charges as factory overhead.

### Containers

All costs incurred on containers for materials received should be included in the purchase price, i.e.

    1. Charges for non-returnable containers.

    2. The difference between the charge for returnable containers and the amount refunded when the container is returned.

### Storage and issuing losses

Many items of stores do not permit the exact measurement of issues, e.g. liquids, where temperature changes may result in an increase or decrease in the apparent volume taken from store. Alternatively, issues may be made in units which are convenient but which do not correspond exactly with the unit in which the stores are purchased. For example, galvanised wire may be purchased by the tonne but issued in coils, each coil being assumed to be of a certain average weight.

Wastage in store may be inevitable because of evaporation or the difficulty of breaking bulk; also, it may be physically impossible to do more than estimate the weight or quantity issued. It is necessary with such commodities to ensure that production is charged with the true cost of the issues and that the book stock is not inflated by reason of the fact that an allowance for wastage or necessary approximation has not been included in the cost of withdrawals from stock.

This can be done by inflating the original price as in the following illustration:

*Received:* 100 kg of Spillit Powder at £0.40 = £40.00.

Anticipated losses are 20 per cent; therefore material cost price $= \dfrac{£40.00}{80 \text{ kg}} = £0.50$ per kg

| *Issues:* | | £ |
|---|---|---|
| Job A | 16 kg at £0.50 = | 8.00 |
| Job B | 25 kg at £0.50 = | 12.50 |
| Job C | 15 kg at £0.50 = | 7.50 |
| | 56 | 28.00 |
| Stock balance | 30 kg at £0.40 | 12.00 |
| Stock loss | 14 kg | — |
| | 100 kg | £40.00 |

Because the amount lost exactly equalled the anticipated loss, the account balances and the full cost of the lost material has been charged out to the three jobs. Any difference in the loss rate would be charged to Costing Profit and Loss Account.

## PRICING ISSUES OF MATERIALS

Where materials have been purchased for a specific job, the purchase invoice value is wholly debited to that job. Where, however, material is purchased for stock it will be issued to several jobs. Sometimes each purchase can be separately identified, e.g. in the footwear industry, it is necessary to keep records of individual deliveries and the use made of these in production, because of the variations in quality that are experienced between bales of the same basic grade.

The cost of the leather in a bale is therefore charged out to the specific jobs on which the leather was used.

In most instances, material is purchased and put into stock with existing material, and thereafter loses its identity. It is not possible to link an issue of material with a particular delivery, but if the materials are completely homogeneous (as stocks of the same item will be—except for small insignificant differences, say between different suppliers' brands), it should not matter.

If the purchase price changes from one delivery to another, the problem arises of which price to use when issuing to production. There are two extremes of opinion in this matter:

1. The current purchase price should be used because transactions must be recorded at current price levels, otherwise false profits or losses may arise. For example, a retailer buys a product for £1.00 and sells at £2.00. If he holds a stock of 100 products when the purchase and selling prices increase to £1.50 and £2.50 respectively, he will make an extra profit when selling his stock, of £0.50 each. However, he will need the extra profit to replenish his stocks and, therefore, although the stock value increases from £100 to £150, his real capital in terms of stock has remained unchanged. His real profit measured at current price levels is still £1.00 each, and, therefore, it is argued, the stock price used in assessing the profit should be £1.50 and not £1.00.

2. The actual cost price should be used because this is the only known fact. It is argued that the use of current prices would be an entirely arbitrary exercise in many cases and, moreover, it presents problems when there is a long production cycle in that material issued today will be used to produce goods which may not be sold until some time ahead. To be consistent the cost price should relate to that existing at the time of sale.

Various conventional methods have been devised for dealing with the problems raised by these schools of opinion and most of them are an attempt at compromise. They fall under four basic types:

1. Actual prices.
2. Average prices.
3. Standard prices.
4. Current prices.

## Actual prices

SPECIFIC PRICE

Where each batch of material delivered retains its separate identity, it is possible to use the actual invoice price to charge out materials to jobs as in the case of batches of leather previously mentioned. To operate the system it is necessary to record the batch numbers on materials requisitions and to keep a running balance of each batch on the stores ledger card.

## FIRST IN FIRST OUT (FIFO)

As the practice of issuing the oldest material first is essential to good storekeeping, it is reasonable to use the price of the earliest delivery until exhausted and then to use the price of the next delivery. The following points about the system should be noted:

1. Deliveries at different prices complicate the stores account because of the need to maintain an analysis of stock by delivery prices.

2. It makes comparison of job costs difficult as two similar jobs may be charged with materials at different prices or one job may be charged with different prices for the same material, e.g.:

Stock of material AB is 5 units at £2.00 each
10 units at £2.50 each

Job 12 is issued with 8 units of AB and will, therefore, be charged with £17.50 materials cost $(5 \times £2.00 + 3 \times £2.50)$.

3. In times of rising prices the charge to production is unduly low, as the cost of replacing the stock consumed will be higher than the price of issue. It may be said, therefore, that the use of "FIFO" methods tends to inflate profits—and hence dividends—at the expense of working capital.

Because of disadvantages (1) and (2) it may perhaps be said that the system is most suited to stores not often used and to finished stocks. It is, however, fairly widely used, and does give a fair commercial valuation of the stock balance.

## LAST IN FIRST OUT (LIFO)

This method is subject to the same practical disadvantages as the FIFO method so far as the difficulty of calculation is concerned and the inequity which may arise between one job and another. It is, of course, an attempt to charge production at current material price levels, but the last price may still be different to the current replacement price. When a buffer stock is maintained, the book value of the buffer stock will be at out-of-date prices as production will be charged at latest delivery prices.

## BASE STOCK

Under this method it is assumed that the minimum stock of a commodity which must always be carried is in the nature of a fixed asset, as in practice it can never be realised while the business continues. This minimum stock is therefore carried at original cost. The stock in excess of this figure would be treated in accordance with one of the other methods. The base stock method, though theoretically sound, is not often met with. One disadvantage of the method is that when measuring the return on capital employed in the business, the stock value will be subject to the same distortion as with the LIFO method.

## Average prices

### WEIGHTED AVERAGE

Under this method, issues of material are priced at the average cost price of materials in hand, a new average being struck whenever a delivery is received. The method tends to smooth out fluctuations in price and reduces the number of calculations to be made, as each issue is charged at the same price until a fresh purchase necessitates the computation of a new average. Although it is necessary to calculate the average price, this is done only after each receipt and the system tends to be simpler to operate than either LIFO or FIFO. It gives an acceptable figure for stock values.

### SIMPLE AVERAGE

This is an average of prices without any regard to the quantities involved. It should only be used when prices do not fluctuate very much and the stock value is small.

### PERIODIC AVERAGES

In a costing system where job costs are prepared infrequently—say every two months—it may be sufficient to price requisitions by taking the average price ruling during the period. The stock records would be maintained on a perpetual inventory basis to ensure adequate control of stock, but the requisitions would all be valued together at the end of the period. The method may be used when stock records are processed by a computer. The computer facility for speedy analysis and calculation would enable, say, one-month's stores transactions to be recorded at one time and the average for the period could be calculated and used to price issues.

## Standard price

This is a price which the management pre-determines for a given period. Purchase invoices are valued in terms of the standard price, and the difference, called a price variance, is posted to a separate account while the standard value is posted to the stock account. All issues are then made at the standard price. While the initial calculation of the standard needs careful consideration, the stock-recording procedure is simplified. In fact it is possible to remove prices and values from stock cards, as the valuing can be a separate exercise.

## Current prices

The principle of this method is that issues are priced at either replacement or realisable price at the date the issue is made. This possesses the following advantages:

1. The result of good or bad buying is disclosed.

2. In view of the fact that many competitors would have had to purchase materials for the contract, a more competitive selling price may be given when tenders are made.

With regard to (2) it must be remembered that cost ascertainment and cost estimating are entirely different matters. The latter is mainly concerned with the probable expenditure which will be incurred, and the price quoted may well be adjusted in the light of market conditions, the strength of competition and other factors. Cost ascertainment, on the other hand, is an attempt to record the actual or historical cost of the job after it has been completed, in as accurate a manner as possible. It may therefore be argued that the cost accounts should not be disturbed because circumstances make it desirable that a certain price should be quoted for work—a competitive price may be given without interference with the costing records; the quoted selling price merely requires to be adjusted or a separate calculation can be made. In addition, the following disadvantages exist:

1. The method departs from cost and, consequently, confusing elements are introduced into the cost accounts.

2. Substantial differences must arise on the stores accounts and dealing with these may complicate the costing system unnecessarily.

3. Where no precise market for particular materials exists difficulty will be experienced in ascertaining current market prices.

This method is suitable only where market prices are ascertainable without difficulty and it is desired, e.g. in the case of large contracts, to keep the cost accounts as far as possible in line with the estimates made, or when a special comparison of the costs involved in alternative circumstances is desired.

The various methods of pricing issues are compared in Fig. 18. It should be noted that the weighted average price is always midway between FIFO and LIFO. When prices are rising the stock value on the LIFO method will always be lower than FIFO or weighted average.

Lest there should be any doubt, it must be emphasised that, whatever method is adopted, it must be consistently used from period to period. The choice of the method depends on various factors among which are:

1. The extent of price fluctuations.

2. The value of material cost in proportion to total product cost.

3. Relative number of stock movements.

4. Custom within the industry or group of companies.

| Date | Receipts Quantity | Receipts Price £ | Receipts Value £ | Issues Quantity | Balance Quantity | FIFO Price £ | FIFO Value £ | LIFO Price £ | LIFO Value £ | Weighted average Price £ | Weighted average Value £ | Standard Price £ | Standard Value £ | Current Price £ | Current Value £ |
|---|---|---|---|---|---|---|---|---|---|---|---|---|---|---|---|
| Jan. 1 | 100 | 1.00 | 100 | | 100 | | | | | | | | | | |
| 2 | 150 | 1.20 | 180 | | 250 | | | | | | | | | | |
| 3 | | | | 100 | 150 | 1.00 | 100 | 1.20 | 120 | 1.12 | 112 | 1.30 | 130 | 1.40 | 140 |
| 4 | 150 | 1.40 | 210 | | 300 | | | | | | | | | | |
| 5 | | | | 100 | 200 | 1.20 | 120 | 1.40 | 140 | 1.26 | 126 | 1.30 | 130 | 1.60 | 160 |
| 6 | 120 | 1.60 | 192 | | 320 | | | | | | | | | | |
| 7 | | | | 150 | 170 | 50 1.20<br>100 1.40 | 200 | 120 1.60<br>30 1.40 | 234 | 1.3875 | 208 | 1.30 | 195 | 1.60 | 240 |
| Stock value | | | | | 170 | 50 1.40<br>120 1.60 | 262 | 20 1.40<br>50 1.20<br>100 1.00 | 188 | 170 1.3875 | 236 | 1.30 | 221 | 1.60 | 272 |
| | | | £682 | | | | £682 | | £682 | | £682 | | £676 | | £812 |

*Value of issues*

FIG. 18.—*A comparison of material-pricing methods.*

NOTE

1. With the weighted average method, small differences may need to be written off due to rounding up or down. The weighted average price has been calculated as follows:

Jan. 2   100 at £1.00 + 150 at £1.20 = £280. Average = $\dfrac{£280}{250} = £1.12$

Jan. 4   150 at £1.40 + 150 at £1.12 = £378. Average = $\dfrac{£378}{300} = £1.26$

Jan. 6   120 at £1.60 + 200 at £1.26 = £444. Average = $\dfrac{£444}{320} = £1.3875$

2. The difference showing on the standard price method is a price variance which would normally be adjusted before debiting the account.

3. The difference on the current price column is due to a revaluation and should be taken to a revaluation account.

## MATERIALS OF SMALL VALUE

In many businesses, material of little individual value may be necessary to the completed article and, in theory, forms part of the prime
cost, e.g. glue and nails in the manufacture of toys, thread for
stitching hat-bands, etc. It is apparent, however, that it would be
inexpedient to requisition such small items separately for each job
or batch. Materials of this character are usually treated as indirect
and charged as factory overhead to the department which uses the
materials.

## ACCOUNTING ENTRIES FOR MATERIALS

### Receipt of goods
The flow diagram in Fig. 19 illustrates the steps required to update
the accounting and stock records when stock materials are received.

### Issue of materials
The flow diagram in Fig. 20 illustrates the steps required to update
the accounting and stock records when materials are issued.

The flow diagrams should be studied together with the following
notes:

1. It is advisable to update the stock records upon receipt of the
goods received note in case there is a delay in receiving the invoice.

2. The use of a materials cost analysis sheet may save numerous
entries in the ledger.

3. Direct materials are debited to work-in-progress accounts and
indirect materials are debited to overhead accounts. An account
would be opened for each job or cost centre as well as total accounts
to control the postings.

4. The accounts department here is taken to mean the whole
accounting function—financial and costing.

SELF-STUDY TEST No. 2

*Materials*

(*Refer to the Appendix on p. 341 for outline solutions.*)

1. List the documents used in the procedure for purchasing materials up
to the stage of receipt into store; give a brief description of the purpose
of each document and indicate in which department it is likely to be prepared.

2. Design a Materials Requisition suitable for the requisitioning of direct
and indirect materials in a large organisation.

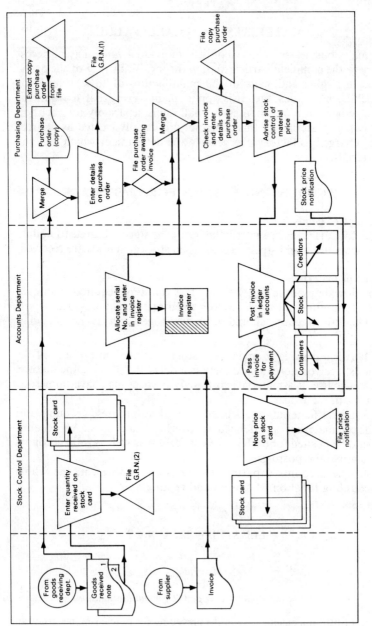

FIG. 19.—*Flow chart of procedure for receiving goods.*

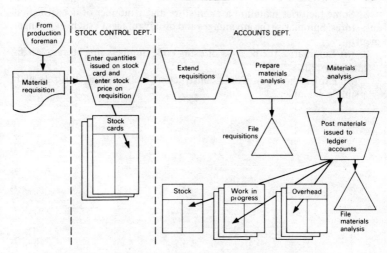

FIG. 20.—*Flow chart of procedure for issuing goods.*

3. (*a*) Define the re-order level; (*b*) Explain its relation to the maximum and minimum stock level; and (*c*) List the factors to be considered in establishing re-order quantities and levels.

4. The following details relate to the Summarised Stock Ledger Account for component PQ for three months ended June 30th:

| Receipts | Qty. | Price £p | Issues | Qty. | Rate £p |
|---|---|---|---|---|---|
| April 1st Stock | 10,000 | 0.60 | April 20th | 20,000 | 0.60 |
| April 15th Stock | 12,000 | 0.625 | May 16th | 2,000 | 0.625 |
| May 12th Stock | 3,000 | 0.632 | May 22nd | 400 | 0.625 |
| June 18th Stock | 20,000 | 0.65 | June 24th | 15,600 | 0.632 |
| | | | June 31st Physical stock: 6,700 units | | |

(*a*) What appears to be the basis for charging issues to production?
(*b*) Comment briefly on the merits of the method.
(*c*) Complete the account and explain your treatment.

5. Materials which are purchased by weight (e.g. kilograms) and issued by measurement (e.g. cubic metre) must give rise to differences on stock-checking. Describe a procedure for control of such differences and for dealing with such materials in the cost accounts.

6. Describe a procedure for controlling and accounting for obsolete stock materials.

7. Explain the imprest system of stores control and describe:

(*a*) the procedure adopted;
(*b*) the conditions under which it should be used; and
(*c*) the expected benefits.

8. Some factories maintain a main store and a number of departmental sub-stores. Summarise the advantages and disadvantages of such an arrangement.

9. (a) Summarise the benefits of using code numbers in a stores classification system.

(b) Explain how you would construct such a code and illustrate with a simple example.

# CHAPTER 4

# Personnel and Labour Cost

## NEW EMPLOYEES

The cost of employing a person goes far beyond his gross wages, some of the additional costs being as follows:

1. Statutory taxes and insurances.
2. Holiday and sick pay.
3. Social expenditure, e.g. pension premiums, canteen and sports clubs.
4. Working space and equipment, e.g. for an office clerk a minimum of 40 square feet (3.5 m$^2$) is required, plus desk, chair, files, etc.
5. Supervision, control and communication.
6. Payroll preparation.
7. Accounting for statutory and voluntary deductions from gross wages.

It is important for every business to keep its direct and indirect employee costs to a minimum. Labour cost control must, therefore, begin at the recruitment stage and should ensure that the number of employees including those in training does not rise beyond actual requirements. Thereafter, control will take the form of keeping costs within accepted standards.

Authorisation for engaging personnel must be clearly defined as part of company policy. A request for additional staff would normally be initiated by a manager after considering his existing and forecast work load. Where the training period is considerable, it is essential to forecast labour requirements very carefully to ensure that the factory is adequately manned when extra output is required.

The line manager will normally send a brief description of the job and personnel specification to the personnel department. Detailed requirements could cover such factors as:

1. Physical: sex, weight, height, hearing, eyesight, voice, etc.
2. Mental or psychological: personality, intelligence, aptitudes, etc.
3. Training: schooling, qualifications, experience, etc.

The personnel manager uses the specification in advertising for, and in selecting, a suitable applicant to fill the vacancy. It is advisable for the line manager to have the final decision in engaging the applicant.

An employee record card will be used by the personnel manager as a permanent record of the engagement, giving details of the clock number allocated to the employee, agreed wage, department in which he will work, etc. All pertinent details of the employee's subsequent career with the firm will be entered on the card. A typical ruling of such a card is given in Figs. 21 and 22.

| P.Q.R. CO. LTD. EMPLOYEE RECORD CARD | |
|---|---|
| Christian or forenames............................................................................ | Clock No. |
| | Surname |
| Address............................................................................ | Date of birth |
| ............................................................................ | N.H.I. No. |
| Tel. No............................................................................ | |
| Married/Single........................................    Children........................................................... | |
| Previous employment........................................................................................................... | |
| ............................................................................................................... | |
| Qualifications/Certificates........................................................................................... | |
| ............................................................................................................... | |
| Engaged by........................................    Wage agreed £....................    Date...................... | |
| Contract of employment and works rules received | |
| Date........................    Signed.......................................... | |

FIG. 21.—*Employee record card (front).*

As part of his induction each employee will receive a copy of the work rules and a written contract of employment. Procedures for time booking and the method of calculating bonus and payment of wages must be clearly explained.

The clock number of the employee is normally retained by him during his employment and acts as a quick reference on all personnel, payroll and works documents. It is helpful to incorporate the code of his department in the employee's clock number as well as his own permanent identity number. The department code can be changed if he moves to another department.

When a new employee is engaged, the payroll department must

| Surname........................................................... | | | | | Clock No. | |
|---|---|---|---|---|---|---|
| Wage and job changes | | | | | General progress | |
| Date | Rate | Details | Dept. | Job or status | Date | Remarks |
| | | | | | | |
| | | | | | | |
| | | | | | | |
| | | | | | | |
| Timekeeping | | | | | | |
| Year | Sickness | Lateness | Other lost time | Remarks | | |
| | | | | | | |
| | | | | | | |
| | | | | | | |
| Date left | | Reasons | | | | |

FIG. 22.—*Employee record card* (*back*).

be given full details, such as income tax form P.45, wage-rate, hours of employment, clock number, age and details of any wage deductions agreed to by the employee.

## TIME-KEEPING METHODS

### Time-recording clocks

Whatever method of remuneration is used, it is necessary, for disciplinary purposes, that some form of time record should be kept for all classes of labour. Moreover, if wages are paid on a time basis the record will be required to ascertain wages. Where possible, time-recording clocks should be used, as they are a quick and accurate method of recording, and facilitate extraction of information for payroll preparation. Also, they reduce the possibility of any manipulation of records by employees, provided the recording is properly supervised. An example of an attendance time card with specimen bookings is given in Fig. 23.

The clock or clocks, together with two racks, an In rack and an Out rack, should be under the supervision of gatekeepers. On arrival, the worker will take his time card from the Out rack, place it in the clock, press a button or depress a lever, and thus record the time of

WEEK ENDING
MAY 28th 19XX

No. 01/14

NAME    JOAN ODDY

SIMPLEX TIME RECORDER CO. (U.K.) LTD.    HALIFAX    Form 85110 (U.K.)

| DAY | IN | OUT | IN | OUT | IN | OUT | Total |
|-----|-----|------|------|------|------|------|-------|
| M | 8 00 | 12 00 | 1 00 | 4 57 | | | 7¾ |
| TU | 8 00 | 12 02 | 12 59 | 5 03 | | | 8 |
| W | 7 59 | 12 01 | 1 00 | 5 01 | | | 8 |
| TH | 7 57 | 12 00 | 12 58 | 5 02 | 5 30 | 6 34 | 9 |
| FR | 8 03 | 12 03 | 12 59 | 5 00 | | | 7¾ |
| | | | | | | | |
| | | | | | | | |

| | | HOURS | RATE | AMOUNT |
|---|---|---|---|---|
| | ORDINARY | 39½ | £2·00 | £79 |
| | OVERTIME | 1 | £2·50 | £2·50 |
| DAYS WORKED 5 | TOTAL HOURS | 40½ | GROSS EARNINGS | £81·50 |

FIG. 23.—*A typical attendance time card.*

his arrival upon the card, which will then be transferred to the In rack. An inspection of the Out racks will reveal absentees, while, if the clock prints in red after the time at which the workers are due to arrive, all late arrivals are pin-pointed. The gatekeepers must take care to see that no worker places a friend's card in the clock in addition to his own in order to cover the friend's late arrival.

On leaving the factory at midday and at night the above procedure will be repeated, the cards being taken from the In racks, punched, and replaced in the Out racks. At the end of the pay week the cards will be collected by the time office and a fresh set for the ensuing week inserted in the racks.

To allow the time card to be inserted in the correct position for printing, the time-recorder incorporates a moving platform which controls the depth to which the card can be inserted.

### Disc method

Another system of time-recording still occasionally met with is the use of metal tags or discs. A numbered disc is assigned to each worker, and hung in numerical sequence on an Out board at the factory gate. On arrival, the worker will take his disc from the Out board and transfer it to the In board. After the time at which all workers are due, the Out board is removed and late arrivals must obtain their discs from the gatekeeper, who will record their time of arrival and forward details to the Wages Office. This system is not so reliable as the time-recording clock; owing to the absence of a written record, disputes frequently arise, while the abstraction of a friend's disc from the Out board may not be difficult.

### Written systems

A third system of time-recording which may be mentioned is the handwritten record. The arrival of each worker is recorded in a book either by the gatekeeper or by the worker himself. The system has little to commend it, as it is cumbersome where a large number of workers is employed, and if the worker records his own time it provides very little check upon late arrivals. A variation is to print the time mechanically and have the employee sign his name against this.

### Recording site

The situation of the time record depends on the size of the factory. Whereas in a small works the time record will be situated at the main gate, in a large works it may be necessary for the employee to travel some distance to his place of work. Therefore, it is realistic to have several recording points within the factory which serve particular departments, although trade unions may object to the practice.

## OUT-WORKERS

In some trades, for example in knitwear and in manufacturing lamp-shades, certain work is performed by workers in their own homes. Time records are not required as the workers are paid according to the work they complete and the time spent on the work is of little interest to the employer. However, it is imperative that rigid control is exercised over the following:

1. Issue of materials and the reconciliation of material drawn from store with the output.
2. Inspection of output and the rejection of defective work.

3. Delivery of output within the time stipulated to ensure an even flow of production and the fulfilment of orders and contracts.

The wages of out-workers will usually be at a higher rate than those paid to piece-workers engaged in the factory, as some compensation must be given for using their own premises, lighting, tools, etc.

Out-workers should not be confused with outside workers, who are employees working outside of the factory on building sites or moving from place to place on small installations or repair work. If these employees report to the factory first for instructions, their arrival times can be recorded in one of the ways previously described, but if they travel direct to the site it may be necessary for them to complete their own time-sheets with some supervision or check on the times, e.g. by a foreman who travels from site to site, or by the customer who is asked to sign the time-sheet which will form the basis of a charge to him. Where workers are engaged upon a site for a long period, e.g. on a civil engineering contract, it is usual for time-recording clocks to be installed at the site.

## REMUNERATION AND INCENTIVES

Wages paid to an employee may be calculated in one of three ways:

1. On the basis of time spent in the factory (time-rates).
2. On the basis of production achieved (piece-work).
3. Using a combination of methods (1) and (2).

In addition, various forms of co-partnership and profit-sharing schemes have been introduced. The schemes vary in detail, but the basic idea is to pay or credit to the labour force, in addition to their normal wages, a sum of money dependent on the year's profits, allocated between employees in relation to earnings, weight sometimes being given to length of service and family commitments.

The method of remuneration adopted must depend largely on the nature of the work performed and, of course, the wage agreement in force. Not all jobs or operations lend themselves to piece-work or bonus arrangements, and frequently only the time basis will be suitable; sometimes this can be supplemented by a shop or departmental bonus based on production or efficiency.

While the subject of wages and methods of remuneration is a complicated and delicate subject, a few observations may be relevant here.

The employer seeks to ensure that his personnel policy will result in maximum cost-effectiveness of labour. This may be achieved as a result of:

1. High rates of good production.
2. Full utilisation of production capacity, i.e. minimum hold-ups due to strikes and disputes.
3. Co-operation by employees in introducing improved production methods.
4. Retention and development of skilled employees.

The employee may be seeking such things as:

1. Regular high wages.
2. Recognition of effort in rewards and promotion.
3. Security of employment.
4. Good conditions of employment.

The employer must consider these matters in deciding his wages policy and it is important to recognise that a wages policy is but one aspect of good labour relations. There is little point in adopting an incentive scheme to reduce unit cost if it subsequently becomes the reason for grievances and stoppages.

### Time rates

Under this system the worker is paid at an hourly, daily or weekly rate, and his remuneration thus depends upon the time for which he is employed and not upon his production. If overtime is worked at the request of the employer, the wage agreement usually provides that hours worked in excess of an agreed number are paid for at a higher rate, e.g. time-and-a-half. The time basis of remuneration for direct labour is appropriate where:

1. The speed of production cannot be influenced by the energy or dexterity of the worker.
2. The quality of work is of paramount importance.
3. It is difficult to measure the work done by the employee.

Although the time system of remuneration is often the only practicable one to adopt, and it is easy to compute and understand, it suffers from the disadvantage of holding out no inducement to the workers to increase production. Constant supervision is required, otherwise considerable wasted time may be paid for, and, as the slow worker receives the same wages as the quick worker, discontent may arise.

It should be noted that, even where the business activity lends itself to payment on a production achieved basis, circumstances may dictate that time-rates are more suitable, e.g.:

1. When an employee is being trained.
2. Where increased production is not required.
3. Where there is a satisfactory return to employees through other incentives.

4. Where production is at a reasonably high level through some means other than an incentive scheme.

Some of the disadvantages of the time basis can be overcome by setting high time-rates. The same system of payment applies but the rates paid are higher than normal. It is possible to attract the best workers in this way and to obtain from them a high level of production, although greater supervision and control is required. High rates are sometimes paid as a result of a productivity deal, which is an agreement between employers and employees whereby, for increases in wages, greater effort is expected from employees. The greater effort may be required due to a reduction in the total work force in a department which must still produce the same amount of work. The difficulty with some productivity deals is that unless they cover all employees, there is a danger that wage differentials between different skills will disappear and result in disagreements.

Where employees' efforts are determined by the speed of the machines they are working or of the conveyor belt feeding them with work, high wages rates may be adopted to justify increasing the speed of the machines or conveyor.

## Production achieved methods

PIECE-WORK

Under this method a fixed rate is paid for each unit produced, job performed or number of operations completed, and the worker's wages thus depend upon his output and not upon the time he spends in the factory. The method meets the objections to the time-rate method, but if it is to work equitably and without friction there must be skilled assessment of the time which a certain job should take under incentive conditions. This assessment is described as rate-fixing, and in deciding the rate for a job the basic time-rate is used with an increase to act as an incentive to the employee. The estimated time is then multiplied by the enhanced time-rate to give the piece-rate.

*EXAMPLE*

Estimated production time = 30 minutes
Basic time-rate             = £1.20 per hour
Allowed increase            = 25 per cent
Enhanced time-rate          = £1.50 per hour
Piece-rate = £1.50 per hour × 30 minutes
            = £0.75

If a job requires particular physical exertion or is unusually unpleasant then an additional allowance may be made to the rate.

Straight piece-work systems are simple to operate and provide a strong incentive. The employer knows the exact cost of production, which is helpful in estimating and planning. However, these systems are rarely found today due to the principal objection that they do not maintain a regular wage for the employee. Thus, a guarantee is normally built into the system that the employee's wages shall not fall below a certain minimum figure, either a guaranteed daily wage or guaranteed weekly wage, the result being that the incentive effects are weakened.

Where the worker has to be transferred to a non-productive job because work is not available, he will be remunerated on a time basis if the National Agreements provide minima below which a piece-worker's wages must not fall.

DIFFERENTIAL PIECE-WORK

Simple piece-work systems offer no particular incentive for the very fast worker because he receives the same rate per unit produced as slower workers.

Various methods have been developed by which faster workers receive a higher rate for all production when operating above a certain target level. F. W. Taylor's scheme had two rates, one below normal time-rates, the other well above them. Merrick later modified this by introducing intermediate levels of performance. Other differential schemes introduced a guaranteed minimum wage, e.g. Gantt and Parkhurst.

The conditions under which a differential scheme may be usefully employed are:

1. When work is of a repetitive, continuous nature.
2. When it is possible to record accurately the output of individual workers.
3. When time standards can be accurately assessed.
4. Where fixed overhead is high in comparison with direct wages.

**Incentive payments**

Incentive schemes or payment by results methods are often criticised by both employers and employees. This is often due to deficiencies in the design, introduction or administration of the scheme, or simply that in the particular circumstances of the business it was really not practicable to use an incentive scheme. Considerable thought must be given before introducing incentives, because anything that affects the size of an employee's pay packet is likely to be suspect straight away and be scrutinised very carefully.

The principles of a good incentive scheme are:

1. The incentive payment must be related closely to the effort involved.
2. There must be full consultation to ensure mutual agreement

between workers and the employer. Any disagreement at a later stage on vital points may wreck the scheme.

3. From the employers and employee's point of view, clearly defined, attainable objectives should be set out.

4. No limits should be placed on additional earnings under the scheme.

5. The employees should not be penalised for matters outside their control.

6. The basis for calculating the bonus must be clear, e.g. on work-study assessments.

7. The level of productivity required by the scheme must be attainable by the average employee.

8. The scheme should be simple to administer.

With time-rates, any additional production above normal levels benefits the employer, whereas with piece-rates the benefit goes to the employee (apart from indirect benefits to the employer). Premium bonus schemes have been developed to produce a compromise, in that any savings are shared between employer and employee. Two examples are the Halsey and Rowan schemes.

### 1. HALSEY

The principle of the Halsey and similar schemes is that the employee receives a fixed proportion of any time which he can save by completing the job in less than the allowed time. The Halsey scheme adopts a proportion of 50 per cent—but this can be varied.

*EXAMPLE*

Allowed time = 30 minutes
Time rate      = £1.20 per hour
Actual time   = 18 minutes

$$\text{Bonus} = \frac{\text{Time allowed} - \text{time taken}}{2} \times \text{time-rate}$$

$$= \frac{30 - 18}{2} \times \frac{£1.20}{60} = £0.12$$

### 2. ROWAN

This scheme uses a formula which ensures that a ceiling is applied to the size of the bonus. The proportion of the time saved which is credited to the employee is based on the percentage which the time taken bears to the time allowed.

*EXAMPLE*

Data as above.

$$\text{Bonus} = \frac{\text{Time taken}}{\text{Time allowed}} \times \text{time saved} \times \text{time-rate}$$

$$= \frac{18}{30} \times 12 \times \frac{£1.20}{60} = £0.144$$

If the time taken in the example was 15 minutes, the bonus under both schemes would be identical, i.e. at £0.15, showing that the ceiling on the Rowan scheme is at double the normal efficiency. If the time taken is then reduced to 6 minutes, the Halsey bonus is £0.24 and the Rowan bonus £0.096. This effect can be seen in the graph, Fig. 24.

The Rowan scheme protects the employer from loose rate-fixing by

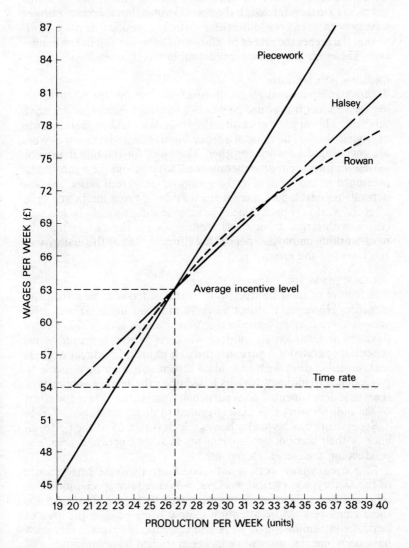

FIG. 24.—*Wages earned under incentive schemes.* For details *see* page 70.

reducing the bonus at high production levels, but for this reason it is unpopular with workers.

## 3. OTHER BONUS SCHEMES

Various schemes of bonus payment will be found in industry and they all use the estimated time for a job as the basic starting point. Points are awarded in some schemes based on efficiency attained, i.e. the relationship of time taken to the estimated time, and the bonus payments are then related to the points gained. Some bonus schemes have incorporated the differential principle applied in piece-work so that the higher the rate of production, the higher will be the bonus-rate. These are known as accelerating bonus schemes.

### GROUP BONUS SCHEMES

Where a group of workers is collectively responsible for manufacturing the product it may not be possible to adopt individual incentive schemes. This applies in contracting industries and in maintenance and repair work. The value of a group bonus scheme is that employees are encouraged to work together. The basis for the bonus may be savings in time spent or sometimes cost savings and the bonus is apportioned to individuals in the group on an agreed basis. Success depends on developing a team spirit and in paying the bonus soon after the work has been done. The scheme will probably be less successful with larger groups and there is always the danger that the hard-working employee reduces his effort to that of the majority of employees in the group.

### BONUS SCHEMES FOR INDIRECT WORKERS

The feature of most indirect work is that it tends to be difficult to measure. However, if direct workers are paid under an incentive scheme there may be considerable unrest unless some kind of extra payment is awarded to indirect workers. Where a group bonus scheme is operated it is normally possible to include indirect workers and, in association with individual schemes, it may be possible to pay a bonus to indirect workers based upon the average efficiency of the whole department. This is particularly important where the effort of the indirect worker is closely geared to direct workers.

Supervisors can be paid a bonus which is related to the performance of their sections or departments in some important area, e.g. production, time saved, scrap, etc.

Employees whose work is not related directly to the performance of the factory, e.g. clerical workers, would require special incentive schemes, but it is often better to resort to higher time-rates for these employees. More attention is now being paid to the area of clerical and administrative work and considerable gains in efficiency have been reported after work has been studied by organisation and methods specialists and incentive schemes introduced.

LIEU BONUS

Employees who are paid under an incentive scheme but who are occasionally required to do work which has not been incorporated in the scheme, may be compensated by a payment "in lieu" of their normal bonus. This will normally be at an average rate. Lieu bonus may also be paid to employees whose work is of such a nature that an incentive scheme would not be appropriate (e.g. toolmakers) although in the same factory incentive schemes are in operation. It is effectively another way of paying higher time-rates.

MEASURED DAY-WORK

Some mention has already been made of the objections raised by some employers and employees to incentive schemes. In spite of this, however, the employer wants a high level of efficiency and the employee wants a high regular wage. Measured day-work is an attempt to secure both without the use of an incentive scheme. The work is studied by work-study engineers and times are agreed. A higher wage-rate is then paid to employees for producing at a rate equivalent to an incentive rate of working. A scheme of this nature requires considerable mutual trust and co-operation.

CALCULATION OF ALLOWED TIMES AND WORK STUDY

We have seen that almost all incentive schemes are based on an allowed time. Ideally this should be calculated by work-study engineers after the job, methods and equipment have been studied to ensure that the best way to do the job has been found.

Work study comprises two complementary activities—method study and work measurement.

Method study is undertaken to improve methods of production and to achieve the most effective use of materials, manpower and plant. The principal stages involved are:

1. Selection of the work. Complex and expensive operations would normally be given priority to obtain maximum benefits.

2. Examination of present methods. All aspects of the work are considered, i.e. purpose, location, sequence and relationship with other work being done, operators and facilities, etc., used.

3. Development of an improved method. This might involve changes in the location and sequence of work, and often designing special production aids to simplify and speed the work.

4. Implementation of the agreed improved method.

5. Follow-up of the improved method to ensure it is being carried out correctly.

Work measurement is undertaken to establish the times required to perform the work. The times may be used for incentive schemes, production planning and estimating selling prices. The stages involved are:

1. Selection of the work.

2. Measurement by an actual timing of the work being done (time study) or by estimating the time to be taken on new work (analytical estimating). The measurement involves timing each basic step of the operation under non-incentive conditions.

3. Establishing the total time for a complete job and including allowances for fatigue and personal needs.

When preparing allowed times for incentive schemes, the time likely to be saved under incentive conditions is calculated to arrive at the net time to be taken under those conditions. Management must then decide how much they are willing to pay employees per hour or week to work at this incentive level. Various factors will be taken into account such as the level of fixed overhead and the extent to which other costs may be expected to rise, e.g. scrap and machine maintenance. Where premium bonus schemes are used, the incentive times are then suitably increased to allow employees to earn a bonus when producing at the incentive level.

*EXAMPLE*

|  | *Minutes per product* |
|---|---|
| Time under non-incentive conditions | 100 |
| Allowances (20%) | 20 |
| Basic time | 120 |
| Time saved under incentive conditions (25%) | 30 |
| Time under incentive conditions | 90 |

In a 40-hour week, the employee is able to produce 20 products under non-incentive conditions (120 minutes basic time). By introducing an incentive scheme, production can be raised by one-third. If wages are at £54 per week there is a gain of £18 per week to the employer.

If the employer wishes to increase the employee's piece-work earnings by £9 per week, the rate for the job would be calculated as follows:

Average wage £54 + £9 = £63.
Production under incentive conditions = $26\frac{2}{3}$ products.

$$\text{Piece-rate} = £\frac{63}{26\frac{2}{3}} = £2.36 \text{ per product.}$$

If the Halsey system is operated, the time allowed would be calculated as follows:

$$\text{Bonus} = \frac{\text{time saved}}{2} \times \text{time-rate}$$

$$£9 = \frac{\text{time saved}}{2} \times \frac{£54}{40}$$

Time saved $= \dfrac{9 \times 2}{1.35} = 13\frac{1}{3}$ hours per week

or $\dfrac{13\frac{1}{3}}{26\frac{2}{3}} = \frac{1}{2}$ hour per product

Time allowed = estimated time + time saved = 90 + 30
$\qquad\qquad\quad$ = 120 minutes

Under the Rowan scheme, the time allowed would be calculated thus:

$$\dfrac{\text{time taken (40 hours)}}{\text{time allowed (40 hours + time saved)}} \times \text{time saved} \times £1.35$$

$$= £9$$

$$\therefore \left( \dfrac{40 \times 1.35}{9.00} \times \text{time saved} \right) - \text{time saved} = 40$$

Time saved $= 8$ hours per week or $\dfrac{8}{26\frac{2}{3}}$ per product $= 18$ minutes

Time allowed $= 90 + 18 = 108$ minutes

The three incentive schemes may be compared graphically with time-rates as shown in Fig. 24 on page 67.

The graph indicates that under the Halsey scheme employees will earn a bonus at a steady rate, whereas under Rowan they earn bonus at a fast rate to begin with and then at a declining rate. The bonus under all these schemes is identical at the point selected as the average production under incentive conditions.

As we are primarily concerned with cost, the graph in Fig. 25 shows the effects on labour cost.

## JOB EVALUATION AND MERIT-RATING

One of the prime difficulties in any wage system is to decide on a fair rate to pay the employee. While wage-rates may be set at national level by collective bargaining, the value of paying above agreed rates for particularly onerous jobs or to particularly good workers is recognised.

Job evaluation is a technique for assessing the relative value of jobs to establish differentials in terms of the amount paid to employees. It is achieved by awarding points to a job based on certain characteristics, e.g. skill, mental effort, physical effort and responsibility. The hourly rate is then adjusted to reflect the total number of points awarded.

Merit-rating goes a stage further than job evaluation in that it allows for differences in performance between employees who are working on similar jobs and would therefore earn the same wages. Typical factors by which workers are assessed are attendance, co-operation, quality of work, initiative and perhaps personal characteristics. As with job evaluation, points are awarded according to the characteristics of the worker, and his wage-rate will reflect the points obtained. The assessment of merit should be done

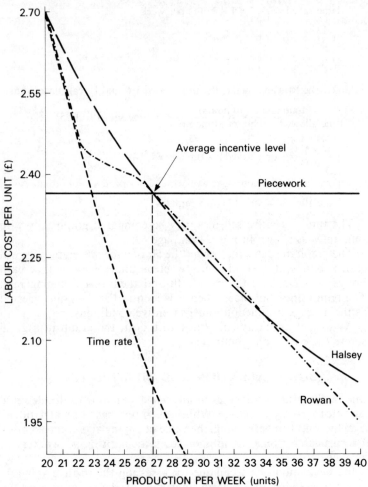

FIG. 25.—*Labour cost per unit under incentive schemes.*

periodically, say, at quarterly or six-monthly intervals, by the manager and foreman.

Provided both job evaluation and merit-rating are seen to be applied fairly, they can be useful to the employee in seeking to improve himself and to the employer in selecting keen workers for promotion or special assignments.

## CO-PARTNERSHIP AND PROFIT-SHARING SCHEMES

Theoretically, a scheme which enables the worker to share in the prosperity of the business and gives him a tangible interest in its welfare is of great benefit to both employer and employed. Some companies give the worker his bonus in the form of shares in the company, and a permanent interest in the future of the business is thus established which is not obtained from a cash distribution.

These schemes, however, usually suffer, *inter alia*, from the following disadvantages:

1. It is difficult to determine the share of profits to be given to each worker, and unless profits are large the share may be so small as to appear to him wholly insignificant.

2. When the share is paid to the workers in cash they tend to regard it merely as a bonus, and not as a reflection of their achievements.

3. As the distribution will, normally, take place only once a year, the advantage to the worker is so distant that he may lose interest in it.

4. If workers participate in profits in relation to years of service, newer employees, who have contributed to the profits of the year may be dissatisfied.

5. Ignorance of finance and accounts may cause suspicion of profits distributed.

6. The share of profits paid out to the workers may be swollen by factors to which they have not contributed, e.g. good buying and skilful salesmanship. Conversely, their share may be depleted by factors for which the workers are in no way responsible, e.g. falling markets, bad administration, etc.

## WAGES OFFICE ROUTINE

### Data required

The calculation of the net wage payable to each employee is based on the following information:

1. Attendance time, analysed between day-work, overtime and shift-work.
2. Rate of pay.
3. Bonus.
4. Sundry payments, e.g. sick and holiday pay, and special allowances.
5. Statutory deductions, i.e. income tax, employee's National Insurance and Graduated Insurance contributions.
6. Voluntary deductions, e.g. sick clubs, pension contributions.

Pure piece-work systems will require only piece-work rates and quantities produced instead of (1)–(3). To compute the income tax due, the employer will require to know the tax code and previous earnings of the employee. The payroll will probably include a record of the employer's National Insurance and any other contribution.

## Static information
Much of the information used in payroll preparation is static, i.e. it does not vary from week to week, such as rates of pay, employees' National Insurance contributions and voluntary deductions. A permanent record of these is therefore kept and referred to when computing the net wage. When changes occur, they must be properly authorised before alterations are made to the permanent record. The tax deduction card is sometimes used to record static information.

## "Dummy" workers
Attendance times recorded in one of the ways previously described should be initially vetted and authorised by the foreman. The wages office must account for everybody employed in the business and one method is to see that for each time record there is also a tax deduction card. This minimises the risk of non-existent or "dummy" employees being inserted on the payroll to defraud the company.

## Calculation of net wage
The attendance record is used to determine the hours to be paid at day-work or overtime rates and any shift premium that may be due. When overtime is necessary authority must be obtained from the works manager. The worker's hourly rate is usually increased for overtime so an incentive is given to provide excuses for late working; unless rigid control is exercised, unnecessary expenditure may be incurred.

A list of workers required for overtime is made out by the foreman and submitted to the works manager for approval. If authorised, the list will be sent to the wages office as authority for payment. Overtime may be paid at time-rates plus one-third, or one-half, or at double rates, dependent upon when it took place. A shift premium arises where, say, an employee works a night-shift of $37\frac{1}{2}$ hours per week and is paid the equivalent of 40 hours; the extra $2\frac{1}{2}$ hours represents the shift premium. Incentive payments are calculated from data supplied and details of sick or holiday pay due are authorised and supplied by the personnel officer. The total gross wage is then used to determine the tax due for the week, and the amount of Graduated Insurance contribution (where applicable). These, plus National Insurance contributions and voluntary deductions, reduce the gross wage to the net wage due to be paid.

## Records used
The employer is required to keep details of tax calculations and will want a detailed payroll to account for gross wages. The employee

should be given details of his wages, and so a useful practical procedure is to produce three documents at the same time. Whether manual or mechanical methods are adopted, it is normally possible to produce carbon copies of any two of the three documents, thus saving time and ensuring agreement in all three records. An example is given in Fig. 26. A separate bonus notification may be given to the employee before he receives his pay slip, to provide details which will enable him to check the figures.

## Payment of wages

The wages office prepares a payroll summary, with an analysis of coins and notes required, passes this to the accountant for drawing the wages cheque and advises the bank of the money required. When the money is received, it is checked and bagged, and at an agreed time the pay envelopes are taken round the factory or collected from the wages office. The foreman should be present to ensure that the envelope is given to the right person and employees may be asked to sign a receipt.

## Prevention of fraud

Rigid control over the calculation and payment of wages must be exercised in order to minimise the risk of fraud. Mention has already been made of dummy workers and the method of exposing them. In addition the following points should be noted:

1. A number of persons should be engaged in the compilation of the records of the wages payable. One member of the wages staff should insert the rate of wages payable on the payroll or time cards, and another should calculate the actual amount payable.

2. The sheets or cards should be passed to the P.A.Y.E. section and the appropriate deductions for income tax and pensions contribution inserted.

3. The payroll should bear the initials of each person concerned in its preparation with details of the work carried out.

4. The reason for all unclaimed pay packets should be established, e.g. absence through sickness, and the packets should be held in the cashier's office for, say, three days, after which they should be opened and the contents paid into a special bank account pending enquiry. Under no circumstances should the wages of one worker be collected by either a fellow-worker or a member of the employee's family without written authority from the worker concerned, and with the consent of the foreman.

5. From time to time a senior officer of the company should personally be present when wages are being paid.

6. Time-cards should be compared at irregular intervals with

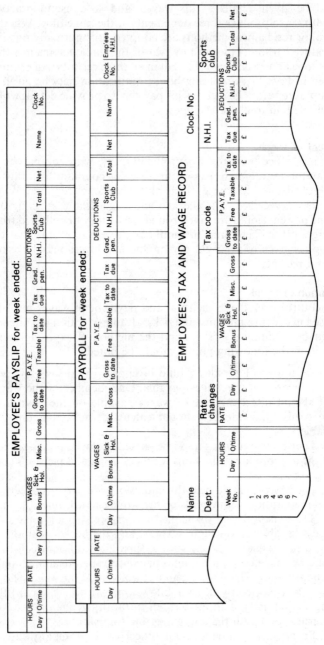

Fig. 26.—*Three wages documents produced simultaneously.*

their income-tax deduction cards, as a further test of the existence of each worker. This check should be carried out by an official in no way connected with the wages office.

The wages due to workers engaged on site contracts should, if possible, be paid by an official from head office, and an occasional visit by one of the senior officials at the time of payment is also desirable.

## P.A.Y.E.

In many firms the wages or personnel office will keep a card for each employee showing his address, age, date of commencement of employment, whether a member of the superannuation scheme and other personal information. The wages office will also keep the tax-deduction cards, enter all changes of tax codes and issue the appropriate forms when an employee leaves.

At the end of the tax year the wages office will prepare summaries of the tax-deduction cards for return to the Inland Revenue and issue to each employee the official form showing earnings, income tax deduction and Graduated Pension contributions.

## ACCOUNTING FOR WAGES

The employer must account for three basic sections of the payroll:

1. Gross wage earned by the employee.
2. Deductions from the gross wage for which the employer is accountable to third parties.
3. Employment costs, e.g. employer's National Insurance and Graduated Pension contributions.

Item (1) represents costs which require analysis and allocation to cost units (direct wages) or to cost centres (indirect wages and salaries). Item (2) does not affect the cost accounts and item (3) is usually treated as overhead and allocated to appropriate cost centres. The basis for gross-wage analysis is the employee's time record, which analyses time between a number of activities during a day or week. The record may take the form of a job card or a time sheet. An employee may record time spent on each job by means of a card which is similar to an attendance time card. When beginning in the morning he clocks his time on the gate card and on the job card. When a job is finished he clocks off that job card and on to another. At the end of the day he clocks off both the job card and the gate card. The total of the hours recorded on the gate card must, therefore, equal the total of the times on the job cards; any discrepancies are investigated by the time clerk.

It is not always practicable to use job cards, e.g. if considerable time must be spent in walking to and from the time office to use the clock. Time-sheets are, therefore, sometimes used and the employee records his time on these manually. The danger with this method is that the employee may not accurately record time, especially if he waits until the end of the day or week to do it. It is advisable, therefore, for the foreman to scrutinise the times shown.

The times recorded must be valued before they can be debited against cost centres and units. The gross-wage rate per hour, however, may be affected by such things as incentive payments, overtime and shift premiums. Furthermore, if the employee is entitled to a holiday, the length of which is somewhat determined by the hours worked during the year, it could be argued that the real cost is greater than the wage rate per hour. Similar arguments apply to employer's National Insurance contributions, etc. The method used to arrive at a wage rate per hour will, therefore, fall between one of the two extremes:

1. Use employees' basic day-work rates and debit all other costs to overhead accounts (perhaps with the exception of abnormal costs, if known).

2. Incorporate all normal wage costs, e.g. incentive payments, overtime premiums, idle time, etc., with the day-work rate, and debit only abnormal costs to the overhead accounts.

The following observations are made on the two methods:

1. If a customer has specifically asked that a job be done quickly, which necessitates overtime working, the overtime premium incurred must be charged to the customer even if it is not debited in the appropriate job cost account.

2. The method of calculation will have a bearing on the incentive payments treatment, e.g. payments out of a group incentive scheme must be averaged over products.

3. Product costs have limited use for management control and it might be more informative to show ancillary employment costs separately in an overhead schedule.

4. When product costs are used for calculating selling prices it is important to include all costs, and although the overhead rate will include a proportion for overtime premium, etc., under method 1, job costs will be more accurate if as much expenditure as possible is treated as direct.

5. Inclusion of an accrual for holiday pay will complicate reconciling the wages charged in the cost accounts with the payroll. It may be simpler to treat it as overhead.

*EXAMPLE*

A worker is paid £1.50 per hour and the 5-day working week contains 40 hours. The daily allowance for approved absence from his place of work, maintenance of his machine, etc., is 12 minutes, and his job cards show the following time analysis:

    P.O. 746 20 hours
    P.O. 747 10 hours
    P.O. 748  8 hours

Time unaccounted for is caused by a power failure. Show how his wages would be dealt with in the cost accounts.

*Method 1*

| | |
|---|---:|
| Wages earned 40 hours at £1.50 per hour | £60.00 |

Allocated as follows:

Productive—

| | |
|---|---:|
| P.O. 746 20 hours at £1.50 per hour | £30.00 |
| P.O. 747 10 hours at £1.50 per hour | 15.00 |
| P.O. 748  8 hours at £1.50 per hour | 12.00 |
| Direct wages charged to job accounts | 57.00 |

Non-productive—
Normal Idle Time Account:

| | |
|---|---:|
| (5 × 12 minutes = 1 hour) at £1.50 per hour | 1.50 |

Abnormal Idle Time Account:

| | |
|---|---:|
| 1 hour at £1.50 per hour | 1.50 |
| Charged to production overhead | 3.00 |
| | £60.00 |

*Method 2*

| | Hours | Rate | |
|---|---:|---:|---:|
| Wages earned | 40 | £1.50 | £60.00 |
| *Less* Normal Idle Time | 1 | — | — |
| Available time | 39 | £1.50 | £60.00 |

The effective rate per hour of available time is

$$£\frac{60.00}{39} = £1.54 \text{ approx.}$$

Allocated as follows:

Productive—

| | |
|---|---:|
| P.O. 746 20 hours at £1.54 per hour | £30.80 |
| P.O. 747 10 hours at £1.54 per hour | 15.40 |
| P.O. 748  8 hours at £1.54 per hour | 12.32 |
| Total direct wages | 58.52 |

Non-productive—
Abnormal Idle Time Account

| | |
|---|---:|
| 1 hour at £1.54 | 1.54 |
| | £60.06 |

It will be seen that under both methods a portion of the worker's earnings is not charged directly to job accounts. In method 1 the cost of normal idle time is separately computed and regarded as an overhead expense for allotment to production with other indirect expenses. Under method 2 the cost of such idle time is merged with the hourly rates, on the assumption that although 40 hours were paid for, the maximum productive hours are 39, and hence the effective rate per hour is $40 \div 39 \times £1.50$, i.e. £1.54. This rate would be used each week until either the rate of pay or the assessment of idle time is altered.

On the other hand, idle time caused by abnormal circumstances is something which, in theory at least, should not occur and which management is, therefore, vitally interested in controlling. Its cost should therefore be distinguished and not merged with the rate charged to production. Pending enquiry, the cost should be charged to a suitably described account (e.g. Power Failure Idle Time Account) and as it cannot be regarded as a productive cost it should be excluded from Cost of Sales and charged as a separate item in the Profit and Loss Account.

### Flow chart of accounting for wages
The flow chart in Fig. 27 shows the main steps in preparing the payroll and posting the financial and cost accounts. The wages control account is useful to reconcile the postings.

## LABOUR REPORTS

Earlier, reference was made to the costs incurred in employing workers. Management requires detailed information on labour performance and costs, as these will materially affect the profitability of the business.

We may consider the reporting of information under the following headings:

1. Idle time, absentees and lateness.
2. Efficiency.
3. Labour turnover.
4. Labour costs.

### Idle time, absentees and lateness
Where workers are remunerated on a time basis a difference between the time for which they are paid and that which they actually spend upon production is bound to arise. This difference is known as idle time, and represents time for which the employer must pay but from which he obtains no direct advantage. The term is not limited in its meaning to time wasted in deliberate slacking, but includes unavoidable losses such as:

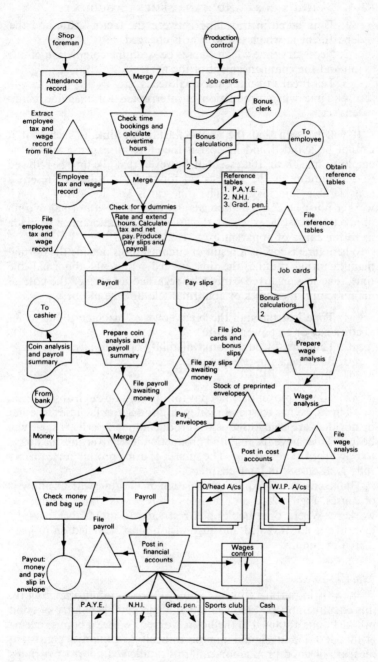

FIG. 27.—*Flow chart of accounting for wages.*

1. Time taken in travelling between the factory gate and the department in which the worker is engaged.

2. Necessary time which elapses between the completion of one job and the commencement of the next.

3. Tea breaks (if any), personal needs, etc.

4. Time when production is interrupted for machine maintenance.

It will be seen that the above wastage of time is such that it cannot be avoided and its cost is therefore an expense which the employer must bear. It is essential, however, that idle time be reduced to a minimum, as the wages paid for such time may represent a considerable sum in total. The time cards and job cards of each worker must be compared constantly and, while a normal margin of idle time must be expected, the fullest investigation must be made as to the cause of apparent excessive idle time.

Where time is lost as a result of circumstances outside the normal manufacturing routine, the time wasted represents abnormal idle time. The loss incurred cannot be regarded as part of the cost of manufacture. Examples of abnormal idle time would be:

1. Time lost through the breakdown of machinery due to inefficiency or to power failure.

2. Time lost through non-availability of materials.

3. Bottlenecks in production.

4. Strikes.

While the employer may not pay for time lost through absenteeism or lateness, he has to spend money on production facilities whether or not they are being used; also, production and perhaps sales will be lost. To achieve the required production level, overtime may have to be worked at added cost. The subject of using production capacity fully is discussed in later chapters.

Management will require information on idle time with an analysis of causes. Figure 28 is an example of a report covering productive workers. Where time booking is restricted to attendance records, idle time is not revealed and supervision must be relied on to keep it to a minimum.

**Efficiency**

While it is important to keep employees occupied in useful work, it is equally important to ensure that an acceptable volume of good production is obtained in the hours worked. Where a bonus scheme is in operation it should not be difficult to obtain a consistent measure of good production in terms of allowed hours or perhaps piece-work earnings. If one type of product is made the number of good products gives a measure of output, but where the products

P.Q.R. CO. LTD.
LOST TIME REPORT

Week ended:........................                           Department:..........................

| Clock No. | Name | Lost time | | | | | | | Prod'n time | % Lost prod'n time | Hours paid |
|---|---|---|---|---|---|---|---|---|---|---|---|
| | | Break down | No material | No work | No drawings | Absentee | Lateness | Total | | | |
| | | | | | | | | | | | |
| | | | | | | | | | | | |
| | | | | | | | | | | | |

FIG. 28.—*Lost time report.*

are diverse, e.g. in a toolmaker's jobbing shop, then problems are encountered. The chapter on Standard Costing will explain how the Standard Hour can be used to measure diverse production but in its absence, sales value of production or added value may be a useful guide.

An efficiency indicator can be prepared at intervals of a day or week by dividing the hours worked into the production. Then if an average or standard efficiency indicator is established, the performance of each employee or section can be measured by calculating the efficiency ratio.

*EXAMPLE*

A factory produces one product which the rate-fixers estimate can be manufactured in 2 hours. In week 4 consisting of 40 hours, Smith and Brown produce 19 and 22 products respectively.

The efficiency indicators are therefore:

Smith $\frac{19}{40} = 0.475$

Brown $\frac{22}{40} = 0.550$

The average indicator is $\frac{20}{40} = 0.500$

The efficiency ratios are therefore:

Smith $\frac{475}{500} = 95\%$

Brown $\frac{550}{500} = 110\%$

**Labour turnover**

Labour turnover is the rate at which employees leave employment, and is evaluated by relating the number of employees leaving during a period of time to the total or average numbers employed in that period. There are various methods of relating these factors:

1. $\dfrac{\text{Employees leaving who have to be replaced}}{\text{Average number employed}}$

2. $\dfrac{\text{All employees leaving}}{\text{Average number employed}}$

3. $\dfrac{\text{All employees leaving plus new employees}}{\text{Average number employed}}$

The second method is to be preferred as it is a better long-term indicator. Method 1 suffers if the business activity goes in cycles as employees will be laid off at a time when business is low, and may subsequently have to be replaced although this may not be known at the time. Method 3 suffers when comparing a department which is expanding with one that is contracting—they may both show similar figures but for different reasons.

By itself the indicator is inadequate; it must be compared with other periods and perhaps other businesses in the same industry. The effects of a high or low turnover rate have then to be considered, e.g. on training cost, on production efficiency and on employee morale.

The personnel department may be asked to prepare a report monthly or quarterly to show the turnover rate and reasons given for leaving. An example is shown in Fig. 29.

P.Q.R. CO. LTD.
LABOUR TURNOVER REPORT

Department.............................    Month:.............................

| Details | This Month | | Cumulative to date | |
|---|---|---|---|---|
| | Men | Women | Men | Women |
| Average number of employees | | | | |
| Number of employees left | | | | |
| Reason for leaving | | | | |
| Higher wages | | | | |
| Job dissatisfaction | | | | |
| Marriage/family | | | | |
| Travelling time | | | | |
| Redundancy | | | | |
| Retirement | | | | |
| Dismissal | | | | |
| Other | | | | |
| Labour turnover rate | | | | |

FIG. 29.—*Labour turnover report.*

## Labour costs

Efficiency indicators are normally based on production hours and quantities, because if wages were used the effect of different rates of pay would distort the figures. However, it is clearly important to analyse the labour cost of production, and therefore, a report such as the one illustrated in Fig. 30 may be presented weekly.

Various other labour costs should be obtained at intervals for management, e.g. training, recruitment, engagement, etc., contained in regular or *ad hoc* reports.

### P.Q.R. CO. LTD.
### LABOUR COST REPORT

Department:.......................................................... Week ended:....................................

| Section | Productive time | | | Paid idle time Hrs | Total time Hrs | Wages paid | | | | Cost per prod'n hour £ |
|---|---|---|---|---|---|---|---|---|---|---|
| | Day work Hrs | O/time Hrs | Total Hrs | | | Time £ | O/time premium £ | Bonus £ | Total £ | |
| Mills | | | | | | | | | | |
| Drills | | | | | | | | | | |
| Auto-lathe | | | | | | | | | | |
| Centre-lathes | | | | | | | | | | |
| Grinders | | | | | | | | | | |
| Miscellaneous | | | | | | | | | | |
| Total | | | | | | | | | | |

FIG. 30.—*Labour cost report.*

### SELF-STUDY TEST No. 3

*Personnel and Labour Cost*

(*Refer to the Appendix on p. 344 for outline solutions.*)

1. Describe a procedure for reconciling job cards, which travel with the work, with employees' weekly time records.

2. List the main documents involved in paying and accounting for direct and indirect labour; indicate briefly the purpose of each document.

3. The rust-proofing department of a company which manufactures metal components comprises nine operatives and a supervisor. The target output of the department is 1,000 units per week of 40 working hours.

Operatives are paid £1.20 per hour plus a share of the departmental bonus, which is calculated weekly as follows:

> 20p per unit in excess of target up to 120 per cent.
> 25p per unit in excess of 120 per cent of target.

Twenty per cent of the bonus is paid to the supervisor whose basic salary is £80 per week and the remainder is divided among the operatives in proportion to the hours worked by each.

Output for the two weeks ended May 23rd and May 30th was:

|  | May 23rd | | May 30th | |
|  | Units treated | Hours worked | Units treated | Hours worked |
|---|---|---|---|---|
| Monday | 224 | 72 | 239 | 68 |
| Tuesday | 236 | 72 | 265 | 72 |
| Wednesday | 242 | 70 | 283 | 72 |
| Thursday | 220 | 64 | 296 | 72 |
| Friday | 260 | 72 | 301 | 72 |

During each of the weeks the department operated a normal working week of 40 hours. Departmental overhead (excluding the supervisor's salary and bonus) is absorbed at the rate of £15 per departmental working hour. Production overhead apportioned to the department is £18,750 for the year of 50 working weeks.

(a) Calculate the proofing cost per unit for each of the two weeks; the cost of material is £0.10 per unit.

(b) Calculate in respect of each of the two weeks the effective hourly rate of pay (including bonus) of the operatives.

(c) Comment briefly upon the results disclosed by your answers to (a) and (b).

4. From the following details calculate the labour cost chargeable to Job No. 873 in respect of an employee who is paid according to:

(a) The Rowan scheme.

(b) The Halsey 50 per cent scheme.

*Job No. 873*

| Time allowed | 5 hours 30 minutes |
| Time taken | 4 hours 25 minutes |
| Rate of pay | £0.90 per hour |

5. Labour costs increase when labour turnover increases. Describe the costs that are affected by a high labour turnover and state the kind of information to include in a report prepared for management to inform them of labour movements.

6. Define and distinguish between job evaluation and merit-rating. List and briefly describe the steps to be taken and the factors to be considered.

7. (a) Give a brief definition of work measurement.

(b) Name and write a brief note on the four principal stages involved in work measurement.

8. A company is considering installing a workers' profit-sharing scheme in lieu of an individual bonus scheme. You are required to specify the disadvantages of each of these schemes and to give an example of each point you list.

# CHAPTER 5

# Expenses

The third element of cost, expenses, represents all costs other than materials and wages. The source document for recording expenses may be an expense invoice, a cash payment or a cost journal voucher. The last-named document would record items such as depreciation of assets and notional items.

## CONTROL OF EXPENSES

Many expenses are incurred at the same time as the other elements of cost. Freight and similar charges incurred in obtaining materials and National Insurance contributions incurred in the employment of labour, are examples. A decision to purchase material or to recruit labour must consider these ancillary costs, and it is at the time when the decision is taken that cost control must function. The decision to employ men or women should allow for different employment expenses; once the decision has been taken the expense is virtually beyond control, at least in the daily aspect of control.

The principle of controlling costs at the decision-point is more important with long-term expenses such as rates and rent, where a decision to occupy a building will involve considerable future costs and cannot be reversed without a major upheaval. This is a feature of many fixed costs and introduces two important points which the cost accountant must consider when providing information for management:

1. Are expenses controllable by the cost centre supervisors for whom they are incurred?
2. Which costs are relevant to a decision?

The first question is considered in the next chapter, on apportioning indirect costs, and the second in the chapter on relevant costs (Chapter 12).

There are a number of expenses, such as telephone charges, postage, power and fuel, where management can influence the amount of cost incurred by giving detailed instructions to employees on when to use a service and ensuring, by supervision and control procedures, that the instructions are complied with. For example, most letters to go by second-class mail and only important letters by first-class mail; requests for copy invoices from local suppliers to be made by telephone; electric ovens only to be used in off-peak times. Such practical measures may reduce expenses, and the effectiveness of control will be apparent when actual expenses are listed monthly for comparison with the budget.

Before proceeding to discuss the methods of relating indirect costs to cost centres and cost units this is a timely place to consider two other expenses, notional charges and depreciation. Notional charges are those which are not incurred in the sense that a debt becomes due for payment, but are included in costs for particular reasons.

Depreciation is the diminution in the value of a fixed asset due to use or the lapse of time. A portion of the purchase price or manufactured value, which represents an estimate of the amount of depreciation, is "released" in an accounting period to be charged against the profits for that period. In a sense it is a prepaid expense as it is incurred in one period for the benefit of future periods; the value is therefore carried forward in the accounts, amounts being released every year during the life of the asset. The various methods of arriving at the depreciation charge will be explained.

Similar problems of charging prepaid costs arise with such costs as advertising, and research and development expenditure. While there is generally a tendency to write the expenditure off as early as possible, strictly, the estimated value attributable to future years should be carried forward and charged against the trading results for those years. The difference in treatment between depreciation and these other prepaid expenses stems from the tangibility of assets compared with, say, an advertising charge. The visible asset remains and has a realisable value whereas, although the effect of advertising may be seen in increased sales, advertising expenditure has no resale value and its effect may be cancelled by the efforts of competitors.

## INTEREST ON CAPITAL

The question of whether or not interest on capital employed in manufacture is to be deemed cost, and as such featured in the cost accounts, is one upon which there is considerable difference of opinion. There is one point, however, upon which opinion should not be divided. If interest is to be considered at all it must not be confined merely to such interest as may actually have been paid by the business. Whether interest is to be paid depends entirely upon the method of capitalisation; if a company relies mainly upon borrowed money, e.g. in the form of debentures, mortgages, loans, etc., upon which it has to pay interest, that does not enable it to charge more for its products than a competitive organisation financed by share capital.

It may be said, therefore, that so far as the cost accounts are concerned, interest should either be ignored entirely or else included in respect of all capital employed, whether such capital requires the payment of interest or not. Where it is decided to exclude interest from the cost accounts, even interest which has been paid must be ignored.

The main arguments advanced for and against the inclusion of a notional charge for interest in cost accounts are summarised below.

### For the inclusion of interest

1. Interest is the reward of capital, and is therefore as much a charge against profits as wages, the reward of labour. It is apparent that profit in the economist's sense cannot be ascertained without due consideration of the question of interest.

*EXAMPLE*

B commences in business as a manufacturer and purchases plant and machinery, tools, material and other necessaries for the sum of £10,000. B raises the capital required by disposing of certain stocks and shares which have previously provided him with an income of £1,000 per annum.

At the end of the first year, B's accounts, after allowing reasonable remuneration for his own services, disclose a profit of £1,000. This profit, however, is only the equivalent of the income he would have received from his original investments, and therefore must be regarded as a return upon the capital he has invested in the business and not as a real profit. If he had borrowed his capital, and as a result interest had been charged against the revenue of the year, no profit would have been disclosed, which actually is the true position.

2. The comparison of operations, processes, etc., without due consideration of the interest factor may lead to erroneous conclusions. For example, if one manufacturer matures his own timber and another purchases his supplies already matured, the first manufacturer will appear to have purchased his materials more cheaply than the second unless interest is considered on the capital which has been locked up in the timber held for maturing.

3. Where interest is taken into consideration, regard is paid to the time element which is one of the most important factors in production.

*EXAMPLE*

Contract No. 1, which involved a total expenditure of £5,000, reveals a profit of £500. Contract No. 2, upon which £3,000 was expended, discloses a profit of £450.

Contract No. 1 took six months to complete, but Contract No. 2 was finished in three months. If the *average* capital locked up in Contract No. 1 for six months was £3,000, and in Contract No. 2, £2,000 for three months, and interest on capital employed is taken into consideration at, say 15 per cent per annum, the real profit made on Contract No. 1 will be £275 only, and that upon Contract No. 2, £375.

From the above illustration it will be seen that where considerable sums of money are locked up in contracts for an extended period the interest factor is of the utmost importance and unless it is taken into consideration, misleading results may be shown.

4. The result of installing expensive machinery to replace hand labour or other machines cannot be gauged accurately without including interest on the capital involved. For example, if £2,000 is expended on the purchase of a machine it must be remembered that in the first years of its life it has cost, at 15 per cent, £300 in respect of interest on the money expended; regard must be had for this fact when considering the advantages gained from the installation of the machine.

## Against the inclusion of interest

1. Whether interest is payable or not is entirely a matter of internal finance, and is not connected with the cost of manufacture. One manufacturer may use only his own capital; another may finance his business by means of loans, bank overdrafts, etc., while a third may raise funds by the issue of debentures, preference shares, etc. Each will adopt the method which he regards as the most economical and satisfactory for his particular requirements; the system adopted will in no way affect manufacturing costs; it will merely affect the balance of profit available for distribution.

*EXAMPLE*

A and B both possess £10,000. A starts a manufacturing business which absorbs the whole of his capital. B commences a similar business, but obtains the necessary capital, on loan at 10 per cent per annum interest. B's private capital of £10,000 is invested in securities yielding 10 per cent per annum.

At the end of the first year of trading A and B each make a profit of £2,000 before charging interest. A will retain the whole of his profit but B must pay £1,000 interest for the use of his capital. B, however, receives £1,000 from his investments and his net position is thus the same as that of A. Other things being equal, it is apparent that B cannot expect the same retainable profit for himself from his business as A will receive from his.

2. If interest, although not paid, is allowed for in the cost accounts, the values of stocks and work-in-progress may include such interest and require adjustment for financial reporting purposes.

3. Considerable difficulty is experienced in determining the exact capital upon which interest should be calculated. The total capital employed in manufacture, e.g. the capital sunk in fixed assets together with the average working capital involved in the form of stocks, and debtors, etc., may be adopted as the basis, or, alternatively, the capital sunk in fixed assets only. Theoretically, there is no doubt

that if interest is to be considered at all it should be calculated upon the total capital employed for the time it is used, which may be most difficult to ascertain.

4. A fair rate of interest is difficult to determine and must necessarily be adjusted to meet market fluctuations; as market rates of interest may vary considerably, numerous adjustments will be required in the cost accounts. Moreover, the risk element may vary between assets or activities and this factor should be considered when determining interest rates. It will also be appreciated that one manufacturer may be in a position to borrow money much more cheaply than another owing to the security he has to offer, the possession of friends willing to make him advances at low rates, etc.

5. The cost accounts are complicated unnecessarily by the inclusion of interest on capital which will entail additional clerical work and may cause misleading statements to be prepared.

It is thought that the arguments against the inclusion of interest, although based largely on expediency and the practical difficulties involved, outweigh the more theoretical arguments in favour of its inclusion. While there is no doubt that profits in the economist's sense cannot be ascertained without regard for interest on the factors of production involved and that a business cannot in the long run survive unless it earns sufficient profits to pay loan interest and a reasonable dividend on its share capital, it does not seem necessary that the cost accounts should be confused by notional calculations based on more or less inexact estimates of capital employed.

*In cost estimation, however, it is advantageous to include an amount to cover interest, especially where the job takes a long period to complete and progress payments are not made.* Furthermore, where a choice between alternative projects is required, and costs per year for the projects vary considerably, costs and income (or, more accurately, cash flows) need to be adjusted by the interest factor.

## RENT OF FACTORY BUILDINGS

Rent paid is undoubtedly an expense which must be charged to production. Sometimes however, the factory premises are owned by the business and no rent is paid. In such circumstances a charge in lieu of rent should be made in the cost accounts in order that a more accurate cost of production may be ascertained. Unless such a charge is made the total cost will be calculated without regard to the expense virtually entailed by reason of the loss of interest on the capital sunk in the factory premises. The annual value of the premises, as assessed for rating purposes, is normally a satisfactory amount to charge in lieu of rent.

It is true that rent is merely a form of interest on capital, and that if a notional charge is made in the cost accounts all other interest should similarly be considered. This argument is, in fact, invariably advanced by those in favour of including interest on capital in the cost accounts. As, however, the actual rent payable, or a charge to be made in lieu, is so much easier to determine than other forms of interest, and is applicable in one form or another to every business, it may with advantage be included in the cost accounts, even if other interest is excluded.

# DEPRECIATION

A summary of the accepted methods of depreciation follows, together with the appropriate formula used to calculate the annual depreciation charge.

## STRAIGHT-LINE METHOD
The method of providing for depreciation by means of equal periodic charges over the assumed life of the asset.

$$(Asset\ cost) \div (Estimated\ life)$$

## REDUCING BALANCE METHOD
The method of providing for depreciation by means of periodic charges calculated as a constant proportion of the balance of the value of the asset after deducting the amounts previously provided.

$$(Written\ down\ balance\ on\ asset\ account) \times (Fixed\ percentage)$$

## PRODUCTION UNIT (HOUR) METHOD
The method of providing for depreciation by means of a fixed rate per unit (hour) of production calculated by dividing the value of the asset by the estimated number of units (hours) to be produced during its life.

$$(Asset\ cost) \div \frac{(Estimated\ production}{units\ or\ hours\ during\ life)} \times \frac{(Annual\ production}{units\ or\ hours)}$$

## REPAIR PROVISION METHOD
The method of providing for the aggregate of depreciation and maintenance cost by means of periodic charges, each of which is a constant proportion of the aggregate of the cost of the asset depreciated and the expected maintenance cost during its life.

$$(Asset\ cost + Estimated\ repairs\ costs\ during\ life) \div (Estimated\ life)$$

## SINKING FUND METHOD
The method of providing for depreciation by means of fixed periodic charges which, aggregated with compound interest over the life of the asset, would equal the cost of that asset. Simultaneously with each periodic charge, an investment of the same amount would be made in fixed-interest securities which would accumulate at com-

pound interest to provide, at the end of the life of the asset, a sum equal to its cost.

$$(\text{Asset cost} - \text{Interest received during life}) \div (\text{Estimated life})$$

ENDOWMENT POLICY METHOD

The method of providing for depreciation by means of fixed periodic charges equivalent to the premiums on an endowment policy for the amount required to provide, at the end of the life of the asset, a sum equal to its cost.

Depreciation equals premium charged by insurance company

REVALUATION METHOD

The method of providing for depreciation by means of periodic charges, each of which is equivalent to the difference between the values assigned to the asset at the beginning and the end of the period.

$$(\text{Previous asset value}) - (\text{Present asset value})$$

SUM OF THE DIGITS METHOD

The method of providing for depreciation by means of differing periodic rates computed according to the following formula: If $n$ is the estimated life of the asset the rate is calculated each period as a fraction in which the denominator is always the sum of the series 1, 2, 3, ... $n$ and the numerator for the first period is $n$, for the second $n-1$, and so on.

$$(\text{Asset cost}) \times \frac{\text{(Estimated life in years} + 1 - \text{age of asset in years)}}{} \div \text{(Sum of years of estimated life)}$$

NOTES: 1. The most popular methods are the first two, due primarily to their simplicity.

2. The asset cost to be written off over the estimated life of the asset is the cost of purchasing (or producing) the asset and will include the cost of architects', and surveyors' fees, etc., transporting the asset, preparing the foundations and installing the asset on site ready for use. Any estimated scrap value, less dismantling and removal costs, would be deducted from the asset cost.

3. The sinking fund method requires an interest rate to be selected.

4. The sinking fund and endowment policy methods provide for replacement of the asset as well as depreciation.

5. The formula for calculating the percentage used in the reducing balance method is: $S = A \left( 1 - \frac{r}{100} \right)^{l}$, where:

$S$ = scrap value
$A$ = asset cost
$r$ = rate of depreciation
$l$ = life in years

*EXAMPLE*

A business acquires a new asset for £1,000. It is estimated that it will last five years, at the end of which it will be sold for £50. The estimated repairs are £200 over the life and the actual repairs for each year are £25, £35, £30, £75 and £35. Show the charges to Profit and Loss Account for each of the five years under the straight line, reducing balance, repair provision and sum of the digits methods.

1. *Straight-line method*

| | |
|---|---:|
| Cost | £1,000 |
| Scrap value | 50 |
| Net cost | £950 |
| Life | 5 years |

Depreciation $(20\%) = £190$

2. *Reducing balance method*

Applying the formula in Note 5 above.

$$£50 = £1,000\left(1 - \frac{\text{rate}}{100}\right)^5$$

Rate $= 45\%$

3. *Repair provision method*

| | |
|---|---:|
| Net cost = | £950 |
| Repairs = | 200 |
| Total cost | £1,150 |

Combined charge per year for five years $= £230$

4. *Sum of the digits method*

Net cost $= £950$

Sum of years $(1+2+3+4+5) = 15$

Year 1 depreciation $= \dfrac{5+1-1}{15} = \dfrac{5}{15} \times £950 = £317$

Year 2 depreciation $= \dfrac{5+1-2}{15} = \dfrac{4}{15} \times £950 = £253$

Etc.

The schedule in Fig. 31 compares the four methods.

There are various reasons for including the depreciation charge in the accounts and accountants differ in the emphasis they place on each and on the relative suitability of the different methods.

1. The annual accounts must be charged with a reasonable proportion of the original cost of the asset before arriving at the annual profit. What is reasonable will depend on the circumstances. If there is political or economic trouble it may be prudent to write assets off quickly. A business with a branch in a country in which revolutions are frequent may well decide that capital investment there is

|  | DEPRECIATION AND WRITTEN DOWN BALANCE PER YEAR | | | | TOTAL ANNUAL CHARGE FOR USE OF ASSET (DEPRECIATION AND REPAIRS) | | | |
|---|---|---|---|---|---|---|---|---|
|  | Straight line £ | Reducing balance £ | Repair provision £ | Sum of digits £ | Straight line £ | Reducing balance £ | Repair provision £ | Sum of digits £ |
| Asset cost | 1,000 | 1,000 | 1,000 | 1,000 |  |  |  |  |
| Year 1 | 190 | 450 | Repairs +25 −230 | $\frac{5}{15}$ 317 | 215 | 475 | 230 | 342 |
|  | 810 | 550 | 795 | 683 |  |  |  |  |
| Year 2 | 190 | 248 | Repairs +35 −230 | $\frac{4}{15}$ 253 | 225 | 283 | 230 | 288 |
|  | 620 | 302 | 600 | 430 |  |  |  |  |
| Year 3 | 190 | 136 | Repairs +30 −230 | $\frac{3}{15}$ 190 | 220 | 166 | 230 | 220 |
|  | 430 | 166 | 400 | 240 |  |  |  |  |
| Year 4 | 190 | 75 | Repairs +75 −230 | $\frac{2}{15}$ 127 | 265 | 150 | 230 | 202 |
|  | 240 | 91 | 245 | 113 |  |  |  |  |
| Year 5 | 190 | 41 | Repairs +35 −230 | $\frac{1}{15}$ 63 | 225 | 76 | 230 | 98 |
| Balance | 50 | 50 | 50 | 50 |  |  |  |  |

Fig. 31.—*Four different methods of depreciation compared.*

so risky that assets are virtually written off when they are purchased. The reducing balance method has the advantage that the balance on the asset account is reduced quickly in the early years; the sum of the digits method has a similar effect on the depreciation charge. These methods do allow for the large reduction in realisable values that immediately takes place with certain assets, e.g. motor-cars. The straight-line method is thought to be reasonable for most assets because it charges depreciation equally each year.

2. The *total* charge for the use of the asset ought to be shared equally over the useful life. Depreciation is only one part of the cost of using an asset and repair costs should be provided for evenly over the life instead of letting them fall heavily in particular years. The repair provision method puts this into effect. It is argued that the reducing balance method achieves this in practice because low depreciation charges in the later years are counterbalanced by heavier repair costs. However, if this does happen it would probably be a rare occurrence.

3. Product costs must include the amount of asset value lost as a result of producing the product. The production hour and production unit methods seek to do this, and where the value of the asset can be exactly related to the units extracted, e.g. in the case of a mine, this is clearly an accurate method. However, not only is it difficult to establish the output during the life of the asset but also this method ignores losses in value due to the asset becoming obsolete. Within certain limits it may make little difference whether the asset is working or not. The revaluation method seeks to achieve a similar aim, but the results could be wildly distorted by the market for the asset, so that the annual depreciation charge would fluctuate from year to year.

4. The real cost of using an asset must be charged in terms of current replacement values. This will ensure that product costs compare with those of competitors using new equipment. Further, by setting additional amounts aside out of profits, there is no risk of the profit being distributed and of money not being available to pay for the increased cost of the new asset. The depreciation charge over and above the amount required to write off the asset would be taken to a Replacement Reserve. This subject is part of the wider aspect of Replacement Theory Accounting, which is outside the scope of this book.

Rarely are estimates borne out by experience and either: (a) the asset is written off too early so that there is no depreciation charge for the last years of its life, or when it is sold it realises more than the estimated scrap value, or (b) it is not written off quickly enough and the sale proceeds are less than the written-down value. If (a) occurs, it may be useful to continue depreciating assets in the cost accounts in order to keep costs comparable between periods and realistic when comparing with competitors' costs. Guidelines for treating various aspects of depreciation are contained in Statements of Standard Accounting Practice or exposure drafts.

## CONTROL OF CAPITAL EQUIPMENT

A complete record of each item of capital equipment is essential in almost any business. Not only will the record be used as the basis for an inventory of fixed assets and for calculating depreciation charges, but the detail provided will assist in management control and decision-making, for example, in planning machine utilisation and in preparing cost budgets. A plant register, similar to the illustration in Fig. 32, is recommended. The columnar form is particularly useful, in that the complete history of the equipment is disclosed at a glance. Further columns can with advantage be added to show, for example, the written-down value for taxation purposes.

| | | | | | P.Q.R. CO. LTD. PLANT REGISTER | | |
|---|---|---|---|---|---|---|---|
| Machine No......................... | | | Location:.............................. | | | Register No.:..................... | |
| Description:......................... | | | Makers:................................ | | | Remarks:........................... | |
| ................................................. | | | Date received:.................... | | | ................................................ | |
| Date | Par-ticulars | Repairs, renewals and main-tenance | Depre-ciation | Written down value | Original value and additions | Calculation of depreciation | |
| | | £ | £ | £ | £ | | |
| | | | | | Purchase and installations | Est. scrap value | £ |
| | | | | | Additions: | Net cost | £ |
| | | | | | | Est. life Annual depreciation | £ |
| | | | | | | Disposal date Proceeds | £ |
| | | | | | | Profit/Loss | £ |

Fig. 32.—*Plant register.*

# CHAPTER 6

# Overhead

## IDENTIFYING COSTS WITH COST UNITS

We have considered the three elements of cost—materials, wages and expenses, and the distinction between direct and indirect costs was referred to in Chapter 1. It is now necessary to pursue this subject further and to study the problems associated with identifying costs with a product or service.

Figure 33 illustrates the procedures involved in processing cost data, using the absorption costing technique, and indicates the greater complexity of the treatment of indirect costs compared with that of direct costs. The main purposes of the technique must be kept in mind, which are:

1. To ascertain the cost of activities in order to help management to operate profitably.
2. To ascertain product costs for use in determining selling prices.
3. To evaluate stocks of work-in-progress and finished goods.

## THE CONCEPT OF COST

In everyday speech the word cost tends to have the same meaning as "price", for example, the purchaser of a suit of clothes for £45 might, if asked the price, say, "It cost £45". But if asked the price of the waistcoat he would have difficulty in answering, because he would need to make certain assumptions in apportioning the £45 which he paid. He might measure the length of cloth and the number of buttons in each garment and make a division of the price on this basis. Alternatively, he might consider that the cost of wages for making the jacket would be higher than for the waistcoat, and allow for that in his computation.

The cost accountant is faced with similar problems. The total costs of the business can be ascertained without much difficulty but they must be related to the multitude of jobs handled. The accountant adopts certain conventions in arriving at historical cost and those he selects will affect his figures. Convention enters into the treatment of each element of cost as will be seen from the following:

1. Raw materials. The charge will vary according to the method selected for the pricing of issues and the treatment of waste.

2. Wages. The charge will be affected by the treatment of overtime payments and idle time.

3. Depreciation. The charge will vary according to the method of depreciation selected.

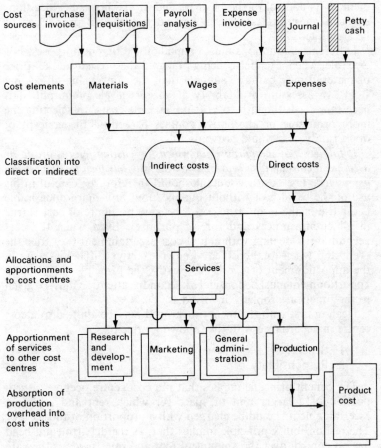

FIG. 33.—*Scheme of processing cost data.*

Different views exist on these problems, and it is impossible to lay down rules which will be theoretically correct for every type of industry or business. The cost accountant must use his knowledge and experience and consider the requirements of management in selecting the methods most suitable. It can, however, be said that the methods selected should be applied consistently and, if a uniform costing system for the industry has been prescribed by its trade association, it should be adopted.

There are, however, other difficulties, and the cost accountant must consider exactly what the term "cost" means and whether this meaning is the same in all circumstances.

The ascertainment of historical cost is only one of the accountant's functions; others include the more important one of assisting management in its control of the business and in making policy decisions on such questions as price fixing and the level of production to be attempted.

Different assumptions must be made for different purposes. For example, when a tender is being prepared the present market price of material may be more suitable than the book value of existing stock. In assessing profitability at various levels of output, it is necessary to distinguish fixed from variable costs. In selecting the more profitable of alternative courses of action, the concept of opportunity cost would prove useful.

*It follows that the purpose for which the costing figures are to be used has a considerable bearing upon the way in which the figures are assembled.* The cost accountant should therefore be careful in his use of the word cost without qualification. Still more undesirable is the use of the term "true cost", because no figure of cost is true in all circumstances and for all purposes. Even when the cost accountant is dealing with actual cost ascertainment (i.e. after the event and when total costs are known exactly), difficulties arise in the apportionment of overhead. Firstly, the principles involved in apportionment must be considered; secondly, attention must be given to the practical problems involved.

Dealing first with the theory, overhead may be allotted to a cost centre in accordance with the following principles:

1. Benefit.
2. Responsibility.

The benefit principle implies that if a cost centre occupies a proportion of a larger unit of space for which rent and rates are ascertainable it should be charged with a proportion of those costs. The responsibility principle implies that, as the departmental head has no control over the amount of rent and rates paid, as they are fixed by decisions of others, his department should not bear any allocation of them. A departmental head can control, at least to some extent, the level of such costs as heating, cleaning and machine maintenance, and these would be chargeable to his department. It is considered that the responsibility criterion is more appropriate for purposes of cost control. Many undertakings have their own service departments, for example, to generate electricity for heating or process purposes. The head of a production department can control the quantity of current used but if the generating plant is inefficient the cost per unit will be unduly high, and, therefore, the cost of current which is the responsibility of the production department, will be excessive. Accordingly, the departmental head might argue that it should be charged to him at Electricity Board rates. This would imply that the excess of the cost of current over that of an outside supply should not be charged against production. A balance would, therefore, remain in the Power House Account, representing the cost of uneconomic operation of the generating plant. It would clearly be in the interest of management to be made aware of this figure when considering the future operation of the plant. The use of the benefit criterion would not disclose this loss. If the department in question used, say, 26 per cent of the current generated as measured by the departmental meters, then 26 per cent of the cost of current would be charged to it and a proportion of the uneconomic cost would be borne by the production department.

These matters are mentioned to illustrate the difficulties inherent in the computation of cost. It is proposed, to simplify the treatment of indirect costs, to leave the question of allotment by responsibility criterion on one side and to assume that, for purposes of actual cost ascertainment, the benefit criterion is used in compiling overhead analyses between departments. Further consideration will be given to the subject when dealing with budgetary control.

## OVERHEAD CLASSIFICATION

With the foregoing in mind, it is necessary now to consider all the indirect costs which are described as overhead and which relate either to the business as a whole or to a particular location or function. They must be charged to cost centres in a fair and reasonable manner bearing in mind the benefit criterion discussed above.

In many businesses, especially when production is highly mechanised, overhead costs are considerable and may well exceed the total cost of productive labour. The importance of accurate allocation of overhead to the various jobs, contracts or departments cannot, therefore, be over-emphasised.

Overhead can be regarded as being incurred in the following major functions:

1. Production.
2. General administration.
3. Marketing.
4. Research.
5. Development.

It may be necessary to subdivide each major function if the size of the business, or management information requirements, demand it. For example, production may be subdivided between different manufacturing divisions. The analysis of overhead will show the cost of running factory A in terms of rents, rates, lighting, depreciation and maintenance. If factory A contains, say, three production shops, with ancillary tool-room, ambulance department, stores and offices, the production overhead attaching to the location will be further subdivided into cost centres, which represent individual departments in factory A. The object is to absorb the costs of the factory into productive cost units, i.e. the particular jobs, contracts or batches which pass through it and the allotment of costs to cost centres is a necessary preliminary to that absorption.

It is essential however, that the cost of obtaining information should not be excessive, and, therefore, a dissection of costs which will theoretically give a great degree of exactness may have to be abandoned for a simpler and quicker, although less accurate, method. For example, the cost of the ambulance room may be included with general works overhead rather than be isolated as a cost of a separate department; thus the labour of ascertaining its cost by analysis is avoided. It is impossible to lay down hard-and-fast rules. Consultation with management will be helpful in determining the degree of accuracy required; figures of reasonable accuracy promptly prepared are usually of greater value than more exact and detailed ones which are not available until long after the event. Furthermore, it is often found that accuracy is not proportional to the degree of analysis attempted.

The following definitions of the costs attributable to major functions are recommended by the Institute of Cost and Management Accountants:

*Production cost.* Prime cost plus absorbed production overhead.

*Marketing cost.* The cost incurred in publicising and presenting to customers the products of the undertaking in suitably attractive forms and at acceptable prices, together with the costs of all relevant research work, the securing of orders and, usually, delivery of the goods to customers. In certain cases, after-sales service and/or order processing may also be included.

*Selling cost.* That portion of marketing cost which is incurred in securing orders.

*Publicity cost.* That portion of marketing cost which is incurred in advertising and promotion as aids to the eventual sales of goods or services.

*Distribution cost.* That portion of marketing cost which is incurred in warehousing saleable products and in delivering products to customers.

NOTE: In most cases, particularly where consumer products are concerned, distribution is regarded as a part of the marketing function but, in exceptional cases—for example, where heavy industrial equipment is supplied—distribution may be regarded as an extension of the production function.

*General administration cost.* The sum of those costs of general management, and of secretarial, accounting and administrative services, which cannot be directly related to the production, marketing, research or development functions of the enterprise.

*Research cost.* The cost of seeking new or improved products, applications of materials or methods.

*Development cost.* The cost of the process which begins with the implementation of the decision to produce a new or improved product or to employ a new or improved method, and ends with the commencement of formal production of that product or by that method.

## Production overhead

The definition of production cost incorporates prime cost, i.e. direct materials, direct wages and direct expenses. Costs which can be immediately classified as production overhead will include:

> Factory rent, rates, lighting and heating.
> Power and fuel.
> Depreciation, repairs and insurance (where such charges relate to production facilities).
> Salaries and related costs of production management.
> National Insurance (employer's contributions).
> Retirement pension premiums.
> Wages of indirect workers.
> Material of little individual value used in production, e.g. screws, nails, bolts, nuts, paint and enamel.
> Oil, rags and other factory supplies.
> Carriage inwards on materials purchased for manufacture (where the charge cannot conveniently be added to the cost of materials).
> Normal wastage of material (where it is not provided for by inflating the price of issues).
> Proportion of estimating department costs.
> Storekeeping and time-keeping.
> Canteen and welfare.
> Tool-room costs.
> Production control and progress department.

Further explanation may be helpful on the treatment of certain costs:

RENT AND RATES

Ascertainment of the total charge for rent and rates should not present any difficulty. It may be necessary, however, to apportion the total between functions and between cost centres within a function, probably on the basis of ground area. Allowance may be made for the fact that the office and sales departments occupy a more valuable part of the site.

#### LIGHTING, HEATING, FUEL AND POWER

Treatment will depend on whether the services are supplied internally or externally. External supplies will be charged by gas/electricity boards, etc. and analysed into convenient natural classifications. The total of each natural classification can then be apportioned between functions and cost centres on an equitable basis.

If the factory generates its own power, it is advantageous to treat the power generating department as a service cost centre. Costs will be charged to the cost centre for subsequent allotment to other cost centres.

#### MAINTENANCE AND REPAIRS TO PLANT AND BUILDINGS

A carefully planned system for the maintenance of plant will minimise the risk of breakdown, with its consequent loss of production. Each machine should be inspected regularly for wear and defects, and such matters as lubrication, greasing and the renewal of small parts attended to. Records of hours run and dates of servicing must be kept, so that each machine is dealt with in its turn. It may be found that out of a battery of, say, ten machines, only nine are in use at any time, the tenth being under maintenance. Such "planned maintenance" goes a considerable way towards preventing a simultaneous breakdown of two or more machines, which would result in excessive pressure on the engineering department and loss of production. At longer intervals, a major overhaul of each machine should be carried out. It is frequently beneficial to analyse separately the cost of:

1. Maintenance.
2. Major overhauls.
3. Repairing breakdowns.

Such analysis will enable management to measure the efficiency with which the programme of maintenance and overhaul has been executed.

Where maintenance and repair work is carried out by the firm's own workmen, adequate records must be kept to give the degree of analysis required, e.g. it may be necessary to ascertain the cost of maintaining each machine or, alternatively, of each batch of similar machines.

Service orders will be issued as authority for the execution of repairs. Expenditure on materials, labour and other direct charges for repairs or maintenance will be debited to a Service Order Account in the same manner as to a Job Account. The prime cost of the work performed is thus disclosed and, an addition may be made for production overhead on one of the bases discussed later in the chapter. Unless this addition is made, the real cost of the work done is not disclosed, but as the total expenditure on the service order is itself an expense, overhead expenses may be ignored.

The cost of the work performed, as shown by the Service Order Account, is charged to the department or departments concerned.

Where capital expenditure work is carried out by the company's own workmen, a Capital Order Account is opened for each contract. Expenditure incurred will be charged to this account in the same way as service orders.

Such Capital Orders do not, of course, represent production overhead, and the appropriate fixed asset account will be debited with the cost. The capital expenditure will affect the charge for depreciation as and when the asset comes into operation.

SALARIES AND RELATED COSTS OF PRODUCTION MANAGEMENT

The amount to be charged in the cost accounts will be the salaries paid, plus auxiliary costs, e.g. the company's superannuation contribution, if any. Directors' fees as such are usually excluded from the costing books, the charge for directors' remuneration being confined to their salaries and other emoluments as executives. If a director divides his time between different functions, e.g. production and administration, his salary and emoluments should be apportioned on the basis of the time devoted to each function.

NATIONAL INSURANCE AND PENSIONS

Employees' contributions, which are deducted from wages payable, will not affect the cost accounts, as the "gross wage" is the true cost of the worker. The contributions made by the employer, however, may be regarded as an indirect expense and allotted to cost centres according to the number and duties of the employees. Details will be provided by the payroll.

INSURANCE OF FACTORY BUILDINGS AND PLANT

Insurance premiums should be apportioned between cost centres on the bases most equitable in the circumstances. Frequently, an inventory of buildings and plant contained in the insurance policy will provide a suitable basis. The schedule to the policy may also indicate the rates for the different risks and, if there is a considerable difference between the rates because of the nature of the processes, account must be taken of this in making the apportionment in order that the department in which the risk is high is charged with the additional cost.

ESTIMATING DEPARTMENT AND DRAWING OFFICE

Expenses incurred in making estimates for the purpose of tendering for contracts are best regarded as marketing expenses. Where, however, the expenses incurred for a particular contract are large they should be charged to the job concerned. In some businesses it may be necessary for draughtsmen and estimators to record their time so that an hourly rate of expense can be computed and charged to the jobs on which they have been engaged. Time spent by the research department in connection with a particular job or contract should be separated from the costs of research and development carried out for the benefit of the business as a whole and regarded as an extension of the costs of estimating or of the drawing office. It must be remembered that time and money must frequently be spent on preparing designs, plans and estimates for the purpose of tendering, which if the tender is not accepted, must be regarded as a general marketing overhead.

ROYALTIES

If royalties based on output are paid for the use of a machine or piece of plant because it incorporates some patented device, the royalty can be regarded as a direct expense and charged to the product concerned. If royalties are calculated on units sold they are more properly regarded as a selling expense.

**Marketing cost**

As indicated by the I.C.M.A. definition, it will be useful in most businesses to divide the function of Marketing into Selling, Publicity and Distribution sub-functions for cost classification purposes. The organisation structure and the significance of marketing cost will determine the arrangement of cost centres within sub-functions.

Typical costs included under each sub-function are as follows:

SELLING
    Salaries, commissions and travelling expenses of salesmen and
        technical representatives.
    Bad debts.
    Upkeep and administration costs of sales offices.

PUBLICITY
    Advertising.
    Catalogues and price-lists.
    Upkeep of showrooms.

DISTRIBUTION
    Carriage and freight outwards.
    Packing charges.
    Delivery vehicle costs.
    Warehousing.

It is impractical to attempt to deal with every foreseeable circumstance but the following examples are indicative of the approach in dealing with contentious items.

CATALOGUES AND PRICE LISTS

The production of a catalogue can be expensive and is often undertaken only at intervals of several years. For costing purposes, expenditure incurred, including the cost of staff to collect the necessary information, may be charged to a suspense account and a proportion allocated each year to publicity costs, so that the full cost of the publication is recovered by the time a new edition becomes desirable. In the financial accounts the cost of catalogues, etc., is usually written off in the year in which it is incurred.

BAD DEBTS

Average bad debts incurred may be ascertained from past experience, expressed as a percentage of credit sales and the resultant sum included in selling overhead.

CASH DISCOUNTS

The question of including cash discounts in the cost accounts is closely related to the question of interest on capital, which has already been discussed. The discount allowed may be regarded merely as interest paid to secure cash resources and, therefore, purely a matter of finance. If this view is taken, the discounts must be treated in the same manner as other interest and excluded from the cost accounts.

REBATES

It is customary in some industries for rebates from selling price to be granted to customers based on their sales for a year or other period. These rebates are frequently on a graduated scale, which increases with the business for the period. Rebates are normally given at the end of the period to which they relate and are in effect trade discounts, and hence a reduction of the selling price. For this reason they are, perhaps, best deducted from the figure of sales. Alternatively, the average percentage which they bear to turnover can be calculated and an appropriate sum included in selling overhead. The reason underlying the second method of treatment is that rebates are given for the reason, *inter alia*, that overheads are proportionately smaller for large customers.

SUBSCRIPTIONS

The treatment of subscriptions in the cost accounts is determined by their nature. Subscriptions to welfare schemes and institutions, for the benefit of production workers, represent a production expense: subscriptions to technical journals should similarly be treated as a production expense. Subscriptions to mercantile agencies and others through whom enquiries may be made as to the financial standing of prospective customers must be treated as a selling expense. Charitable donations from which no direct benefit is obtained by employees are regarded as appropriations of profit and excluded from the cost accounts.

## General administration costs

Costs coming under this heading will include the following:

> Office rent and rates.
> Office lighting, heating and cleaning.
> Depreciation of office buildings, furniture and fittings.
> Repairs to office buildings and equipment.
> Salaries of office staff.
> Telephone and postage.
> Insurance of office premises, contents, etc.
> Salaries of administrative directors.
> Printing and stationery.
> Audit fees.
> Legal charges.
> Bank charges.

As opposed to production expenses, there will probably be a smaller degree of fluctuation in these expenses, most of which will be largely fixed in nature.

It may be necessary to analyse the total cost of general administration into cost centres, depending upon the nature of the business. Selling and distributing costs are sometimes included with administration overhead but, as selling costs should be dealt with on an entirely different basis from distribution costs, the practice is to be deprecated.

## Research and development cost

Expenditure on research into improving product design or production methods must be distinguished from that incurred in the search for new products. The functions will be controlled by a technical director who will have various departments reporting to him.

Typical costs of the functions would be:

> Laboratory technicians.
> Work-study engineers.
> Raw materials, etc., used in research.
> Depreciation of equipment.
> Technical journals.
> Research association subscriptions.
> Experimental production runs.
> Patent fees.

## Items excluded from cost accounts

Certain items to be found in the financial accounts of a business will not be charged in the Cost Accounts. Such items fall into three main classes:

1. *Appropriations of profit.* Under this heading will be found the following:

(*a*) Income tax and corporation tax.

(*b*) Transfers to reserves.

(*c*) Charitable donations where the employees of the company derive no direct benefit therefrom.

(*d*) Dividends.

(*e*) Directors' fees (as distinct from emoluments as executives).

(*f*) Amounts written off goodwill, preliminary expenses, underwriting commission, debenture discount, expenses of capital issues, etc.

(*g*) Appropriations to sinking funds created for the redemption of loans.

(*h*) Allocations to depreciation account over and above the normal charge (but note the discussion on depreciation in the previous chapter).

2. *Matters of pure finance.* Items of this nature will include:

(*a*) Interest received on bank deposits.

(*b*) Interest, dividends, etc., received on investments.

(*c*) Rents receivable (but *see* page 91).

(*d*) Profits and losses on sales of assets.

3. *Adjustments.* The basis on which expenditure is charged in the cost accounts frequently varies from that adopted for the financial accounts. Depreciation of plant under construction cannot be charged in the cost accounts, as there is no process to which the expense can be debited, but for reasons of prudence such depreciation may be provided for in the financial accounts. Also, as already stated, only an annual proportion of the cost of preparing a trade catalogue may be included in the Cost Accounts whereas it will be written off at once in the financial books. The differences caused by varying methods of treatment must be carefully computed and brought into the statement reconciling the profit shown by the two sets of accounts. In similar fashion, any differences in overhead and other charges (which have perhaps been brought into the Cost Accounts at their anticipated amounts) must be compared with the actual charge as shown by the financial accounts prepared "historically" after the close of the trading period. Any differences must be allowed for in the reconciliation.

## CONTROL OF OVERHEAD

In this chapter, considerable space is devoted to ensuring that overhead is absorbed in products in order to determine as accurately as possible the actual cost. Such production costs can be used for calculating selling prices and evaluating stocks and work-in-progress. However, as overhead often forms a considerable proportion of total cost, management must consider very carefully the effect that its decisions will have on the level of overhead. This matter is dealt with in greater detail in the chapter on Relevant Costs, where a consideration is given to the incidence of fixed and variable overhead. At this stage it is important to reflect on the degree of detail required in the analysis of overhead to assist management decisions. Overhead control statements showing detailed expenses will be presented regularly and this is the subject of part of the chapter on Budgetary Control. In addition, overhead will sometimes require *ad hoc* analysis to provide data for special investigations.

Management needs to check periodically that it is employing the best methods, equipment and services, etc., in order to maximise profit. The cost accountant will therefore often need to produce information on the cost of alternatives. It may be useful to consider briefly the type of information required by management:

*Production overhead*
1. The cost of operations and the effect on costs of suggested changes.
2. The cost of internally provided services compared with outside services, e.g. electricity generation.
3. The effect on overhead of an improved layout of plant and machines.
4. The ideal order size for the factory.
5. Those products involving disproportionate overhead when incurred through, say, inspection, storage or handling.

*General administration overhead*
1. The cost of alternative methods of communication, e.g. letters, telephone calls, internal memoranda, and personal visits.
2. The cost of mechanisation compared with hand methods in invoice preparation, ledger posting, payroll preparation, correspondence work, etc.
3. The measurement of output in offices, related to overhead incurred.
4. The comparative costs of centralised and decentralised services, e.g. typing pools.

*Marketing overhead*
1. Comparative costs of selling in various areas.
2. Minimum order size to be accepted.
3. Comparative costs of various distribution methods.
4. Cost of representation, e.g. cost per salesman's call.
5. Comparative costs of different containers and packages.

*Research and development overhead*
1. Cost of each development project compared with the budgeted allowance.
2. Estimated savings in cost to be obtained from improvements, and the cost incurred in developing improvements.

## OVERHEAD ALLOTMENT

### Allotment procedures
Direct costs normally present little difficulty in being allocated to cost units; material requisitions and workers' time-sheets will give sufficient indication of where the costs are to be charged. With indirect costs, however, whole items of costs may need to be divided between various cost centres and accumulated cost centre costs will then be allotted to cost units. The procedure for allotting indirect costs to cost units embraces allocation, apportionment and absorption, which are defined as follows:

*Cost allocation.* The allotment of whole items of cost to cost centres or cost units.

*Cost apportionment.* The allotment to two or more cost centres of proportions of common items of cost on the estimated basis of benefit received.

*Overhead absorption.* The allotment of overhead to cost units by means of rates separately calculated for each cost centre. In most cases the rates are predetermined.

A schedule (*see* Fig. 34) will be prepared of the total indirect costs incurred for the accounting period. These costs will first be classified according to function, i.e. production, general administration, marketing, research and development; certain general costs may require apportionment between functions. Each particular cost centre will then be allotted with its own costs and a cost centre total obtained (this is sometimes known as primary distribution). Those cost centres which provide services, e.g. canteen, will then be apportioned to production cost centres (the secondary distribution) and the total on each production centre may then be absorbed into cost units.

### Bases for apportionment
Mention was previously made of various bases used to charge cost centres with an equitable proportion of costs. In some instances it will be possible to charge the whole of an expense invoice to a cost centre, e.g. a charge for repairing a machine in the cost centre, but other invoices will be apportioned over a number of cost centres, e.g. a rental charge for factory space. The basis of apportionment will depend on the information available and since much of the information will probably be imperfect, the cost accountant will need to

## PRODUCTION OVERHEAD
## DEPARTMENTAL DISTRIBUTION SUMMARY
### Period No..................

| Cost | Amount £ | Basis of apportionment | Remarks | Dept. A £ | Dept. B £ | Dept. C £ | Dept. D £ | Can- teen £ | Power house £ |
|---|---|---|---|---|---|---|---|---|---|
| Rent and rates | 100 | Floor space | Site value taken into consideration | 30 | 25 | 27 | 10 | 2 | 6 |
| Lighting | 20 | Number of points | No allowance for wattage | 5 | 5 | 4 | 2 | 2 | 2 |
| Heating | 25 | Number of radiators | – | 8 | 4 | 5 | 3 | 5 | – |
| Indirect wages | 212 | Actual | – | 30 | 30 | 26 | 26 | 40 | 60 |
| Depreciation | 55 | Plant register | Straight line basis | 20 | 10 | 10 | 6 | 2 | 7 |
| Repairs and maintenance | 115 | As estimated | By works manager | 33 | 40 | 12 | 15 | 5 | 10 |
| Power | 120 | – | – | – | – | – | – | – | 120 |
| Oil, rag, etc. | 5 | No. of machines | – | 1 | 1 | 1 | 1 | – | 1 |
| Insurance | 15 | Insured amounts | As per schedules to fire policies | 5 | 3 | 2 | 2 | 1 | 2 |
| Canteen expenses | 10 | – | – | – | – | – | – | 10 | – |
| Supervisory labour | 150 | Time occupied | Estimated | 60 | 60 | 10 | 10 | – | 10 |
| National insurance | 100 | Actual | Number of men | 25 | 25 | 25 | 21 | 2 | 2 |
| Works Manager's salary | 300 | Time occupied | Estimated | 120 | 120 | 15 | 30 | – | 15 |
| Technical Director's salary | 400 | Time occupied | Estimated | 200 | 100 | 50 | 50 | – | – |
| Sundries | 25 | Estimated | – | 10 | 5 | 5 | 5 | – | – |
| £ | 1,652 | | | £ 547 | 428 | 192 | 181 | 69 | 235 |
| Apportionment of Canteen in proportion to men | | | | 18 | 18 | 18 | 15 | –69 | |
| Apportionment of Power House per meter readings | | | | 90 | 80 | 65 | – | | –235 |
| Departmental Totals | | | | £ 655 | 526 | 275 | 196 | | |

FIG. 34.—*Departmental distribution summary.*

Figure 34 demonstrates the process of indirect costs being allotted to production cost centres—including services—and the various apportionment bases used. The apportionment of the canteen and powerhouse costs to production departments assumes that these services do not benefit marketing, administrative or development functions. If they did, then the total cost would be apportioned to these as well as to production.

exercise his own judgment. For example, an invoice for electricity should be apportioned on the basis of electricity consumed as measured by meters in each cost centre. These are not always available, and, therefore, the nearest basis would be the power of the machines and wattage of lights. However, some machines may only be used occasionally and consume only a small amount of electricity. Consequently, actual or estimated running times of machines may be used to weight the power figures.

It would be impossible to give an exhaustive list of the bases of apportionment to be used for each element of indirect cost, but the following principles may assist:

1. Apportion on the basis of the unit measure of service consumed, e.g.

| Cost | Apportionment basis |
|------|---------------------|
| Electricity. | Meter readings. |
| Canteen costs. | The number of meals served to employees from the different cost centres |
| Rental charges. | Square feet (metres) of space occupied. |
| Maintenance workers. | Hours spent in each cost centre. |

2. Where (1) is not practicable, apportion on the basis of a factor which approximates to the amount of service consumed, e.g.

| Cost | Apportionment basis |
|------|---------------------|
| Electricity. | Power of machines multiplied by running times. |
| Canteen costs. | Number of employees or wages paid. |
| Maintenance workers. | Value of plant serviced or power of machines. |
| Manager's salary. | Number of employees, total wages or output of cost centre. |

## Apportionment of service cost centres

It often happens that when apportioning service departments, a proportion of one service department finds its way back to another service department which has itself already been apportioned. There are various methods of dealing with this problem:

### 1. CONTINUOUS APPORTIONMENT OR REPEATED DISTRIBUTION

In this method the process of apportioning service departments is continued until the figures are immaterial.

*EXAMPLE*

The overhead of a factory has been analysed to the point of primary distribution.

| | | |
|---|---|---|
| Production departments: | Machine | £10,000 |
| | Assembly | £4,000 |
| Service departments: | Canteen | £2,000 |
| | Powerhouse | £3,000 |

The canteen is to be apportioned on the basis of employees:

| | Employees | % |
|---|---|---|
| Machine | 240 | 60 |
| Assembly | 140 | 35 |
| Powerhouse | 20 | 5 |
| | 400 | 100 |

The powerhouse is to be apportioned on the basis of electricity used:

| | Thousand kilowatts | % |
|---|---|---|
| Machine | 270 | 75 |
| Assembly | 36 | 10 |
| Canteen | 54 | 15 |
| | 360 | 100 |

The apportionment would proceed as follows:

| | Machine | Assembly | Canteen | Powerhouse |
|---|---|---|---|---|
| Primary apportionment | £10,000 | £4,000 | £2,000 | £3,000 |
| Apportion: Canteen | 1,200 | 700 | −2,000 | 100 |
| Powerhouse | 2,325 | 310 | 465 | −3,100 |
| Canteen | 279 | 163 | −465 | 23 |
| Powerhouse | 18 | 2 | 3 | −23 |
| Canteen | 2 | 1 | −3 | |
| Total service depts. | £3,824 | £1,176 | | |
| Total prod. overhead | £13,824 | £5,176 | | |

## 2. ALGEBRAIC METHOD

Using the above data, we can prepare two formulae:
let $a$ = total canteen overhead including the share of powerhouse.
let $b$ = total powerhouse overhead including the share of canteen.

Then $a = £2,000 + \dfrac{15 \times b}{100}$ . . . . . . . . . . . . . (1)

$b = £3,000 + \dfrac{5 \times a}{100}$ . . . . . . . . . . . . . (2)

Multiply (2) by 15 per cent, then $\dfrac{15 \times b}{100} = £450 + \dfrac{75 \times a}{10,000}$ . . . . (3)

Substituting in (1):

$$a = £2,000 + £450 + \frac{75 \times a}{10,000}$$
$$= £2,470$$

Substituting in (2):

$$b = £3,000 + \frac{5 \times 2,470}{100}$$
$$= £3,123$$

The machine department receives 60 per cent of canteen, i.e. $60\% \times £2,470 = £1,482$, plus 75 per cent of the powerhouse, i.e. $75\% \times £3,123 = £2,342$. The total is therefore £3,824.

Similarly the assembly department receives 35 per cent of the canteen, i.e. $35\% \times £2,470 = £864$, plus 10 per cent of the powerhouse, i.e. $10\% \times £3,123 = £312$. The total is therefore £1,176.

## 3. SIMPLIFIED METHOD

By this method service departments receiving little service from other departments are apportioned first *and receive no apportionments from other service departments*. Thus in the above example the powerhouse would be apportioned first:

| | Machine | Assembly | Canteen | Powerhouse |
|---|---|---|---|---|
| Primary apportionment | £10,000 | £4,000 | £2,000 | £3,000 |
| Apportion: Powerhouse | 2,250 | 300 | 450 | −3,000 |
| Canteen | 1,550 | 900 | −2,450 | |
| Total service depts. | £3,800 | £1,200 | | |
| Total production over-head | £13,800 | £5,200 | | |

Applied sensibly this method makes the exercise much easier and the margin of error is so small as to be irrelevant, especially when one considers the amount of averaging done to arrive at the original totals.

### PRELIMINARY TRANSFER METHOD

Where there may be a significant margin of error under the simplified method, an estimated figure can be transferred into the service departments which are apportioned first from other service departments. Thus, in the example, an estimated figure of, say, £150 may be transferred into the powerhouse from the canteen and then no subsequent apportionment is made once the service department has been apportioned.

|                        | Machine  | Assembly | Canteen | Powerhouse |
|------------------------|----------|----------|---------|------------|
| Primary apportionment  | £10,000  | £4,000   | £2,000  | £3,000     |
|                        |          |          |         |            |
| Preliminary transfer   |          |          | −150    | +150       |
| Apportion: Powerhouse  | 2,363    | 315      | 472     | −3,150     |
| Canteen                | 1,467    | 855      | −2,322  |            |
|                        |          |          |         |            |
| Total service depts.   | £3,830   | £1,170   |         |            |
| Total production over- |          |          |         |            |
| head                   | £13,830  | £5,170   |         |            |

The estimated preliminary transfer would be calculated on the basis of past experience or perhaps the budgeted overhead.


## ABSORPTION OF PRODUCTION OVERHEAD IN COST UNITS

In a manufacturing cost centre, all units produced may be identical, in which case the total cost could be shared equally over the total production. Thus if the total production of Department B (in Fig. 34) for the period was 1,500 units, overhead per unit would be £526 ÷ 1,500 = £0.351. Furthermore, if all the cost units passed through every department, production overhead could be allotted to cost units merely by dividing the total cost by total units, i.e. in Fig. 34, £1,652 ÷ 1,500 = £1.10 per unit.

However, the units are not usually identical and different facilities are used in their manufacture. Consequently, if a unit rate were used, some units would be overcharged and others undercharged. Thus, to arrive at an equitable allotment of overhead to cost units, the initial problem is to identify the main factor which causes the overhead to be incurred and then to measure output in terms of that factor. If 75 per cent of the overhead were caused by storing and handling materials, it would be reasonable to measure output in terms of the direct material consumed—either in quantity or in value, and charge cost units with overhead according to the direct material consumed to produce the cost unit. This situation would be very rare and other absorption methods would normally be used.

The questions which the cost accountant needs to answer in determining the best method of absorption are:

1. Are the manufacturing processes mechanised or manual?
2. Is there a wide divergence between rates of pay?
3. What are the principal constituents of overhead and how are they incurred?

It will probably be found that most overhead costs vary with time, e.g. rent, rates and salaries, and therefore that twice as much expenditure is normally incurred in a period of four weeks as in a period of two weeks. It may therefore be claimed that if one job takes twice as long as another it should bear twice the charge for production expenses, as the space, facilities and organisation of the factory have been used in that proportion. It is thus necessary to determine a means of measuring the time the job takes in passing through each cost centre. Overhead can then be expressed as a function of this, and if the time spent on individual jobs is fairly computed the overhead charge per job can be more accurate.

### Percentage on direct wages

This method has more to commend it than either the prime cost or the materials bases considered later, for the following reasons:

1. Automatic consideration is given to the time factor; the greater the charge to a job for wages, the longer will have been the time spent upon that job.

2. Labour rates are usually more constant than material prices.

3. Variable overhead will to some extent vary with the number of employees, and hence with the charge for wages.

This method, which has the advantage of simplicity, will operate as shown by the following Job Account.

Job No. ..........

| | |
|---|---:|
| Direct materials | £143 |
| Direct labour | 125 |
| Direct expenses | 10 |
| Prime cost | 278 |
| Production overhead (say 100% on direct labour) | 125 |
| Production cost | £403 |

The method is widely used in practice but suffers from the disadvantage that it does not take into account variations, if any, in the rates of remuneration for different types of labour, and therefore the wages incurred on different jobs are not necessarily in the same ratio as the hours spent.

The question of overtime will also disturb the position. Higher hourly rates will be paid to workers in respect of overtime but overhead will not increase in the same proportion; many costs will, in fact, remain constant.

A further disadvantage of the percentage on wages method is that no distinction is drawn between production by hand and that by machine. It is apparent that work performed by machinery will involve heavy charges in the form of power, depreciation, etc., which will not be incurred where work is done by hand. Similarly, one job may require the services of expensive machinery while another may be performed by a cheap machine. The difference in the cost of the two services is, however, ignored—a disadvantage not peculiar to the percentage methods.

Accordingly, unless all labour employed earns similar hourly rates and production is uniform, the percentage on direct labour method of apportionment will not prove completely equitable. In few factories will these circumstances exist but, in some, certain departments will answer these requirements and the method can therefore be adopted usefully for absorption where a separate charge for overhead is made by each department. A more accurate charge is obtained where the hours expended upon production are considered irrespective of the wages paid. This method is considered in detail under the heading "Direct Labour-Hour Rate" on page 121.

## Percentage on direct materials

This method is only equitable where overhead costs are significantly related to material costs. Except in such an unlikely set of circumstances, the method is illogical and unfair for the following reasons:

1. The cost of materials is often subject to considerable fluctuations which will not be accompanied by similar fluctuations in overhead. The basis must necessarily therefore be unstable. Even where only one type of article is produced, this factor must be considered if material prices are subject to considerable fluctuation, as the accuracy of the percentage adopted will be vitiated.

2. The mere fact that a job consumes material of a very expensive nature is no justification for the assumption that the overhead appropriate to that job will be proportionately heavier. An analysis of the overhead costs would probably show that storage and handling costs were a small proportion of the total, and even if they were substantial they would be related to weight or volume rather than price.

3. As stated above, the overhead attributable to any job tends to vary with the time expended on it, since most expenses, e.g. rent, rates and salaries, accrue on a time basis. Time, therefore, is the most important factor to be considered in the allocation of overhead to production, but this factor is ignored completely if the charge for overhead is based upon materials consumed.

The disadvantages of this method, and the grossly inaccurate results which may be obtained, are illustrated by the following example.

*EXAMPLE*

The following are the cost statements relating to two standard jobs. Production overhead has been charged to these jobs at 20 per cent on the cost of materials consumed.

### JOB NO. I

| | |
|---|---:|
| Materials consumed | £200 |
| Direct wages (10 hours hand labour at £1.20 per hour) | 12 |
| | |
| Prime cost | 212 |
| Production overhead (20% on materials consumed) | 40 |
| | |
| Production cost | 252 |
| Gross profit (16% on sales) | 48 |
| | |
| Selling price | £300 |

### JOB NO. II

| | |
|---|---:|
| Materials consumed | £20 |
| Direct wages (20 hours machine operation at £1.20 per hour) | 24 |
| | |
| Prime cost | 44 |
| Production overhead (20% on materials consumed) | 4 |
| | |
| Production cost | 48 |
| Gross profit (52% on sales) | 52 |
| | |
| Selling price | £100 |

From a superficial examination of these statements it would appear that Job No. II is the more profitable activity, particularly in view of the large amount invested in materials for the performance of Job No. I, and the consequent risk and loss of interest on the capital involved. As a result of such an examination, the tendency of the manufacturer might reasonably be to concentrate his efforts upon the marketing of Job No. II to the gradual exclusion of Job No. I. Such a policy would lead to disastrous results, as from a detailed examination the following facts emerge:

1. The time occupied upon Job No. II has been twice that expended upon Job No. I. Other things being equal, it may reasonably be said that the overhead attributable to Job No. II is therefore twice the amount attributable to Job No. I.

2. As machine labour has been employed upon Job No. II, such expenses as depreciation of plant and machinery, repairs and power, must have been incurred, and represent a charge which should be made to the job if the true cost is to be ascertained. In the case of Job No. I, however, hand labour only has been employed, involving but a small cost for the use of tools, etc.

On the facts it would appear that although the total indirect expenses of the business may have been charged to production, the individual jobs have not borne their correct proportions, it being apparent that Job No. II ought to be charged with a far greater sum in respect of overhead expenses than Job No. I.

The inequity of the "Percentage on Materials Basis" is further emphasised where the price of raw material is subject to considerable fluctuation.

*EXAMPLE*

The following cost statements are prepared for the manufacture of an identical article, at different raw material prices. Overhead is absorbed at a percentage of raw materials.

| Raw materials at: | £0.25 per kg | £0.40 per kg | £0.50 per kg |
|---|---|---|---|
| Materials consumed 200 kg | £50 | £80 | £100 |
| Direct wages (20 hours at £1.20) | 24 | 24 | 24 |
| Prime cost | 74 | 104 | 124 |
| Production overhead (20% on materials) | 10 | 16 | 20 |
| Production cost | £84 | £120 | £144 |

The increase in the price of raw materials has caused the loading for works overhead to increase from £10 to £20, although the time taken for the jobs (as shown by the wages charge) has remained constant. This is particularly unfair if, as is probable, overhead consists chiefly of items which vary with time.

## Percentage on prime cost

Apart from the simplicity of operating this method, the main argument in its favour is that both materials and labour give rise to overhead and therefore both should be taken into consideration when arriving at the charge to be made to each job for overhead.

Unless, however, a standard article is produced, requiring a constant quantity of materials and number of hours engaged upon its manufacture, the method produces inaccurate results because of the following disadvantages:

1. Two items, i.e. materials and labour, both of which as separate bases possess many disadvantages, have been combined.

2. Where the cost of materials is the predominating item of prime cost, insufficient allowance is made for the time factor.

3. As with other percentage methods, the additional costs occasioned by the use of expensive machinery, etc., on certain jobs is ignored.

*EXAMPLE*

| *Job A* | | *Job B* | |
|---|---|---|---|
| Direct materials | £150 | Direct materials | £20 |
| Direct wages (25 hours at £1.20 per hour) | 30 | Direct wages (100 hours at £1.20 per hour) | 120 |
| Prime cost | 180 | Prime cost | 140 |

| Production overhead (50% on prime cost) | 90 | Production overhead (50% on prime cost) | 70 |
|---|---|---|---|
| Production cost | £270 | Production cost | £210 |

It will be seen that although Job B has taken four times as long to produce as has Job A, this is not reflected in the charges made for overhead.

## Hourly rates of overhead recovery

It will now be appreciated that although the adoption of a simple method for overhead recovery may in some cases give reasonable and useful results, it is essential, if a greater degree of accuracy is required in the cost accounts, that some other method be used.

Where a greater degree of accuracy is required and it is desired to charge each individual job with a share of overhead on such a basis that all the facts of each case are taken into consideration, one of the two following methods should be employed:

1. The machine-hour rate.
2. The direct labour-hour rate.

These methods are not as simple as those previously considered and the provision of the necessary data is perhaps more lengthy and expensive, but they must be adopted in those businesses whose production is not uniform and where, therefore, a percentage method would yield inaccurate results.

### THE MACHINE-HOUR RATE

In order to apply this method the total machine hours worked in the cost centre must be recorded. Where one employee operates one machine, the time-sheets will provide the required information. However, an employee may operate two or three automatic or semi-automatic machines and a separate record is necessary to record the machine running times. Similarly, there may be some machines which are operated by two or more employees and the machine hours cannot be obtained from one employee's time-sheet. In practice, difficulties can arise where the number of men operating the machine varies with the complexity or size of the job. Then it may be necessary to use a machine-hour rate based on the time of the principal operator, and a labour-hour rate for the total hours of all the other operators.

### THE DIRECT LABOUR-HOUR RATE

It will be appreciated that the machine-hour rate method of absorbing overhead in production can be adopted only for those departments in which machinery represents the predominating factor of production. For the recovery of overhead of those departments in which hand labour is employed some other method must be adopted.

The overhead of such departments will be ascertained from the Departmental Distribution Summary. If all the workers are engaged upon similar tasks the total overhead for a period will be divided by the total estimated working hours of all the workers for that period and an hourly rate of overhead per worker thus ascertained. Where the workers engaged in the department are employed on different tasks and are thus responsible for different proportions of the total departmental overhead, each worker or group of workers may be considered as a separate cost centre. If the operative unit is a group or gang of workers, provided that the proportion of skilled and unskilled workers in the group remains constant, a labour-hour rate may be determined for the group as a whole. In such circumstances the time taken by the whole group is ascertained, details of each worker's time being of no significance.

## Comparison of various absorption methods

The analysis of actual overhead incurred given in Fig. 34 shows £655 for Department A. The output of Department A for the period may be expressed as follows:

| | |
|---|---:|
| Direct materials consumed | £13,100 |
| Direct wages (1,965 hours) | 3,275 |
| | |
| Prime cost | £16,375 |
| | |
| Machine running time | 1,310 hours |
| Units produced (varying sizes) | 131 |

The overhead absorption rate which would recover the cost of Department A in the charge to production could, therefore, be any one of the following:

Per unit: £655 ÷ 131 = £5 per unit.
Percentage on direct wages: £655 ÷ 3,275 = 20 per cent.
Percentage on material cost: £655 ÷ 13,100 = 5 per cent.
Percentage on prime cost: £655 ÷ 16,375 = 4 per cent.
Machine hour rate: £655 ÷ 1,310 = 50p per machine hour.
Labour hour rate: £655 ÷ 1,965 = 33p per labour hour.

If any of the above methods is used, the total overhead will be absorbed. However, if the units produced are not identical, each unit will absorb a different amount.

Consider the following cost unit, produced in the relevant period:

| | | |
|---|---|---:|
| Direct materials | | £45.00 |
| Direct wages: 2 operators | | |
| 10 hours at £2.00 | £20.00 | |

10 hours at £1.50          15.00

                                      ——          35.00

Prime cost                          £80.00

Machine time: 10 hours

Depending on the absorption method used, the following overhead would be charged to the product:

| | |
|---|---|
| Per unit | £5.00 |
| Percentage on direct wages | £7.00 |
| Percentage on direct materials | £2.25 |
| Percentage on prime cost | £3.20 |
| Machine hour | £5.00 |
| Labour hour | £6.67 |

The reason for the differences in the amount of overhead absorbed is that the products are not uniform; consequently, each cost unit represents a different quantity in terms of the measurement in which output is expressed, e.g. labour hours, £s of material.

**Individual machine-hour rates**

In the preceding example, production departments have been treated as cost centres but, where a production department comprises different types of operation, absorption by means of a departmental overhead rate may suffer from the same drawback as a factory absorption rate, i.e. insufficient recognition of the variation in cost of different operations. To avoid this, departmental overhead may be further apportioned over the main types of operation used in production. A separate absorption rate is then calculated for each operation. The operation may be performed by either hand or machine. The number of separate operations for which overhead absorption rates are calculated will depend on the nature of production. A large number of rates makes heavy demands on the clerical work, but too few may result in inaccurate product costs.

The schedule in Fig. 35 shows the apportionment of overhead for Department B over machines, and should be studied together with the following notes.

Analysis of overhead to machines:

| *Expense* | *Basis of distribution* |
|---|---|
| Rent and rates, lighting and heating | Effective floor space occupied, i.e. allowing for reasonable space to operate the machine and a proportion of aisles, gangways, etc. |
| Depreciation | Actual depreciation per machine according to information disclosed by the plant register. |
| Repairs and maintenance | As for depreciation. |

| Supervisory labour | The degree of supervision required by each machine. If, for example, a foreman, paid £100 per week, supervises the production of four machines, each will be charged £25 per week for this service. If, however, half of the foreman's time is occupied by one machine and the remainder equally upon the other three, his wages must be apportioned as 3:1:1:1. |
| Power | Actual consumption as shown by meter readings or estimated consumption ascertained from past experience, having regard to power of machine, etc. |
| Sundry supplies, oil, rag, etc. | Past experience. |
| Management salaries | Past experience. |
| Insurance | Insured values, having regard to any special risks involving increased premiums. |

Where operatives can be identified with a particular machine group, it may be convenient to include their direct wages as part of the machine group cost. Thus, production will be charged with a rate per machine hour which comprises labour plus overhead.

## Fixed and variable overhead

In calculating overhead absorption rates, it is advisable to separate fixed from variable overhead. The classification is essential information for cost control purposes and will be used for many other purposes (a later chapter will deal with the subject of relevant cost information in detail). There may be certain instances where the rates are separately applied in absorption, e.g. a piece of equipment loaned from a plant department to a production department may be charged out on the basis of one rate for the use made of the equipment, to absorb maintenance costs, driver's wages, fuel and lubricants, etc., and another rate to absorb the fixed or standing costs, e.g. depreciation, insurance, licences, etc. The former rate would be multiplied by the running hours each period, and the latter rate based on a fixed time period, e.g. a rate per week.

## PREDETERMINED OVERHEAD ABSORPTION RATES

In considering the calculation of overhead absorption rates, the basic aim was to absorb total overhead in products. In practical terms the cost accountant would have to wait until the end of the accounting period, collect all the cost and production data, and proceed to allot the actual costs to cost centres and cost units. The effect of this practice would be that:

1. Product costs cannot be determined until some considerable time after the end of the accounting period.

2. The overhead absorption rate will probably vary each period due to fluctuations in overhead incurred, volume of production and efficiency of the factory.

In order, therefore, that management may be provided with reasonably accurate and *timely* product costs, which are not distorted

| DEPARTMENT B ANALYSIS OF DEPARTMENTAL OVERHEAD Period No.................... | | | | | | |
|---|---|---|---|---|---|---|
| Apportionment of overhead per departmental distribution summary (Fig. 34) | Amount £ | Basis of apportionment | Machine group A £ | Machine group B £ | Machine group C £ | Machine group D £ |
| Rent and rates | 25 | In proportion to floor space | 8.25 | 4.25 | 4.25 | 8.25 |
| Lighting | 5 | In proportion to floor space | 1.50 | 1.25 | 1.25 | 1 |
| Heating | 4 | In proportion to floor space | 1 | 1 | 1 | 1 |
| Indirect wages | 30 | In proportion to workers | 15 | 5 | 5 | 5 |
| Depreciation | 10 | Per plant register | 5 | 1.50 | 1.50 | 2 |
| Repairs and maintenance | 40 | Estimated | 15 | 10 | 10 | 5 |
| Power | 80 | Per meters | 20 | 20 | 20 | 20 |
| Oil, rag, etc. | 1 | Equally | 0.25 | 0.25 | 0.25 | 0.25 |
| Insurance | 3 | Per insured values | 1 | 0.50 | 0.50 | 1 |
| Supervisory labour | 60 | Degree of supervision required | 30 | 15 | 10 | 5 |
| National Insurance | 25 | In proportion to workers | 8 | 6.50 | 6.50 | 4 |
| Works manager's salary | 120 | In proportion to time spent | 45 | 45 | 15 | 15 |
| Technical director's salary | 100 | In proportion to time spent | 60 | 20 | 10 | 10 |
| Sundries | 5 | Estimated | 2 | 1 | 1 | 1 |
| Canteen expenses | 18 | In proportion to workers | 6 | 4.50 | 4.50 | 3 |
| | £526 | | £218 | £135.75 | £90.75 | £81.50 |

FIG. 35—*Sub-analysis of departmental overhead.*

by seasonal fluctuations, a predetermined absorption rate is calculated. This is a rate calculated in advance of the period in which it is to be used, by dividing the anticipated period overhead by the anticipated period production. Production may be measured on any of the absorption bases already described, e.g. prime cost, labour hours, etc.

The procedure is to record for each job the amount of the absorption base that has been incurred on it. When the job is finished, or at the end of the accounting period, this amount is then multiplied by the predetermined absorption rate, and the total overhead absorbed recorded on the job cost account. If the job is completed, the prime cost plus absorbed overhead will be transferred out of Work-in-Progress Account to Finished Goods or Cost of Sales Accounts. If it is unfinished it will be carried forward at prime cost plus absorbed overhead to the next accounting period. The total overhead absorbed is credited to the overhead account.

The use of predetermined rates can be extended to apportionments from service departments, so that each service cost centre is credited with the amount of service given multiplied by the predetermined rate. In this way it is possible to obtain simple measures of the efficiency of operating the service.

The subject of predetermined rates leads logically to standard costing and budgetary control because we are now in the field of applying planned costs instead of historic costs. Before leaving the subject it is necessary to consider the problems involved in computing the predetermined rate.

**The length of the period**
It is possible to calculate predetermined rates at the beginning of every accounting period. This would perhaps ensure that the rates were close to those which would be calculated after the event. The rate could fluctuate widely from period to period, however, and make pricing and cost comparison difficult.

*EXAMPLE*
A company forecasts its overhead expenditure and production at the beginning of each month and uses the predetermined rate in calculating selling prices.

The following information related to three successive months:

| Month | Overhead forecast | Production forecast | Absorption rate per unit |
|---|---|---|---|
| August | £2,500 | 1,000 units | £2.5 |
| September | 3,000 | 1,500 units | 2.0 |
| October | 4,500 | 3,000 units | 1.5 |
| | £10,000 | 5,500 | |

Where production is seasonal, the effect of fixed costs in the total overhead will force overhead rates up in slack periods and down in busy periods. Where prices are based on cost, further difficulties would be encountered in selling in slack periods because of the higher cost. A solution is to extend the period to, say, a year, and if in the above example the overhead and production for the three months were representative of the year, an average rate of £1.8182 per unit could be used. Obviously in individual cases it may be almost impossible to forecast twelve months ahead and so a compromise must be effected. Considerable care must be used as, if selling prices are linked to costs, inaccurate forecasting can easily have disastrous results.

### Estimated overhead
Overhead can be divided into three main classes:

1. *Fixed*. Those costs which for all practical purposes do not vary with the volume of production, except over very wide limits. Examples are factory rent and factory manager's salary. Unless a further factory is rented or the salary increased, neither of these costs will change, whatever the level of production.

2. *Variable*. Those costs which vary in proportion either to production or (in the case of selling overhead) to sales. Examples are electric power (if purchased at a rate per unit), commission paid to agents and similar items where the correlation, although not so close as with power and commission, is close enough to allow them to be regarded as variable overhead.

3. *Semi-variable*. These costs comprise a class of expenditure which, although affected by variations in production or sales, does not vary directly therewith. Examples are telephone charges (which are composed of a basic rent, plus a charge per call) and office salaries (where an increase or decrease in the volume of orders might result in the engagement or dismissal of an invoice typist, the size of the clerical staff being otherwise unaffected).

This threefold division of overhead costs is of the greatest importance in costing and although the matter is dealt with at length in later chapters, some consideration must here be given to it.

### EXAMPLE
A manufacturer has forecast production and overhead at three levels of working: single shift; single shift with overtime; double shift. The result is as follows:

|                 | 1 Shift | 1 Shift + o/t | 2 Shifts |
|-----------------|---------|---------------|----------|
| Output in units | 50,000  | 75,000        | 100,000  |

| Appropriate overhead: | *1 Shift* | *1 Shift+o/t* | *2 Shifts* |
|---|---|---|---|
| Fixed | £10,000 | £10,000 | £10,000 |
| Semi-variable | 1,500 | 2,000 | 2,250 |
| Variable | 5,000 | 7,500 | 10,000 |
| | £16,500 | £19,500 | £22,250 |
| Total overhead per article | £0.33 | £0.26 | £0.2225 |
| Variable overhead per article | £0.10 | £0.10 | £0.10 |

Depending upon the level of output selected as most probable, the charge for overhead would vary between £0.33 and £0.2225 per article. In calculating a realistic overhead rate, reference must be made to past expenditure and allowance made for changes in the production level and known cost changes, e.g. wage awards in the industry.

## Estimated production
The estimated level of output could be based on:

1. Average output of past years.
2. A diminished output due to trade depression or other causes.
3. An increased output due to a more vigorous selling policy.
4. Normal production capacity.
5. Standard output.

These methods are considered in detail:

### 1. AVERAGE OUTPUT OF PAST YEARS
Under this method the average output of past years is ascertained and if a number of years is taken, a fairly reliable basis may be determined. The system is suitable for small concerns owing to its simplicity and the fact that the overhead of such concerns, being small, will not be affected to any considerable extent by the volume of turnover. The basis must be reviewed from time to time in order to give effect to a progressive increase or decrease in output.

### 2. DIMINISHED OUTPUT
The object of this method is the recovery of total overhead regardless of the volume of trade. If it is considered that the output for the current period will be reduced considerably by reason of a trade depression, the rates per unit for overhead must be increased in order that, on the reduced output, the total indirect costs may be absorbed. The method is dangerous as a fall in output results in higher prices being quoted, which will perhaps result in further loss of business, with the consequent need to quote still higher prices.

### 3. INCREASED OUTPUT
An increased output with stable standing charges may mean that the business has passed the break-even point and is operating satis-

factorily. It is thus able, if its policy so dictates, to reduce selling prices and still further increase sales and production, provided that the increase can be attained without an unacceptable rise in its so-called fixed costs.

## 4. NORMAL CAPACITY

Under this method the normal capacity of the works, i.e. the maximum feasible output, is adopted every year as the basis upon which the overhead rates are calculated, irrespective of temporary fluctuations. The method is generally regarded as superior to methods 1 and 3 for the following reasons:

(*a*) If a factory is working to only half of its capacity it cannot be said that the reduced output has incurred the whole of the fixed expenses. It is apparent that the real cost of a job should be the same whether a factory is busy or slack.

(*b*) Comparison of the results of one year with those of another is rendered valueless if fluctuating output is allowed to disrupt the charges made to production for fixed expenditure.

(*c*) The loss due to idle plant, etc., can only be ascertained if production is charged with expenditure on the basis of normal output. In other words, the cost of plant lying idle should be treated as a loss of profit and not as an expense of production. If the diminished output method is adopted, the cost of idle machines is charged to production, although such machines may not even have been used thereon.

(*d*) Selling prices are frequently based upon information provided by the cost accounts. If overhead costs are deemed to be high during slack periods and low during periods of activity, it follows that high selling prices would be quoted at the very time when the lowest possible price must be submitted if orders are to be obtained.

(*e*) It is in periods of depression that the fullest use of the cost records should be made by a manufacturer. With their aid the lowest permissible margin of profit on the lowest possible output can be computed, and thus there will be less danger of losing an order by tendering too high a price or of accepting an order at too low a price. This advantage will not be obtained if the costing records are confused by an entirely new redistribution of fixed expenditure.

(*f*) If fixed overhead were charged to production on the basis of actual output, stocks of finished goods and work-in-progress would be valued at the conclusion of a period of low production at a higher figure than would have been the case if production had been greater. Inventory values would thus be inflated.

The above remarks are illustrated by the following example.

*EXAMPLE*

*Trading and Profit and Loss Account*
*for the year ended................*

| | | | |
|---|---:|---|---:|
| Material consumed | £100,000 | Sales (100,000 units) | £200,000 |
| Direct wages | 50,000 | | |
| Production overhead | 30,000 | | |
| Office expenses | 9,000 | | |
| Marketing costs | 6,000 | | |
| Net profit | 5,000 | | |
| | £200,000 | | £200,000 |

The normal output of the factory is 150,000 units. Fixed production overhead is £18,000. Office expenses are for all practical purposes constant. Marketing costs are constant to the extent of £3,000, and the balance varies directly with sales.

If expenditure is charged to production on the basis of normal output it is apparent that only part of the costs shown in the above account really relates to the production of the period; the balance has been unfruitful, as shown below:

| | Total | Per unit |
|---|---:|---:|
| Materials consumed | £100,000 | £1.00 |
| Direct wages | 50,000 | 0.50 |
| Prime cost | 150,000 | 1.50 |
| Production overhead: | | |
| Two-thirds of fixed overhead | 12,000 | 0.12 |
| Variable overhead (assumed to have been incurred by reason of production for the year) | 12,000 | 0.12 |
| Production cost | 174,000 | 1.74 |
| Office expenses: | | |
| Two-thirds of fixed expenses | 6,000 | 0.06 |
| Marketing costs: | | |
| Two-thirds of fixed costs | 2,000 | 0.02 |
| Variable costs | 3,000 | 0.03 |
| Cost of sales | 185,000 | 1.85 |
| Real profit on actual output | 15,000 | 0.15 |
| Sales | £200,000 | £2.00 |

*Reconciliation with Profit shown by Financial Accounts*

| | | |
|---|---:|---:|
| Profit shown by cost accounts | | £15,000 |
| *Less:* Unrecouped production overhead | £6,000 | |
| Unrecouped office expenses | 3,000 | |
| Unrecouped marketing costs | 1,000 | |
| | | 10,000 |
| Profit shown by financial accounts | | £5,000 |

It will be seen from the above that 100,000 units have been produced and sold at a profit of £15,000. Indirect costs include a total of £10,000 which should have been recouped by the production of a further 50,000 units, but which have been lost owing to the absence of the necessary output. The diminution in the company's profit is thus shown to be due, not to inefficient production, but to lack of output.

## 5. STANDARD OUTPUT

The standard output of a factory differs from the normal output, which is an ill-defined concept and not necessarily related to the conditions which will prevail in the future. Circumstances may arise, e.g. a change in the rate of V.A.T. or the introduction of a completely new process of manufacture, which will make the so-called normal output of the past unsatisfactory as a guide for the future.

The standard output will be computed only after careful thought has been given to: (a) the availability and cost of all the factors of production; (b) the likely volume of sales; and (c) the adequacy of the financial resources. Further consideration is given to this problem in the chapter on standard costing.

### Estimated production efficiency

Where overhead is absorbed on the basis of units of production, if actual expenditure and actual production are in line with forecast, there will be no unabsorbed overhead. Where, however, the forecast production is in terms of, say, labour hours, the forecast must assume a given rate of production, and if there is any difference between the forecast and actual rate of production, the product costs will change.

*EXAMPLE*

The Easy-going Company Ltd. has forecast the following production information for the year:

| | |
|---|---|
| Production overhead (allowable) | £10,000 |
| Labour hours | 20,000 |
| Production units | 2,000 |

The actual results were:

| | |
|---|---|
| Production overhead | £15,000 |
| Labour hours | 30,000 |
| Production units | 2,500 |

Overhead was absorbed into production on the basis of labour hours, i.e. £0.50 per hour, therefore the 2,500 units will be charged with the full £15,000 of overhead. In terms of normal costs the 2,500 units should only have cost £12,500 in terms of overhead because the forecast absorption rate based on production units would have been £5 per unit. The cost of the lower rate of working has therefore been £2,500, but unless some form of standard costing is employed, this would not be apparent.

## TREATMENT OF UNABSORBED OVERHEAD

It has been pointed out that there will almost certainly be a difference between actual overhead incurred and overhead absorbed. This will arise because of errors in the forecast of expenditure and/or production. Where production is seasonal, an average absorption rate will have been calculated with the knowledge that there would be an under- or over-absorption each month, but that these should cancel out for the year as a whole.

*EXAMPLE*

Using the figures from the example on page 126, the results would appear as follows if the forecasts were accurate:

| Month | Production units | Overhead absorbed (£1.8182 per unit) | Actual overhead | (Under) or over absorption |
|-------|------|------|------|------|
| August | 1,000 | £1,818 | £2,500 | (£682) |
| September | 1,500 | 2,727 | 3,000 | (273) |
| October | 3,000 | 5,455 | 4,500 | 955 |
| | 5,500 | £10,000 | £10,000 | Nil |

In the accounts therefore the under- or over-absorbed overhead could be carried forward from one month to another. Any difference remaining at the end of the year should be written off to the Profit and Loss Account. The accountant may not be in a position to know what, if any, under- or over-absorbed overhead to carry forward unless he knows why it has been caused. Once again, standard costing can be employed to give him this information.

## ABSORPTION OF GENERAL ADMINISTRATION OVERHEAD

Adoption of a scientific and complicated system for charging general administration costs to products is considered to be a wasteful exercise. While such costs must be subjected to control procedures, little benefit is derived by detailed analysis and allotment procedures based on benefit. General administration costs are usually treated as period costs and charged in total to Profit and Loss Account.

If a proportion of general administration cost is to be reflected in product costs for pricing or stock valuation purposes, the addition of an agreed percentage to production cost will usually be adequate.

## ABSORPTION OF MARKETING OVERHEAD

In businesses where marketing overhead is small, manufacturers may prefer to exclude such expenditure entirely from their cost accounts and rely upon the addition of a sufficient margin of profit to allow for its recovery. It is apparent, however, that in many businesses overhead of this nature is considerable and may even approach the cost of production. Where this is so, it is imperative that detailed information is available from the cost accounts. The ascertainment of a basis upon which to absorb marketing overhead is a difficult problem. The costs of selling and publicity must first be separated from those of distribution, as they are likely to be incurred in different ways.

### Selling and publicity costs

Pure selling costs do not, as do the bulk of distributive costs, vary directly with the number of articles sold; neither do they vary with the cost of such articles. For example, a manufacturer produces two articles, A and B, at a production cost of £10 and £1 respectively. Article A possesses a ready market and in fact practically sells itself, but £0.50 is normally spent on advertising article B before it is sold. It is apparent that to take a percentage on production cost of these articles as representative of selling overhead would be most inaccurate.

Further points which must be considered are the following:

1. Such expenditure as advertising is largely determined by the policy of the management and may be varied from time to time for reasons in no way connected with the costs of manufacture or the volume of sales. The directors of a company may decide to spend £20,000 or £500,000 upon an advertising campaign, the amount to be expended being determined by the resources available for the purpose and the possible market for the company's product.

2. The class of trade and the type of customer to whom a product is sold will determine the extent of credit to be granted. Extended credit involves considerable loss of interest on the capital locked up in book debts and although this may not strictly be regarded as a selling cost it must be taken into consideration when fixing selling prices.

### Distribution costs

Most distributive costs, e.g. packages, casks, freight, carriage, insurance, etc., vary with the quantity of articles sold. As with selling costs, however, distributive costs will not normally vary with the cost of manufacture. The following factors will affect the costs of distribution:

1. The bulk, weight, etc., of the articles sold.
2. The necessity for costly packing, e.g. fragile articles, articles subject to deterioration, exported goods.

3. The locality in which customers reside. If all customers are within a short radius of the factory, thus enabling the business to effect all deliveries by van, heavy railway and sea freights will not occur.

4. The means of transport, whether road, rail, sea freight, etc.

5. The promptness of delivery and degree of service expected by the customer.

It should be apparent from the above remarks that if more than one type of article is sold the costs of selling and distribution must be considered separately. The following principles may be adopted:

1. *Advertising.* The extent to which each individual product is advertised may be capable of identification and the cost allocated directly to specific products.

Where a company's products are advertised generally without mention of any specific article it is impossible to ascertain the benefit each product derives therefrom. The total expenditure upon advertisements of this nature may be considered as a whole and apportioned over products in a more or less arbitrary manner.

2. *Commissions.* Commissions payable to travellers, salesmen, agents, etc., will usually be an agreed amount or percentage, and therefore the amount payable for each type of article is a known quantity.

3. *Travellers' salaries.* Where each traveller devotes his attention to the sale of one type of article only his salary can be allocated directly to the products concerned. If travellers canvass orders for any or all of the company's products, their salaries and expenses may be apportioned to products on one of the bases mentioned later.

4. *Freight, carriage, insurance, etc.* Such charges will vary from product to product, and although the distance for which the goods must be carried will influence the expense to be incurred, a fair average charge can be arrived at on the basis of past experience.

5. *Packing costs.* These costs will depend upon the product, and the cost per article can thus be ascertained. The wages of packers and the costs of the packing department can be apportioned over the articles packed, allowing for the time spent upon each type of package.

6. *Showroom rent, lighting, and other costs.* Costs of this nature cannot, normally, be identified with any particular article sold, and must, therefore, be treated as a whole and charged to products on one of the undermentioned bases. In some businesses it may be desirable to treat showroom and associated costs in the same manner as advertising costs.

It will be seen that marketing costs may be subdivided into two classes, viz.

Those which vary directly with the quantity or value of articles sold, i.e. which are incurred only when the article is sold.

Those which are not incurred by reason of any particular article and represent fixed overhead expenses incurred whether an article is sold or not.

Expenditure coming within the first category represents a definite sum per article sold, and may be added to cost of production in the form of a direct charge. Expenditure of the type included in the second category, however, may be apportioned over the articles sold on one of the following bases:

## 1. RATE PER ARTICLE

If this method is adopted the total fixed selling costs are divided as equitably as possible, over the types of product sold. Each cost is considered separately and the benefit derived therefrom by each article determined. The expenses of the showroom are best apportioned by means of a percentage on the selling prices of the articles concerned, unless circumstances show this to be inequitable. The total fixed expenditure allocated to each type of article is then divided by the quantity of the article sold to give a rate per article. The method is more equitable than the percentage on production cost method. Some attention is paid to the relative benefit obtained by each article from the fixed expenditure incurred and those expenses which vary directly with the article sold are considered separately.

Expenditure might, therefore, be apportioned as under:

|  | *Products* | | |
| --- | --- | --- | --- |
|  | A | B | C |
| Fixed selling costs | £4,400 | £5,800 | £2,000 |
| Sales (units) | 10,000 | 100,000 | 80,000 |
| Rate per article | £0.44 | £0.058 | £0.025 |
| Direct selling and distributive costs: | | | |
| Commissions | 0.10 | 0.050 | 0.025 |
| Freight and carriage | 0.05 | 0.0375 | 0.0625 |
| Packages | 0.15 | 0.0625 | 0.125 |
| Insurance | 0.0125 | 0.0125 | 0.0125 |
| Total cost per article | £0.7525 | £0.2205 | £0.25 |

An addition will thus be made to the cost of production of each article of A, B and C sold, of £0.7525, £0.2205 and £0.25 respectively, as a charge for marketing expenses.

## 2. A PERCENTAGE ON THE SELLING PRICE OF EACH ARTICLE

Fixed selling costs may be charged by way of a percentage on the selling price. The percentage will be ascertained from an analysis of past accounts, taking the selling costs and actual turnover as the basis. Thus, if the fixed selling costs of a business are £2,000 per annum and the turnover £100,000 per annum, an addition should be made to the cost of production of each article sold of 2 per cent on the selling price. Costs which vary with the articles sold, should, as before, be treated as a direct charge.

This method can be adopted successfully only where the products of a business are sold at standard prices and the proportion of each type of product is constant.

### 3. A PERCENTAGE ON PRODUCTION COST

For the reasons already explained, this method is usually unsound unless a business produces one commodity only. In such cases the method has the advantage of simplicity. Where selling costs are small the method may also be adopted, even though various articles are produced, as little advantage would be gained by the employment of a more complicated system, but even then, expenses which vary with articles sold should be treated as direct charges.

In conclusion, the scientific allocation of marketing expenses is, in many businesses, impossible and any attempt to make such an allocation may entail the expenditure of considerable time in achieving results which are useless, and even misleading. The important point is to arrange the data on these costs in such a way as to help management to manage the business profitably.

## ACCOUNTING FOR OVERHEAD

The subject of cost book-keeping is dealt with in Chapter 13, but at this stage a simple example of the treatment of overhead may help to clarify the basic procedure.

*EXAMPLE*

A manufacturing company maintains a cost ledger in addition to a financial ledger. The following information has been extracted for the company's activities for the last four-week period.

| | Salaries | Wages | Stock issues | Purchase invoices | Expenses invoices | Petty cash | Depre- ciation |
|---|---|---|---|---|---|---|---|
| Direct costs: | | | | | | | |
| Dept. I | | | £35,000 | £40,000 | £20,000 | £1,000 | |
| Dept. II | | 20,000 | | | | | |
| Production overhead: | | | | | | | |
| Dept. I | £1,500 | 2,500 | 3,000 | | 500 | | £1,500 |
| Dept. II | 1,500 | 1,500 | 5,000 | | 3,900 | | 6,100 |
| Production services | | 5,000 | 4,500 | | 2,500 | | 500 |
| General services | | 2,500 | 2,500 | | 3,250 | | 750 |
| Marketing overhead | 10,000 | | 5,000 | | 11,000 | £1,000 | 500 |
| Administration | | | | | | | |
| overhead | 15,000 | | 6,000 | | 18,850 | 500 | 650 |
| Stock | | | | 79,000 | | | |
| | £28,000 | £66,500 | £66,000 | £99,000 | £41,000 | £1,500 | £10,000 |

The General Services Department is to be apportioned as follows:

| | |
|---|---|
| Production Dept. I | 22.2% |
| Production Dept. II | 33.4% |
| Production services | 5.5% |
| Selling overhead | 16.7% |
| Administration overhead | 22.2% |
| | 100.0% |

The Production Services Department is to be apportioned as follows:

| | |
|---|---|
| Production Dept. I | 38.5% |
| Production Dept. II | 61.5% |
| | 100.0% |

The overhead of Production Dept I is absorbed on the basis of 50 per cent on Direct Wages. The overhead of Production Dept. II is absorbed on the basis of £2 per machine hour. 13,250 machine hours were recorded in the period. There were no opening stocks. Closing stocks were:

| | |
|---|---|
| Materials | £13,000 |
| Work-in-progress | £12,000 |
| Finished stock | £18,000 |

*Wages and Salaries Account*

| | | | |
|---|---|---|---|
| Gross wages or pay-roll | £66,500 | Direct wages: Dept. I | £35,000 |
| Salaries | 28,000 | Dept. II | 20,000 |
| | | Indirect wages & salaries | |
| | | Production Dept. I | 4,000 |
| | | Production Dept. II | 3,000 |
| | | Production services | 5,000 |
| | | General services | 2,500 |
| | | Marketing overhead | 10,000 |
| | | Administration overhead | 15,000 |
| | £94,500 | | £94,500 |

*Stock Account*

| | | | |
|---|---|---|---|
| Creditors | £79,000 | Direct material | £40,000 |
| | | Indirect material | |
| | | Production Dept. I | 3,000 |
| | | Production Dept. II | 5,000 |
| | | Production services | 4,500 |
| | | General services | 2,500 |
| | | Marketing overhead | 5,000 |
| | | Administration overhead | 6,000 |
| | | Balance c/d | 13,000 |
| | £79,000 | | £79,000 |
| Balance b/d | £13,000 | | |

*Expenses Account*

| Creditors | £41,000 | Direct expenses | £1,000 |
|---|---|---|---|
| Petty cash expenses | 1,500 | Indirect expenses | |
| Depreciation | 10,000 |    Production Dept. I | 2,000 |
| | |    Production Dept. II | 10,000 |
| | |    Production services | 3,000 |
| | |    General services | 4,000 |
| | |    Marketing overhead | 12,500 |
| | |    Administration | |
| | |      overhead | 20,000 |
| | £52,500 | | £52,500 |

*Work-in-Progress Account*

| Wages Account Dept. I | £35,000 | Finished Stock Account | £148,000 |
|---|---|---|---|
| Wages Account Dept. II | 20,000 | Balance—unfinished work | |
| Stock Account direct | |    c/d | 12,000 |
|    material | 40,000 | | |
| Purchases | 20,000 | | |
| Expenses Account | | | |
|    direct expenses | 1,000 | | |
| | | | |
| Production overhead | | | |
|    absorbed: | | | |
| Dept. I 50% on direct | | | |
|    wages | 17,500 | | |
| Dept. II £2 per hour | 26,500 | | |
| | £160,000 | | £160,000 |
| Balance b/d | £12,000 | | |

*Production Overhead Account: Production Dept. I*

| Indirect wages & | | Overhead absorbed in | |
|---|---|---|---|
|    salaries | £4,000 |    work-in-progress | |
| Indirect material | 3,000 |    (50% on direct wages) | £17,500 |
| Indirect expenses | 2,000 | | |
| Production services | 5,000 | | |
| General services | 2,000 | | |
| Profit & Loss Account | | | |
|    —over-absorption | 1,500 | | |
| | £17,500 | | £17,500 |

*Production Overhead Account: Production Dept. II*

| | | | |
|---|---|---|---|
| Indirect wages & salaries | £3,000 | Overhead absorbed in work-in-progress (£2 per machine hr.) | £26,500 |
| Indirect material | 5,000 | Profit and Loss Account— under-absorption | 2,500 |
| Indirect expenses | 10,000 | | |
| Production services | 8,000 | | |
| General services | 3,000 | | |
| | £29,000 | | £29,000 |

*Production Services Account*

| | | | |
|---|---|---|---|
| Indirect wages & salaries | £5,000 | Production Dept. I | £5,000 |
| Indirect materials | 4,500 | Production Dept. II | 8,000 |
| Indirect expenses | 3,000 | | |
| General services | 500 | | |
| | £13,000 | | £13,000 |

*General Services Account*

| | | | |
|---|---|---|---|
| Indirect wages & salaries | £2,500 | Production Dept. I | £2,000 |
| Indirect materials | 2,500 | Production Dept. II | 3,000 |
| Indirect expenses | 4,000 | Production services | 500 |
| | | Marketing overhead | 1,500 |
| | | Administration overhead | 2,000 |
| | £9,000 | | £9,000 |

*Marketing Overhead Account*

| | | | |
|---|---|---|---|
| Indirect wages & salaries | £10,000 | Profit & Loss Account | £29,000 |
| Indirect materials | 5,000 | | |
| Indirect expenses | 12,500 | | |
| General services | 1,500 | | |
| | £29,000 | | £29,000 |

*Administration Overhead Account*

| | | | |
|---|---|---|---|
| Indirect wages & salaries | £15,000 | Profit & Loss Account | £43,000 |
| Indirect materials | 6,000 | | |
| Indirect expenses | 20,000 | | |
| General services | 2,000 | | |
| | £43,000 | | £43,000 |

*Finished Stock Account*

| | | | |
|---|---|---|---|
| Completed produc'n | £148,000 | Trading Account | £130,000 |
| | | Balance c/d | 18,000 |
| | £148,000 | | £148,000 |
| Balance b/d | £18,000 | | |

*Trading and Profit and Loss Account*
*for the 4-week period ended....*

| | | | |
|---|---|---|---|
| Cost of sales | £130,000 | Sales | £209,000 |
| Gross profit c/d | 79,000 | | |
| | £209,000 | | £209,000 |
| Marketing overhead | £29,000 | Gross profit b/d | £79,000 |
| Administration overhead | 43,000 | Over-absorbed overhead in Dept. I | 1,500 |
| Under-absorbed overhead in Dept. II | 2,500 | | |
| Net profit | 6,000 | | |
| | £80,500 | | £80,500 |

NOTE:

1. In the above accounts, the transaction has been described rather than the contra account. In an interlocking system of cost accounts, entries, which affect financial accounts, e.g. creditors, petty cash, provisions for depreciation, would be debited or credited to a "Cost Ledger Contra" account in the cost ledger.

2. The transfers from Work-in-Progress to Finished Stock and from Finished Stock to Trading Account (cost of sales) are balancing figures after recording closing stocks.

## SUMMARY

It is necessary at this point to qualify the treatment of overhead described in this chapter before passing on to specialised forms of costing adapted to the needs of different industries or for use in particular circumstances.

The cost accountant must bear in mind the purpose of his computations. He must avoid undue complications in his methods and must be aware of the pitfalls inherent in historical cost accounting, especially in so far as the treatment of fixed overhead is concerned. The detailed consideration of the apportionment of such expenses in this chapter is of necessity somewhat artificial. In an undertaking comprising many productive and ancillary departments the procedure outlined may, besides being extremely complicated, yield results quite divorced from reality.

There are, however, circumstances in which the apportionment must be attempted, for example in the preparation of estimates or quotations or in compiling product costs for stock valuation. It is important that the student should be aware of the techniques involved in charging overhead to departments and to the production of those departments.

This latter procedure is perhaps the more open to criticism and later chapters deal with methods which meet some of the objections.

## SELF-STUDY TEST No. 4

*Expenses and Overhead*

(*Refer to the Appendix on p. 348 for outline solutions.*)

1. State how you would deal with the following items in the cost accounts of a manufacturing company:

    (*a*) depreciation and obsolescence of machinery;
    (*b*) bad debts:
    (*c*) rent, where premises are owned by the company;
    (*d*) advertising.

2. List the advantages which may be expected from an efficiently operated plant and equipment record.

3. In many manufacturing companies, overhead is divided between: (*a*) production; (*b*) general administration; (*c*) marketing.

Explain why such a division is made and how such costs differ.

4. Pressings Ltd. operate four identical machines in Department H. The following data is supplied:

    (*a*) Each machine:

| | |
|---|---|
| Purchase cost | £3,000 |
| Estimated working life | 10 years |
| Estimated scrap value thereafter | £250 |
| Estimated running time (50 weeks) | 2,000 hours per annum |

    (*b*) Wages of each of two operators (each operator is in charge of two machines): £64 per week.

(c) 30 units of electric current are consumed per hour, £0.05 per unit.

(d) Repairs and maintenance per machine, £400 per annum.

(e) Other factory overhead attributable to the four machines together, £5,000 per annum.

Compute a machine-hour rate in respect of each machine.

5. In the process of allotting overhead expenditure to manufacturing departments, one has to deal with: (a) expenditure readily identifiable with each department and with no other; (b) expenditure common to all departments and needing to be apportioned on an equitable basis.

Name three important classes of expenditure falling into each of these divisions.

Also, explain very briefly the basis you would suggest for allotting to each department the following:

(a) depreciation of plant and machinery;
(b) factory store-keeping cost;
(c) lighting and heating;
(d) supervision.

6. In two businesses of comparable size and structure making the same kind of product the ratios of overhead to direct labour vary considerably. What differences of method would account for this?

Would you expect the business having the higher ratio to be the more efficient of the two, or the more inefficient?

Give your reasons.

7. The following costs have been estimated for the forthcoming year by a manufacturing company which operates a "batch" costing system. The manufacturing process is executed by labour, machines or a mixture of both.

| | |
|---|---|
| Rent and rates | £56,000 |
| Repairs and maintenance (machinery) | 4,200 |
| Repairs and maintenance (buildings) | 1,850 |
| Fuel, gas and water (heating and general) | 22,000 |
| Electric power (for machinery) | 12,600 |
| Raw materials used | 378,600 |
| Maintenance of patterns, jigs and fixtures | 2,320 |
| Direct wages | 525,000 |
| Interest on bank overdraft | 3,080 |
| Storekeeping expense | 5,890 |
| Production management | 7,600 |
| Depreciation (machinery) | 80,100 |
| Depreciation (buildings) | 5,000 |
| Wages of foremen, timekeepers and inspectors | 10,200 |
| Carriage inwards | 11,400 |
| Carriage outwards | 15,500 |
| Salesmen's commissions | 13,000 |
| Salesmen's travelling expenses | 13,400 |
| Designing and estimating | 18,340 |
| General expenses | 17,160 |
| Management and secretarial | 23,000 |
| Advertising | 32,700 |
| General office | 9,830 |
| Sales | 1,500,000 |

Additional information:

Machine hours worked during the year: 697,500 (budgeted 700,000).
Direct labour hours worked during the year: 810,000 (budgeted 800,000).
Area of buildings:

| Factory buildings | 80,000 m² |
|---|---|
| Offices | 20,000 m² |

You are required to:

(a) divide overhead into the following classifications: (i) Production (items to be recovered by a machine-hour rate); (ii) Production (items to be recovered on a direct labour-hour basis); (iii) Marketing; (iv) Administration and Finance.

(b) State how the cost in each of the above classifications will be absorbed and calculate the rate of absorption.

(c) Job No. 156 has been charged with £70 of raw material, 50 hours' machine time and 150 hours of direct labour representing £165 wages. Calculate the total cost of the job.

8. A firm is working at full capacity within the normal 40-hour week for 50 weeks a year. Eighty operatives are employed and are paid £1.80 per hour. Overtime working is not permitted.

The firm wants to expand production and is recruiting twenty part-time workers to attend for four hours on each of five evenings of the week. The part-timers would be paid the normal hourly rate plus one-third. It is expected that the arrangement would apply for the whole of the forthcoming year, i.e. 50 weeks.

The time spent by each operative on production is estimated at 95 per cent of the time for which operatives are paid.

Production Overhead for the forthcoming year has been estimated as follows:

|  | *Without the extra shift* | *Addition for extra shift* |
|---|---|---|
| Materials handling | £8,000 | 20% |
| Power | 6,000 ⎱ | Proportionate to |
| Consumable stores | 4,000 ⎰ | direct labour hours |
| Lighting and heating | 2,000 | 12½% |
| Production control | 5,000 | £900 |
| Plant maintenance | 3,000 | 25% |
| Depreciation | 8,000 | 10% |
| Miscellaneous expenses | 4,000 | 5% |

You are required to:

(a) prepare the Production Overhead Schedule for the forthcoming year assuming the evening shift is worked;

(b) calculate the production overhead absorption rate using the: (i) direct labour hour basis; (ii) percentage of direct labour cost basis.

9. The recovery of overhead as part of the cost of production may include not only costs directly allocated to the production department, but also a share of service department costs.

Describe the methods by which service department costs may be apportioned.

# CHAPTER 7

# Specific Order Costing

In Chapter 1 brief mention was made of the two basic costing methods —specific order costing and operation costing. Specific order costing is used where costs can be identified with and allocated to a specific job or order produced, whereas operation costing is used where all the products are identical and costs are averaged over products.

Job costing will be undertaken in a manufacturing department where each order is different, e.g. in a printing firm. The job may consist of one item or a number of items, in which case the job cost becomes strictly a batch cost, and the cost of each item is found by dividing the total batch cost by the quantity in the batch. An attempt is made to find the profit or loss on each job, and also to compare actual costs incurred with estimated costs.

Most of the jobs executed by a manufacturing firm will be started and finished within an accounting period of, say, one year. There are, however, certain industries, e.g. aircraft manufacture and ship-building, where the job will take a much greater time to complete. Also there are other industries where the work will be done outside the factory at certain sites, e.g. civil engineering and building firms. Contract costing methods are used for such undertakings.

## JOB COSTING

Procedures for recording material used and time worked on jobs in the factory have been described, as have the methods of allotting overhead to cost units. The work to be done will be initiated by a production authorisation from the production control department which instructs the factory to produce and supplies details of the quantity and quality of material, machines to be used, anticipated production times, etc. At the same time the cost department should be informed so that it may prepare a Job Cost Account on which to record the cost of materials from material requisitions and in-voices, and wages incurred from time-sheets. Where production control has prepared a detailed specification of the job and the estimator has used this in preparing a quotation for the customer, the account can be ruled in such a way as to indicate at a glance what stage has been reached on the job, and how the actual cost compares with the estimate.

## H.F.L. CO. LTD.

| Customer | | Customer Order No. | Job No. |
|---|---|---|---|
| Job description | | | Date started |
| | | | Date completed |

| Actual cost | | Estimate |
|---|---|---|

| | | | | | £ | £ | £ | £ |
|---|---|---|---|---|---|---|---|---|

**MATERIALS**

| Quantity | Description | Code or Inv. No. | Price | Per |
|---|---|---|---|---|
| | | | | |
| | | | | |
| | | | | |

**WAGES**

| | Operation | M/c hours | Cost centre | Lab. hours |
|---|---|---|---|---|
| 1 | | | | |
| 2 | | | | |
| 3 | | | | |

**DIRECT EXPENSES**

| Invoice No. | Details |
|---|---|
| | |
| | |

**PRIME COST**

**FACTORY OVERHEAD**

| Cost centre | Absorption rate | Base | Quantity |
|---|---|---|---|
| | | | |
| | | | |

Factory cost

Selling overhead

Administration overhead

Total cost

Profit/loss

Selling price

Fig. 36.—*Job cost account.*

NOTE. If required, separate sections could be provided for materials issued from store and materials purchased direct for the job.

An example of a Job Cost Account is given in Fig. 36. The job number allocated by the production control department must appear on all requisitions, time-sheets, purchase invoices and sales invoices. The cost data will be prepared in a form suitable for posting to the Job Cost Account. Materials cost and wages analysis sheets may be prepared as mentioned in the chapters relating to those cost elements. Thus, the total materials or wages incurred for an accounting period are summarised for debit to Job Cost Accounts. The disadvantage with this method is that although it saves posting each individual requisition, the Job Cost Account does not show details of materials used and, if there are any subsequent investigations, it will be necessary to search through all the materials and wages analyses.

When the job is finished, a finished goods note should be raised by the production department and approved by the inspector. If the products are to go into a finished parts store, a note must be signed by the storekeeper; alternatively they may be taken direct to the packing department to be prepared for despatch, in which case the packing foreman will sign for the goods. The finished goods note should then be passed to the cost department which will close the Job Cost Account and calculate the profit or loss on the job. The benefit of showing the estimate alongside the actual figures is in providing a comparison for control purposes and in checking if all costs incurred have been recorded.

The overhead to be absorbed by the job may be calculated when the job is finished or analysed over jobs at the end of each accounting period. The total absorbed is credited to the Overhead Control Account. A Work-in-Progress Control Account will be kept in the Cost Ledger and this may be subdivided according to the main types of work done.

*EXAMPLE*

F. Linch (Hooks) Ltd. is a small company which produces special-purpose lifting equipment. In the month ending September 30th the following details were obtained on the month's production and costs.

|  | Job XEL 9 | Job YME 2 | Job IMA 1 | Job URA 12 | Total |
|---|---|---|---|---|---|
| Stores issues | £40.10 | £35.35 | £68.75 | £151.40 | £295.60 |
| Wages | 69.20 | 71.40 | 21.40 | 82.90 | 244.90 |
| Purchases | — | 45.00 | 5.00 | — | 50.00 |

Job URA 12 was completed during the month and sent to the customer. The sales value was £1,000. Overhead is absorbed on the basis of 200 per cent on prime cost. The overhead incurred during the month was £1,250.

Write up: 1. Job Cost Accounts; 2. Work-in-Progress Control Account; 3. Overhead Control Account; 4. Cost Ledger Profit and Loss Account.

JOB COST LEDGER

### JOB XEL 9

| Date | Stores issues £ | Purchases £ | Wages £ | Prime cost £ | Overhead £ | Total £ | Profit £ | Sales £ | Remarks |
|---|---|---|---|---|---|---|---|---|---|
| 30/9 | 40.10 | – | 69.20 | 109.30 | 218.60 | 327.90 | | | |

### JOB YME 2

| Date | Stores issues £ | Purchases £ | Wages £ | Prime cost £ | Overhead £ | Total £ | Profit £ | Sales £ | Remarks |
|---|---|---|---|---|---|---|---|---|---|
| 30/9 | 35.35 | 45.00 | 71.40 | 151.75 | 303.50 | 455.25 | | | |

### JOB IMA 1

| Date | Stores issues £ | Purchases £ | Wages £ | Prime cost £ | Overhead £ | Total £ | Profit £ | Sales £ | Remarks |
|---|---|---|---|---|---|---|---|---|---|
| 30/9 | 68.75 | 5.00 | 21.40 | 95.15 | 190.30 | 285.45 | | | |

### JOB URA 12

| Date | Stores issues £ | Purchases £ | Wages £ | Prime cost £ | Overhead £ | Total £ | Profit £ | Sales £ | Remarks |
|---|---|---|---|---|---|---|---|---|---|
| 30/9 | 151.40 | – | 82.90 | 234.30 | 468.60 | 702.90 | 297.10 | 1,000.00 | Closed 30/9 |

Work-in-Progress at month end:

| | |
|---|---|
| XEL 9 | £327.90 |
| YME 2 | 455.25 |
| IMA 1 | 285.45 |
| | £1,068.60 |

Total per Work-in-Progress Control

### Work-in-Progress Control Account

| | | | |
|---|---|---|---|
| Stores issues | £295.60 | Profit & Loss Account | £702.90 |
| Wages | 244.90 | Balance c/d | 1,068.60 |
| Purchases | 50.00 | | |
| Overhead | 1,'81.00 | | |
| | £1,771.50 | | £1,771.50 |
| Balance b/d | £1,068.60 | | |

### Overhead Control Account

| | | | |
|---|---|---|---|
| Overhead incurred | £1,250.00 | Overhead absorbed | £1,181.00 |
| | | Profit & Loss Account: | |
| | | under-absorption | 69.00 |
| | £1,250.00 | | £1,250.00 |

### Costing Profit and Loss Account

| | | | | |
|---|---|---|---|---|
| Overhead | | Profit on Job URA 12 | | |
| under-absorbed | £69.00 | Sales | £1,000.00 | |
| Net profit | 228.10 | Cost | 702.90 | £297.10 |
| | £297.10 | | | £297.10 |

## CONTRACT COSTING

Contract or terminal costing is the term applied to the system adopted by businesses which carry out substantial building or constructional work. Special features are:

1. The contractor carries out a small number of large contracts in the course of a year.

2. The contracts are carried out away from the contractor's premises, with perhaps some initial assemblies prepared at the premises, e.g. pre-cast concrete frames, window and door frames.

3. The contracts may continue over more than one accounting period.

4. Specialist sub-contractors may be employed, e.g. ventilation engineers, lift manufacturers, flooring specialists, etc.

5. Payment by the customer for various stages of the contract will be made only on receipt of an architect's certificate for the completed stage. A deduction, called retention money, will be

withheld by the client until a specific period of time, agreed in the original contract, has elapsed.

6. Penalties may be incurred by the contractor for failing to complete the work in the agreed time.

7. The contract price is normally estimated in advance. Additional work found necessary may be charged on a cost-plus basis. In addition, the contractor may be able to pass on to the client additional costs incurred as a result of wage awards.

### General principles

Before attempting to outline the costing system and book-keeping entries, the purposes should be clarified. These may be *inter alia*:

1. Comparison of actual cost with estimated cost.
2. Detailed analysis of costs to provide a basis for "cost-plus" pricing.
3. Calculation of profit which may reasonably be taken each year on a long-term contract.
4. Guidance to management on the utilisation of resources.

In principle each contract can be regarded as a large job within a job-costing system. A detailed record of costs attributable to the contract may take the form of an account or analysis sheets to provide memorandum detail for an overall Contract Control Account. The Contract Control Account would therefore be similar to the Work-in-Progress Control Account shown on p. 148.

As with job costing, there will be overhead costs of administration and central services, e.g. plant, which may be charged to contracts on some equitable basis. In addition, Work-in-Progress Accounts may be kept for the manufacture of common items used at various sites, e.g. window frames and roof trusses. Such items may be charged to contracts at either actual or standard cost.

Whatever accounting structure is adopted, the cost analysis will be similar and will have regard to the purposes outlined above. Although the contract itself can be regarded as a cost unit, sub-units will often be used for cost analysis. These will form natural divisions of work, e.g. in a building contract the sub-units may be:

    (*i*) Foundations.
   (*ii*) Steelwork.
  (*iii*) Walls.
  (*iv*) Roof.
   (*v*) Electrical installations.
  (*vi*) Plumbing.
 (*vii*) Floors.
(*viii*) Painting and decorating.

The choice of sub-units should be those used in the analysis of the estimated costs prepared before submitting a quotation to the client.

Normally each contract will be allocated a special contract number and sub-codes will identify each sub-unit. Additional work not originally included in the contract price will be given a separate code in order to accumulate the exact cost which may form the basis of an additional charge to the customer. A specimen analysis which may be used is given in Fig. 37.

## Materials

A considerable proportion of the material used will be purchased specifically for the contract and will be delivered direct to the site; invoices for these materials will be posted direct to the Contract Account.

Other materials will be delivered to a central stores for subsequent issue to contract sites or to central fabricating departments. Stores records will be kept for these materials, all movements being recorded on goods received notes and requisitions.

It may be difficult to allocate certain materials, e.g. sand, ballast, bricks, etc., to sub-units, as they will be delivered to the site for use on two or more sub-units. Ideally, site stock records would be kept for bulk materials and all issues controlled and recorded by requisitions. However, storage facilities at sites are often far from ideal and workmen may be free to obtain materials when they need them. Under those conditions perhaps the only practical solution is to analyse the contract by sub-units related to the type of work, e.g. bricklaying, concreting, etc.

In view of the money involved, the accounting function will need to ensure that strict control is maintained over receipt of and payments for materials. Stock records, especially any held at sites, should be regularly verified by physical stocktaking.

Transfers of materials between sites must be accompanied by a transfer note to be finally routed to the cost department; the value of the materials will be ascertained and the transfer made between the contract accounts. Occasionally, materials may be sold at the site if they are defective or surplus to requirements and are not sent back to the supplier. The sale proceeds may be credited to the Contract Account, or an account may be opened to which the cost of materials is transferred and the proceeds credited.

## Labour

In a factory, control of workmen may be facilitated by the proximity of the foreman, the flow along an automated production line or an incentive scheme linking output with wages; conditions at a construction site are often, however, not conducive to effective control. The

## CONTRACT LEDGER

Completion date.................................  Contract No.....................  Site.....................

Terms for instalments.........................  Contract price.................  Work certified:

Retention money...............................                                    Date.................  £.................

                                                                                  Date.................  £.................

                                               Etc.                               Etc.

| Date | Par- ticulars | Folio | Materials £ | Wages £ | Sub- con- tracts £ | Prime cost £ | Plant £ | Estab- lish- ment ch'gs £ | Total £ | Date | Par- ticulars | Folio | Materials £ | Wages £ | Sub- con- tracts £ | Prime cost £ | Plant £ | Estab- lish- ment ch'gs £ | Total £ |
|---|---|---|---|---|---|---|---|---|---|---|---|---|---|---|---|---|---|---|---|
|  |  |  |  |  |  |  |  |  |  |  |  |  |  |  |  |  |  |  |  |
|  |  |  |  |  |  |  |  |  |  |  |  |  |  |  |  |  |  |  |  |
|  |  |  |  |  |  |  |  |  |  |  |  |  |  |  |  |  |  |  |  |

FIG. 37.—*Contract ledger.*

NOTES

1. The columns for materials and wages may be subdivided if required, e.g. to show different classes of labour.

2. As the credit columns will rarely be used, they may be dispensed with, credit entries can be deducted on the debit side, either entered in red or in a section reserved for the purpose at the foot of the account.

3. A separate sheet may be kept for each sub-unit of the contract with a control sheet to record total costs.

site may cover a wide area with employees being lost to view; difficulties may be encountered in supplying material at the right time and place; co-ordination of work will be a problem, i.e. ensuring that work is done in such a sequence that workmen are not standing idle. Some workmen may of course have to travel from one part of the site to another, while, when small contracts are undertaken, they will travel between sites.

The costing system will seek to achieve an accurate analysis of labour costs and also an assessment of the utilisation of the labour force. In view of the difficulties at the site, the cost accountant must ask himself whether he can rely on an analysis of time worked provided by the worker. Assuming the worker makes an effort to record his time accurately, the circumstances of his work may preclude him from doing this until some time after the event. These factors will need to be considered when selecting sub-units of the contract for cost analysis. If the sub-units are confined to the main stages in the contract, cost analysis will be easier; it may not be necessary for workers to complete time-sheets, as the foreman will know what parts of the contract each worker has been assigned to each day, and he can analyse the time records accordingly.

It is essential to keep accurate records of time-keeping to ensure that wages are paid for actual attendance and where possible time-recording clocks could be used. Where this is impracticable the foreman remains responsible for recording workers' attendance time. When workmen travel between sites, it will be important to separate travelling time from time spent working. This information will normally be provided by a time-sheet completed by the worker and authorised (where possible) by responsible officials at each site.

If the contract is small and has not been divided into sub-units for cost analysis, all labour costs incurred at the site can be considered direct. If the contract has been sectionalised, however, some workmen will be indirect, e.g. supervisors, storemen and site office staff, and such costs may need to be apportioned to sub-units.

At the contractor's premises, there may be direct workers engaged on assembling structures required at the site and also indirect workers in stores, transport and maintenance departments, etc. There will also be indirect wages and salaries incurred in the central administrative offices.

The payroll will be prepared from an assortment of time records and the gross wages posted to the contract accounts or sub-units, and various overhead accounts. The wage computation may include a bonus payment from a group bonus scheme, and where possible this should be charged direct to the contract.

It will be advisable for the accounts function to arrange spot checks from time to time on the adequacy of the time-recording systems to minimise the risks of fraud.

**Plant**

The contracting industry is perhaps less mechanised than the manufacturing industry due to the nature of the work, but a contractor will nevertheless seek to purchase or hire plant when the scale of operations and site conditions permit the plant to be economically employed.

Records must be maintained of plant to ensure that none is lost or improperly disposed of and that the contract is duly charged for the use of the plant. A plant register should be kept and movements between individual sites, and also between the central yard and sites, recorded. A complete physical inventory of plant should be made at suitable intervals, all discrepancies being investigated.

It is important to adopt a realistic method of depreciation for purchased plant to take account of the rough conditions in which the plant may be required to operate, e.g. out in all weathers and perhaps working over rough terrain.

The following methods are in use for charging contracts for the use of plant:

(a) The cost of the plant issued to the site (or, if old plant is issued, the written-down value thereof as shown by the plant register) may be charged direct to the Contract Account concerned.

(b) A charge for the hire of the plant may be made to each contract, based upon the time the plant is in use.

The former method may be used for plant which will be required for daily use at the site for an extended period or which will be completely worn out before the contract is completed. In other words, the capital cost of the plant may be regarded as an expense specifically incurred for the contract. If, however, the plant is transferred either to the central yard or to another contract it should be revalued and credited to the Contract Account accordingly. If the plant is sold the Contract Account should be credited with the proceeds.

Where a contract extends over a number of years, the plant charged to the Contract Account must be revalued at the close of each financial period in order that the cost of the contract to date may be ascertained. The depreciated value of the plant will be credited to the Contract Account and carried down as a balance to a new period. In this way the depreciation which has taken place is duly charged to the account.

*EXAMPLE*

Plant costing £2,000 is issued to a contract on January 1st and at December 31st it is ascertained that £75,000 has been expended upon the contract (excluding plant) and that the plant is valued at £1,500 at the close of the year. The Contract Account would appear as under. (For simplicity the Contract Account is shown in ordinary account form without analysis columns.)

*Contract Account*

| Jan. 1 | | Dec. 31 | |
|---|---|---|---|
| Plant issued to site | £2,000 | Value of plant c/d | £1,500 |
| Jan./Dec. | | Dec. 31 | |
| Sundry expenditure | 75,000 | Work-in-progress c/d | 75,500 |
| | £77,000 | | £77,000 |
| Jan. 1 Plant b/d | 1,500 | | |
| Jan. 1 | | | |
| Work-in-progress b/d | 75,500 | | |

It will be seen from the above illustration that the depreciation of £500 has been added automatically to the cost of the work-in-progress.

The second method of charging depreciation to the contract, i.e. a charge based on the use made of the plant, is of course similar to the charges which would be incurred if the plant had been hired instead of purchased. The advantages of the method are:

1. Full deployment of the plant is encouraged as the site fore-man will not want to be charged for plant standing idle.
2. It will be possible to compare the economics of purchase against hire.
3. If the rate used is the market rate, the efficiency of the plant department can be established.

The method may be kept simple by using a rate which covers depreciation only, but it may be advantageous to include all charges for plant, i.e. driver, fuel and lubricants, insurance, maintenance and repairs. The rate may be divided between standing costs, charged on a weekly basis, and running costs, charged on an hourly basis. Alternatively, the rate may be based on the market rate paid to hiring companies for the particular type of plant.

Costs included in the hiring rate will be debited to the Plant Account. The account will be credited with the hours of use multi-plied by the hiring rate and the various Contract Accounts debited. The balance on the Plant Account represents a profit or loss on plant operations and will reflect the efficiency of the plant department and the adequacy of the rate used. It will be necessary to set up a provi-sion account for unrealised profit, i.e. in respect of plant charges included in work-in-progress, as any profit on the Plant Account is internal to the contractor's business.

The utilisation of plant may assume considerable importance for a large contractor and relevant data must be forthcoming to ensure adequate control. Some contractors have found that greater effici-ency is obtained by converting the plant department into an autono-mous business run on normal commercial principles.

## Overhead

While most costs will be chargeable directly to contracts and sub-units, there will be some charges which are incurred for the contract as a whole, e.g. site supervision, or for the business as a whole, e.g. central offices.

Further treatment may not be required for the first category, i.e. they have been located to contracts and it may not be considered necessary to apportion the costs over sub-units of the contract. Such costs will be treated as part of work-in-progress until the contract is completed. The contractor may prefer not to apportion such costs as central administration to contracts but simply to write them off during the year in which they are incurred. This will be particularly so where the costs are relatively small.

If the contractor feels the need to charge individual contracts with a share of general overhead a percentage on prime cost should be adequate as a basis for recovering overhead. Alternatively, any one of the methods outlined in Chapter 6 could be used, e.g. a percentage on direct wages, or a labour-hour rate. It may be informative to use an estimated absorption rate, calculated with reference to budgeted overhead and activity.

Whether or not indirect costs are charged in the cost accounts, allowance must be made for them in the preparation of estimates, or the prices quoted will not cover all costs concerned.

## Extras

In many contracts, modifications, additional work or variations of the work originally contracted for are required by the contractee. This additional work, being outside the original contract, will be the subject of a separate charge. Extras of this character often form an important item, and the contractee's written confirmation of the extra work to be undertaken and the price to be paid, or the basis upon which such work is to be charged, must be obtained.

As extras are frequently charged for on a cost-plus basis, it is important to isolate such expenditure to support charges to the customer. An additional sub-unit code will need to be issued so that all costs can be collected.

## Sub-contracts

Work of a specialised character, e.g. steelwork, heating installations, lifts and special flooring, is usually carried out by sub-contractors who are responsible to the main contractor. Such work forms a direct charge to the contracts concerned. If an agreed charge is made by the sub-contractor, detailed records will not be required for labour, materials, etc., which are provided by the sub-contractor. If the sub-contractor is responsible for labour only, careful control of the materials used must be instituted to avoid waste, pilferage, etc.

Payment to sub-contractors will be made upon receipt of an invoice which may be accompanied by an architect's or surveyor's certificate. The certificate will indicate the amount of money to be paid, which will be less than the total value of work completed. The amount deducted is called retention money. The contractor must ensure that the full value of sub-contracted work is charged to the Contract Account and not merely the amount which is paid. This will be important when calculating profits. The amount paid to the sub-contractor will be debited to the Contract Account and the retention money can be treated as an accrued expense.

**Architect's certificate**
It will be appreciated that when a contractor is engaged on a contract for a long time, his financial resources could become severely strained. A large amount of working capital would be required if he did not receive payment until the completion of the contract. It is normal practice, particularly in the case of large contracts, for the contractee to pay the contractor sums of money on account during the period of the contract.

These sums will be paid against certificates issued by architects acting for the contractee, certifying the value of the work so far performed. Before issuing such a certificate, the professional representative of the contractee will satisfy himself that the work has been carried out in a proper manner and that the amount of the proposed certificate is amply covered by the value of the work to date.

The terms of the contract frequently provide that the whole of the amount shown by the certificate shall not be paid immediately but that a percentage thereof shall be retained by the contractee until some time after the contract is completed. The sum retained is called *retention money*. The object of this retention is to put the contractee in a favourable position should faulty work arise or penalties become payable by reason of late completion of the contract.

The following alternative methods may be employed for recording the certificates received:

1. Credit the Contract Account with the value and debit the personal account of the contractee with the net amount payable. Retention money is debited to a Retention Money Account.
2. Credit the Contract Account with the value and debit the personal account of the contractee. After the net amount payable is received, the balance on the contractee's account will represent the retention money.
3. Enter the certificates on a memorandum record until the final certificate is received when either method 1 or 2 above may be employed. When payments are received from the contractee they

are credited to his account and carried forward as a credit balance from one accounting period to another.

It should be noted that under method 2, the balance on the contractee's account for the retention money must not be treated as a debt in the Balance Sheet. Legally it is not due until the period of time stated in the contract has elapsed. Similarly, under method 3, the credit balance on the contractee's account representing interim payments must not be included under creditors. There is no liability to repay as it has been received in accordance with the terms of the contract.

The effect of crediting the Contract Account with the value of the certificates received will be to create a profit or loss as the balancing figure; the account virtually becomes one of many trading accounts from which profit is transferred to the main Profit and Loss Account.

*EXAMPLE*

Contracts A and B were begun and completed during the year and cost £1,000 and £1,500 respectively. The contract prices were £2,000 and £1,750 respectively:

*Contract A*

| | | | |
|---|---|---|---|
| Cost incurred | £1,000 | Customer A: | |
| Profit & Loss Account | 1,000 | Contract price | £2,000 |
| | £2,000 | | £2,000 |

*Contract B*

| | | | |
|---|---|---|---|
| Cost incurred | £1,500 | Customer B: | |
| Profit & Loss Account | 250 | Contract price | £1,750 |
| | £1,750 | | £1,750 |

*Profit and Loss Account*

| | | |
|---|---|---|
| | Profit on contracts: A | £1,000 |
| | B | £250 |

Where contracts remain unfinished at the year end a proportion of the profit may be taken.

## The balance sheet

In preparing the Balance Sheet for a contractor special attention must be given to the requirements of S.S.A.P. 9. So far as the contractor is concerned, incomplete contracts are regarded as work-in-progress and the cost (plus any profit for which credit has been taken) so described on the Balance Sheet. All cash received and due for receipt (progress payments) on account of such contracts must be shown as a deduction from the work-in-progress figure and the net amount extended. This principle should be followed whether or not the Contract Account is credited with the value of the work certified.

Thus if £245,632 has been expended on uncompleted contracts at December 31st, and £200,000 has been received on account, in cash, from the contractees, the position would be shown in the contractor's Balance Sheet as follows:

| | | |
|---|---:|---:|
| Work-in-progress, at cost | £245,632 | |
| *Less:* Cash received on account | 200,000 | |
| | | £45,632 |

Where the contractee has failed to pay an amount authorised by the contract, this amount only may be shown as a debt in the Balance Sheet. Similarly if the contractee pays money in advance, i.e. more than the amount authorised by the certificates, this may be shown under creditors (or deducted from debtors).

If the total expenditure on contracts to date includes the value of plant and materials at sites, these items may be segregated and shown separately in the Balance Sheet, thus:

| | | |
|---|---:|---:|
| Plant at sites, at cost | £25,000 | |
| *Less:* Provision for depreciation | 9,504 | |
| | | £15,496 |
| Materials in hand at sites | | 5,312 |
| Work-in-progress, at cost | 224,824 | |
| *Less:* Cash received on account | 200,000 | |
| | | 24,824 |
| | | £45,632 |

## Profit on uncompleted contracts

In manufacturing industry generally, production orders are costed separately or in groups and profit or loss taken after the orders are completed and invoiced. Where an order for a large number of units extends over two or more years, deliveries will normally be made as the units are completed. The profit or loss on each delivery can then be calculated and taken into account. Each delivery in fact becomes a sale in its own right and payment in full becomes due according to the stated credit terms. Any units returned as defective and requiring rectification or replacement will be charged to the accounts of the year in which they arise.

In the contracting industry the situation is more difficult as, when contracts take a number of years to complete, their cost, and hence the profit earned, cannot be ascertained precisely until the construction is completed. Moreover, the contract may provide that a proportion of the price (the retention money) is not payable till six months or more after completion, for reasons already explained, and the final cost may not be known until the end of that period as subsequent problems or bad workmanship in later stages may result in additional costs being incurred on parts of the contract originally thought to be complete. If work-in-progress is valued at cost at each Balance Sheet date during the period of construction, it is clear that no profit would be shown by the Contract Account till the job was completed and the final account agreed.

Such a course, though no doubt desirable, may lead to considerable fluctuations in the contractor's annual profits, for the number and size of contracts completed would vary from year to year. Such fluctuations would be especially marked in the case of a contractor who only occasionally enters into large contracts. Accordingly, if a reasonable proportion of profit on uncompleted contracts is taken to the credit of Profit and Loss Account each year, profits on large contracts will tend to accrue more evenly.

The problems associated with incomplete contracts have resulted in certain principles being formulated to determine the profit or loss to be taken into the accounts. They fall under three headings:

1. Adopt a conservative policy.
2. Take account of the cash received.
3. Take account of the total estimated profit when it is possible to foresee future costs.

These factors will now be considered in detail.

## A conservative approach

TAKE NO PROFIT ON THE EARLY STAGES

Each stage may subsequently incur additional costs as changes become necessary and the early stages will clearly be the most vulnerable in this respect. It is impossible to be specific as to what constitutes the early stage, as each business will treat the matter differently. However, as a guide, it may be conceived as the period from the commencement of the contract to the end of the next financial year in the case of medium- and long-term contracts (more than three years), or perhaps a proportion, say 20 per cent of the total contract. In the case of short-term contracts, i.e. about two years, the business may find that it has sufficient contracts to take profit on completion only, without unduly distorting the total annual profits.

Since no credit for profit is taken, work-in-progress at an early stage will be valued at cost. Any excess of the cost of certified work over certified value will immediately be taken to the Profit and Loss Account, and the work-in-progress would be written down to the value of the certificates issued. Thus if costs of £10,000 have been incurred, certificates issued to a value of £7,500, and uncompleted work valued at cost of £2,000 the loss would be shown in the Contract Account as follows:

### Contract Account

| | | | | | |
|---|---|---|---|---|---|
| Costs to date | £10,000 | Work-in-progress c/d: | | | |
| | | Cost of work certified | £8,000 | | |
| | | Work not certified | 2,000 | | |
| | | | 10,000 | | |
| | | Less: Loss to date | 500 | | |
| | | | | £9,500 | |
| | | Profit & Loss Account | | 500 | |
| | £10,000 | | | £10,000 | |

| | | | |
|---|---|---|---|
| Work-in-progress b/d | | | |
| Work certified | £8,000 | | |
| Work not certified | 2,000 | | |
| | | £10,000 | |
| Less: anticipated loss | | 500 | |
| | | £9,500 | |

#### PROFIT TO BE TAKEN ONLY ON WORK CERTIFIED

The surveyor or architect will value the work done on the site periodically and issue a certificate. If the certificate date does not coincide with the end of an accounting period the cost of the work done from the date the certificate was issued to the end of the accounting period must be ascertained. This can be done by apportioning costs to periods before and after the certificate date or by analysing costs to periods.

#### EXAMPLE

Recorded costs on a contract were £10,000 as at September 30th and £12,700 as at December 31st. Certificates were issued at December 1st to the value of £13,000.

| Calculation of profit: | | |
|---|---|---|
| Certificates issued | | £13,000 |
| Total cost | £12,700 | |
| Cost of uncertified work: $\frac{1}{3}$ £(12,700–10,000) | 900 | |
| | | 11,800 |
| Profit | | £1,200 |

One third of the costs incurred from September 30th to December 31st are reckoned to have been incurred during December.

### ANTICIPATE ADDITIONAL EXPENDITURE ARISING

Specific or general provisions may be set up to anticipate additional expenditure arising on work certified as complete. In the absence of these a proportion of the profit may be withheld as a precautionary measure. One-third of the profit is normally recommended as a suitable arbitrary deduction. Thus in the above example the profit taken to Profit and Loss Account for the year would be £800, £400 being held in reserve. If the certificates issued are brought into the accounts, then the profit not taken to the Profit and Loss Account will be shown as a credit balance in the Contract Account, as profit in suspense. If the certificates are not brought into the accounts the profit not taken is not disclosed. The Contract Accounts under each method using the above figures are as follows:

1. Certificates brought into the accounts:

*Contract Account*

| Costs incurred | £12,700 | Contractee's Account: | |
| Profit & Loss Account | 800 | certificates issued | £13,000 |
| Profit in suspense c/d | 400 | Work not certified c/d | 900 |
| | £13,900 | | £13,900 |
| Work not certified b/d | £900 | Profit in suspense b/d | £400 |

2. Certificates not brought into the accounts:

*Contract Account*

| Costs incurred | £12,700 | Work-in-progress c/d: | |
| Profit & Loss Account | 800 | not certified | £900 |
| | | certified | 12,600 |
| | £13,500 | | £13,500 |
| Work-in-progress b/d | | | |
| not certified | £900 | | |
| certified | 12,600 | | |

Whichever method is adopted, attributable profit must be separately disclosed in the Balance Sheet, i.e.:

| Work-in-progress: | |
| At cost to date | £12,700 |
| *add* Attributable profit | 800 |
| | £13,500 |

**Cash received**

The contractee is entitled to withhold retention money and may in addition sometimes delay payment of the amount certified as payable. Some contractors reduce the profit taken by the proportion that the cash received bears to the amount certified.

Thus, in the above example, if the cash received is £12,350, i.e. 95 per cent of the amount certified, the profit of £1,200 would be reduced by one-third to £800 and reduced further by 5 per cent to £760. The formula for taking profit may therefore be stated as follows:

Apparent profit (certificate − cost of certified work)

$$\times \tfrac{2}{3} \times \frac{\text{Cash received}}{\text{Certificates issued}}$$

The arguments put forward for adjusting profit by the proportion of cash not received are as follows:

1. To avoid the possibility of the financial resources of the business being dangerously depleted by distributions of profit not realised in cash.

2. Additional costs may have to be incurred if faulty work arises and has to be rectified before the retention money is received.

3. The contractees may become insolvent.

Arguments against this adjustment should, however, be considered:

1. Calculations of profit should not be affected by considerations of dividend policy. Normal accounting practice is to reduce profit by bad debts only, not by an amount related to unpaid sales invoices.

2. The provision of one-third is likely to be sufficient cover against faulty work.

3. If the solvency of the contractee is in doubt, a provision against the whole amount outstanding should be made, i.e. a specific provision.

4. If a general provision is required for bad debts, it should be related to the total amount outstanding and the contractor's past experience.

**Estimated profit**

When a contract has reached an advanced state, the contractor may be in a position to estimate future costs with some degree of accuracy. These costs, including contingencies, plus actual expenditure to date, will reveal the estimated total cost of the contract. By deducting this figure from the contract price, the estimated net profit on the contract will be disclosed. It is the practice of some contractors to take credit for a proportion of this profit based on one of the following methods:

1. By dividing the total estimated profit in the proportion which the total of the certificates issued to date bears to the contract price (i.e. in accordance with "sales" values).

2. By dividing the total estimated profit in the proportion which the cost of the work so far performed bears to the estimated total cost.

Whatever method is adopted it should be applied consistently from year to year so as not to disturb the trend of profits.

It must also be borne in mind that any profit taken credit for in a previous year must be allowed for when calculating the amount of profit for later years.

On the whole, it is considered that the first method above is normally to be preferred, the adjustment for an unsatisfactory cash position being made where required.

*EXAMPLE*

At December 31st, £97,000 has been expended upon a contract and certificates have been received to the value of £110,000. The cost of work performed, but not yet certified, is £3,000. Up to the end of the previous year, profit of £6,000 had been taken on the contract. It is estimated that the contract will take a further three months to complete and that it will incur additional expenditure of £20,000. The total estimated expenditure is to include a provision of $2\frac{1}{2}$ per cent for contingencies. The contract price is £140,000, and £100,000 has been received in cash to date.

The proportion of profit to be taken to the credit of Profit and Loss Account at December 31st is ascertained as follows:

| | |
|---|---:|
| Total expenditure to date | £97,000 |
| Estimated additional expenditure | 20,000 |
| | 117,000 |
| Provision for contingencies ($2\frac{1}{2}\%$ on total estimated expenditure $= \frac{2.5}{97.5}$ of £117,000) | 3,000 |
| Estimated total expenditure | £120,000 |
| Contract price | £140,000 |
| Estimated total expenditure | 120,000 |
| Estimated total profit | £20,000 |

The cumulative profit taken to the Profit and Loss Account to December 31st would be:

First method:

$$\frac{\text{Value of work certified}}{\text{Contract price}} = \frac{£110,000}{£140,000} \times £20,000 = \underline{£15,700} \text{ (approx.)}$$

Second method:

$$\frac{\text{Cost of work to date}}{\text{Estimated total cost}} = \frac{£97,000}{£120,000} \times £20,000 = \underline{£16,200} \text{ (approx.)}$$

The profit credited to the Profit and Loss Account for the year would be either of those figures less £6,000 which has already been credited for previous years. If required the above profits could be reduced as follows:

First method:

$$\frac{\text{Cash received}}{\text{Work certified}} = \frac{£100,000}{£110,000} \times £15,700 = £14,300 \text{ (approx.)}$$

or

Second method:

$$\frac{\text{Cash received}}{\text{Work certified}} = \frac{£100,000}{£110,000} \times £16,200 = £14,700 \text{ (approx.)}$$

Using the first method without any adjustment for cash, the contract would appear in the Balance Sheet at December 31st as:

| | |
|---|---:|
| Long-term contracts in progress: | |
| At cost to date: | £97,000 |
| *Add* attributable profit | 15,700 |
| | 112,700 |
| *Deduct* progress payments | 100,000 |
| | £12,700 |

## Budgeted profit

The methods of taking profit outlined in this chapter embrace the main principles to be adopted. In practice the actual methods used may vary considerably from those advocated here. One method which may be adopted takes account of the total budgeted profit on the contract rather than the actual profit. One advantage of the method is that where there are numerous sub-units in the contract and the contractor knows that the profit on each varies considerably, the profit is spread over the life of the contract in proportion to the work done. Thus, if the budgeted profit on a contract is £20,000 and certificates have been issued for three-quarters of the total contract price, £15,000 could be taken to the Profit and Loss Account for profit earned to date. Normally a provision would be made—say, one-third—so that £10,000 would in fact be taken. The method is simple to use, but the contractor must ensure that the budget is accurately prepared.

## BATCH COSTING

As has been explained, a production order can be for an item or a number of items. The latter represents a batch and the total batch cost must be divided by the quantity to give a cost per item. A Job Cost Account will be prepared for the batch and the costing entries will be similar to those used in job costing.

Problems may sometimes arise where batches of dissimilar products are brought together so that a common operation can be performed on them in order to save setting time on the machine. A typical example would be batches of products which require heat treatment and a number of batches are put into the oven together. Loading and unloading time, and the oven costs, must be apportioned to the batches on some equitable basis. However, if the cost per unit is considered small, an easy solution would be to include such costs in general production overhead. A further problem may arise if at the end of the accounting period part of a batch is unfinished and costs have to be apportioned between completed and uncompleted units. This is a common process costing problem which is dealt with in the next chapter.

## SELF-STUDY TEST No. 5

*Specific Order Costing*

(*Refer to the Appendix on p. 352 for outline solutions.*)

1. According to the factory job cost ledger, Job No. 84 has incurred the following prime costs:

Materials (Direct)

30 kgs at £6 per kg

Wages (Direct)

Department A 18 hours at £1.75 per hour.
Department B 32 hours at £1.50 per hour.

Budgeted overhead for the year, based on normal capacity, is as follows:

Variable overhead

Department A £4,500 for 9,000 direct labour hours.
Department B £12,500 for 10,000 direct labour hours.

Fixed overhead

Total budgeted direct labour hours for whole factory 22,000
Total budgeted expenditure £28,600.

You are required

(*a*) to calculate the cost of Job No. 84.
(*b*) Estimate the percentage of profit obtained if the price quoted to the customer was £500.

2. British Contractors Ltd. undertook three contracts, one on January 1st, one on July 1st and one on October 1st. On December 31st, when the accounts were made up, the position was as follows:

|  | 1 | 2 | 3 |
|---|---|---|---|
| Contract price | £200,000 | £135,000 | £150,000 |
| Expenditure: |  |  |  |
| Materials | 36,000 | 29,000 | 10,000 |
| Wages | 55,000 | 56,200 | 7,000 |
| General expenses | 2,000 | 1,400 | 500 |
| Plant installed | 10,000 | 8,000 | 6,000 |
| Materials on hand | 2,000 | 2,000 | 1,000 |
| Wages accrued | 1,700 | 1,800 | 800 |
| General expenses accrued | 300 | 200 | 100 |
| Work certified | 100,000 | 80,000 | 18,000 |
| Cash received | 75,000 | 60,000 | 13,500 |
| Work finished but uncertified | 3,000 | 4,000 | 1,050 |

The plant was installed on the dates of the contracts and depreciation is taken at 10 per cent per annum. Prepare the respective contract accounts and the relevant entries in the Balance Sheet. Columnar form may be used and the dates may be omitted.

3. Cost cards relating to jobs completed by a service engineer during last year are summarised as follows:

| | | |
|---|---|---|
| Materials issued | | £92,800 |
| Direct wages | | 68,000 |
| Overhead: | | |
| 20% on material | £18,560 | |
| 100% on direct labour | 68,000 | |
| | | 86,560 |
| Carriage | | 2,540 |
| Profit (15% of sales value) | | 44,100 |
| Sales | | £294,000 |

The Financial Accounts for the year show:

| | | | |
|---|---|---|---|
| Sales | | | £294,000 |
| Opening stocks and work-in-progress | £36,000 | | |
| Purchases of materials | 102,600 | | |
| | 138,600 | | |
| *Less:* | | | |
| Closing stocks and work-in-progress | 40,200 | | |
| | | £98,400 | |
| Factory wages | | 102,000 | |
| Factory expenses | | 40,000 | |
| | | | 240,400 |
| Gross profit | | | 53,600 |
| *Less:* | | | |
| General office expenses | | 16,800 | |
| Estimating and selling expenses | | 7,200 | |
| Carriage | | 2,400 | |
| | | | 26,400 |
| Net profit | | | £27,200 |

The following analyses are relevant:

(*a*) The Stocks and Work-in-progress figures are made up as follows:

|  | Opening | Closing |
|---|---|---|
| Stocks of materials | £12,000 | £12,400 |
| Work-in-progress |  |  |
| Material | 18,000 | 18,200 |
| Labour | 6,000 | 9,600 |

(*b*) Factory wages consist of £77,600 for Direct labour, and £24,400 for Indirect labour.

(*c*) Included in the Purchases of materials figure is £4,200 for consumable stores used during the year.

Prepare a statement to reconcile the two profit figures and suggest possible causes of the discrepancies.

# CHAPTER 8

# Operation Costing

In the previous chapter on specific order costing, the reader will have observed that each cost unit was different. In consequence, considerable analysis work was undertaken to arrive at an accurate cost of the various units worked on in the accounting period. There are, of course, many businesses where such analysis is not necessary, because the products are identical and it can be assumed that, since all products are processed in the same way, they must all cost the same. In fact it would be impossible to identify a particular item of cost with a particular product and, therefore, the total cost of processing is divided by the total number of units produced to give an average product cost. The averaging of cost is a basic feature of operation costing.

Operation costing is applicable when standardised or basically similar goods (process costing) or services (service costing) are produced.

## PROCESS COSTING

In many businesses a product passes through several distinct stages of manufacture; manufacture in such industries is said to be "continuous" if plant or machinery is so arranged that production of a standard article proceeds for a long period of time, interrupted only when the plant or machinery must be shut down for repairs or when it is decided to alter the product either by re-tooling or by a change in technique or specification. The word "continuous" is applied to this type of production in distinction to "batch" production, in which only a limited number of articles, i.e. a "batch" of a particular specification, is to be produced.

Industries, in which the material handled is liquid or semi-solid, e.g. chemicals, paint and rubber, may face particular problems concerning the treatment of joint and by-products.

### Characteristics
1. Because of the continuous nature of the process and the uniformity of the output, it is unnecessary and impossible to identify a particular unit of output with a time of manufacture. The cost of any particular unit must therefore be taken as the average cost of manufacture over a period.

2. Wastage, possibly due to scrap, chemical reaction or evaporation, is unavoidable but must be reduced as near as possible to the theoretical minimum.

3. In order to obtain accurate average costs, it is necessary to measure production at various stages of manufacture.

4. Process costs for a period are apportioned between completed output (transferred to stock or the next process) and unfinished production at the end of the period (work-in-progress).

## General principles

### COST CENTRE

A cost centre will normally be set up for each stage of operation that can be separately identified. This may be at an inspection point, where the quality of the production is checked before further processing, and scrap and waste removed. It may be at a stage where semi-completed units are stored awaiting further processing. Expenditure for each cost centre is collected and at the end of the accounting period the cost of the completed and uncompleted units is calculated and the completed units are then transferred into a stock account, or to a further process cost centre.

### COST UNITS

The cost unit must be logically chosen and often will vary with the type of process. Where liquids are used and processed, production will be measured by volume: where solids are processed, weight will be measured. At later stages the measurement may be in actual units of product completed.

### MATERIALS

The raw material and sundry supplies required for each process may be requisitioned from store in the usual manner, unless this procedure is too cumbersome. A requisition in bulk is usually made and a stock of material thus kept in the department itself. Requisitions may be made on the departmental stock, but for materials of little individual value, stocks in hand may be checked frequently and the consumption compared with the output. Where material is used by only one process and it is difficult to measure the amount of material drawn for production, the difficulty can be overcome by checking the stock at the end of each period and calculating the usage, i.e. stock at the beginning of the period, *plus* receipts during the period, *minus* stock at the end of the period, *equals* consumption. This of course requires the store to be so arranged that a reasonably accurate stock check can be made.

### LABOUR

Where workers are engaged continuously upon one process, the allocation of wages is simple. The payroll should provide the necessary analysis for each Process Account to be debited with labour expended. The general control routine, outlined in Chapter 4, will be followed.

It will frequently be found that direct labour is only a small element of production cost in process businesses, as the worker's task is often only supervisory, e.g. reading dials or gauges and regulating cocks or valves. It is usually impossible for the worker to increase the speed of the process by his own efforts and such workers are therefore usually remunerated on a time basis. If a worker is engaged on the supervision of one or more processes it may be necessary to apportion his time in accordance with time-sheets.

OVERHEAD

Expenses incurred wholly for a particular process will be charged direct. Each Process Account may also bear a share of general production overhead computed in accordance with the principles outlined in Chapter 6.

*EXAMPLE*

A product passes through three distinct processes to completion. These processes are numbered 1, 2 and 3. During the week ended January 15th, 500 litres are produced. The following information is obtained

|  | Process 1 | Process 2 | Process 3 |
|---|---|---|---|
| Materials | £3,000 | £1,500 | £1,000 |
| Labour | 2,500 | 2,000 | 2,500 |
| Direct expenses | 500 | 100 | 500 |

Indirect costs for the period were £1,400, apportioned to the processes on the basis of wages. No work-in-progress or process stocks existed at the beginning or end of the week.

PROCESS NO. 1

Description................    Week ended Jan. 15, ....

Output 500 litres

| Particulars | Cost per litre | Total | Particulars | Cost per litre | Total |
|---|---|---|---|---|---|
| Materials | £6.00 | £3,000 | Output transferred to Process No. 2 | £13.00 | £6,500 |
| Labour | 5.00 | 2,500 | | | |
| Direct expenses | 1.00 | 500 | | | |
| Indirect costs | 1.00 | 500 | | | |
| | £13.00 | £6,500 | | £13.00 | £6,500 |

PROCESS NO. 2

Description................    Week ended Jan. 15, ....

Output 500 litres

| Particulars | Cost per litre | Total | Particulars | Cost per litre | Total |
|---|---|---|---|---|---|
| Process No. 1 | £13.00 | £6,500 | Output transferred to Process No. 3 | £21.00 | £10,500 |
| Materials | 3.00 | 1,500 | | | |
| Labour | 4.00 | 2,000 | | | |
| Direct expenses | 0.20 | 100 | | | |
| Indirect costs | 0.80 | 400 | | | |
| | £21.00 | £10,500 | | £21.00 | £10,500 |

PROCESS NO. 3

Description.................          Week ended Jan. 15, ....
Output 500 litres

| Particulars | Cost per litre | Total | Particulars | Cost per litre | Total |
|---|---|---|---|---|---|
| Process No. 2 | £21.00 | £10,500 | Output transferred | | |
| Materials | 2.00 | 1,000 | to Finished Stock | £30.00 | £15,000 |
| Labour | 5.00 | 2,500 | | | |
| Direct expenses | 1.00 | 500 | | | |
| Indirect costs | 1.00 | 500 | | | |
| | £30.00 | £15,000 | | £30.00 | £15,000 |

## Valuing unfinished work

When production is in batches, or represents a continuous process, it is almost certain that, at the end of an accounting period, some of the items in a batch or in the flowline will be partially completed. Such units will obviously bear a smaller share of the costs incurred during the period than will completed units. In order to average costs over output units, the most logical approach is to express unfinished work in terms of *equivalent whole units*. The following example will illustrate the procedure.

### EXAMPLE

Faggash Ltd. manufacture metal ashtrays. The ashtrays are cut and pressed to shape in the machine shop and passed to the Finishing department where they are cleaned, sprayed and polished. On July 1st, 1,000 ashtrays were transferred from Machining to Finishing at a cost of 50p each.

During July, the finishing operations were completed on 800 ashtrays, which were transferred to Finished Stock, and 200 ashtrays were in progress at the end of July; it was estimated that the 200 were half-completed. The cost of operating the Finishing department for July was £270.

The month's cost of £270 has been spent on processing 1,000 ashtrays but the 200 in progress should only be charged with 50 per cent of the average finishing cost per ashtray, i.e. £270 is apportioned over:

800 units, 100 per cent complete; and
200 units, 50 per cent complete

which is the same as apportioning £270 over 900 (800 plus 200 × ½) equivalent whole units, giving an average Finishing department cost per unit of 30p.

The 800 ashtrays transferred to Finished Stock will be valued, therefore, at the average machining plus finishing cost per unit, i.e. 50p + 30p = 80p per unit and the 200 ashtrays in progress will have a cost valuation of 65p per unit, i.e. the full machining cost per unit plus half the average finishing cost per unit.

The Finishing department Process Account would appear as follows:

| Details | Units | per unit | | Details | Units | per unit | |
|---|---|---|---|---|---|---|---|
| | | £p | | | | £p | |
| Machining dept. | 1,000 | 0.50 | £500 | Finished stock | 800 | 0.80 | £640 |
| July costs | — | | 270 | Work-in-progress c/d. | 200 | 0.65 | 130 |
| | 1,000 | | £770 | | 1,000 | | £770 |

Sometimes, work-in-progress units may be at different stages of completion for different cost elements. In the above example, cleaning, spraying and polishing may be treated as separate cost elements; further analysis could disclose that the Finishing department cost of £270 comprised:

| | |
|---|---|
| Cleaning | £96 |
| Spraying | 90 |
| Polishing | 84 |
| | £270 |

and that the 200 ashtrays in progress represented:

(a) 80 units cleaned, sprayed and half-polished;
(b) 60 units cleaned and one-third sprayed; and
(c) 60 units one-third cleaned.

Then, in order to apportion cost, a statement of equivalent whole units would be prepared by cost element, as follows:

| | Input Units | Equivalent Units Produced | | | |
|---|---|---|---|---|---|
| | | Machining | Cleaning | Spraying | Polishing |
| Finished Stock | 800 | 800 | 800 | 800 | 800 |
| Work-in-progress (a) | 80 | 80 | 80 | 80 | 40 |
| Work-in-progress (b) | 60 | 60 | 60 | 20 | — |
| Work-in-progress (c) | 60 | 60 | 20 | — | — |
| Total | 1,000 | 1,000 | 960 | 900 | 840 |
| Process costs | | £500 | £96 | £90 | £84 |
| Cost per unit | | 50p | 10p | 10p | 10p |

The value of transfers to Finished Stock represents 800 units at the total process cost per unit of 80p and the value of work-in-progress would be calculated thus:

| | |
|---|---|
| 200 equivalent units machined at 50p per unit | £100 |
| 160 equivalent units cleaned at 10p per unit | 16 |
| 100 equivalent units sprayed at 10p per unit | 10 |
| 40 equivalent units polished at 10p per unit | 4 |
| | £130 |

Note that, irrespective of the stage of completion in the Finishing department, the value placed upon work-in-progress in that department will always include a full charge per unit in respect of previous process (in this instance, machining) costs.

## Opening and Closing Work-in-Progress

The reader will appreciate that cost apportionment can require intricate calculations when a process comprises several cost elements and unfinished work is involved at the beginning and end of a period. The following example illustrates the treatment.

*EXAMPLE*

In a finishing shop one man is employed in cleaning, spraying and polishing machines received from the assembly shop. Each machine takes about twelve hours to finish and the man is paid £80 for a forty-hour week. In the first week he completes three machines and spends four hours on a fourth. This can be represented graphically as follows:

Week 1:

| Machine A | Machine B | Machine C | Machine D |
|-----------|-----------|-----------|-----------|

Hours worked:  12         12         12         4

Machine D is one-third complete and therefore the unit cost for A, B, C and D is $£\frac{80}{3\frac{1}{3}} = £42$. We knew this, of course, because 12 hours at £2.00 per hour = £24.

In the second week the following work is done:

Week 2:

| Machine D | Machine E | Machine F | Machine G |
|-----------|-----------|-----------|-----------|

Hours worked:  8          12         12         8

The total units produced can be said to be $\frac{8}{12} + 1 + 1 + \frac{8}{12} = 3\frac{1}{3}$ units and therefore the unit cost is the same i.e. £24. In this illustration our method of working has been to *divide the cost by the equivalent number of units on which it has been incurred.*

This is best represented as a statement:

|  | *Equivalent units* |
|---|---|
| Opening work-in-progress—units awaiting completion | $\frac{8}{12}$ |
| Completed input | 2 |
| Closing work-in-progress—units completed | $\frac{8}{12}$ |
| Total | $3\frac{1}{3}$ |
| Total cost | £80 |
| Cost per unit | £24 |

The figure for opening work-in-progress represents the proportion completed in the current week. The figure for completed input represents the machines started and finished during the week (i.e. machines E and F). Alternatively, the statement of equivalent production for the week could be expressed as:

Transfers to finished Stock   (machines D, E and F)    3

*Add*: Closing W.I.P.            (machine G)              $\frac{2}{3}$

$3\frac{2}{3}$

*Less*: Opening W.I.P.          (machine D)              $\frac{1}{3}$

$3\frac{1}{3}$

In practice we may not have known the number of hours worked on machine D, and a competent person would have assessed the proportion of the machine that was finished, i.e. one-third. The total value attributable to machine D is made up by taking $\frac{4}{12} \times £24$ in week $1 = £8$, plus $\frac{8}{12} \times £24$ in week $2 = £16$. It has been assumed for simplicity that the rate of working and the costs incurred are constant in both weeks.

Let us now suppose that in week 3 the employee is paid £120 per week under a productivity deal and that his rate of output increases to about ten hours per machine. The work may be represented as follows:

| Machine G | Machine H | Machine I | Machine J | Machine K |
|---|---|---|---|---|
| | | | | |

Proportion completed in week:    33%      100%      100%      100%      67%

The total units produced during the week are therefore $33\% + 100\% + 100\% + 100\% + 67\% = 4$ units and the unit cost is therefore £30. The cost of completing machine G is $33\% \times £30 = £10$ and the costs brought forward were $\frac{2}{3} \times £24 = £16$, giving a total of £26.

The account for week 3 would appear as follows:

*Finishing Shop—Week 3*

|  | Units | £ |  | Units | £ |
|---|---|---|---|---|---|
| Work-in-progress b/f | 1 | 16 | Production | 4 | 116 |
| Units introduced | 4 | — | Work-in-progress c/f | 1 | 20 |
| Wages | — | 120 |  |  |  |
|  | 5 | 136 |  | 5 | 136 |

NOTE. For the purpose of the example, material costs have been ignored.

The production valuation has been calculated as follows:

| | | |
|---|---|---|
| Work-in-progress b/f | £16.00 | |
| Costs of completion | 10.00 | |
| | | £26.00 |
| Units introduced and completed in week 3 ($3 \times £30$) | | 90.00 |
| | | £116.00 |

The closing work-in-progress represents 67 per cent of £30 = £20.

It should be noted that in this example we know that a machine unfinished at the end of the week will be worked on and finished in the following week. Therefore the costs brought forward from one week are included in the value of production for the next week. This is often true, but not always. If a solution flows into a processing tank where it is mixed with other ingredients and then flows on, it is impossible to say that work-in-progress at the end of a period will be finished in the next period, because the work-in-progress units cannot be identified at a later point in time. For this reason some accountants prefer to add all costs brought forward to the costs incurred in the next period and then spread the total over equivalent units finished. If this were done in week 3 of the above example the total debit of £136 would have been spread over 4⅔ units to give an average cost of £29.14 per unit. The closing work-in-progress would be valued at 67 per cent of £29.14 = £19.42. This method is known as the *Weighted Average* method whereas the former (more popular) method is known as the *First In First Out* (FIFO) method.

The following example introduces various cost elements which are incurred at different stages in production.

*EXAMPLE*

In the manufacture of "Blink" two ingredients B and L are introduced at the commencement of the process and a third ingredient K, a colouring agent, is fed in towards the end of the mixing cycle. The following details relate to production during September:

| | | | |
|---|---|---|---|
| Materials used: | B | 200 kg | £600 |
| | L | 300 kg | £90 |
| | K | | £479 |
| Wages | | | £150 |
| Overhead | | | £89 |

Work-in-progress at August 31st, 100 kg, £290 (100 per cent complete for B and L, 50 per cent for wages and overhead, 25 per cent for K).

Work-in-progress at September 30th, 80 kg (100 per cent complete for B and L, 60 per cent for wages and overhead, 30 per cent for K).

Production of Blink, 480 kg. All waste material has no value and is to be charged to production.

Each cost element must be divided by the equivalent number of units on which it has been incurred. Therefore the first stage is to find the equivalent units which will represent the work done during the month.

EQUIVALENT UNITS

| | Total units | B & L | K | Wages + overhead |
|---|---|---|---|---|
| Opening work-in-progress units awaiting completion | 100 | — | 75 | 50 |
| Completed input | 380 | 380 | 380 | 380 |
| Waste (not to be valued) | 40 | — | — | — |
| Closing work-in-progress—units completed | 80 | 80 | 24 | 48 |
| | 600 | 460 | 479 | 478 |
| Costs incurred | | £690 | £479 | £239 |
| Cost per unit | | £1.5 | £1.0 | £0.5 |

The costs per unit are then multiplied by the equivalent units.

COST ALLOCATION

|  | Total | B & L | K | Wages + overhead |
|---|---|---|---|---|
| Opening work-in-progress | £100 | — | £75 | £25 |
| Completed input | 1,140 | £570 | 380 | 190 |
| Closing work-in-progress | 168 | 120 | 24 | 24 |
|  | £1,408 | £690 | £479 | £239 |

*Blink Process Account—September*

|  | kg | £ |  | kg | £ |
|---|---|---|---|---|---|
| Work-in-progress b/f | 100 | 290 | Production | 480 | 1,530 |
| Materials: B | 200 | 600 | Waste | 40 | — |
| L | 300 | 90 | Work-in-progress c/f | 80 | 168 |
| K | — | 479 |  |  |  |
| Wages | — | 150 |  |  |  |
| Overhead | — | 89 |  |  |  |
|  | 600 | £1,698 |  | 600 | £1,698 |

The value of production is made up as follows:

| | | |
|---|---|---|
| Opening work-in-progress b/fwd | £290 | |
| Cost of completing work-in-progress | 100 | |
| | —— | |
| | 390 | (100 kg) |
| Completed input | 1,140 | (380 kg) |
| | £1,530 | (480 kg) |

## Process losses and wastage

In many process industries, loss is unavoidable because of scrap, chemical change or evaporation. It is imperative that records be kept to disclose these losses so that inefficient processing may be remedied. It is frequently possible to compute, from technical data, what the process loss should be under theoretical conditions, although in practice losses are almost certain to vary from the theoretical figures.

Where wastage occurs at a late stage in manufacture, it is apparent that the financial loss is greater than the mere cost of the raw material concerned, owing to the labour, power, etc., which has been expended in earlier processes and from which no advantage has been derived.

It is generally accepted that the costing system should distinguish normal from abnormal process losses. That amount of loss which is theoretically unavoidable because of the nature of the material or the process is a normal process loss, and must be treated for costing purposes as an additional charge to the usable units produced. Any loss arising in excess of this margin must be regarded as abnormal and charged to an appropriate account pending investigation. *This implies that the fullest quantity records of material passing through the processes should be maintained and reconciliation effected between the input and output of each process.* Any deficiency shown by the reconciliation will represent:

1. *Normal process losses*, consisting of:

(*a*) Losses inherent in the material or process due to chemical changes or other physical reasons.

(*b*) Unavoidable spoiled quantities or units, withdrawals for test or sampling, if unrecorded, and, possibly, losses inherent in large-scale processing.

2. *Abnormal process losses*, consisting of deficiencies of finished products due to carelessness, bad plant design or operation, or other errors. This type of loss or wastage should receive close investigation by management.

NORMAL PROCESS LOSS

The process in which the wastage occurs must be credited with the quantity and with any value which can be placed upon the scrap or residue. In assessing scrap value, the following facts should be considered:

1. Certain waste materials, e.g. iron or steel borings and turnings, possess such a small scrap value that it would be impractical to try to ascertain the exact amount to be credited to each process. Such scrap may be accumulated over a period and the proceeds credited to Production Overhead or to Sundry Income.

Where the scrap possesses no value or is dealt with as described above, the loss in weight or volume must be shown in the Process Account and the cost per unit of the satisfactory production increased accordingly. Thus if 1,000 kg of material are issued to a process at a cost of 50p per kg, and manufacturing expenses incurred amount to £220, the cost per kg produced would be 72p. If, however, in the course of manufacture, normal waste occurs to the extent of 100 kg and the scrap possesses no value, the reduced weight has cost 80p per kg, the wastage representing an additional expenditure of 8p per kg. Shown in the form of a cost statement the position would appear as under:

COST STATEMENT. PROCESS X

|  | kg | Cost per kg | Total |
|---|---|---|---|
| Materials consumed | 1,000 | £0.50 | £500 |
| Manufacturing expenses |  | 0.22 | 220 |
|  | 1,000 | 0.72 | 720 |
| *Less:* Wastage | 100 | 0.08 | — |
| Cost of production | 900 | £0.80 | £720 |

2. In some processes, a proportion of the output, e.g. residue, must be reworked, either in the process concerned or in an earlier one. Such residue or scrap is worth no more than the crude material to which it corresponds; the expenditure attributable to it has thus been wasted and must be treated as an additional expense incurred for the benefit of the usable output. Its value as crude material is credited to the Process Account and charged either to the process to which it is relegated or to the corresponding stock account. Assuming that a process treating 2,000 kg of crude material yields 1,900 kg of finished product and 100 kg requires re-processing, the Process Account would appear as under:

*Process Account*

| | kg | Cost per kg | Total | | kg | Cost per kg | Total |
|---|---|---|---|---|---|---|---|
| Materials | 2,000 | 0.50 | 1,000 | Residue transferred to | | | |
| Labour | | 1.00 | 2,000 | crude stock | 100 | 0.50 | 50 |
| Overhead | | 0.25 | 500 | Output | 1,900 | 1.82 | 3,450 |
| | 2,000 | £1.75 | £3,500 | | 2,000 | — | £3,500 |

3. If, in the previous example, the 100 kg was suitable only for return to an earlier process than that represented by the account, it would be credited at the value of the crude material entering that earlier process. This would inflate the cost of the output still further, as the following calculation shows:

Cost of processing 2,000 kg (as per above account)   £3,500
 *Less:* Value of 100 kg residue to be introduced into an earlier
   processes which uses raw material costing £0.10 per kg
   100 kg at £0.10   10

Cost of 1,900 kg output (£1.837 per kg)   £3,490

4. Scrap or waste produced will frequently have no value as a raw material but may have a saleable value as a waste product. Then the sales value of the scrap will be credited to the account of the process from which it is derived.

In general, therefore, it can be said that normal or unavoidable waste should be recorded in terms of quantity only and its process cost, less any value which can be placed upon the waste either as sale for scrap or as raw material for an earlier process, absorbed by the good units produced. The quantity of loss or waste which can be considered normal will be computed by reference to the specification of the material and the experience gained in processing similar material in similar conditions. All other waste must be considered abnormal.

ABNORMAL PROCESS LOSS

Such losses are due to special circumstances and the extent thereof will vary. If processing is carried out efficiently there should be no abnormal loss but, if mishaps occur, losses may be substantial. If the cost of spoilt or lost units were absorbed by good production it is clear that unit costs would fluctuate and impair the usefulness of such costs; in addition, the values placed upon stocks could be distorted by abnormalities. To overcome this and also to disclose the cost of abnormal wastage, it is necessary to adopt the following procedure:

1. Allow for normal wastage (if any) in the manner described above.
2. Apportion the process cost between good units and those lost for abnormal reasons.
3. Credit the cost of abnormal losses to the Process Account and debit an Abnormal Loss Account, for investigation. The balance on Abnormal Loss Account will be charged to Costing Profit and Loss Account as a loss of an exceptional nature, and will therefore not become a charge against production.

*EXAMPLE*

Fifty units are introduced into a process at a cost of £50. The total additional expenditure incurred by the process is £30. Of the units introduced, 10 per cent are normally spoilt in the course of manufacture; scrapped units possess a sales value of £0.25 each. Owing to an accident only 40 units are produced.

*Process Account*

|  | Units | £ |  | Units | £ |
|---|---|---|---|---|---|
| Units introduced | 50 | 50.00 | Normal wastage | 5 | 1.25 |
| Process expenses |  | 30.00 | Abnormal wastage | 5 | 8.75 |
|  |  |  | Output | 40 | 70.00 |
|  | 50 | £80.00 |  | 50 | £80.00 |

The cost of the abnormal wastage is calculated as follows:

Normal cost of 45 units = £80 − (5 × £0.25) = £78.75
Normal cost of 1 unit = £78.75 ÷ 45     = £1.75
Cost of abnormal wastage: 5 × £1.75     = £8.75

If the abnormal wastage possesses the same scrap value as the normal wastage, £1.25 of the loss will be recovered, reducing the actual loss incurred to £7.50. Any sum so realised will be credited to the Abnormal Wastage Account. The complete position is disclosed by the following journal entries:

JOURNAL

| | | | |
|---|---|---|---|
| Processed Stock Account | Dr. | £70.00 | |
| Normal Wastage Account | Dr. | 1.25 | |
| Abnormal Wastage Account | Dr. | 8.75 | |
| To Process Account | | | £80.00 |

Output of 40 units and spoilage transferred.

| | | | |
|---|---|---|---|
| Cash | Dr. | 2.50 | |
| To Normal Wastage Account | | | 1.25 |
| Abnormal Wastage Account | | | 1.25 |

Being sale for scrap of units spoilt.

| | | | |
|---|---|---|---|
| Costing Profit and Loss Account | Dr. | 7.50 | |
| To Abnormal Wastage Account | | | 7.50 |

Net cost of abnormal wastage written off.

It will be appreciated that the margin allowed for normal wastage must necessarily be an estimate, and slight differences are bound to occur between the actual output of a process and that anticipated. The differences will not always represent increased wastage; on occasions the actual total loss or wastage will be less than that expected. In those circumstances the *abnormal process gain* must be adjusted in a similar manner to abnormal wastage. When the actual wastage differs consistently from that fixed as normal, the allowance for the latter should be adjusted.

The effect of transferring abnormal losses or gains from Process Accounts at cost is that yield variations do not distort the cost per unit of good production.

*EXAMPLE*

100 units are introduced into a process at a cost of £200 and expenditure of £96.50 is incurred. From past experience it is ascertained that wastage normally represents 15 per cent of units introduced; waste product has a scrap value of £0.50 per unit. If the actual output is 90 units the Process Account would appear as under:

*Process Account*

| | Units | £ | | Units | Per unit | £ |
|---|---|---|---|---|---|---|
| Units introduced | 100 | 200.00 | Normal wastage | 15 | £0.50 | 7.50 |
| Process expenses | | 96.50 | Output | 90 | 3.40 | 306.00 |
| Abnormal gain | | | | | | |
| (£3.40) | 5 | 17.00 | | | | |
| | 105 | £313.50 | | 105 | | £313.50 |

The value of the abnormal gain is ascertained as under:

Normal cost of 85 units (£296.50 − (15 × £0.50)) = £289.00
Normal cost of 1 unit (£289.00 ÷ 85)       = £3.40
Value of abnormal gain (5 × £3.40)        = £17.00
Value of production (90 × £3.40)         = £306.00

If actual output had been 100 units, the Process Account would be as follows; it will be seen that the cost per unit of output is unchanged as abnormal fluctuations in yield do not distort its cost.

### Process Account

| | Units | £ | | Units | Per unit | £ |
|---|---|---|---|---|---|---|
| Units introduced | 100 | 200.00 | Normal wastage | 15 | £0.50 | 7.50 |
| Process expenses | | 96.50 | Output | 100 | 3.40 | 340.00 |
| Abnormal gain (£3.40) | 15 | 51.00 | | | | |
| | 115 | £347.50 | | 115 | | £347.50 |

In practice, the Abnormal Process Gains Account may be dispensed with, amounts being credited to the Abnormal Wastage Account. It may be found that over a period abnormal losses and gains tend to compensate each other, but any balance on the account must be transferred to Costing Profit and Loss Account.

The credit for abnormal process gain is not wholly profit because the value is arrived at after assuming that the normal wastage of 15 units is saleable. In fact, this is not so, because the actual number of units available for sale as scrap is the difference between the normal loss and the abnormal gain; the credit for normal waste is not realised in cash because the quantity shown was not actually lost. In the example above only $15 - 5 = 10$ units are available for sale as scrap and so only £5 will be received. If this sum is credited to Normal Wastage Account a debit balance of £2.50 remains, which must be transferred to Abnormal Gains Account, reducing the balance thereon to £14.50. In the second example there is no overall wastage and hence no scrap available for sale. Accordingly, the debit balance of £7.50 on Normal Wastage Account must be transferred to Abnormal Gains Account, reducing the balance thereon to £43.50.

It must be emphasised that these adjustments merely affect the wastage and gains accounts. The process accounts set out above record the position in accordance with the assessment of normal loss.

It may be necessary to open separate accounts for normal and abnormal wastage and process gains in respect of each process. Sums realised for the sale of scrap will be credited to the Normal Wastage Account concerned, which should balance after making the adjustment necessary when abnormal gains arise, as explained above.

The principles are further illustrated by the following example:

### EXAMPLE

A product passes through three distinct processes, A, B and C. From past experience it is ascertained that wastage is incurred in each process as under:

Process A:  2%
Process B:  5%
Process C:  10%

The percentage of wastage is computed on the number of units entering the process concerned; wastage of processes A and B is sold at £25 per 100 units and that of process C at £50 per 100 units.

The following information is obtained for the month of February:

20,000 units of crude material were introduced in Process A at a cost of £8,000.

|  | Process A | Process B | Process C |
|---|---|---|---|
| Materials consumed | £8,000 | £1,500 | £1,000 |
| Direct labour | 4,500 | 2,000 | 2,000 |
| Direct expenses | 4,100 | 450 | 420 |
|  | Units | Units | Units |
| Output | 19,500 | 19,250 | 16,000 |
| Finished product stock: |  |  |  |
| February 1 | 3,000 | 2,750 | 4,000 |
| February 28 | 2,500 | 4,000 | — |
| Stock valuation, February 1st, per unit | £1.175 | £1.340 | £1.710 |

Stocks are valued and transferred to subsequent processes at weighted average costs.

Process and stock accounts would appear as under:

### Process A

|  |  | Units | £ |  |  | Units | £ |
|---|---|---|---|---|---|---|---|
| Feb. 1 | Units introduced | 20,000 | 8,000 | Feb. 28 | Normal wastage | 400 | 100 |
|  | Materials |  | 8,000 |  | Abnormal wastage | 100 | 125 |
|  | Labour |  | 4,500 |  | Product A Stock |  |  |
|  | Expenses |  | 4,100 |  | Account | 19,500 | 24,375 |
|  |  | 20,000 | £24,600 |  |  | 20,000 | £24,600 |

### Product A Stock Account

|  |  | Units | £ |  |  | Units | £ |
|---|---|---|---|---|---|---|---|
| Feb. 1 | Stock b/f | 3,000 | 3,525 | Feb. 28 | Process B | 20,000 | 24,800 |
| Feb. 28 | Process A | 19,500 | 24,375 |  | Stock c/f | 2,500 | 3,100 |
|  |  | 22,500 | £27,900 |  |  | 22,500 | £27,900 |

### Process B

|  |  | Units | £ |  |  | Units | £ |
|---|---|---|---|---|---|---|---|
| Feb. 28 | Input of material A | 20,000 | 24,800 | Feb. 28 | Normal wastage | 1,000 | 250 |
|  | Materials |  | 1,500 |  | Product B Stock |  |  |
|  | Labour |  | 2,000 |  | Account | 19,250 | 28,875 |
|  | Expenses |  | 450 |  |  |  |  |
|  | Abnormal process |  |  |  |  |  |  |
|  | gain | 250 | 375 |  |  |  |  |
|  |  | 20,250 | £29,125 |  |  | 20,250 | £29,125 |

### Product B Stock Account

|  |  | Units | £ |  |  | Units | £ |
|---|---|---|---|---|---|---|---|
| Feb. 1 | Stock b/f | 2,750 | 3,685 | Feb. 28 | Process C | 18,000 | 26,640 |
| Feb. 28 | Process B | 19,250 | 28,875 |  | Stock c/f | 4,000 | 5,920 |
|  |  | 22,000 | £32,560 |  |  | 22,000 | £32,560 |

### Process C

|  |  | Units | £ |  |  | Units | £ |
|---|---|---|---|---|---|---|---|
| Feb. 28 | Input of material B | 18,000 | 26,640 | Feb. 28 | Normal wastage | 1,800 | 900 |
|  | Materials |  | 1,000 |  | Abnormal wastage | 200 | 360 |
|  | Labour |  | 2,000 |  | Product C Stock |  |  |
|  | Expenses |  | 420 |  | Account | 16,000 | 28,800 |
|  |  | 18,000 | £30,060 |  |  | 18,000 | £30,060 |

### Product C Stock Account

|  |  | Units | £ |  |  | Units | £ |
|---|---|---|---|---|---|---|---|
| Feb. 1 | Stock b/f | 4,000 | 6,840 |  |  |  |  |
| Feb. 28 | Process C | 16,000 | 28,800 |  |  |  |  |
|  |  | 20,000 | £35,640 |  |  |  |  |

### NOTES

1. The cost of the abnormal wastage in Process A has been calculated as follows:

Normal output: 19,600 units (98% of 20,000)
Normal cost of normal output: £24,500

Cost of abnormal wastage: $\dfrac{£24,500}{19,600} \times 100 = £125$

2. The cost of the abnormal gain in Process B has been calculated as follows:

Normal output: 19,000 units (95% of 20,000)
Normal cost of normal output: £28,500

Cost of abnormal gain: $\dfrac{£28,500}{19,000} \times 250 = £375$

3. The cost of the abnormal wastage in Process C has been calculated as follows:

Normal output: 16,200 units (90% of 18,000)
Normal cost of normal output: £29,160

Cost of abnormal wastage: $\dfrac{£29,160}{16,200} \times 200 = £360$

4. The following accounts would also be prepared in respect of Process B:

### Abnormal Process Gains Account

|  |  | Units | £ |  |  | Units | £ |
|---|---|---|---|---|---|---|---|
| Feb. 28 | Normal Wastage Account Profit & Loss Account | 250 | 62.50 312.50 | Feb. 28 | Process B | 250 | 375.00 |
|  |  | 250 | £375.00 |  |  | 250 | £375.00 |

### Normal Wastage Account

|  |  | Units | £ |  |  | Units | £ |
|---|---|---|---|---|---|---|---|
| Feb. 28 | Process B | 1,000 | 250.00 | Feb. 28 | Cash, £25 per 100 Abnormal Process Gains Account | 750 250 | 187.50 62.50 |
|  |  | 1,000 | £250.00 |  |  | 1,000 | £250.00 |

If the actual price realised for scrap differs from the normal price, a balance will arise on the Normal Wastage Account, which may require investigation prior to write-off.

5. Unit costs of material in closing stocks at February 28th and material transferred to subsequent processes have been calculated as follows:

$$\text{Process A} \qquad \qquad \text{Process B}$$

$$\frac{\text{Stock value b/f} + \text{Production cost}}{\text{Stock units b/f} + \text{Completed units}} : \frac{£3,525 + £24,375}{3,000 + 19,500} = £1.24 \qquad \frac{£3,685 + £28,875}{2,750 + 19,250} = £1.48$$

6. Accounts in debit and credit form have been used in the example to emphasise the double-entry aspect of the process accounts. The columnar form of presentation may be thought preferable and the figures in respect of Process A, for example, would appear as follows:

PROCESS A COST STATEMENT

| PERIOD............ | Units | £ |
|---|---|---|
| Input to process: |  |  |
| Raw material | 20,000 | 8,000 |
| Other materials |  | 8,000 |
| Direct labour |  | 4,500 |
| Direct expenses |  | 4,100 |
|  |  | 24,600 |
| Less: Normal wastage at scrap value | 400 | 100 |
| Cost of normal production (£1.25) | 19,600 | 24,500 |
| Less: Abnormal wastage | 100 | 125 |
| Production transferred to Process A |  |  |
| Stock | 19,500 | £24,375 |

## Losses, by-products and joint products

In a manufacturing process where materials are converted to form a saleable product, the results of the process may be classified in one of four ways.

1. All the original material finds its way into the final product, i.e. the total quantity is accounted for.

2. Some of the original material is processed incorrectly resulting in a residue which may or may not have any saleable value. This is termed scrap or waste, and occasionally it may be possible to reprocess this material.

3. Some of the original material is lost, e.g. by evaporation.

4. The original materials lose their identity and emerge as several different products, e.g. various solids, gases and liquids. This may be due to chemical change or physical change, e.g. where metal rings are stamped from sheet metal and an offcut results. The various products will assume different importance according to their respective market values. Those products which have relatively unimportant value are termed by-products and those which have a sufficiently high saleable value are recognised as main products.

The manufacturer is clearly concerned to obtain maximum profit and, therefore, where it is within his power to improve the result of the process by a different mix of ingredients or by different processing methods he will do so. This may in fact require that a mathematical model be set up to calculate the greatest profit from a variety of alternative courses of action.

The accounting problem is expressed graphically in Fig. 38.

So far as the cost accountant is concerned, his object is to:

1. Provide information on manufacturing performance.
2. Compute unit costs to value stocks and assist in establishing selling prices.

**Measuring performance**
In order to help management to control manufacturing performance, the cost accountant must consider the normal or standard results of the process. He must then provide a costing system which is able to monitor the performance of the process against the standards. This approach has been described in relation to normal and abnormal gains and losses. The cost accountant must also note where the bulk of cost is incurred and concentrate on detailed measurement of this.

**Computing unit costs**
In certain processes, e.g. coal-gas production and chemical refining, secondary products and valuable residues arise in the course of manufacturing the main product. Although it may be possible to

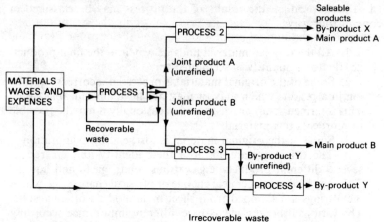

FIG. 38.—*Flow of materials and costs in processing business.*

The manufacturer has a factory and distribution organisation to sell products A and B. There are four processes, the principal one being process 1. Both products emerge from this process as does scrap and waste material which can be put back for re-processing. Both products require refining and, as a result of refining product A, in process 2 a by-product X emerges, which is sold wholly to an associated company. Product B is refined in process 3 from which by-product Y emerges as well as some waste material which has no value. By-product Y has a market value after it is refined in process 4.

influence the quantities of these products by the method of manufacture adopted, the physical nature of the raw material usually makes the emergence of certain secondary products unavoidable. For example, under normal methods of gas manufacture, coke and tar must also be produced. These are considered to be by-products. Such products often possess significant value, but the total amount may be small in relation to the main product.

The costs of processing are of course joint until the various products are physically separated. Moreover, in some sections of the chemical industry what is regarded as the main product of one manufacturer may be the by-product of another. Sometimes, altered market conditions place a different emphasis upon the relative importance of the products.

It must be appreciated at the outset that the computation of product costs is an arbitrary exercise. The cost accountant can obtain information from production and technical departments on the nature of the process and the product, but the final approach will rest to a large extent on his own judgment. Virtually he will decide whether products can be classified into by-product or main product categories. By-products can be dealt with simply, whereas main products may require more complex treatment.

1. TREATMENT OF BY-PRODUCTS

(*a*) *Additional revenue*. Proceeds of selling the by-product are treated as additional profit and are taken direct to the Profit and Loss Account.

(*b*) *Reduction in cost*. Sale proceeds, less handling costs, are credited to the Process Account to reduce the cost of the main product.

*EXAMPLE*

In the manufacture of "Sog" for March, 3,000 kg of plastic material at £0.20 was mixed with 200 litres of a solvent at £1.15 to produce 2,000 units of the main product. 50 units of a by-product, "Gunge", were also produced. Wages and other costs amounted to £170. The price of Sog was £1 per unit and Gunge could be sold for £1 per unit after it had been through a cleansing process costing £0.60 per unit. In the month 1,000 units of Sog were sold, the balance being held in stock, and the whole of the production of Gunge was sold. Compute the profit for March.

METHOD 1: *Treating the by-product as additional revenue*

| | | |
|---|---:|---:|
| Sales of Sog: 1,000 at £1.00 | | £1,000 |
| Process cost: | | |
| 3,000 kg of plastic at £0.20 | £600 | |
| 200 l of solvent at £1.15 | 230 | |
| Wages, etc. | 170 | |
| Total production cost | £1,000 | |

Cost per unit $\dfrac{£1,000}{2,000} = £0.50$

| | | |
|---|---:|---:|
| Cost of sales, 1,000 at £0.50 | | 500 |
| | | 500 |
| Sales of Gunge 50 at £1.00 | £50 | |
| *Less:* Cleansing costs 50 at £0.60 | 30 | |
| | | 20 |
| Total profit: | | £520 |

METHOD 2: *Crediting the proceeds to the process account*

| | | |
|---|---:|---:|
| Sales of Sog: 1,000 at £1.00 | | £1,000 |
| Process costs—as above | £1,000 | |
| *Less:* Net proceeds of Gunge | 20 | |
| Net production cost | £980 | |

Cost per unit $\dfrac{£980}{2,000} = 0.49$

| | | |
|---|---:|---:|
| Cost of sales, 1,000 at £0.49 | | 490 |
| Total profit: | | £510 |

It can be seen that, where stock levels fluctuate, monthly profits will be distorted, and of course a distortion would also result when production of the by-product is not always in the same proportion to production of the main product. The selling price and cleansing costs of the by-product might also fluctuate and cause distortions. However, since the value of the by-product is so small, it cannot materially affect the result. If the second method is used, it is advisable to use a normal basis, i.e. credit the Process Account with the normal value of normal production of the by-product as previously explained in the section on normal and abnormal losses.

2. TREATMENT OF MAIN PRODUCTS PRODUCED JOINTLY
Each main product represents a major proportion of the output and sales value of the company. An attempt will therefore be made to apportion joint costs, if only to calculate a stock valuation.

(a) *Apportion costs by physical measurement.* A common unit of measurement is adopted, e.g. weight or volume, and the joint cost is apportioned on this basis. The argument for this method is that the raw material (and appropriate processing costs) eventually forms part of all products and ought therefore to be averaged over total production. This may not be entirely true of course. The cost of raw material may well vary between output products with the content of low-value and high-value properties, e.g. mineral-bearing ores.

EXAMPLE
The following data relate to a manufacturing process for June.

| Product | Units produced | Units sold | Selling price | Total cost |
|---------|---------------|------------|---------------|------------|
| Flug | 100 | 90 | £6 | |
| Swosh | 200 | 150 | £2 | £900 |

Calculate the month's profit, apportioning the costs by units produced.

Unit cost: $\dfrac{£900}{100+200} = £3$ per unit.

TRADING STATEMENT

| | Flug | Swosh | Total |
|---|---|---|---|
| Sales: units | 90 | 150 | 240 |
| Sales: value | £540 | £300 | £840 |
| Cost | 270 | 450 | 720 |
| Profit/*Loss* | £270 | *£150* | £120 |

The stock value of Swosh is £3 per unit, whereas the market price is £2. Therefore if the stock was written down to market price, the profit would be reduced by £50 to £70.

(b) *Apportion costs by the market value of production.* Joint costs are apportioned to products on the basis of their total market values.

The result is therefore that the profit margin, expressed as a percentage of sales value, is the same. It is of course an arbitrary method but the results may be more realistic. In using the method, costs occurring after the point of separation should be deducted from the market value before apportioning the joint cost.

*EXAMPLE*

Assuming the facts as in the previous example, compute the profit, apportioning costs by market value.

|  | Sales value of production | Total cost | Unit cost |
|---|---|---|---|
| Flug, 100 at £6 = | £600 | £540 ($\frac{6}{10}$) | £5.40 |
| Swosh, 200 at £2 = | 400 | 360 ($\frac{4}{10}$) | £1.80 |
|  | £1,000 | £900 |  |

The £900 total process cost has been apportioned in the ratio 6:4, i.e. the relative proportions of each product's sales value to total sales value.

TRADING STATEMENT

|  | Flug | Swosh | Total |
|---|---|---|---|
| Sales: units | 90 | 150 | 240 |
| Sales: value | £540 | £300 | £840 |
| Cost | 486 | 270 | 756 |
| Profit | £54 | £30 | £84 |

If Flug were processed after the point of separation and 100 units were processed costing an additional £50, the apportionment of the joint cost would be as follows:

|  | Sales value of production | Joint costs | Other costs | Total cost | Unit cost |
|---|---|---|---|---|---|
| Flug £600 − £50 = £550 | £520 | £50 | £570 | £5.70 |
| Swosh | 400 | 380 | — | 380 | £1.90 |
|  | £950 | £900 | £50 | £950 |  |

In both methods it is important to establish which costs are strictly joint costs, i.e. any costs which are incurred wholly or largely for one product should be dealt with separately from the others.

*EXAMPLE*

Using the same figures as in the previous example, if we assume that costs of £75, included in the total, were incurred wholly for the production of Swosh, the apportionment would be as follows, assuming the market values were adopted.

|  | Sales value of production | Joint costs | Other costs | Total costs | Unit cost |
|---|---|---|---|---|---|
| Flug | £600 | £495 | — | £495 | £4.950 |
| Swosh | 400 | 330 | 75 | 405 | £2.025 |
|  | £1,000 | £825 | £75 | £900 |  |

The cost accountant may feel that he can obtain a more realistic result by using both the quantity basis and the market-value basis. Thus, for instance, he might apportion raw material cost on the basis of market value, and processing costs on the basis of total weight produced.

## SERVICE COSTING

No doubt the reader will by now have realised that the concept of operation costing is not restricted to those businesses engaged in manufacturing a homogeneous product. Many firms have a power generating department which supplies power, and possibly heat, to production departments. Even if job costing is used in the manufacturing departments, operation costing can be applied to the electricity-generating plant and to similar departments. The term "service costing" is applied to operation costing of services as opposed to products and may be used for a service undertaking or for a service cost centre within an undertaking. Costing principles are identical in that total costs are averaged over the total amount of service given. A difficulty encountered with service costing is the measurement of the service. In a transport firm, for example, the service could be measured in terms of weight or volume carried, or miles travelled or a combination of units.

A characteristic of service undertakings, e.g. hospitals, theatres, travel agencies and schools, is the high proportion of costs which are fixed in nature. For example, the costs of operating a theatre are virtually unaffected by the size of the audience, and the establishment and staffing costs of a hospital are unaffected by fluctuations in the number of occupied beds. The development of service costing methods should, therefore, be applied more to the compilation of reliable statistical data than to the calculation of theoretical profit rates. It is frequently informative to use more than one cost unit.

For example, in hospital cost accounting, standing charges will be related to the number of available bed days, while housekeeping and other variable costs will be associated with the number of occupied bed days.

## TRANSPORT COSTING

Each service undertaking will develop its own cost accounting system and the principles outlined in this book will be appropriate to most businesses. A transport service, however, tends to be common to many businesses and the subject merits closer attention.

### The objects

Unlike most business activities to which costing treatment may be applied, the operation of transporting goods, by its very nature, takes place outside the confines of the factory, and so outside the direct supervision of management. Control aspects of motor transport costing, therefore, assumes great importance, i.e.

1. Vehicles must be so deployed and routed that journeys are completed expeditiously and "light" running reduced to a minimum. The vehicle should be suitable for its purpose, and so far as possible should run with complete loads.

2. Waste and other losses in connection with fuel, tyres and other running expenses should be minimised.

3. Vehicles must be properly maintained and operated, not only to secure good performance and to comply with regulations but also to minimise breakdowns and the consequent loss of carrying capacity.

Control information is to a large extent statistical, mileages and standard journey times assuming considerable importance. It is, however, usually impossible in this type of costing to draw a distinction between costs and statistics, and the student must consider factors other than the mere attribution of costs.

Further problems arise if, as is usually the case, vehicles are maintained, serviced and repaired by a department of the transport undertaking. It is essential that the repair department should embrace a system of job costs so that the cost of each job can be computed and, if desired, compared with the price an outside contractor would charge. The repair department should be efficient, so that vehicle time lost through servicing, overhauls, etc., is reduced to a minimum.

The objects of motor transport costing may be summarised as follows:

1. To provide information from which the efficiency with which the vehicles are routed may be judged, i.e.:

(*a*) All journeys should be carried out in a reasonable time, allowing for the distance between the points of collection and delivery and the time spent in loading and unloading.

(*b*) So far as possible, complete loads should be made up.

(*c*) Return loads should, so far as possible, be arranged so that "light" running is minimised.

2. To provide information for quotations and the fixing of rates.

3. To relate road transport costs, as an element of distribution costs, to individual products, when transport is ancillary to the main business.

4. To provide cost comparisons between:

(*a*) The firm's own transport fleet and alternatives, e.g. hiring, whether of road or rail services.

(*b*) The operation of different types or makes of vehicles.

5. To facilitate control of standing charges and running costs.

### Standing charges and running costs

It is important that the distinction between fixed or standing charges and running expenses should be observed in motor transport costing. Standing charges are those which are incurred irrespective of the mileage run, e.g. insurance, licences and administration. It is unscientific and misleading to allocate such charges to specific journeys on the basis of mileage. On the other hand, such expenses as fuel, lubricants, repairs and maintenance vary more or less in direct proportion to mileage, and so a cost per mile may be computed. Total operating cost is, therefore, composed of two elements, viz. standing charges and running expenses, and each must be computed separately. Special considerations apply to wages and to depreciation.

SELF-STUDY TEST No. 6

*Operation Costing*

(*Refer to the Appendix on p. 354 for outline solutions.*)

1. Explain the term equivalent unit; describe how equivalent units are relevant to process costing.

2. (*a*) The input of Process Y for the month of May was 1,000 kg of raw material at £3 per kg. Process costs for the month were £4,800. 800 kg were completed and transferred to Process Z; 200 kg were unfinished at the end of the month (complete for materials; 80 per cent complete for processing costs.)

Prepare the Process Account for Process Y.

(b) In June, 800 kg of raw material were input to Process Y at £3.50 per kg; process costs were £4,500. 800 kg were transferred to Process Z and 200 kg (materials 100 per cent complete, processing 50 per cent complete) were in progress at the end of June.

Prepare the June Process Y account using: (i) the FIFO method; and (ii) the weighted average method.

3. Explain the difference between normal and abnormal losses in process.

4. The management of Crackers Ltd. is concerned about the effect of spoilage on the final cost of the product. Production consists of subjecting a material to four successive processes. The product costs for a recent typical week were as follows:

| Process | Process cost | Units processed | Units of good output |
|---------|--------------|-----------------|----------------------|
| A | £30.00 | 100 | 95 |
| B | 142.50 | 95 | 80 |
| C | 90.00 | 80 | 70 |
| D | 61.25 | 70 | 65 |
| Total | £323.75 | | |

Calculate the process cost per good unit produced assuming that:
   (a) all spoilage is considered to be normal;
   (b) all spoilage is considered abnormal;
   (c) that 10 per cent of input is considered to be a normal loss in each process; and
   (d) as for (c) except that spoiled units can be sold for scrap at 50p each.

5. A chemical undertaking manufactures a number of products. The early processes in the manufacturing chain are joint for all products.

The Cost Department allocates the joint costs of these processes to the various products on the basis of the final sales value of each product.

A director argues that this procedure is a waste of time and money, because it provides no information on which any useful action can be taken.

You are asked to give your reasoned opinion.

6. Suggest cost units which could be used to measure performance in the following businesses:
   (a) an hotel;
   (b) a private nursing home;
   (c) an electrical goods wholesaler; and
   (d) a travel agent.

7. You are asked to advise a wholesale distributor how to prepare comparative costs of running his fleet of motor vehicles, which consist of three different classes of vehicles. The information he requires is:
   (a) the cost of the fixed charges per km and per tonne-km for each vehicle and class of vehicle;
   (b) the cost of the fluctuating charges per km and per tonne-km for each vehicle and class of vehicle.

Draw up a schedule to show the types of cost you would expect within each category. Figures are not required.

# CHAPTER 9

# Budgetary Control

## INTRODUCTION

Reference has already been made to the value of budgets, e.g. in setting predetermined overhead rates and in controlling expenditure. It is necessary to deal now with budgetary control at length, because it is one of the principal tools used by management in fulfilling its responsibilities. To begin with, it will be useful to consider the following definitions from the *Terminology* of the Institute of Cost and Management Accountants.

> *Budgets.* Financial and/or quantitative statements, prepared and approved prior to a defined period of time, of the policy to be pursued during that period for the purpose of attaining a given objective. They may include income, expenditure and the employment of capital.

Everyone is familiar with the idea of a budget. In private life few people embark on a project involving expenditure without some idea of what it will cost, even if this is never committed to paper. For example, a person considering a holiday would ascertain the cost of fares and make an estimate of hotel charges and other incidental expenditure. On the total of this, i.e. the budget, would depend his decision as to whether the proposed holiday should be abandoned, curtailed, or spent at home rather than abroad. On returning, the holiday-maker might compare his actual expenditure with his budget to find out why he had spent more or less than he planned. He might find that although the total cost of his holiday was within his estimate, an increased charge for hotel accommodation had been offset by travelling second-class instead of first-class, as he originally planned. In other words, an adverse variance on accommodation account has been set off against a favourable variance on travelling account.

Such an example can be extended by assuming that the traveller, at the end of his first week's holiday, discovered that his hotel was more expensive than anticipated, owing to an increase in its scale of charges. He might, perhaps, change to a cheaper hotel. In other words, the disclosure of an adverse variance at the time it occurred enabled him to alter his plan for the succeeding weeks so as to keep within his budget.

> *Budgetary Control.* The establishment of budgets relating the responsibilities of executives to the requirements of a policy, and

the continuous comparison of actual with budgeted results either to secure by individual action the objective of that policy or to provide a basis for its revision.

The following important features should be noted:

1. *Executive responsibility*. All managers have a specific job to do and their work must at all times be directed towards the overall objectives of the business, i.e. the policy. The result is co-ordinated rather than unco-ordinated effort.

2. *The requirements of a policy*. Unless the management has specific aims in view and takes action to attain those aims, its development and growth (if any) will be haphazard and fragmentary, and resources of assets and skills will not be used to maximum advantage. The budget is a statement of policy concerning the position the business plans to attain, rather than a forecast of how outside influences will affect the firm.

3. *Comparison of actual with budgeted results*. Control can only take effect where there is a plan, because no one can be said to be in control of a situation if he does not know where he is going. From the starting point of the plan, therefore, control takes effect by measuring the results of an activity and comparing the actual results against budget. Where there are significant divergences from budget, management can take action to correct them.

4. *The revision of policy*. It is only by understanding the forces that affect the performance of the business that the management can realistically steer an acceptable course for the future. Policy must never be static but must take into account the difference between required objectives and attainable objectives. Unforeseen factors may cause management to amend its policy in the short term in order to make the best of the prevailing situation.

## THE CONTROL PROCESS

Figure 39 illustrates the process of management. Note the following:

1. The diagram illustrates the way in which an appraisal of the present situation and the immediate past, an assessment of the influence of outside factors, e.g. political or economic, and the necessity for moving into new fields, e.g. products or processes, are brought together in determining policy.

2. With a more complicated diagram it would be possible to illustrate the difference between day-to-day control, which requires decisions at operational level, and long-term overall control at top management level.

3. The importance of the control loop for the accountant is that he is concerned predominantly with measurement as an aid in appraisal. Accounting reports must be prepared promptly in order

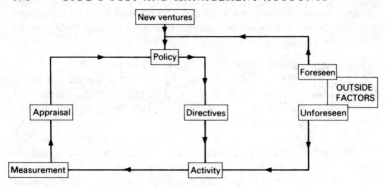

FIG. 39.—*The control loop.*

to help management to decide the action required, if any, to correct divergences from the policy as shown in the budget.

## BUDGETARY CONTROL AND MANAGEMENT

Terms are used to describe topics related to budgetary control which are an expansion of the general subject. It will be useful to mention some of these topics briefly here.

### Corporate and long-range planning
There is sometimes a tendency for budgetary control to operate where there is little or no attempt to specify long-term aims. In this situation the budget may be no more than an anticipation of the effects of past decisions and outside influences. The decisions themselves may well have been made on a piecemeal basis without seeking to co-ordinate all activities to achieve a given objective. Corporate planning seeks to overcome this weakness by determining the objectives of the business and developing plans designed to achieve those objectives. The principal objective will be to increase profits as measured by return on capital employed or earnings per ordinary share but subsidiary objectives, such as maintaining and improving product quality, obtaining a dominance in the market for the company's products, making better use of the resources of capital, management and workers, will exist.

An important aspect of corporate planning is the assessment of the strengths and weaknesses of the company in respect of matters like labour relations, ability to obtain capital, competence of managers, etc; it is the weaknesses which must be overcome and the strengths which must be exploited if the company is to attain its objectives. It is from this assessment that specific plans will be developed to take the business from a present performance of, say, profits of 10 per cent on capital employed to 20 per cent within the next fifteen years. This side of planning may be called *strategic planning* as it involves a strategy to achieve defined goals which in themselves form part of the overall corporate plan. It may be further analysed between new activities (*project planning*) and existing activities (*operational planning*). With the former, there is a need to choose between alternative projects which have been proposed and, with the latter, management is concerned to develop existing operations to improve their contribution towards the desired objectives.

## Management by objectives (MBO)

The importance of co-ordinating the efforts of executives in achieving policy objectives has been stressed. A serious problem that can arise in an organisation that uses budgetary control is that it can be seen as a pressure device, calculated to force workpeople to attain seemingly impossible ends. The result might be that when reports are issued showing the success or failure of supervisors and managers in achieving their budget, those with adverse results tend to look round for scapegoats in order to remove the blame from themselves, and in general the result of applying budgetary control is to aggravate human problems within the firm. There is need therefore to appreciate the psychological implications of a control system. Much of the problem can be overcome by the participation of managers and supervisors in preparing their own budgets. If there is real participation and it is not just a formal acceptance of top management's requirements, managers are encouraged to play an active role in achieving the company's corporate objectives. Each manager in fact has his own objective to meet which he has previously formulated with his immediate superior. He is therefore given considerable responsibility which will help his own development as a manager. Before it can be applied successfully, management by objectives requires a corporate plan within which to operate and also a clearly defined organisation structure of managers able to play a truly managerial role.

So far as the accountant is concerned he will need to produce information to help managers formulate objectives, e.g. controlling overhead, reducing wastage, eliminating excessive labour cost, etc., and thereafter to present information *to help the manager to assess his own performance*. The emphasis will not be on using budgetary control as a stick to goad managers into action, but as a tool to help them control their particular spheres of activity.

## Management by exception

An important principle in any control system is that, as a result of measuring a specific quantity, a signal is given that a particular result is unacceptable and the signal prompts corrective action. It may be anything from the temperature controller in a central-heating system to quality control in a productive process. The same is true of sales and costs. Once a budget has been formulated and agreed, there is no need to give detailed information of actual results to managers. Their job is to control against a plan and, if the plan is being achieved, they are doing their job successfully. When the actual differs from budget there is then a need to show where this has happened and, as far as possible, why. The manager must focus his attention on problem areas and he does not want to sift through a mass of figures to find these. By reporting variances from budget the accountant guides the manager into the problem areas, and so it is the exceptions that the manager concentrates on to the exclusion of those items which fall within the budget.

## FORECASTING

Since decisions by management often have long-term effects it is important that they should be based upon a true understanding of the past with a logical estimate of the future. In a small business, detailed knowledge of the business and its environment will be possessed by perhaps one man, but in a larger one this is unlikely to be so and there is therefore a need for a formal fact-finding process. It is likely that there will be a host of factors which could adversely affect the company's future or, alternatively, which could be exploited if the company were prepared in advance to take advantage of them. Typical questions that the management must consider are: What changes in the business environment will be experienced from now until the corporate plan is achieved, and what problems and/or opportunities will these bring? What changes in the abilities and structure of the company will have taken place over this same time-span? Are these external and internal changes fully taken into account in the company's long-term objectives?

Our purpose here is not to consider forecasting at length but to relate it to budgeting. Basic problems will be highlighted and two major areas of forecasting then considered, i.e. sales and production.

### Forecasting problems

*Difficulties in recognising trends and patterns.* Trends which arise slowly are often difficult to measure, and business cycles present problems in interpreting at which point in the cycle the business or economy exists, i.e. on the upward or downward gradient or at a turning point.

*Difficulties in comparing different time periods.* An appraisal of past results must take into account any factors which distort the comparison of one month with another, e.g. holidays, strikes, effects of weather, etc.

*Difficulties in predicting the influence of various changes.* Many external factors will affect the market for a company's products, e.g. political and economic changes, customer habits and opinions, competitors' actions, technological advances, etc. In addition to these the effect of changes in the company's policies will need to be anticipated.

## The sales forecast

Factors affecting the sales forecast of a particular company may include the following:

1. Population changes.
2. Changes in prosperity in specific areas indicated by personal incomes, company profits, etc.
3. Competition and technological change.
4. Political factors, e.g. trade alliances, development projects, import and export regulations.
5. Movements in commodity prices.
6. Sales promotion policy.
7. Scarcity of factors of production.
8. Efficiency and structure of distribution arrangements.
9. Customer goodwill.
10. Company pricing policy.
11. Age of products and development of new products.

Information for forecasting sales will come from a variety of sources. Salesmen can be expected to have the greatest local knowledge and a procedure for passing relevant market information to the sales manager should be developed in order to take advantage of opportunities. Trends in the overall economic climate can be gauged by reading press reports and trade journals. Special surveys by external agencies or by the company's own staff may be required before major policy changes are formulated.

## The production forecast

Production activity must be geared to the sales forecast, but production management will have considerable scope for planning activities to improve efficiency. Factors, apart from the sales forecast, which may affect the production forecast include the following:

1. Availability of material and price trends.
2. New materials, processes and methods being developed or likely to be developed.
3. Availability of funds to finance production.
4. Labour relations and influences of unions.
5. Government directives on redundancy, development areas, etc.
6. Labour costs and economies of overtime and shift working.

7. Use of single- or multi-purpose machinery.
8. Availability of production services.

**Other forecasts**

The sales and production forecasts will be studied and policies will be developed and budgets prepared to express the policies in monetary and quantitative terms. The effect of the policies must be anticipated in areas such as plant maintenance, data processing, storage space, finance, etc., and plans developed to cater for requirements.

## ESTABLISHING A BUDGETARY CONTROL SYSTEM

Before a system can be developed, three main aspects require definition; the budget period, the budget structure and what factors limit the business activity.

### The budget period

This is the period for which a budget can be prepared and used and its length will depend on the type of business, the length of the manufacturing cycle from raw material to finished product, the ease or difficulty of forecasting future market conditions, and other factors.

The period need not be of the same length for each section of the business. For example, if complicated and expensive plant is used it may be necessary to budget capital expenditure for five to ten years ahead, although the manufacturing budget period is three months or less. Frequently a budget for a long period represents a general objective and is supplemented by short-period budgets, prepared in greater detail. The short-period budgets will be compared period by period with the long-term budget so that management can monitor progress along the general lines laid down. Where necessary, the long-term budget can be amended in the light of later experience.

It is generally agreed that, for satisfactory control, budgets need to be reviewed and modified regularly to reflect changes in conditions. Many businesses, therefore, operate a continuous budgeting system whereby as the results for a specific period become available, a budget for a corresponding future period is prepared. For example, at the end of the first quarter, a budget will be developed to cover the remaining three quarters of the current year together with the first quarter of the ensuing year.

Students should distinguish between a budget period and a control period. The control period is a period in respect of which comparisons are made between budgeted and actual results. It is usually the same as the costing period.

**Budget structure**

The overall budget structure will consist of a master budget which is prepared from and summarises the functional budgets. Each functional budget will be broken down into budget centres related to the organisation structure and control requirements.

A budget centre is a section of an organisation defined for the purposes of budgetary control. Thus, a machine shop might be a budget centre because overhead is not budgeted for machine groups. The machine groups may be cost centres, i.e. cost rates would be obtained for absorbing overhead but costs would not necessarily be recorded at machine-group level. It is important to define responsibility over budget centres and, in preparing budgets, the emphasis will be on responsibility rather than on the benefit criterion. Ideally, costs should be charged to budget centres before apportionment to other centres to help in identifying responsibility for costs.

**The limiting factor**

When plans are being made there will invariably be a factor which governs, or sets a limit to, the quantity which can be made or sold. The limiting factor (also known as "key factor" or "principal budget factor") is usually customer demand, i.e. the total quantity which the market will absorb, taking into account the price and quality of the product, competition, the general purchasing power of the public, advertising, etc.

The limiting factor may be, however, a shortage of one of the productive resources, e.g. plant capacity, the supply of labour of the right grades, or the availability of scarce materials. Management may deliberately impose limiting factors, e.g. by being unwilling to purchase machinery or by restricting production in order to keep up prices.

Whatever the cause, the limiting factors must be kept in mind in preparing the budgets, to facilitate the integration of one budget with another and to ensure that functional budgets are capable of achievement.

Limiting factors can be changed by management action. If, for example, the volume of sales of an article is subject to the limiting factor of plant capacity, the purchase of additional plant will allow production to be increased. Output of the new plant may increase total productive capacity to more than can be sold and sales would replace plant capacity as the limiting factor.

## ADMINISTRATION FOR BUDGETARY CONTROL

**The budget committee**

It will be apparent that a co-ordinating authority is necessary to resolve difficulties and disputes which arise between functional heads and also to take decisions involving increases or decreases in production, price changes and the like. It must be borne in mind that the aim of budgeting is to produce an integrated plan for all the various sections of the business and adjustments, e.g. to make sales and production match each other, are often necessary. Decisions of this nature are the function of the managing director, though he will normally appoint a committee of functional heads, the budget committee, to advise him. If, however, vital matters of policy are involved the decisions must be made by the board of directors.

The co-ordination of budgets is sometimes a difficult task, and the accountant (referred to in this connection as the budget controller or officer) must give the maximum assistance both to individual functional heads and to the committee as a whole. Limiting factors must first of all be considered and decisions taken where necessary to amend them, e.g. by the purchase of additional plant, the engagement of further sales representatives, or the arranging of extra shifts. Conflicting views must be harmonised, the final decision resting with the managing director. When the necessary decisions have been made, the budget controller prepares the draft master budget, submitting it to the committee for consideration. The budget should then be passed to the board, for approval. The master budget will disclose the anticipated profit and consequent changes in the financial position of the company, and these matters will receive careful consideration from the board in the light of the company's dividend policy, its long-term expansion plans and other matters.

If the board is dissatisfied with the state of affairs shown by the budget, e.g. if the profit is considered inadequate or full use is not made of the company's plant and equipment, it may be referred back to the budget committee for the functional budgets to be recast. For example, a higher level of sales may be required. This may involve the employment of additional representatives, a more intensive advertising campaign or the appointment of new agents. Higher sales volume, in its turn, will make additional calls upon production and any limiting factors must be removed, for example, by working overtime or by the purchase of additional plant. Increased demands will be made upon the cash budget to pay for new machinery and to finance higher stocks and debtors. Revised budgets for all sections must, therefore, be prepared and the new master budget submitted to the board for approval. When finally accepted, the budget becomes the operating plan of the business for the period it covers, acting as authority for each functional head to take the necessary steps to implement it. The budget also provides the criterion by which performance will be judged and it is this aspect of control which is such an important feature of the system.

## The budget manual

It is necessary that all involved in budgeting and using control reports understand what is required of them and a budget manual will be most useful in achieving that understanding. It may be merely an extension of the accounts manual and it should include at least the following items of information:

### 1. STATEMENT OF OBJECTIVES AND PROCEDURES

The purpose of operating budgetary control should be made clear so that the ends are never obscured by the means. The procedure for forecasting and budgeting will be described to the extent of explaining how specific forecasts will be prepared and the critical information that must be obtained beforehand.

### 2. BUDGET STRUCTURE AND CODES

The organisation structure should be set out clearly in the manual so that those responsible for each functional budget and budget centre can be identified; also the manual should show which cost centres are included in each budget centre together with assigned codes.

### 3. BUDGET TIMETABLE

A great deal of work needs to be done before the budget receives approval from the board; it must be clearly scheduled so that each contributor knows when their part must be finished in order not to hold up the production of the master budget. A typical timetable might be as follows, assuming sales to be the limiting factor:

| Date required by | Persons responsible | Required | Recipient |
|---|---|---|---|
| Oct. 5 | Sales representatives. | Area sales forecasts. | Manager. |
| Oct. 19 | Sales manager. | Summary sales forecast. | Budget committee. |
| Oct. 19 | Accountant. | Current year's forecast results. | Budget committee. |
| Oct. 26 | Budget committee. | Review of sales forecast; current year's results; long-term budget. | Directors. |
| Oct. 28 | Directors. | Approval of sales forecast. | Budget committee. |
| Nov. 9 | Production manager. | Forecast production costs—material, labour and overhead; capital requirements. | Budget controller. |
| Nov. 9 | Sales manager. | Forecast selling and distribution costs; capital requirements. | Budget controller. |
| Nov. 9 | Technical director. | Forecast research and development costs; capital requirements. | Budget controller. |
| Nov. 9 | Company secretary. | Forecast administration costs; capital requirements. | Budget controller. |
| Nov. 9 | Managing director. | Forecast advertising costs. | Budget controller. |
| Nov. 23 | Budget controller. | Master budget summary—profit forecast and balance sheet; monthly cash forecast. | Budget committee. |
| Nov. 25 | Budget committee. | Review master budget. | Directors. |
| Nov. 30 | Directors. | Approval of master budget. | Budget committee. |
| Dec. 7 | Budget controller. | Detailed budgets. | Functional heads. |

### 4. FORMAT, FREQUENCY AND DISTRIBUTION OF REPORTS

It will be informative to indicate how reports are prepared, what figures are included and how they are calculated, especially variances. The manual will also show when reports are due to be prepared and who receives them.

5. EXPENDITURE AUTHORISATION
It would be useful to specify who in the organisation is responsible for authorising particular items of expenditure.

## FUNCTIONAL BUDGETS

In a manufacturing business, the following budgets are usually necessary:

| Budget | Prepared by: |
|---|---|
| Sales | Sales manager |
| Production | Production manager |
| based on: | |
| Plant utilisation budget | Plant superintendent |
| Labour budget | Personnel manager |
| Material purchases budget | Chief buyer |
| Overhead: | |
| Production | Production manager |
| General administration | Chief accountant |
| Marketing | Marketing manager |
| Cash | Chief accountant |
| Capital expenditure | Managing director |
| Research | Head of research department |

It has been emphasised that it is necessary, after the various budgets have been brought into an integrated relationship with each other, to prepare a master budget which shows how each interlocks and what the financial results will be. The master budget provides in effect the estimated Profit and Loss Account for the budget period and the estimated Balance Sheet as at the end thereof. Before dealing with the preparation of the master budget in detail, the various functional budgets must be considered. Illustrations of typical budgets are shown, and these are integrated into a final master budget. It is necessary to explain how the budgets are integrated, as it is clear that each must interlock, and that no budget must make assumptions which conflict with those in others.

The inter-relationship of the principal budgets is illustrated in Fig. 40.

### Sales budget
This is probably the most important budget, as it is usually the most difficult to forecast or to attain. As already stated, the sales manager, with his intimate knowledge of customers, competitors, new lines and trade conditions, will be responsible for its preparation. He will

draw fully upon the knowledge and advice of his product or regional managers, who will, in turn, consult salesmen or technical representatives for detailed assessments of possibilities. The sales manager will take into account the effect of national or local advertising campaigns and, exercising the best possible judgment, will prepare a draft budget setting out what he is reasonably confident of selling in the budget period.

An example of a sales budget is shown in Fig. 41.

Similar budgets would be prepared for other products, and to illustrate the manner in which the various budgets interlock, it may be assumed that these show the following totals:

| | | |
|---|---|---|
| Product Q | 60,000 units | £260,000 |
| Product R | 72,000 units | £230,000 |

Where possible it is preferable to budget by four-weekly periods or calendar months, especially where an overall increase is expected. It will help the production managers to plan their own requirements more realistically.

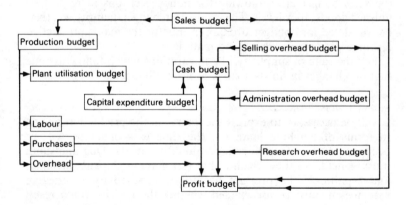

FIG. 40.—*Inter-relationship of budgets.*

NOTES

1. It has been assumed that sales are the limiting factor in the above chart, so that most other budgets stem from this.

2. The production budget is based on the sales budget but there may be policy changes on stock levels, so that the budgeted production could be in excess of or less than budgeted sales.

3. The capital expenditure budget is a long-term budget but the production budget may reveal plant shortages which have to be remedied in the short term.

4. The administration overhead and research overhead budgets tend to be unrelated to sales activity but must be kept within limits dictated by general policy.

| SALES BUDGET – PRODUCT P 12 months to March 31st 19........ | | | | | | | | | |
| Previous Year | | | | | | Budget | | | |
| Area | Budgeted | | | Actual | | | Remarks | Quantity | Price £ | £ |
| | Quantity | Price £ | £ | Quantity | Price £ | £ | | | | |
| N | 10,000 | 5 | 50,000 | 9,000 | 4 | 36,000 | Competition | 9,000 | 4 | 36,000 |
| S | 40,000 | 5 | 200,000 | 30,000 | 5 | 150,000 | New traveller | 38,000 | 5 | 190,000 |
| E | 30,000 | 5 | 150,000 | 35,000 | 5 | 175,000 | Strong demand | 40,000 | 5 | 200,000 |
| W | 20,000 | 5 | 100,000 | 24,000 | 5 | 120,000 | Loss of large customer | 20,000 | 5 | 100,000 |
| Export | 8,000 | 4 | 32,000 | 12,000 | 4 | 48,000 | New agents | 14,000 | 4 | 56,000 |
| | 108,000 | | £532,000 | 110,000 | | £529,000 | | 121,000 | | £582,000 |

Fig. 41.—*Sales budget.*

## Production budgets

Initially, a production budget in quantity only will be developed from the sales budget after allowing for policy decisions in respect of finished goods stock levels. The production budget quantity will then be translated into budgeted requirements for the major productive resources, i.e. plant, labour and materials.

For the sake of simplicity, the illustrations which follow assume that no changes in finished stock levels are budgeted.

PLANT UTILISATION

It will be necessary to express the figures in the production budget in terms of machine load, i.e. the time each machine will be occupied in manufacturing the required products. Due allowance must be made for time which will be lost in tooling up, maintenance and repairs. If the product has to be handled by a series of machines it must be ascertained whether the budget would result in a balanced load or whether excessive demands will be placed on certain machines, thus causing bottlenecks in the flow of production. This provides an example of a matter which must be referred to the budget committee for decision as to whether to (*a*) reduce the sales budget; (*b*) purchase new machinery; (*c*) work extra shifts; or (*d*) use sub-contractors.

*EXAMPLE*

Based on the sales and production budget for Product P in Fig. 41 and the corresponding budgets for products Q and R, the machine time budget would be as Fig. 42, assuming the following times are taken for each operation.

| Product | Turning (minutes) | Fettling (minutes) | Finishing (minutes) |
|---------|-------------------|--------------------|---------------------|
| P | 15 | 12 | 6 |
| Q | 30 | 15 | 6 |
| R | 7½ | 5 | 6 |

### MACHINE TIME BUDGET
### 12 months to March 31st 19........

| | Budgeted sales | Equivalent machine time | | |
|---|---|---|---|---|
| | | Turning | Fettling | Finishing |
| | units | hours | hours | hours |
| Product P | 121,000 | 30,250 | 24,200 | 12,100 |
| Product Q | 60,000 | 30,000 | 15,000 | 6,000 |
| Product R | 72,000 | 9,000 | 6,000 | 7,200 |
| | | 69,250 | 45,200 | 25,300 |
| Available hours | | 72,000 | 55,000 | 22,000 |

FIG. 42.—*Machine time budget.*

NOTES

1. Turning. The estimated demand is very near to the available hours. The turning department must be very closely supervised if the budget is to be achieved.

2. Fettling. There is ample capacity and additional work could be undertaken.

3. Finishing. Capacity is inadequate to meet the demand. Some overtime must be worked or the sales budget amended.

4. The figures for equivalent machine time will be used to calculate the labour budget and also to budget for variable production overhead.

LABOUR

It will be necessary for the personnel officer to obtain the labour, adequate in numbers and grades, to achieve the production budget. Any difficulties will have been referred to the budget committee in case modifications to the sales budget are necessary. If labour must be trained, arrangements must be planned so that the necessary skill is achieved at the right time. The number of maintenance workers, fitters, etc., necessary must also receive consideration; unless an adequate staff is employed, it may be impossible to keep the plant in good working order.

The man hours required for planned production will be determined on the basis that output will conform to predetermined standards. The labour budget prepared must disclose the following information:

1. The numbers of each grade or class of worker required to achieve the output in each period into which the budget is divided.

2. The anticipated cost of such labour in each period.

3. The period of training which will be necessary if workers previously unversed in the processes are to be trained.

The labour budget based on the machine time budget above is shown in Fig. 43.

## LABOUR BUDGET
### 12 months to March 31st 19........

| Department | Machine hours | Equivalent labour hours | Rate per hour | Total value | No. of operatives (1,500 hours) |
|---|---|---|---|---|---|
| | | | £ | £ | |
| Turning | 69,250 | 5,771 | 1.80 | 10,388 | 4 |
| Fettling | 45,200 | 7,533 | 1.20 | 9,040 | 6 |
| Finishing | 22,000 | 7,333 | 1.80 | 13,199 | 5 |
| Overtime | 3,300 | 1,100 | 2.70 | 2,970 | |
| | 139,750 | 21,737 | | £35,597 | 15 |

Distribution over products:

Product P

| | | £ | £ |
|---|---|---|---|
| Turning | 2,521 hours at £1.80 | 4,538 | |
| Fettling | 4,033  ″  ″ £1.20 | 4,840 | |
| Finishing | 4,033  ″  ″ £1.917 | 7,732 | 17,110 |

Product Q

| | | | |
|---|---|---|---|
| Turning | 2,500 hours at £1.80 | 4,500 | |
| Fettling | 2,500  ″  ″ £1.20 | 3,000 | |
| Finishing | 2,000  ″  ″ £1.917 | 3,835 | 11,335 |

Product R

| | | | |
|---|---|---|---|
| Turning | 750 hours at £1.80 | 1,350 | |
| Fettling | 1,000  ″  ″ £1.20 | 1,200 | |
| Finishing | 2,400  ″  ″ £1.917 | 4,602 | 7,152 |
| | | | £35,597 |

FIG. 43.—*Labour budget.*

#### NOTES

1. In the turning department one man operates twelve machines. There are 1,500 productive hours in the budget period and so four operators are necessary. Similarly, one operative controls six fettling machines and one man operates three finishing machines.

2. The rate per hour is the rate paid adjusted for normal idle time, holidays, etc., i.e. it relates to the productive hours.

MATERIALS BUDGET

The production budget quantities must be converted in terms of raw materials and components so that the chief buyer can develop a purchasing plan. If semi-manufactured components are to be purchased from outside suppliers they must be ordered in good time so that they are available when necessary. Consideration must be given to materials which are in short supply and the effect on the budgets determined. The buyer must appraise market conditions and recommend whether stocks are to be increased or reduced. The budget will be prepared to show the quantities and values of materials required for budgeted production, taking into account:

1. Planned increases or decreases in stocks of raw materials and component parts during the budget period.

2. The dates by which materials required must be available related to the production budget.

3. The anticipated prices of materials.

4. The period of credit allowed.

The information thus disclosed will enable the buying department

| MATERIALS PURCHASE BUDGET 12 months to March 31st 19....... | | | | | | | |
|---|---|---|---|---|---|---|---|
| Product | | | Consumption | Stock increase (decrease) | Purchases | | |
| P | Q | R | | | Quantity | Rate | Amount £ |
| **Casting** | | | | | | | |
| P | | | 123,420 | 10,000 | 133,420 | £3.00 | 400,260 |
| 123,420 | | | | £30,000 | | | |
| (£370,260) | | | | | | | |
| Q | 61,200 | | 61,200 | (5,000) | 56,200 | £2.00 | 112,400 |
| | (£122,400) | | | (£10,000) | | | |
| R | | 73,440 | 73,440 | 10,000 | 83,440 | £2.25 | 187,740 |
| | | (£165,240) | | £22,500 | | | |
| **Component** | | | | | | | |
| 1 | (2)246,840 | (1)61,200 | 308,040 | 30,000 | 338,040 | £0.35 | 118,314 |
| (£86,394) | (£21,420) | | | £10,500 | | | |
| 2 | (1)123,420 | (1)73,440 | 196,860 | (20,000) | 176,860 | £0.15 | 26,529 |
| (£18,513) | | (£11,016) | | (£3,000) | | | |
| 3 | | (4)244,800 | 244,800 | | 244,800 | £0.25 | 61,200 |
| | | (£61,200) | | | | | |
| | £475,167 | £205,020 | £176,256 | £50,000 | | | £906,443 |

FIG. 44.—*Materials purchase budget.*

NOTES

1. To allow for waste and spoilage, castings and components required for production have been increased by 2 per cent.

2. The budgeted changes in stock are due to consideration of market trends, availability of storage space, etc.

to plan its programme well in advance and purchase under better conditions. Definite responsibility is imposed upon the buying department to ensure that materials are available when required.

Figure 44 illustrates a materials purchase budget based on the sales/production budget in Fig. 41.

## Overhead budgets

Overhead budgets will be prepared for major functions, and by individual budget centres within functions.

PRODUCTION OVERHEAD

The managers of each of the production budget centres are responsible for preparing their overhead budgets but they will need

| PRODUCTION OVERHEAD BUDGET 12 months to March 31st 19...... | | | |
|---|---|---|---|
| | Previous year's budget £ | Previous year's actual £ | Current budget £ |
| Controllable overhead: | | | |
| Materials: Cleaning materials (V) Oils and lubricants (V) Small tools (V) Stationery (V) Sundries (V) | | | |
| Labour: Supervisory (F) Clerical (F) Setters (V) Cleaners (F) | | | |
| Apportionments: Boiler house (V) Electricity generator (V) Maintenance dept. (V) | | | |
| TOTAL CONTROLLABLE | £ | £ | £ |
| Uncontrollable overhead: | | | |
| Expenses: Rent and rates (F) Insurance (F) Depreciation (F) | | | |
| Apportionments: Building services (F) Factory management (F) | | | |
| TOTAL UNCONTROLLABLE | £ | £ | £ |
| TOTAL OVERHEAD | £ | £ | £ |
| Machine hours Overhead per hour | £ | £ | £ |

FIG. 45.—*Production overhead budget.*

considerable help and advice from the budget controller. He will advise them on past figures and give guidance on price increases, etc. The managers themselves must judge their requirements for services, etc., for the budget period in order to meet the production budget. It is important to differentiate fixed from variable overhead in order to provide a more suitable budget for control purposes. Furthermore, it is advisable to differentiate between controllable and uncontrollable overhead. The former will be budgeted by the manager with some help from the budget controller, but the latter would probably be apportionments prepared by the budget controller himself (*see* Fig. 45).

| ADMINISTRATION OVERHEAD BUDGET 12 months to March 31st 19...... | | | |
|---|---|---|---|
| Cost analysis | Previous year's budget £ | Previous year's actual £ | Current budget £ |
| Material: | | | |
|    Stationery | | | |
|    Sundries | | | |
| Salaries & wages: | | | |
|    Management & supervisory | | | |
|    Clerical | | | |
|    Cleaners | | | |
|    Sundries | | | |
| Expenses: | | | |
|    Rent and rates | | | |
|    Telephone | | | |
|    Postage | | | |
|    Travelling | | | |
|    Insurance | | | |
|    Depreciation | | | |
|    Bank charges | | | |
|    Audit fees | | | |
|    Subscriptions | | | |
|    Donations | | | |
|    Entertaining | | | |
| Apportionments: | | | |
|    Building services | | | |
|    Maintenance dept. | | | |
|    Welfare dept. | | | |
| | £ | £ | £ |

FIG. 46.—*Administration overhead budget.*

In order to prepare the master budget, a production overhead figure of £106,990 has been assumed which includes £8,000 for depreciation. Overhead absorption rates could be calculated as £0.60, £1.00 and £0.80 per machine hour for the turning, fettling and finishing departments respectively, using the analysis of hours shown in Fig. 42; budget overhead could be distributed to products as follows:

|   | Turning | Fettling | Finishing | Total |
|---|---|---|---|---|
| P | £18,150 | £24,200 | £9,680 | £52,030 |
| Q | 18,000 | 15,000 | 4,800 | 37,800 |
| R | 5,400 | 6,000 | 5,760 | 17,160 |
|   | £41,550 | £45,200 | £20,240 | £106,990 |

GENERAL ADMINISTRATION OVERHEAD

This budget will be prepared by the chief accountant and approved by the managing director. It is probable that most administrative expenditure will prove to be fixed in nature, but any variable amounts

| MARKETING OVERHEAD BUDGET 12 months to March 31st 19....... | | | |
|---|---|---|---|
| Cost analysis | Previous year's budget £ | Previous year's actual £ | Current budget £ |
| Representation: | | | |
| Salaries | | | |
| Commission | | | |
| Entertaining | | | |
| Travelling | | | |
| Total | £ | £ | £ |
| Sales office: | | | |
| Office supplies | | | |
| Salaries | | | |
| Postage | | | |
| Telephone | | | |
| Rent & rates | | | |
| Total | £ | £ | £ |
| Publicity: | | | |
| Salaries | | | |
| Office costs | | | |
| Press | | | |
| Journals | | | |
| Television | | | |
| Cinema | | | |
| Samples | | | |
| Sundries | | | |
| Total | £ | £ | £ |
| Warehousing, packing & despatch: | | | |
| Salaries | | | |
| Packing wages | | | |
| Drivers wages | | | |
| Vehicle costs | | | |
| Sundries | | | |
| Total | £ | £ | £ |
| Grand total | £ | £ | £ |

FIG. 47.—*Marketing overhead budget.*

should be distinguished for control purposes. The budgets will be prepared in similar manner to those for production overhead and will be analysed by budget centre as appropriate.

It is assumed for the purpose of the master budget that general administration overhead for the budget period amounts to £30,000.

A specimen form of administration overhead budget is given in Fig. 46.

MARKETING OVERHEAD

The major sections of the marketing overhead budget are likely to be:

>    Representation.
>    Sales Office.
>    Publicity.
>    Warehousing, Packing and Despatch.

There may be further subdivisions by product or sales areas. The marketing manager will be generally responsible but, where large sums are involved in advertising, it is likely that the managing

## RESEARCH & DEVELOPMENT COST BUDGET
### 12 months to March 31st 19.......

| Cost analysis | Projects | | | | Total |
|---|---|---|---|---|---|
| | X100 | X101 | X102 | X103 | |
| PROJECT COSTS | £ | £ | £ | £ | £ |
| Materials: | | | | | |
|   Raw materials | | | | | |
|   Small tools | | | | | |
|   Oils & lubricants | | | | | |
|   Sundries | | | | | |
| Salaries: | | | | | |
|   Chemists | | | | | |
|   Technicians | | | | | |
|   Others | | | | | |
| Expenses: | | | | | |
|   Professional fees | | | | | |
| TOTAL | £ | £ | £ | £ | £ |
| GENERAL COSTS | | | | | |
|   Supervisory salaries | | | | | |
|   Laboratory costs | | | | | |
|   Technical publications | | | | | |
|   Office costs | | | | | |
|   Subscriptions | | | | | |
| | | | | TOTAL £ | |
| | | | | GRAND TOTAL £ | |

FIG. 48.—*Research and development cost budget.*

director will want to exercise personal control. The specimen form shown in Fig. 47 is illustrative; in practice, it is likely that further detail would be required, e.g. for warehousing costs.

For the purposes of the master budget, a total of £29,000 is assumed for marketing overhead.

RESEARCH AND DEVELOPMENT

Research and development expenditure is governed by the policy of the board of directors and the head of the technical division may be allowed discretion only as regards allocating the overall figure between various projects. The expenditure can therefore be budgeted

---

### MASTER BUDGET – OPERATING PROFIT
### 12 months to March 31st 19........

| Sales: | Units | £ |
|---|---|---|
| Product P | 121,000 | 582,000 |
| Product Q | 60,000 | 260,000 |
| Product R | 72,000 | 230,000 |
| | 253,000 | £1,072,000 |

| Production costs: | £ | |
|---|---|---|
| Labour | 35,597 | |
| Materials | 906,443 | |
| Overhead | 106,990 | |
| | 1,049,030 | |

| Stock (increase)/decrease: | | |
|---|---|---|
| Raw materials | (50,000) | |
| Work-in-progress | — | |
| Finished goods | — | |

| Cost of sales | | 999,030 |
|---|---|---|
| | | 72,970 |

| General administration | 30,000 | |
|---|---|---|
| Marketing overhead | 29,000 | |

| | | 59,000 |
|---|---|---|
| OPERATING PROFIT | | 13,970 |

FIG. 49.—*Master budget—operating profit statement.*

by cost element, or by specific projects, or by a combination of the two methods as shown in Fig. 48.

## Master budget—operating profit

The functional budgets prepared so far can be summarised to provide the operating profit section of the master budget, as illustrated by Fig. 49.

## Capital expenditure budget

The plant utilisation budget will have indicated if existing facilities are adequate to meet production requirements. If they are insufficient, short-term emergency measures will be necessary to prevent production bottlenecks but, if it appears that facilities are inadequate in the long-term, additional equipment must be purchased. Capital

---

NOTES TO FIG. 49

1. Where a business maintains a wide variety of stocks of materials and finished products, the stock (increase)/decrease figure will be supported by a detailed Stocks Budget.

2. Analysis of production costs by product is unnecessary for the Master Budget as the statement analyses the budgeted operating profit by functional responsibility, i.e. sales, labour, materials and overhead. Functional budgets will be supported by budget centre budgets which further analyse responsibility.

3. Selling prices and cost rates established for operating budgets can be used as basic standard cost data, e.g. for product P:

|  |  | £ per unit |
|---|---|---|
| Selling price (average: £582,000 ÷ 121,000 units) |  | £4.81 |
| Direct labour: |  |  |
| Turning—average, £4,537 ÷ 121,000 | 0.04 |  |
| Fettling—average, £4,840 ÷ 121,000 | 0.04 |  |
| Finishing—average, £7,733 ÷ 121,000 | 0.06 |  |
|  |  | 0.14 |
| Direct materials: |  |  |
| Casting P—1 at £3.00 | 3.00 |  |
| Component 1—2 at £0.35 | 0.70 |  |
| Component 2—1 at £0.15 | 0.15 |  |
|  | 3.85 |  |
| *Add:* 2 per cent for scrap | 0.08 |  |
|  |  | 3.93 |
| Production overhead absorption rate: |  |  |
| Turning: 15 mins. at £0.60 per m/c hr. | 0.15 |  |
| Fettling: 12 mins. at £1.00 per m/c hr. | 0.20 |  |
| Finishing: 6 mins. at £0.80 per m/c hr. | 0.08 |  |
|  |  | 0.43 |
| Production cost |  | £4.50 |

budgeting involves planning, over a long period, for the acquisition of finance and for investment in specific capital projects which will facilitate achievement of the longer-term objectives of the business. The principles and techniques are part of a much wider area of study which is outside the scope of this book. At this stage we need only consider the extract from the capital budget which represents planned expenditure in the short-term budget period. A suitable form for such a "capital expenditure" budget is shown in Fig. 50.

For the purpose of preparing the master budget, £19,000 has been budgeted for capital expenditure.

### CAPITAL EXPENDITURE BUDGET
### PRODUCTION DIVISION
### 12 months to March 31st 19.......

| | Apr. | May | June | July | Aug. | Sept. | Oct. | Nov. | Dec. | Jan. | Feb. | Mar. | Total |
|---|---|---|---|---|---|---|---|---|---|---|---|---|---|
| Buildings: | | | | | | | | | | | | | |
| Machine shop extension | | | | | | | | | | | | | |
| Contractor | | | | | | | | | | | | | |
| Approval No. | | | | | | | | | | | | | |
| Date of contract | | | | | | | | | | | | | |
| Payments          £ | | | | | | | | | | | | | |
| Plant: | | | | | | | | | | | | | |
| Automatic presses | | | | | | | | | | | | | |
| Supplier | | | | | | | | | | | | | |
| Approval No. | | | | | | | | | | | | | |
| Date of contract | | | | | | | | | | | | | |
| Payments          £ | | | | | | | | | | | | | |
| Sundry equipment: | | | | | | | | | | | | | |
| Additional tools  £ | | | | | | | | | | | | | |
| Replacements tools £ | | | | | | | | | | | | | |
| TOTAL             £ | | | | | | | | | | | | | |

FIG. 50.—*Capital expenditure budget.*

### Financial budgets

The most carefully prepared plans are incapable of fulfilment if adequate cash is not available at the right time. The preparation of a cash budget or forecast is therefore of the utmost importance both in the short-term budget period and, especially, in a longer period. The aim of most businesses is a planned and constant expansion and, unless a long-term cash forecast is made, progress may well be frustrated by an unanticipated lack of funds. Increased sales usually implies a need for increased investment in raw materials, work-in-progress, finished stocks and debtors, so that additional finance may have to be obtained either from the money market or from other sources. The long-term budget will enable the necessary arrangements to be made in good time.

Preparation of such a long-term forecast is part of the capital budgeting procedure previously mentioned but a short-term cash budget will be a vital part of the budgetary control system. A cash budget, in the form of a Receipts and Payments Statement by quarter, is illustrated, based on the budgets given in the examples in this chapter. The cash budget also takes into account the following:

1. *Quarterly analysis.* Analysis of the various budgets, rounded to the nearest thousand pounds, shows:

|  | Total budget | First quarter | Second quarter | Third quarter | Fourth quarter |
|---|---|---|---|---|---|
| Sales | 1,072 | 240 | 296 | 296 | 240 |
| Labour | 36 | 9 | 9 | 9 | 9 |
| Materials | 906 | 213 | 240 | 240 | 213 |
| Production overhead | 107 | 24 | 30 | 30 | 23 |
| General administration | 30 | 7 | 8 | 8 | 7 |
| Marketing | 29 | 6 | 8 | 8 | 7 |
| Capital expenditure | 19 | 11 | 4 | 4 | — |

NOTE: (*i*) Material purchases include the planned stock increase of £50,000.

(*ii*) Production overhead budget includes £2,000 per quarter for depreciation.

2. *Credit terms.* (*a*) Sales are all on 2 months' credit; (*b*) Purchases are all on 1 month's credit; (*c*) Labour and overhead costs are paid in the month in which they arise.

3. *Opening balances.* Balances at the beginning of the budget period were; (*a*) Debtors £150,000; (*b*) Creditors £70,000; (*c*) Cash £75,000.

In practice, the effect of budgeted operations and the short-term capital budget will be translated into a cash forecast, probably analysed by months. The forecast will indicate shortages or surpluses of funds so that action can be planned to alleviate shortages or use surpluses; the cash budget will then reflect the results of such action.

Complex businesses will probably need to prepare detailed budgets for debtors, creditors and stocks as a preliminary to the cash budget and for subsequent control purposes.

## Master budget—balance sheet
The final stage in the development of an integrated plan is to project the effect of the budgets prepared so far in the form of a balance sheet as at the end of the budget period. Appropriations of profit

and any other non-operating items expected will need to be incorporated in the budgeted balance sheet.

## CONTROL BY BUDGET

Management is concerned with deviations for the following reasons:

1. To detect errors in the budget due to incorrect assumptions, carelessness, etc.

2. In order to take remedial action. For example, if deliveries of raw material are not received in accordance with the purchasing programme, follow-up action with the suppliers must be taken or alternative sources of supply found. Unless this is done, production may be impeded.

3. To revise future plans if necessary. For example, if because of an unforeseen event, e.g. a protracted rail strike, despatch of finished products becomes impossible, it may be necessary to (a) reduce production or (b) accumulate heavy stocks of finished products. Alternative (a) may cause reductions in the labour force and in the buying programme. Alternative (b) might imply the need to provide additional working capital to finance the stocks. A sudden unforeseen demand for products might warrant an

|  | CASH BUDGET 12 months to March 31st 19...... | | | |
|---|---|---|---|---|
|  | All amounts in £'000s | | | |
|  | 1st qr. | 2nd qr. | 3rd qr. | 4th qr. |
| Receipts: |  |  |  |  |
| Sales | 230 | 259 | 296 | 277 |
| Other | — | — | — | — |
|  | 230 | 259 | 296 | 277 |
| Payments: |  |  |  |  |
| Purchases | 212 | 231 | 240 | 222 |
| Wages | 9 | 9 | 9 | 9 |
| Overhead | 35 | 44 | 44 | 35 |
| Capital | 11 | 4 | 4 | — |
| Other | — | — | — | — |
|  | 267 | 288 | 297 | 266 |
| Surplus/(deficit) for quarter | (37) | (29) | (1) | 11 |
| Opening cash balance | 75 | 38 | 9 | 8 |
| CLOSING CASH BALANCE | 38 | 9 | 8 | 19 |

FIG. 51.—*Cash budget.*

increased programme of production, which in turn would call for additional raw material, labour and finance.

It is, therefore, essential for management to receive regular control reports to show how events are keeping pace with budget. The frequency of preparation will depend upon the nature of the business. If sales can be determined with reasonable accuracy for a long period ahead, monthly or even quarterly comparisons may be adequate. In businesses dependent on incalculable factors, e.g. the weather, weekly control reports may be essential. Control reports will usually

---

NOTES TO FIG. 51

1. Receipts for sales represent the following:

| 1st qr. | | 2nd qr. | | 3rd qr. | | 4th qr. | |
|---|---|---|---|---|---|---|---|
| Opening debtors | 150 | $\frac{2}{3}$ first qr. | 160 | $\frac{2}{3}$ second qr. | 197 | $\frac{2}{3}$ third qr. | 197 |
| $\frac{1}{3}$ first qr. | 80 | $\frac{1}{3}$ second qr. | 99 | $\frac{1}{3}$ third qr. | 99 | $\frac{1}{3}$ fourth qr. | 80 |
| | 230 | | 259 | | 296 | | 277 |

2. Similarly, payments for purchases:

| Opening creditors | 70 | $\frac{1}{3}$ first qr | 71 | $\frac{1}{3}$ second qr. | 80 | $\frac{1}{3}$ third qr. | 80 |
|---|---|---|---|---|---|---|---|
| $\frac{2}{3}$ first qr. | 142 | $\frac{2}{3}$ second qr. | 160 | $\frac{2}{3}$ third qr. | 160 | $\frac{2}{3}$ fourth qr. | 142 |
| | 212 | | 231 | | 240 | | 222 |

3. Payments for overhead comprise production, general administration and marketing, less depreciation.

4. The reduction in the cash balance of £56,000 arises as follows:

|  |  |  | £ 000's |
|---|---|---|---|
| Cash generated by operations: | | | |
| Operating profit | | 14 | |
| *Add* depreciation | | 8 | |
| | | — | 22 |
| Applications of funds: | | | |
| Materials stock increase | | 50 | |
| Capital expenditure | | 19 | |
| Increase in debtors | | | |
| Closing balance | 160 | | |
| Opening balance | 150 | | |
| | — | 10 | |
| | | — | (79) |
| Source of funds. | | | |
| Increase in creditors $(71-70)$ | | 1 | |
| | | — | |
| | | | 56 |
| Closing cash | | | 19 |
| | | | — |
| Opening cash | | | 75 |

be in the form of figure tabulations though sometimes the necessary information may be conveyed more cogently by graphs or charts.

It is impossible to do more than provide examples of typical control reports; in essence, the report structure will reflect the responsibility definition recognised in the development of budgets.

The following principles should be applied in their preparation:

1. The report should be clearly headed and the period covered shown. The unit, viz. cash, tonnes, litres, etc., should be indicated.

2. Like must be compared with like, and there must be no ambiguity of description. For example, there should be no doubt whether a sales control report refers to "deliveries made and invoiced" or to "orders received".

3. Information not relevant to the purpose for which the report is prepared should be omitted, so that conclusions from the report can be drawn quickly and with certainty.

4. The report should not attempt to portray so much information that clarity is lost. If the information to be conveyed is complicated, more than one statement may be desirable. For example, to show actual sales compared with budget, analysed over both "areas" and "commodities", a separate statement for each analysis would improve clarity.

5. The information included should be limited to the sphere of the person to whom it is furnished. The data to be given to a foreman would normally be confined to that affecting his particular shop, but the factory manager would require broader information covering all departments for which he is responsible.

6. Promptness is to be preferred to absolute accuracy; the purpose is not merely to convey information but to convey it promptly and to the person who has the authority to take action.

7. All reports should be reviewed periodically to ensure that they are still useful and to ascertain whether they should be expanded, contracted, or discontinued.

*EXAMPLE*

| Sales Report Sales Invoiced Week 3, 19... (A) = Adverse variance, (F) = Favourable variance | | | | | | | | |
|---|---|---|---|---|---|---|---|---|
| | *This week* | | | | *Cumulative to date* | | | |
| *Area* | *Budget* | | *Actual* | *Variance* | *Budget* | | *Actual* | *Variance* |
| | *Units* | *£* | *£* | *£* | *Units* | *£* | *£* | *£* |
| N | 1,000 | 2,000 | 1,900 | 100(A) | 3,000 | 6,000 | 6,500 | 500(F) |
| S | 750 | 1,575 | 1,640 | 65(F) | 2,400 | 4,040 | 4,650 | 610(F) |
| E | 1,100 | 2,200 | 2,000 | 200(A) | 3,000 | 6,000 | 5,800 | 200(A) |
| W | 1,400 | 2,800 | 2,950 | 150(F) | 4,200 | 8,400 | 9,100 | 700(F) |
| Export | 700 | 2,100 | 2,100 | — | 2,000 | 6,000 | 5,850 | 150(A) |
| | 4,950 | £10,675 | £10,590 | £85(A) | 14,600 | £30,440 | £31,900 | £1,460(F) |

It would appear that in all areas except E sales are satisfactory. The reason for the fall in E should be investigated and action taken to stimulate sales.

*EXAMPLE*

The budgeted and actual sales for a budget period are reported to the sales manager as follows:

| Product | Budgeted sales (units) | Actual sales (units) | Variance (units) |
|---------|---------|---------|---------|
| A | 400 | 415 | 15 (F) |
| B | 700 | 600 | 100 (A) |
| C | 600 | 590 | 10 (A) |
| D | 900 | 1,050 | 150 (F) |
| | 2,600 | 2,655 | 55 (F) |

Products A and C are selling in accordance with budget, and the sales manager, therefore, finds it unnecessary to give much attention to these lines. Product B, however, is falling behind budget, and the sales manager must investigate the reasons. These reasons may include:

1. Increased competition.
2. A change in fashion.
3. Slow deliveries.
4. Uncompetitive prices.
5. Seasonal fluctuations.
6. Inadequate advertising.

As a result of this investigation, the sales manager will act to stimulate the sales of product B. Should this not be possible, the managing director, subject to policy constraints, will authorise a revision of the sales budget, which may entail amendments to the production and labour budgets and possibly to the financial budget.

Product D is selling substantially in excess of budget. Unless this is regarded as temporary, the production budget must be revised which in turn may involve amendments to the raw materials budget and possibly to the labour and financial budgets.

*EXAMPLE*

| Unit Scrap Report, Week 4, 19... | | | | |
|---------|---------|---------|---------|---------|
| | | | | Percentage of scrap |
| Operation | Good production | Budgeted scrap | Actual scrap | Budget | Actual |
| A | 7,500 | 75 | 82 | 1.0 | 1.1 |
| B | 5,000 | 100 | 90 | 2.0 | 1.8 |
| C | 2,500 | 50 | 75 | 2.0 | 3.0 |
| D | 8,000 | 120 | 240 | 1.5 | 3.0 |
| | 23,000 | 345 | 487 | 1.5 | 2.1 |

It would appear that excessive scrap is arising in operations C and D. This may be due to:

1. Carelessness on the part of the operators.
2. Defective maintenance of machines C and D.
3. Unsatisfactory raw material.
4. An inadequate allowance in the standard.

Management would endeavour to discover the reasons for the unsatisfactory results of operations C and D. A and B are seen to be proceeding satisfactorily.

*EXAMPLE*

| Outstanding Order Position, end of Week 7, 19... | | | | | | |
|---|---|---|---|---|---|---|
| Product (*tonnes*) | F | | G | | Total | |
| | *Budget* | *Actual* | *Budget* | *Actual* | *Budget* | *Actual* |
| Orders in hand Jan. 1 | 1,000 | 1,000 | 500 | 500 | 1,500 | 1,500 |
| Received | 1,200 | 1,300 | 1,000 | 700 | 2,200 | 2,000 |
| | 2,200 | 2,300 | 1,500 | 1,200 | 3,700 | 3,500 |
| Despatched | 1,700 | 1,500 | 1,100 | 900 | 2,800 | 2,400 |
| Orders in hand Feb. 24 | 500 | 800 | 400 | 300 | 900 | 1,100 |

It would appear that deliveries of product F are not keeping pace with the budget, even allowing for the increased orders received. The orders for Product G have fallen considerably but deliveries have apparently improved. Enquiries to ascertain reasons would be instituted.

The preceding examples emphasise the following important aspects of budgetary control:

1. Disclosure by accountancy methods of deviations; from budget, which may be expressed in terms of cash, quantity, hours, etc.
2. Investigation of the reasons for such deviations.
3. The taking of action to correct unsatisfactory deviations.
4. Revision of future plans to reflect trends disclosed by budget comparisons.

## FLEXIBLE BUDGETS

So far in this chapter, we have assumed that the budget prepared for the budget period will be used to measure actual performance. It will be obvious, however, that all budgets will be affected, to a greater or lesser degree, by the level of activity chosen for the master budget. In the illustration of budget development, the planned level of sales was the starting point to which all other budgets were related.

It is unlikely that the planned level of sales will be exactly attained; consequently, any comparison of actual performance against budget will immediately give rise to deviations which relate to a change in the volume of activity. Such changes are likely to be outside the control of most functional heads and budget centre managers; to rely on a fixed budget as a standard of comparison might be unsatisfactory, if not actually misleading, as fluctuations in output might lead to violent deviations from the budget which are outside the control of the person responsible for the budget.

It is usual, therefore, to adopt the flexible budgetary technique. A flexible budget is defined in the *Terminology* issued by the Institute of Cost and Management Accountants, as follows:

*Flexible Budget.* A budget which, by recognising the difference in behaviour between fixed and variable costs, in relation to fluctuations in output or turnover, is designed to change appropriately with such fluctuations.

If flexible budgeting is adopted, a series of budgets would be compiled to cover the range of levels of activity possible. It is clear that the division of costs and expenses into fixed and variable is crucial in such budgets, because:

Variable costs will tend to remain constant *per unit of output*, although if greater output leads to cheaper material costs or wage reductions per unit because of the increased "tempo" of the factory, such variable costs per unit of output may fall.

Fixed costs will tend to remain constant *in total*, although considerably increased output may lead to an increase *in total* if, for example, additional costs in storage space or supervisory staff are necessary.

Before the flexible budget can be prepared it is necessary to decide upon a unit in which to express the level of activity, so that variable costs may be computed and consideration given to the possibility of additions to the fixed costs. In functional budgets, units of production may be taken as a measurement of activity, but in departmental budgets it is frequently convenient to express output in labour or machine hours.

## EXAMPLE

Prepare a flexible budget from the following information:
Possible levels of activity—

|  | Up to 140,000 units | 140,000 to 160,000 units | 160,000 to 200,000 units |
|---|---|---|---|
| Sales price | £1.00 | £1.00 | £0.975 |
| Variable unit costs: |  |  |  |
| Material | £0.40 | £0.3875 | £0.375 |
| Labour | £0.20 | £0.20 | £0.1915 |
| Overhead | £0.10 | £0.10 | £0.10 |
| Fixed costs | £30,000 | £30,000 | £35,000 |

| *Flexible Budget, period ...............* | | | |
|---|---|---|---|
| Level of activity (in units) | 140,000 | 160,000 | 200,000 |
| Sales price per unit | £1 | £1 | £0.975 |
| Estimated revenue | £140,000 | £160,000 | £195,000 |
| Variable costs: |  |  |  |
| Material | 56,000 | 62,000 | 75,000 |
| Labour | 28,000 | 32,000 | 38,300 |
| Overhead | 14,000 | 16,000 | 20,000 |
| Fixed costs | 30,000 | 30,000 | 35,000 |
|  | 128,000 | 140,000 | 168,300 |
| Budgeted profit | 12,000 | 20,000 | 26,700 |
|  | £140,000 | £160,000 | £195,000 |

Such budgets primarily indicate the profits which should arise from each level of activity but, for the purpose of controlling costs, it is necessary to relate the appropriate budget to the level of activity achieved when this is ascertained at the end of the budget period. At activity of, say, 180,000 units actual costs would be compared with the following amended budget:

| Variable costs: | | |
|---|---|---|
| Materials | $180,000 \times £0.375 =$ | £67,500 |
| Labour | $180,000 \times £0.1915 =$ | 34,470 |
| Overhead | $180,000 \times £0.10 =$ | 18,000 |
|  |  | 119,970 |
| Fixed costs |  | 35,000 |
| Total costs |  | £154,970 |

## EXAMPLE

A department operates 12 machines; the working week is 35 hours, and normal estimated productive time is 80 per cent. Prepare a flexible departmental expense budget for the week on the following assumptions:

1. Normal production time is achieved.
2. Production time falls to (a) 60%, (b) 70%.
3. Production time increases to 90%.

Variable costs of production at the above levels of activity amount to £1 per productive hour. Fixed expenses are £100 per week for all levels of production up to and including 80 per cent, but if production increases beyond that figure they will increase by £24.

NOTE: Available machine hours per week: $12 \times 35 = 420$.

| Flexible Departmental Expense Budget Week ending ............. | | | | |
|---|---|---|---|---|
| Percentage utilisation budgeted | 60 | 70 | 80 | 90 |
| Effective machine hours | 252 | 294 | 336 | 378 |
| Departmental expenses: | | | | |
| Variable | £252 | £294 | £336 | £378 |
| Fixed | 100 | 100 | 100 | 124 |
| | £352 | £394 | £436 | £502 |

Comparisons for control purposes would be made with the appropriate budget when the actual machine hours are ascertained at the end of the week.

## THE APPLICATION OF BUDGETARY CONTROL

Budgetary control properly applied can be immensely valuable to those in charge of a business. It is, however, not without dangers unless skill and intelligence are exercised both in devising the budgets and in implementing the plans to achieve them.

A business is a dynamic thing. Conditions both inside and outside the firm are constantly changing. A budget is a framework and must not be allowed to hinder, by undue rigidity, the development of the business. New opportunities must be grasped and the budget must not be used as an excuse for rejecting them. On the other hand a continual and haphazard branching out of a business without regard to any unifying principle can deflect the attention of those employed from the main objectives, and may therefore be dangerous. Budgetary control should ensure that new and unforeseen opportunities are channelled to members of the organization capable of giving them proper consideration. Such opportunities should be neither accepted immediately nor rejected out of hand; the existence of budgets should assist in deciding whether they can be properly accepted in the light of the overall plans for the business.

## SELF-STUDY TEST No. 7

*Budgetary Control*

(*Refer to the Appendix on p. 358 for outline solutions.*)

1. What advantages do you consider would be likely to follow the adoption of Budgetary Control by a manufacturing business?

2. What is the distinction between a fixed budget and a flexible budget?

3. What do you understand by a master budget? Into what sections is it usually divided, and what are the purposes of the division?

4. Summarise the main duties of: (*a*) the budget committee; and (*b*) the budget controller.

5. List, and write a short note on the main items you would expect to find in a budget manual.

6. What are the major factors to be assessed before a sales forecast is prepared?

7. What budget centres would you expect the marketing cost budget of a large consumer product manufacturer to be divided into?

8. A company making for stock in the first quarter of the year is offered overdraft facilities. The relevant budget figures follow:

|  | *Sales* | *Purchases* | *Wages* |
|---|---|---|---|
| November | £60,000 | £41,500 | £4,900 |
| December | 64,000 | 48,000 | 5,000 |
| January | 36,000 | 81,000 | 4,000 |
| February | 58,000 | 82,000 | 3,800 |
| March | 42,000 | 89,500 | 5,200 |

Budgeted cash at the bank at January 1st is £8,600.

Credit terms of sale are payment by the end of the month following the month of supply. On average, one half of the sales are paid on the due date, while the other half are paid during the next month. Creditors are paid during the month following the month of supply.

You are required to prepare a cash budget for the quarter January 1st to March 31st, showing the amount of overdraft required at the end of each month.

9. A retail department store sells mixed nuts in either a 500 gm plain package or in a 250 gm fancy package. The nuts are purchased on bulk and the two types of packages are bought separately. The nuts are boxed by shop staff during slack periods.

As part of a stock reduction scheme, the store manager is asked to prepare, for September and October:

    (*a*) sales budget for plain and fancy mixed nuts; and

    (*b*) purchases budget for mixed nuts and packages.

No price changes are anticipated but sales of plain mixed nuts and fancy mixed nuts are up by 5 per cent and 10 per cent respectively compared with last year.

The following data are relevant:

Selling prices per package: Plain   £1.50

Fancy   £1.00

Purchase prices: Mixed nuts 80p per kg

Plain package 10p  ,,

Fancy package 20p  ,,

| Stocks: | At August 31st | Budgeted at October 31st |
|---|---|---|
| Mixed nuts | 2,000 kg | 400 kg |
| Plain packages | 1,400 | 600 |
| Fancy packages | 2,000 | 800 |
| Last year's sales: | September | October |
| Plain | 8,000 | 14,000 |
| Fancy | 8,000 | 24,000 |

Prepare the budgets as required.

# CHAPTER 10

# Standard Costing

The benefits to be derived from the comparison of departmental performances over a period with a budget prepared before the commencement of that period have been considered in the previous chapter. A logical extension of budgetary control is standard costing, in which the principles of comparing "actual with plan" are applied to the *costs of products and services* as well as to functions and responsibility centres. Standard costing also provides a basis for disclosing the causes of deviations from plan and measures their cost in terms of money. Such a system is particularly useful in repetitive industries, i.e. where a small range of products uses a limited number of fundamental mechanical operations, but it is also possible and valuable to apply standards to jobbing industries, as it will probably be found that the manufacture of special products involves common processes or operations for which standards can be set.

## OBJECTS

It is customary for financial accounts to show comparative figures for the previous accounting period and, similarly, cost statements are often provided with columns for comparative figures which will also be those of previous periods if standard costing is not in operation. While valuable information can be afforded by these comparisons, misleading conclusions may be drawn, as the figures of earlier periods tend to be regarded as standards by which current efficiency can be judged. When comparing results with a previous period, therefore, it must be remembered that:

1. Changing money values, alterations in V.A.T. rates, etc. will complicate any analysis.
2. The expenditure of the previous year may have been extravagant, or abnormally low, due to factors which no longer apply.
3. The installation of new facilities and changes in methods of production will affect costs.

Prices, wage-rates, factory capacity and efficiency are matters which are constantly changing and a comparison of this year's figures with those of last year discloses merely whether costs have increased or diminished. Such comparisons do not show whether the change is entirely due to a single factor, e.g. increased prices, or whether it is the net result of various changes, not all of which may operate in the same direction. For instance, a change in wages cost may be due to a combination of some or all of the following factors:

1. Wage-rates, either changes in the rates themselves or employment of different grades of labour.
2. Efficiency of working, whereby a greater or smaller output per hour has been achieved.
3. Hours of working.
4. Idle time caused by production hold-ups, strikes, power failures and the like.

In one period, an increase in wage-rates may be coupled with greater efficiency or fewer working hours, and any comparison with the previous period will show, not the increased or decreased costs caused by each of these factors, but merely the net result. Such an overall comparison is almost useless for purposes of control as it does not disclose the savings in labour which the efforts of the works manager may have achieved, or the unavoidable additional costs caused by increases in negotiated wage-rates.

Similarly for materials, an overall comparison may show that the cost per unit manufactured is unchanged. This apparent stability may in reality be the result of lower prices (due to the skill of the chief buyer) offset by increased wastage (due to bad supervision by the works manager). Preparation of standard costs permits the cost of deviations from plan to be disclosed and classified as to causes, so that management is immediately informed of the sphere of operation in which remedial action is necessary. The deviations are termed variances. Standards are set before the commencement of a period and cover all aspects of production.

## THE CONCEPT OF "STANDARD"

A great advantage of preparing budgets is in crystallising the intentions of management for the future of the business. A similar advantage arises from using standard costs. In many industries a product could be produced from a variety of materials, using a variety of machines manned by different skills of labour. For example, nuts and bolts may be machined from different types of steel using either automatic, semi-automatic or manually operated lathes. The final product might be quite acceptable regardless of how it has been manufactured. The cost, however, may differ considerably according to the material and production method used. To arrive at a standard cost, it is necessary for production management to specify how a product will be manufactured and an important consideration will be the minimum cost consistent with producing an acceptable product. Various management techniques will be employed, e.g. value analysis and method study, and finally a standard production specification will be prepared indicating the material, machines and labour required and, possibly, the standard batch quantity to be produced.

The definition of standard cost included in the terminology issued by the I.C.M.A. summarises its concept and purpose:

"A predetermined cost calculated in relation to a prescribed set of working conditions, correlating technical specifications and scientific measurements of materials and labour to the prices and wage rates expected to apply during the period to which the standard cost is intended to relate, with an addition of an appropriate share of budgeted overhead. Its main purposes are to provide bases for control through variance accounting, for the valuation of stocks and work in progress, and, in exceptional cases, for fixing selling prices."

## IDEAL OR ATTAINABLE STANDARDS?

Standards should be realistic and therefore capable of attainment and not based on mere aspirations. On the other hand, they should not be fixed too low and thereby be too easily achievable, which could result in false complacency. For example, standards of production could be based upon what is possible under:

1. The best possible conditions of management and performance, i.e. assuming the maximum possible efficiency.
2. Existing conditions.
3. Conditions capable of achievement with existing resources by the exercise of prudent management.

Of these, (1) is probably unrealistic, (2) does not reflect improvements which can be made and (3) therefore provides the considerations upon which standards are usually based. It must be emphasised that standards must not be confused with ideals. For example it might be found that last year a certain shop produced 11,100 units. It is estimated that this year it could produce 15,000 units if there are no plant breakdowns or delays in the supply of material. Under existing conditions, however, only 12,000 units per annum can be produced but it is considered that if management improves certain weaknesses, an output of 13,750 could be achieved. The standard output would probably be set at 13,750 units.

## COMPONENTS OF STANDARD COST

The general conception of a standard costing system is one in which a standard cost is accumulated for each product, comprising the standard cost of materials and wages used together with a predetermined share of budgeted production overhead.

The basic two constituents of cost elements for which standards are specified are the price and the quantity. The production engineer will specify the quantity of materials required, allowing for waste and scrap, and the purchasing manager will set a standard price based on current prices and estimated changes during the next budget period. Labour times will be set by the rate-fixer or work-study engineer and a bonus allowance may be included. Wage rates will be set according to the type of labour required and anticipated average rates for the future year. Direct expenses, if any, will be similarly assessed and overhead absorption rates will be calculated as appropriate.

The standard specification can be an invaluable piece of information in the business. It can be used by production control for scheduling production and for machine loading. The purchasing manager will use it to obtain details of material requirements. Standard times can be used as a basis for an incentive scheme, and clearly the sales department will find standard cost data useful for price-fixing purposes.

An example of a standard cost specification is given below.

*EXAMPLE*

STANDARD COST SPECIFICATION

| **Product: XYZ Fitting** | *Unit price* | *Per dozen* |
|---|---|---|
| Material: | | |
| 250 kg alloy to B.S.S. -- | £0.40 kg | £100.00 |
| Packing material, 12 cartons | £0.30 each | 3.60 |
| | | 103.60 |
| *Less:* Standard scrap recovery, 25 kg at £0.10 | | 2.50 |
| | | 101.10 |
| Labour: | | |
| Shop No. 1: Lathe A 50 hours | £1.50 hour | 75.00 |
| Lathe B 10 hours | £1.40 hour | 14.00 |
| Shop No. 2: Miller F 20 hours | £2.00 hour | 40.00 |
| Grinder 8 hours | £1.00 hour | 8.00 |
| Inspection 0.5 hours | £0.90 hour | 0.45 |
| | | 238.55 |
| Overhead: standard absorption: | | |
| Fixed, 88 hours at £1.00 | | 88.00 |
| Variable, 88 hours at £0.80 | | 70.40 |
| Standard cost per dozen | | £396.95 |

Prepared: Date ................................. By ................ Approved.....

NOTE: 1. If Shops 1 and 2 were treated as separate cost centres, separate standard overhead absorption rates would be calculated.

2. The standard product specification may also incorporate the standard selling price and batch quantity, if appropriate.

## OVERHEAD STANDARDS

In building up a standard product cost an allowance is included for overhead costs and the important distinction between fixed and variable overhead must be borne in mind. It is usually possible to identify variable overhead with the production of an article, because it is assumed that it does not occur unless production is embarked upon and that it rises or falls in proportion thereto. If the package per article costs £0.05 no cost occurs if no production takes place, and the cost per article will be £0.05, however many articles are made.

Fixed overhead, which is assumed to be constant in total whether production is zero or at the maximum output of the factory, can be budgeted in total before production takes place but the amount to be included in a standard product cost depends upon the budgeted output. For example, if fixed costs for the budget period are £2,000 an output budget of 2,000 articles would necessitate the inclusion of £1 per article. If, however, the output budget provided for 4,000 articles the amount to be included would be £0.50 per article, as the amount of £2,000 would be unchanged. Similarly, if only 1,000 articles were budgeted for, it would be necessary to include £2 per article.

The fixed overhead can therefore be regarded as the cost of the overall establishment. By budgeting for a certain output, the cost of the establishment per unit can be determined, i.e. the establishment costs are made to suit the budgeted output. If output differs from budget, it may be said that the establishment no longer fits the changed circumstances and its costs are either too large or too small as the case may be. Only the standard allowance per unit manufactured may be charged to production and any amount over- or under-recovered may be said to be a measure of the amount by which the establishment is too large or too small for the production actually achieved.

As production may be expressed in standard hours, it is possible to calculate a rate of fixed overhead per standard hour and, if a variety of articles are manufactured, this may well be the only satisfactory method.

A third class of overhead is termed semi-variable. These move in sympathy with production, though not in exact relation thereto. For example, electricity may be purchased at a price comprising a fixed standing charge plus a charge for each unit consumed. If, therefore, consumption is doubled the total bill will increase, but not by 100 per cent. In dealing with semi-variable costs it is probably best to divide each into its fixed and variable components and to include each part with the appropriate group.

## PERIOD COVERED BY STANDARD COST

A great deal of work goes into the preparation of standard costs and, therefore, once they have been set, there will be a reluctance to revise them very often. However, the standard must reflect current conditions especially where it is used for machine loading, setting selling prices or calculating material requirements; in addition, out-of-date standards lose much of their value as a target for performance. Normally standards will be revised annually to coincide with the budgeting process, i.e. new overhead absorption rates will be calculated every year. It is likely that most revisions will arise from price changes and such changes can be accumulated for a major periodic revision. However, it is advisable that standard times, material quantities, etc., are reviewed regularly so that the standard cost reflects current workshop practice.

## EVALUATING PRODUCTION IN TERMS
## OF STANDARD COSTS

Just as the standard relationship which exists between the kilometre and the mile permits distances expressed in one system to be converted into the other, so the use of standards makes it possible to express:

1. Finished production in terms of the quantity or value of raw materials necessary to make it, and vice versa.

2. Finished production in terms of hours or costs of labour engaged in its manufacture, and vice versa.

3. Fixed overhead in terms of the quantity postulated in the standard output, or as a percentage of the labour cost, or at a rate per hour.

*EXAMPLE*
The specification of a finished article is as follows:

  5 kg of raw material
  2 hours of labour

If raw material costs £0.50 per kg and the wage rate is £1.50 per hour, express production of 150 finished articles in terms of raw material and labour.

The standard cost of the article is as follows:

| | | |
|---|---|---:|
| Raw material: | 5 kg at £0.50 per kg | £2.50 |
| Labour: | 2 hours at £1.50 per hour | 3.00 |
| | | £5.50 |

150 articles therefore have a standard cost of $150 \times £5.50 = £825.00$, made up of:

| | | |
|---|---|---|
| Raw material: $150 \times £2.50$ | | £375.00 |
| Labour: $150 \times £3.00$ | | 450.00 |
| | | —— |
| | | £825.00 |

It is also possible to say that 150 articles represent:

| | |
|---|---|
| Raw material: $150 \times 5$ kg | 750 kg |
| Labour: $150 \times 2$ hours | 300 hours |

*EXAMPLE*

Estimates show that fixed overhead for the budget period will total £1,500. It is estimated that production will be 6,000 articles and that each article will require 10 kg of material at £0.75 per kg and 2 hours of labour at £1.50 per hour. Express production in terms of materials, labour and fixed overhead, and express fixed overhead as (*a*) a rate per hour; (*b*) as a percentage of the labour cost.

| | Standard cost per article | Standard cost of 6,000 articles | Standard quantity for 6,000 articles |
|---|---|---|---|
| Materials, 10 kg at £0.75 per kg | £7.50 | £45,000 | 60,000 kg |
| Labour, 2 hours at £1.50 | 3.00 | 18,000 | 12,000 hrs |
| Fixed overhead, £1,500 ÷ 6,000 | 0.25 | 1,500 | 12,000 hrs |
| | —— | —— | |
| | £10.75 | £64,500 | |

(*a*) Fixed overhead per hour:

To complete 6,000 articles requires $6,000 \times 2$ hours $= 12,000$ hours

$$£1,500 \div 12,000 = £0.125 \text{ per hour}$$

Alternatively, each article requires 2 hours of labour and the standard absorption rate for fixed overhead is £0.25 per article.

(*b*) Fixed overhead as a percentage of the labour cost:

$$£\frac{1,500}{18,000} \times 100 = 8\tfrac{1}{3}\%$$

An understanding of the relationships which the use of standards makes possible is vital, and the student should make sure that he fully understands the foregoing examples.

**The standard hour**

Production can be expressed in many different ways, e.g. dozens, tonnes, litres and units, but it is essential to have a common measurement in which the output of differently measured articles can be expressed. The factor which is common to all operations or processes is "time" and it will be seen that, if a constant rate of production is assumed, outputs, however diverse, can be expressed in terms of the time necessary to manufacture them. This measurement is called the standard hour, which is "a hypothetical unit pre-established to represent the amount of work which should be performed in one hour at standard performance" (I.C.M.A.). A standard hour, therefore, is not a measurement of time but of the work content of a clock hour. For example, if the standard time required to produce 10 litres of article A and 18 kg of article B is respectively 5 and 6 clock hours, a standard hour is equivalent to 2 litres of A or 3 kg of B; an output of 100 litres of A and 150 kg of B would each represent 50 standard hours, irrespective of the time actually taken to produce them.

The standard hour is a convenient way of expressing output of a variety of products in common terms.

*EXAMPLE*

A company packs three household preparations Splonk, Splosh and Splurge, of which 200, 100 and 50 cartons respectively can be packed in 1 hour. There are 20 operatives working a 40-hour week in the 10-week budget period and the company proposes to pack 400,000 cartons of Splonk and a similar quantity of Splosh. How many cartons of Splurge may also be packed? Ignore idle time.

|  |  | *Clock hours* |
|---|---|---|
| Hours in budget period | | |
| $20 \times 40 \times 10 =$ | | 8,000 |
| Used to pack: | | |
| Splonk  $400,000 \div 200 = 2,000$ | | |
| Splosh  $400,000 \div 100 = 4,000$ | | |
| | —— | 6,000 |
| Hours available for packing Splurge | | 2,000 |
| Output of Splurge | | |
| $2,000 \times 50 = 100,000$ cartons | | |

## The productivity (or efficiency) ratio

It was stated above that production may be measured in standard hours irrespective of the clock hours taken to achieve it.

If output differs from standard for the hours worked, i.e. if the rate of production changes, an alteration in efficiency is implied which can be measured by means of the efficiency ratio. This is defined by the Institute of Cost and Management Accountants as follows:

*Productivity (or efficiency) ratio.*   The standard hours equivalent to the production achieved, whether completed or not, divided by (or expressed as a percentage of) the actual direct working hours.

*EXAMPLE*

The production budget of a manufacturing company is as follows:

Period ..................

| | Units of Output | Standard hours per unit | Budgeted production in standard hours |
|---|---|---|---|
| Ashtrays | 1,000 | ¼ | 250 |
| Cigarette lighters | 500 | 2 | 1,000 |
| Pipes | 600 | 1 | 600 |
| Budgeted standard hours | | | 1,850 |

The actual production is as follows:

| | Units of Output | Standard hours per unit | Actual production in standard hours |
|---|---|---|---|
| Ashtrays | 1,200 | ¼ | 300 |
| Cigarette lighters | 600 | 2 | 1,200 |
| Pipes | 400 | 1 | 400 |
| Value of production expressed in standard hours | | | 1,900 |

The actual direct working hours are:                                     2,000

The productivity ratio is therefore:

$$\frac{\text{Standard hours equivalent to the work produced}}{\text{Actual direct working hours}} \times 100$$

$$= \frac{1,900}{2,000} \times 100 = 95\%$$

A lower degree of efficiency was achieved than was budgeted, for at standard performance the production in terms of standard hours should have been 2,000, i.e. equivalent to the hours worked. It will be noted that, in calculating the efficiency ratio, no account is taken of budgeted production, merely the standard rate of performance. If the efficiency ratio is more than 100, higher efficiency has been obtained than was allowed in the budget, i.e. production *for the hours worked* is greater than standard.

## The capacity ratio

In order to operate profitably, a business needs to maintain an efficient rate of manufacture and also to ensure that facilities are fully utilised, i.e. that resources are not wasted. A measure of the use that is made of resources is the Capacity Ratio. The ratio is defined by the Institute of Cost and Management Accountants as:

*Capacity ratio.* The actual number of direct working hours divided by (or expressed as a percentage of) the budgeted number of standard hours.

Assuming that there is good reason for pitching the budget below maximum capacity, this ratio indicates the extent to which planned utilisation has been achieved. In the example, the ratio is 108.1 per cent showing that the budget has been exceeded, i.e.

$$\frac{\text{Actual direct working hours}}{\text{Budgeted standard hours}} = \frac{2,000}{1,850} = 108.1\%$$

**The production volume ratio**
While the productivity ratio indicates how efficiently the hours actually worked have been used, and the capacity ratio indicates the extent to which the capacity of the factory has been utilised, there is a need to equate these two ratios. The production volume ratio indicates the effective utilisation of capacity by measuring production in terms of standard hours instead of actual hours. It is defined by the Institute of Cost and Management Accountants as follows:

*Production volume ratio.* The number of standard hours equivalent to the production achieved, whether completed or not, divided by (or expressed as a percentage of) the budgeted number of standard hours.

NOTE: The term "activity ratio" is synonymous but it is not recommended as the word "activity" is capable of different interpretations.

Using the figures in the previous example, the production volume ratio is:

$$\frac{\text{Standard hours equivalent to the production achieved}}{\text{Budgeted standard hours}} \times 100$$

$$= \frac{1,900}{1,850} \times 100 = 102.7\%$$

A higher volume of production was achieved than was budgeted for as, although it was expected that production would be 1,850 standard hours, 1,900 standard hours were in fact produced.

## VARIANCE ANALYSIS

**The purpose**
It will be appreciated that standard costs are based upon a number of assumptions. If it turns out that any or all of these assumptions are falsified by events the standard cost will be either exceeded or not attained, and the cause and amount of the deviation must be

ascertained. These deviations from standard are termed *variances*, and their calculation and classifications is one of the most important features of standard costing. Variances must be classified so that their cause is disclosed to management in order that remedial action of the right nature and in the right direction can be undertaken and responsibility duly allocated. If, for example, an adverse materials price variance is disclosed, management will require an explanation from the chief buyer. It may be possible to find an alternative and cheaper source of supply either of the same or of a substitute material or, on the other hand, the increase, if permanent, may make it desirable to increase the selling price of the finished articles in which the material is used.

A reduction in output would, if caused by diminished efficiency, be the responsibility of the production manager. If the fall in output is the result of a reduction in the working hours it might be due to a shortage of workers, to strikes and other stoppages, or to a deliberate reduction resulting from falling sales.

An important aspect of analysing and reporting variances is the need to separate controllable from uncontrollable variances. The test is whether or not the variances can be identified as the primary responsibility of a specified person. One needs to look carefully at the circumstances before labelling variances. For example, a materials price variance for goods purchased from associated companies may be the result of the holding company's policy and therefore cannot be strictly identified with the purchasing manager. Responsibility implies freedom to choose between alternative avenues of action, and therefore the cost accountant may need to look further than the organisation chart to see where decisions are really made.

**Variance accounting**

It is obvious that the concepts and principles related to standard costing are identical to those involved in budgetary control. Consequently, it will be advantageous to combine budgetary control, standard costing and variance analysis into one integrated technique which embraces all business activities and incorporates the principles of comparing actual with plan in the accounting system.

The description given to a comprehensive technique of this kind is "Variance Accounting", which is defined in the I.C.M.A. *Terminology* as:

"A technique whereby the planned activities of an undertaking are expressed in budgets, standard costs, standard selling prices and standard profit margins, and the differences between these and the comparable actual results are accounted for. Management is periodically presented with an analysis of differences by causes and responsibility centres, such analysis usually commencing with the operating profit variance. The technique also includes the establishment of a suitable arrangement of accounts in the principal ledger."

### Components of the Operating Profit Variance
At this stage, it is not necessary to explore all the ramifications of variance accounting but before explaining how the basic variances are calculated, it may be helpful to indicate, in broad outline, the component parts of the Operating Profit Variance.

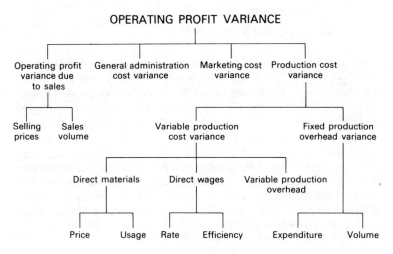

Fig. 52.—*Variance analysis—components of operating profit variance.*

It must be emphasised that the above chart indicates the main variance classifications. Each business will develop, within the overall structure, its own sub-analysis appropriate to the nature of production and to the relative significance of cost items.

For example, wage rate variances may be analysed into overtime premium, bonuses, etc., while materials price variances may be analysed into goods and carriage variances. The criterion is whether the analysis helps management.

### The Operating Profit Statement
When a variance accounting system is operated, an Operating Profit Statement can be extracted from the accounts in the following outline format:

*Operating Statement*
*Month of* ................... 19...

Budgeted sales
Standard cost of budgeted sales

   Budgeted margin
± Sales Volume variance

Standard margin on actual sales
± Selling price variances
   Production cost variances

Actual margin
− Administration and
    Marketing costs

Actual operating profit

To simplify variance accounting, it may be assumed that stocks of raw materials, work-in-progress and finished goods are valued at standard cost. Thus, cost variances are calculated on actual production during the period and any unsold production carried forward at standard cost.

*EXAMPLE*

Grumbles Ltd. manufacture one product, the Whine, which has a standard selling price of £20 and a standard cost of £15. The sales and production budget for period I was for 100 units; actual sales were 80 units at £21 each and 90 units were produced at a total cost of £1,400. There were no opening stocks. The Operating Statement (to actual margin) would be:

| | | |
|---|---:|---:|
| Budgeted Sales: 100 units at £20 | | £2,000 |
| Std. cost of budgeted sales: 100 at £15 | | 1,500 |
| Budgeted margin: 100 at £5 | | 500 |
| *Deduct*: Sales volume variance: 20 at £5 | | 100 |
| Std. margin on actual sales: 80 at £5 | | 400 |
| *Add:* Selling Price Variance: 80 at £1 | 80 | |
| *Deduct:* Production Cost Variances | | |
| (90 units at £15 each–£1,400) | (50) | |
| | | 30 |
| *Actual margin* | | £430 |

The actual margin represents:

| | | |
|---|---:|---:|
| Sales (80 at £21) | | 1,680 |
| Production cost | 1,400 | |
| Closing stock (10 units at £15) | 150 | |
| | | 1,250 |
| | | £430 |

The reader will note that the production budget is ignored when cost variances are calculated. The difference between budget (100 units) and actual production (90 units) is reflected at standard cost in the sales volume variance offset by the stock increase.

## THE ADVANTAGES OF STANDARD COSTING

Before passing to a detailed consideration of variances, it is appropriate to summarise the principal advantages which may be obtained from a system of standard costing.

1. A ready method is provided of comparing actual costs with those which are considered capable of achievement.

2. The cost of deviations from standard and the amount attributable to each cause is disclosed.

3. Establishment of standard costs encourages investigation of improved methods and cost reduction.

SELF-STUDY TEST No. 8

*Standard Costing*

(*Refer to the Appendix on p. 360 for outline solutions.*)

1. What benefits would you expect from the introduction of a standard costing system?

2. Explain the difference between an ideal standard and an attainable standard. Do you consider that an ideal standard provides a satisfactory measure of performance?

3. Explain the term "management by exception".

4. List, and write a brief note on each, five of the main factors to be considered in setting direct material standards.

5. Calculate, from the figures below, the capacity ratio, the production volume ratio and the productivity ratio:

|  | *Actual* | *Budget* |
|---|---|---|
| Production units: | | |
|     Product A | 420 | 400 |
|     Product B | 360 | 400 |
| Standard times per unit | | |
|     Product A | | 10 hours |
|     Product B | | 20 hours |
| Hours worked on production | 12,600 | 12,000 |

6. List the main steps in preparing a standard fixed overhead absorption rate for a product which is worked on in three budget centres.

# CHAPTER 11

# Analysis of Variances

## INTRODUCTION

As indicated by Fig. 52, the Operating Profit Variance comprises:

Sales.
Production Cost.
Marketing Cost.
General Administration Cost.

This chapter will concentrate on the traditional analysis of the Production Cost Variance into its main components; other aspects of variances affecting profit, and more complex analysis procedures, will be examined in general terms.

## THE PRODUCTION COST VARIANCE

### Cost elements

A standard product cost is obtained by accumulating cost standards for each cost element, i.e. Direct materials, Direct wages, Variable overhead and Fixed overhead. Consequently, it is appropriate to treat each element separately and to recognise the different ways in which standards are set and costs incurred.

### Comparison base

It is important to note that the variances for Direct materials, Direct wages and Variable overhead are calculated by comparing actual production costs with the flexible budget, i.e. the standard cost of production actually achieved. It would be unrealistic to compare actual variable costs with costs expected for a higher or lower level of production but fixed overhead, by definition, is expected to be unchanged in total irrespective of the level of production activity and, therefore, the budget for fixed overhead is unaffected by output changes.

### Work-in-progress

Subsequent illustrations generally assume that achieved production represents complete units. Frequently, however, quantities of unfinished work will remain in operation at the end of a period but the procedures involved in dealing with unfinished work do not affect the principles of variance analysis and can be ignored at this stage.

## DIRECT MATERIALS COST VARIANCES

### Price and quantity variances

In Chapter 10 reference was made to the following simple formula:

$$Price \times quantity = cost$$

Thus the two major cost variances which may arise, for direct materials and for direct wages, are price and quantity variances. This can be shown graphically as follows:

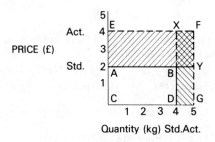

FIG. 53.—*Price and quantity variance (1).*

When analysing Direct materials cost, the quantity variance is termed "usage variance".

*EXAMPLE*

Standard specification for product: 4 kg of raw material at £2 per kg.
Actual consumption of raw material: 5 kg of raw material at £4 per kg.
Standard cost is represented by the unshaded area ABDC, i.e. $4 \times £2 = £8$. Actual cost is represented by the area EFGC, i.e. $5 \times £4 = £20$, and the variance (shaded) is therefore $£20 - £8 = £12$. In analysing the cause of the variance, the increase in price would appear to be represented by the area EXBA, i.e. $(£4 - £2) \times 4 = £8$, and the increase in quantity by the area BYGD, i.e. $(5 - 4) \times £2 = £2$. However, this ignores the area XFYB, i.e. $(£4 - £2) \times (5 - 4) = £2$ and it can be seen that this is common to both the price and quantity increases.

To simplify the analysis, a principle is adopted by which the common area is attributed to the price variance, as shown in Fig. 54.

The principle may, therefore, be stated as follows:

Price variance = (actual price − standard price) × actual quantity.

Quantity variance = (actual quantity − standard quantity) × standard price.

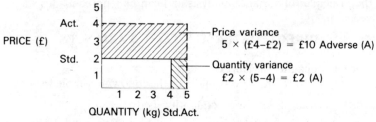

FIG. 54.—*Price and quantity variance* (2).

This principle will hold even where there is an increase in quantity but a decrease in price.

*EXAMPLE*

Standard specification for product = 4 kg of raw material at £2 per kg. Actual consumption of raw material: 5 kg at £1 per kg.

$$\begin{array}{ll}
\text{Standard cost} & = £2 \times 4 = £8 \\
\text{Actual cost} & = £1 \times 5 = £5 \\[4pt]
\hline
\text{Total variance} & = £3\,(F) \\[4pt]
\hline\hline
\text{Analysis: Price variance} & = £5\,(F) \\
\text{Quantity variance} & = £2\,(A)
\end{array}$$

Here, a common area is created, the price variance being inflated by an extra £1 which is treated as a favourable variance whereas the quantity variance is inflated by £1 which is treated as an adverse variance. The convention is necessary to maintain a consistent approach.

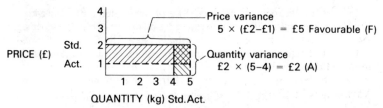

FIG. 55.—*Price and quantity variance* (3).

## Calculation of variances

A logical approach to variance analysis may be to present the information in the form of a tabulation which reconciles actual cost to standard.

*EXAMPLE*

The standard direct material specification for product Beta is to use 5 kg of raw material X at £6 per kg. Last month, 30 Betas were produced from 160 kg of X, which cost £940 in total. Calculate material price and usage variances:

| | | |
|---|---|---:|
| 1. | Actual Materials Cost | £940 |
| | *Direct materials price variance* (1 − 2) | 20 (F) |
| 2. | Actual materials used at standard price (160 kg at £6) | 960 |
| | *Direct materials usage variance* (2 − 3) | 60 (A) |
| 3. | Standard material cost of actual production | |
| | (30 Betas × 5 kg at £6) | £900 |

Note that the actual price per kg does not need to be calculated. In practice, materials could be obtained from a number of different suppliers at varying prices.

## Purchase price variances

The price variance may be segregated at one of the following times:

1. At the time of purchase, i.e. when the material is taken into stock.

2. At the time of issue from stock, i.e. when the material is put into production. Under this method, the actual cost of issues must be determined, using FIFO or one of the other actual cost methods explained in Chapter 3.

Each method possesses advantages which may be summarised as follows.

Advantages of Method 1—segregation at the time of purchase:

(*a*) The price variance is immediately disclosed.

(*b*) Stock accounts may be maintained in terms of quantities only, as issues and the balance in stock are valued at standard cost.

(*c*) The price variance need be calculated only once for each invoiced delivery.

Advantages of Method 2—segregation at the time of issue:

(*a*) As stock accounts are maintained at actual cost, the balances comply with conventional accounting principles.

(*b*) The price variance is written off in the period when the materials are consumed. This is probably more equitable than Method (1), under which it is written off in the period of purchase, because if favourable price variances occur profits are anticipated and stock is, in effect, over-valued. It is possible, however, to hold the price variance in suspense and to release a proportion into the period accounts according to consumption.

The two methods are illustrated by the following Journal entries.

1. *Where stocks are maintained at standard cost:*

JOURNAL

| | | | |
|---|---|---|---|
| Raw Materials Account | Dr | £90.00 | |
| Materials Price Variance Account | | 15.00 | |
| To Sundry creditors | | | £105.00 |
| 120 kg of material of standard cost £0.75 per kg purchased at £0.875 per kg | | | |

| | | | |
|---|---|---|---|
| Work-in-Progress Account | Dr | £30.00 | |
| To Raw Materials Account | | | £30.00 |
| Issue of 40 kg of material at standard cost. | | | |

2. *Where issues to production are priced at standard cost but stores accounts are maintained at actual cost:*

| | | | |
|---|---|---|---|
| Raw Materials Account | Dr | £105.00 | |
| To Sundry creditors | | | £105.00 |
| 120 kg of material purchased at £0.875 per kg | | | |

| | | | |
|---|---|---|---|
| Work-in-Progress Account | Dr | 30.00 | |
| Materials Price Variance Account | | 5.00 | |
| To Raw Materials Account | | | 35.00 |
| Issue of 40 kg of material at standard cost and price variance attributable thereto. | | | |

It will be appreciated that individual journal entries would not be made in practice. Suitable analysis columns are provided in the Purchases Journal or Materials Issues Summary to accumulate variances for periodical posting in total to Materials Price Variance Account. If variances are segregated at purchase, purchase invoices would be sent to the pricing clerk in the cost department or stock records department and the standard price would be entered on the invoice. Alternatively the pricing may be done in the purchasing department so that the purchasing manager can keep in touch with price movements.

If variances are segregated on issue of materials, the requisitions would be priced at both actual and standard price by the stores records clerk.

A materials price variance may result from one of the following reasons:

1. An overall movement in material prices through national wage awards, increases in customs duties, etc.
2. Difference between the standard and actual order quantities resulting in a gain or loss of quantity discounts.
3. Materials obtained from a different supplier.
4. Differences between standard and actual carriage costs, e.g. freight, insurance, etc.

5. Differences between the standard and actual quality of material.

A report showing the analysis of significant price variances by cause would be prepared periodically. The format in Fig. 56 could be typical.

| PURCHASE PRICE VARIANCE REPORT | | | | | | | | |
|---|---|---|---|---|---|---|---|---|
| Month ended.....................19........ | | | | | | | | |
| Variances above 5% of standard | | | | | | | | |
| Purchase order No. | Supplier | Material code | Variance | | | | | Remarks |
| | | | Total | General price | Qty. dis. | Supplier | Carriage | |
| | | | | | | | | |
| | | | | | | | | |
| | | | | | | | | |
| Total variances below 5% of standard | | | | | | | | |
| Total all variances | | | | | | | | |

FIG. 56.—*Purchase price variance report.*

## Material usage variance

As issues to production are priced at standard cost, any variation in usage must be priced on the same basis. If in the previous example a further 4 kg of material were necessary to complete the job, the following Journal entry (or its equivalent) would be made.

1. *Where stocks are maintained at standard cost.*

JOURNAL

| | | |
|---|---|---|
| Materials usage variance | Dr £3.00 | |
| To Raw Materials Account | | £3.00 |
| 4 kg of materials at standard cost (£0.75 per kg) used in excess of standard. | | |

2. *Where issues to production are priced at standard cost but stores accounts are maintained at actual cost.*

| | | |
|---|---|---|
| Materials usage variance | Dr £3.00 | |
| Materials price variance | 0.50 | |
| To Raw Materials Account | | £3.50 |
| Materials used in excess of standard, and price variance thereon. 4 kg at £0.875 per kg, the standard cost being £0.75 per kg. | | |

It may be instructive to consider the joint effect of the two foregoing variances, assuming Method 2, i.e. segregating variances at the time of issue to production, is adopted.

JOURNAL

| | | | |
|---|---|---|---|
| Work-in-Progress Account | Dr | £30.00 | |
| Standard quantity at standard price (40 kg at £0.75) | | | |
| Materials Price Variance Account | | 5.50 | |
| Standard use 40 kg | | | |
| Excess use      4 kg | | | |
| ‾‾ | | | |
| 44 kg at £0.125 | | | |
| | | | |
| Materials Usage Variance Account | | 3.00 | |
| Excess use at standard price (4 kg at £0.75) | | | |
| To Raw Materials Account | | | £38.50 |

## Isolating materials usage variance

A materials usage variance may arise from:

Quality of material.
Material handling by the operator.
Production methods.
Substituted materials.
Mixture of materials.

Segregation of the usage variance should be done as early as possible so that any necessary corrective action may be taken. Ideally, the material requisition should be prepared in advance of production and show the standard quantity required; should the operator require more, a special requisition authorising the additional issue is prepared. The authorising procedure should ensure that it is brought to the attention of the supervisor who can immediately investigate the reasons, and the cost department merely values the additional material and reports total variances periodically.

*EXAMPLE*

In the manufacture of plastic components, a scrap rate of 10 per cent of production is normally allowed. The weight of a finished component is 2 kg, and the number of components required for a particular order is 1,000.

The storekeeper must issue $1,000 \times 2$ kg = 2,000 kg to cover the basic requirements *plus* 200 kg to cover the normal scrap. If the operator returns for more material, an "excess requisition note" would be used. Alternatively, if some material were returned to store, it would be supported by a surplus requisition note indicating a favourable usage variance.

The ideal situation may not arise in practice because the processing method may be to put in a certain fixed quantity of material (perhaps to fill a processing tank) and output will vary according to operator handling, weather conditions, etc. In addition there may be a long process cycle so that the results of the process are not known until some considerable time after the time of input. Consequently, the usage variance can only be calculated at the end of the cycle.

Faced with different situations, the cost accountant must design a suitable system in order to calculate and report usage variances as quickly as possible.

A further difficulty that can arise in practice is in dealing with work-in-progress. Where the usage variance is isolated at the time of issue the problem can be overcome; i.e. work-in-progress is valued at standard. However, where the variance is only revealed at the end of the production cycle, the usage variance is only taken on the finished units, unless it is possible to evaluate the work-in-progress at standard costs.

## EXAMPLE

A small range of plastic components is produced in large quantities by a pressing shop. Sheets of plastic material are issued to each of several operators to produce as many components as possible. The operators cut out the components on a press and then carry out a finishing operation by smoothing the component with sandpaper. Finished components are taken from the operator at the end of each day and at any one time unpressed sheets of material and components in an unfinished form make up the work-in-progress. In the last week 50 batches of 100 sheets of material at £1 per sheet were issued to operators and 30 batches were finished in the week. The standard number of components per sheet is 10 and in the week 29,000 components were produced. The variance would be calculated as follows:

| | |
|---|---|
| Total issues of material (5,000 sheets) | £5,000 |
| *Less:* 20 batches of unfinished material in work-in-progress | 2,000 |
| Actual cost of finished components | 3,000 |
| Standard cost of components 29,000 × £0.10 | 2,900 |
| *Material usage variance* | £100(A) |

Any excess usage of material on the components not yet finished would not be revealed until the following week. If it were practicable to count the unfinished components remaining on the shop floor at the end of the week, as well as the sheets of uncut material, the usage variance could be isolated as it arose.

## EXAMPLE

Taking the facts from the previous example, but assuming the uncut sheets on the shop floor were 495 and there were 14,950 unfinished components, the usage variance would be calculated as follows:

| | |
|---|---|
| Total issues of material (5,000 sheets) | £5,000 |
| *Less:* Uncut sheets (495) | 495 |
| Total cut sheets | 4,505 |

Production: Finished components    29,000
             Unfinished components  14,950
                                    ───────
             Total                  43,950 at £0.10    4,395
                                                       ───────

*Material usage variance*                              £110(A)
                                                       ═══════

## DIRECT WAGES COST VARIANCES

As with direct materials, the direct wages cost variance comprises two major factors, price and quantity. The variances are termed "direct wages rate variance" and "direct labour efficiency variance" respectively.

Inefficiency in the use of materials arises when an excessive weight or quantity is consumed and, except from the point of view of interest on capital invested in stocks, the time factor does not apply. As wages paid are related to the time spent on a job or process, the efficiency of productive time, i.e. the amount of output per clock hour, is of the utmost importance. Not only can the hourly rate of pay vary and thus cause a rates of pay variance but the true value of the labour, measured in terms of output, can also vary from standard and give rise to an efficiency variance.

**Rate variance**
In building up a standard product cost, standard rates of pay must be assumed. It may, however, prove necessary to employ a more highly skilled worker than was originally envisaged, so that the actual cost of a clock hour will be greater than was anticipated. It might also be necessary for overtime to be worked in order to meet a delivery date, or the bonus element of the hourly or weekly rate might prove higher or lower than that allowed for in the standard. It is therefore necessary to segregate this variance in the same way as a materials price variance.

*EXAMPLE*
The standard for a particular job includes 40 hours of direct labour at a standard rate of £2 per hour, but the rate is subsequently increased to £2.20 per hour. The following Journal entry will be made:

JOURNAL

| | | | |
|---|---|---|---|
| Work-in-Progress Account | Dr | £80.00 | |
| Standard hours at standard rate (40 at £2) | | | |
| Direct Wages Rate Variance Account (40 at £0.20) | | 8.00 | |
| To Direct wages | | | £88.00 |
| (Actual payment for clock hours) | | | |

A rate variance also arises where employees are remunerated on a simple piece-work system if the piece-work price is increased or reduced.

When a number of operatives, who are of different grades and therefore receive different rates of pay, work as a team, an average direct labour rate is generally established as a standard for the team. If a member of the team is replaced by a higher or lower grade operative, a rate variance will arise. Unless such instances are likely to occur frequently and are significant, variances of this nature may be reported as part of the sub-analysis of rate variance by cause.

### Efficiency variance

Variances can arise if the rate of production, i.e. the efficiency of the factory, changes. Such changes can reflect: (a) alterations in the amount of effort each worker puts into his task; and, even more important, (b) the degree of administrative and organisational skill exercised by the management in providing good working conditions, e.g. a regular flow of work, proper machine maintenance and adequate lighting.

However caused, changes in the rate of production give rise to an efficiency variance. It will be observed that if in a working week of 40 hours an employee working at standard efficiency should produce 400 units the whole of his wages will be absorbed by that production. Any additional production, though charged to Production Account at a figure based on the standard wages cost, cannot be credited to Wages Account, and so gives rise to a favourable efficiency variance. Conversely, if his efficiency has diminished because only 350 units were produced in the week only $350 \div 400$ of his weekly wage can be charged to production. The wages cost of 50 units which, because of the reduced efficiency of the worker, cannot be charged to production must be written off as an adverse efficiency variance.

The increase or decrease in efficiency can be expressed in its time content, i.e. in a working week of 40 hours, the employee should produce 40 standard hours of production. The shortfall in production of 50 units therefore represents 5 standard hours $\left(50 \times \dfrac{40}{400}\right)$ and the value of the labour efficiency variance is calculated by multiplying the standard hours lost by the standard labour rate.

### Idle time

Generally, the standard time will incorporate an allowance for normal stoppages, e.g. setting up the machine, waiting for materials, calls of nature, etc., and it is impractical to attempt to identify variances due to such causes. Occasionally, however, idle time may occur through identifiable abnormal circumstances, for example, a power failure; the labour cost of abnormal idle time can be valued (hours lost at standard direct labour rate) and reported as a cause of the efficiency variance.

## Calculating wage cost variances
The tabulation method can be adopted to identify wage rate and labour efficiency variances.

*EXAMPLE*

The weekly budget prepared by the production controller of a machine shop is as follows:

|  | *Day work (40 hours)* |
|---|---|
| Four skilled operatives | 160 |
| Ten semi-skilled operatives | 400 |
|  | 560 hours |

Production: Product X 330 units at 1 hour each
Product Y 460 units at $\frac{1}{2}$ hour each

Wage-rates are £2.50 and £1.80 for skilled and semi-skilled operatives respectively. In week 39 you are presented with the following data:

Five skilled and nine semi-skilled operatives were paid £1,180 for a 40-hour week.
A power failure halted production for 2 hours.
Production was 300 of product X and 440 of product Y.

You are required to calculate the direct wage variances for week 39.
The first step is to calculate the standard direct wages rate for the machine shop:

| Budgeted wages: Skilled 160 hrs at £2.50 | £400 | |
|---|---|---|
| Semi-skilled 400 hrs at £1.80 | 720 | |
|  | —— | £1,120 |
|  | | |
| Budgeted standard hours: X − 330 at 1 hr | 330 | |
| Y − 460 at $\frac{1}{2}$ hr | 230 | |
|  | —— | 560 hours |
|  | | |
| Standard rate: | | £2.00 per hr |

The wages rate and efficiency variances can then be calculated:

| 1. Actual direct wages cost | £1,180 |
|---|---|
| Direct wages rate variance (1 − 2) | 60(A) |
|  | —— |
| 2. Actual hours at standard rates (14 × 40 × £2) | 1,120 |
| Direct labour efficiency variance (2 − 3) | 80(A) |
|  | —— |
| 3. Standard labour cost of production (300 × 1 hr + 440 × $\frac{1}{2}$ hr = 520 standard hours at £2) | £1,040 |

When variances are reported and commented on, two known causes can be evaluated from the information given:

1. The adverse rate variance includes £28 excess cost (40 hours at the difference between the hourly rates) caused by using a skilled man when a semi-skilled man would be adequate.
2. The adverse efficiency variance includes £56 of wasted labour cost (14 employees × 2 hours × £2 per hour) caused by the power failure. It must be assumed that the budget did not allow for such an occurrence.

## Isolating wages variances

The method of isolating wages variances depends on the type of business. Wage-rate variances can normally be obtained fairly easily by valuing the hours shown on the payroll at the standard wage-rate and deducting the standard from the actual gross wages payable. A report on wage-rate variances might be prepared as shown in Fig. 57.

### WAGES RATE REPORT
Finishing Dept.    Month.....................19........

| | Skilled men | | Semi-skilled men | | Female | | Apprentices | | Supervision | | Total | |
|---|---|---|---|---|---|---|---|---|---|---|---|---|
| | Hrs | £ | Hrs | £ | Hrs | £ | Hrs | £ | Hrs | £ | Hrs | £ |
| Normal time | | | | | | | | | | | | |
| Overtime | | | | | | | | | | | | |
| Bonus | | | | | | | | | | | | |
| Extra allowances | | | | | | | | | | | | |
| Gross pay | | | | | | | | | | | | |
| Standard rate per hour | | | | | | | | | | | | |
| Standard cost | | | | | | | | | | | | |
| Wage rate variance | | | | | | | | | | | | |

FIG. 57.—*Wages rate report.*

NOTES

1. The above hours and wages represent attendance time. Sick pay and holiday pay are excluded as they would normally be debited to an overhead account.

2. The standard wage rate would include a normal amount of overtime premium and bonus.

For a company which makes a few products from several processes the actual hours worked and the production achieved at each process centre are recorded and variances can be extracted for each process.

*EXAMPLE*

A packing station prepares selected farm produce for shipment abroad. There are three products A, B and C and each one passes through washing, grading and bagging operations. The standard times per 100 are as follows:

|  | A | B | C |
|---|---|---|---|
|  | Min. | Min. | Min. |
| Washing | 10 | 10 | 15 |
| Grading | 15 | 20 | 10 |
| Bagging | 10 | 10 | 12 |

Output for the week was 2,700 of product A, 3,300 of product B and 2,400 of product C. Actual times recorded at each operation were 1,550 hours for washing, 2,150 hours for grading and 1,700 hours for bagging. The standard wage-rate per hour for the station is £2.40. The efficiency variance could be reported as in Fig. 58.

**LABOUR EFFICIENCY REPORT**

Week ended...................

| | Production units | Washing hours | Grading hours | Bagging hours | Total hours |
|---|---|---|---|---|---|
| Product A | 2,700 | 450 | 675 | 450 | 1,575 |
| Product B | 3,300 | 550 | 1,100 | 550 | 2,200 |
| Product C | 2,400 | 600 | 400 | 480 | 1,480 |
| | | | | | |
| Total standard hours | | 1,600 | 2,175 | 1,480 | 5,255 |
| Actual hours | | 1,550 | 2,150 | 1,700 | 5,400 |
| Hours lost/gained | | 50 | 25 | (220) | (145) |
| Efficiency variance | | £120(F) | £60(F) | £528(A) | £348(A) |

FIG. 58.—*Labour efficiency report.*

The reasons for the excess number of hours in the bagging operation would need to be established. If a record were kept of time lost through, say, machine breakdown or lack of materials, etc., hours lost could be evaluated and included in the report.

In a company engaged in jobbing manufacture, e.g. specialised electrical fittings, the costing system would normally be more complex. Products may be manufactured in small batches and employees may work on several different batches during the course of a day. The time record, on which the employee enters the time worked on each batch would be used to evaluate the standard hours of production of each day. The evaluation would need to be done by experienced clerks working with a manual giving details of machine times and allowances for special types of work. The time record might then be used to prepare the payroll and also by the cost department to evaluate standard cost and report on the variances. A suitable ruling would be as shown in Fig. 59.

**TIME SHEET**

Department:................................ Week ended:...........................

Machine group:........................... Employee No.:........................

Employee's name:...........................................................................

| Job No. | Description | Quantity | Time started | Time finished | Total time | Standard time |
|---------|-------------|----------|--------------|---------------|------------|---------------|
|         |             |          |              |               |            |               |
|         |             |          |              |               |            |               |
|         |             |          |              |               |            |               |
|         |             |          |              |               |            |               |
|         |             |          |              |               |            |               |

FIG. 59.—*Typical time sheet.*

A time sheet used in this way becomes a very important control document. The efficiency variance, i.e. the difference between the actual time and standard time, can be summarised by department, machine group, employee, job number or product type. One problem, of course, is the volume of paperwork to be handled and in order to summarise the information some form of high-speed data-processing equipment is often required.

## VARIABLE OVERHEAD VARIANCES

Variable production overhead is that which, in the aggregate, tends to vary in direct proportion to changes in the volume of output. Some of the items comprising variable overhead are power, steam and compressed air for the process, coolants and lubricants for machines, consumable items like small tools, cleaning rag, protective clothing, etc. It is obvious that factors other than volume of output can influence the cost of the above items but, when the standard product cost is developed, the various influencing factors need to be reconciled so that a standard rate of variable overhead *per unit* can be established. Consequently, when analysing the variance, the actual total of variable overhead is compared with the amount expected for the *actual* volume of output; both actual and plan are related to the same volume of output and, therefore, only prices can vary. Thus, it is considered that only an expenditure variance needs to be calculated; any additional information can be obtained by analysing variations in individual items of variable overhead.

## Variable production overhead expenditure variance

The prices of items comprising variable overhead may change and cause an expenditure variance. Since variable overhead is expected to fluctuate with activity the actual expenditure must be compared with an allowance related to the actual volume of output in the period.

*EXAMPLE*

Budgeted variable overhead for a factory was £10,000 each month and budgeted production was 2,000 units. In June, actual production was 2,750 units and actual variable overhead £14,500. Since variable overhead is expected to rise with production, the expenditure variance is calculated by deducting the allowed overhead from the actual overhead:

| | |
|---|---:|
| Actual variable overhead | £14,500 |
| Allowed overhead $\dfrac{£10,000}{2,000} \times 2,750 =$ | 13,750 |
| Variable production overhead expenditure variance | £750(A) |

## Efficiency variance

It has been mentioned that a standard cost will include some items of variable overhead based on the rate of working of a machine or an employee. Where the actual rate of working differs from the standard an efficiency variance can be calculated, because it is assumed that the overhead has been incurred in proportion to the hours spent on production rather than to the output achieved.

*EXAMPLE*

Using the figures from the previous example and assuming that (*a*) all the items included as variable overhead are expected to vary with machining time; (*b*) that each unit requires 10 hours of machining time, and (*c*) that the actual hours worked were 26,000, the following statement can be prepared:

| | | Hours | £ |
|---|---|---:|---:|
| (i) | Actual variable expenditure | 26,000 | 14,500 |
| | Expenditure variance (ii)–(i) | — | 1,500(A) |
| (ii) | Allowed variable expenditure on actual hours | 26,000 | 13,000 |
| | Efficiency variance (iii)–(ii) | 1,500 | 750(F) |
| (iii) | Standard variable overhead value of production | 27,500 | £13,750 |

The standard variable overhead rate per hour:

$$\frac{\text{Budgeted overhead}}{\text{Budgeted hours}} = \frac{£10,000}{2,000 \times 10} = £0.50$$

The efficiency variance is a memorandum calculation which attempts to sub-analyse the expenditure variance by indicating the effect on variable production overhead of changes in production efficiency. It would only be prepared at the specific request of management. A great deal depends on the items included in the classification "variable", which may be somewhat arbitrary and there is little value in working to an unreal precision.

### Overhead utilisation variance

In a production department a number of services will be required, e.g. steam, power, compressed air. In a business using standard costing, services will be charged to the production departments at the standard rate per unit of service used. The cost of services will be included in the overhead budget of the department, and when analysing the expenditure variance it may be possible to separate the excess utilisation of services as a controllable variance.

## FIXED PRODUCTION OVERHEAD VARIANCES

### Fixed production overhead volume variance

The fixed production overhead volume variance is the difference between the standard fixed overhead absorbed in production achieved and the budgeted fixed overhead for a specific control period. The volume variance together with the expenditure variance comprises the overhead variance.

Fixed production overhead represents the cost of the production organisation or establishment. It is budgeted in total and then apportioned over the budgeted production to arrive at a standard absorption rate per production unit. In contrast, variable expenses are normally compiled in the reverse direction, i.e. the totals are computed by multiplying the cost per unit (based on the specification) by the budgeted production.

The costs of the organisation are thus made to fit each unit of production but this fit is exact only if the budget is exactly attained. If output falls short, variable costs abate in proportion but fixed costs remain constant, and it may therefore be said that the organisation, and hence its costs, are excessive in relation to the diminished output, i.e. there are unused machines, space and facilities, and, in theory, less fully occupied supervisors and managers. Such unrecouped fixed costs may be substantial.

Conversely, if production exceeds budget, overhead will be over-recouped; in other words, the excess production will in effect be achieved without any charge for fixed overhead. The amount by which the budgeted fixed overhead is unrecouped or over-recouped (over- or under-absorbed), is termed the volume variance.

*EXAMPLE*

Production is budgeted at 10,000 standard hours and fixed overhead at £2,000. Compute the standard fixed overhead cost per standard hour and the overhead over- or under-recouped if production (*a*) increases to 11,000, (*b*) falls to 9,500.

Fixed overhead per standard hour: $\frac{£2,000}{10,000} = £0.20$

| | | |
|---|---|---:|
| (*a*) | Budgeted fixed overhead | £2,000 |
| | Recoverable from production | |
| | 11,000 × £0.20 | 2,200 |
| | Volume variance | £200(F) |
| (*b*) | Budgeted fixed overhead | 2,000 |
| | Recoverable from production | |
| | 9,500 × £0.20 | 1,900 |
| | Volume variance | £100(A) |

In the above example reasons for the changes in production output are not given, and it is therefore not possible to sub-analyse the volume variance.

The changes in production output may arise from any or all of the following factors:

1. Hours worked, and hence the effective capacity of the factory, may have altered due to:

(*a*) Short time or overtime working.

(*b*) The working of more or fewer shifts.

(*c*) A change in the number of days in the period, compared with budget, due to calendar vagaries, or public holidays.

(*d*) A variation in idle time, temporary shortages of work, power cuts, and the like, compared with that allowed for in the budget.

2. Greater or less efficiency, viz. a change in the rate of production.

3. A combination of any of the causes in 1 with 2. For example, fewer hours may have been worked, though the rate of production per hour has increased.

The fixed overhead volume variance, therefore, can be subdivided into two main components:

(*a*) Capacity: the value, at standard, of additional or less working hours available.

(*b*) Productivity: the value, at standard, of increased or reduced production output in the working hours available.

In most production organisations, separate fixed overhead absorption rates (and variances) are prepared by budget centres. Management would need to consider, therefore, whether any further analysis of the volume variance is justified by its value as information.

The above sub-variances, and the fixed overhead expenditure variance, (the difference between actual and budgeted fixed overhead for a period) will now be dealt with in detail.

## Fixed production overhead expenditure variance

The expenditure variance represents the difference between budgeted fixed overhead for a specific control period and the amount of actual fixed expenditure attributed and charged to that period. It may be due to inaccurate budgeting (e.g. the omission of an item) or an unforeseen change in price.

Using the previous example, if actual fixed overhead for the period amounted to £2,400 then the expenditure variance would be £400 adverse, whether actual production was 9,500, 10,000 or 11,000 standard hours. The *control period* is unaltered even though output may vary.

Individual expenditure variances would be calculated for each budget centre and any further sub-analysis would normally be restricted to identifying the items of overhead cost which show significant changes compared to budget.

## Capacity variance

The capacity of a department or factory is expressed in terms of those hours which could result in production. That is to say, if 10,000 productive hours are budgeted for but only 7,500 are worked the capacity of the factory in the budget period has diminished by one-quarter. Accordingly, one-quarter of the time available to recoup fixed overhead is lost and can be valued at the absorption rate to arrive at an adverse capacity variance.

In general terms, the fixed overhead capacity variance is arrived at by multiplying the standard fixed overhead rate per hour by the difference between the budgeted and actual hours worked. If reference is now made to the previous example and it is assumed that hours worked have altered to 11,000 and 9,500 respectively, it will be seen that the variance can be arrived at as follows:

(a) Excess hours:
$$11,000 - 10,000 = 1,000$$
Capacity variance: 1,000 at £0.20      £200(F)

(b) Deficient hours:
$$10,000 - 9,500 = 500$$
Capacity variance: 500 at £0.20      £100(A)

In other words, the whole of the variances are attributable to changes in capacity, because the hours worked are equal to the standard hours produced, i.e. standard productivity has been achieved.

It will be noted that the variances may also be arrived at by proportion. In example (a) production has increased by 10 per cent, so the variance is 10 per cent of the budgeted overhead figure or £200.

The value of the capacity variance is calculated by multiplying hours gained or lost by the standard absorption rate. Similarly, a value, in terms of fixed overhead absorption, may be placed on any known factors which contribute to the capacity variance, e.g. overtime, shiftwork, machine breakdown, by valuing the hours gained or lost from such factors.

**Productivity variance**

Fixed overhead absorbed represents the overhead charge appropriate to the standard hours of production. If actual production in standard hours is different from hours actually worked, a change in the rate of production, i.e. a change in productivity, has occurred. Accordingly, the fixed overhead productivity variance can be measured by multiplying the excess or deficiency of production in standard hours by the overhead absorption rate. If reference is once more made to the example on page 258 and it is assumed that the hours worked have remained at 10,000 while production has (a) increased and (b) decreased, the variances can be arrived at as follows:

(a) Excess production
    11,000 − 10,000 = 1,000 standard hours
    Productivity variance 1,000 at £0.20                            £200(F)

(b) Deficient production
    10,000 − 9,500 = 500 standard hours
    Productivity variance 500 at £0.20                              £100(A)

In other words, the whole of the volume variance is due to changes in productivity, as there has been no change in the hours worked.

**Fixed overhead variances summarised**

A fixed overhead rate per hour is determined by the following budgeted data:

1. Level of expenditure in period.
2. Productive hours.
3. Units produced per hour.

The above factors are considered therefore when analysing the fixed overhead variance and the analysis can be prepared in the form of a statement, illustrated by the following example:

*EXAMPLE*

A factory prepares its monthly fixed overhead budget by taking one-twelfth of the annual budget (£34,560). The average number of working days in a month is 20 and the factory employs 15 operators who normally work an 8-hour day. Unproductive time is budgeted at 20 per cent. One product is made and the standard production rate is 2 units per hour. The standard fixed overhead absorption rate has therefore been calculated as follows:

$$\frac{\text{Budgeted overhead}}{\text{Budgeted output}} = \frac{£34,560}{12 \times 20 \times 15 \times 8 \times \frac{80}{100}} = £1.50 \text{ per hour}$$

In the month of June the following information is available:

| | |
|---|---|
| Hours paid | 2,350 |
| Unproductive hours | 400 |
| Production | 3,600 units |
| Fixed overhead | £3,050 |

| | Hours | Units | £ |
|---|---:|---:|---:|
| Actual fixed overhead | | | 3,050 |
|   Expenditure variance | | | 170(A) |
| Budgeted overhead | 1,920 | 3,840 | 2,880 |
|   Capacity variance | 30 | 60 | 45(F) |
| Overhead absorbed on hours worked | 1,950 | 3,900 | 2,925 |
|   Productivity variance | | 300 | 225(A) |
| Overhead absorbed in production | | 3,600 | £2,700 |

NOTE:

(*i*) As a single product is manufactured, the overhead absorption rate can be expressed as £0.75 per unit.

(*ii*) Production of 3,600 units represents 1,800 standard hours, i.e. 150 standard hours of production were lost through lower productivity.

(*iii*) The volume variance comprises capacity plus productivity and represents the difference between budgeted overhead and overhead absorbed in production.

(*iv*) Unproductive time was 17 per cent $\left(\frac{400}{2,350}\right)$ compared to budget of 20 per cent and is a cause of the favourable capacity variance. Alternatively, standard unproductive time may be reflected in the production rate which would be for 2 units to be produced in 1 hour $\times \frac{100}{80}$. The absorption rate then becomes £1.20 per standard hour and the difference in unproductive time would be reflected in the productivity variance.

## Accounting for overhead variances

Standard overhead absorption rates are generally established for each budget centre and, therefore, it is appropriate to account for variances in the same way. Actual fixed and variable overhead incurred is charged to a budget centre overhead account, which is credited with the overhead absorbed in production at the standard rate (charged to W.I.P. or Finished stock). The difference on the overhead account thus represents the total overhead cost variance, which can then be analysed as required and cleared by distribution to individual variance accounts.

The expenditure variance will usually be subject to additional analysis to identify the major items of cost making up the variance.

## SALES VARIANCES

### Sales volume variance

The sales variance, or to give it its full title, the Operating Profit Variance Due to Sales, comprises a price variance and a volume variance. Referring back to the Operating Profit Statement in Chapter 10, it is evident that, when comparing actual sales with the sales budget, additional revenue obtained from an increase in the volume sold will be offset by additional production costs incurred to produce the extra volume. Similarly, an adverse sales volume variance in terms of sales value will be partly compensated for by a favourable cost of sales variance.

To simplify analysis, the sales volume variance is based on the standard margin, i.e. standard selling price less standard production cost per unit. Any difference between actual and standard production costs of sales will, of course, be accounted for as cost variances.

### EXAMPLE

The GHQ Company budget is to sell 1,000 tanks per month at the standard selling price of £100. The standard production cost is £60 per unit. 1,100 tanks were sold in May at standard selling price.
The Sales volume variance is:

| | |
|---|---:|
| Actual sales at standard margin (1,100 × 40) | £44,000 |
| Budgeted sales at standard margin (1,000 × 40) | 40,000 |
| Operating profit variance due to sales volume | £4,000(F) |

### Sales price variance

The sales price variance (full title, Operating Profit Variance Due to Selling Prices) is calculated by multiplying the actual units sold by the difference between the actual and standard selling price. In the previous example, if actual sales revenue for May were £107,000, the sales price variance represents:

|  |  |  |
|---|---|---|
| 1. | Actual sales at actual prices (1,100 units) | £107,000 |
|  | Sales price variance (1 − 2) | 3,000(A) |
| 2. | Actual sales at standard prices (1,100 × £100) | £110,000 |

The variance is reported in full as a reduction to the budgeted operating profit; the additional margin expected on the 100 units sold in excess of plan will be accounted for in the volume variance.

## Sales variances in a multi-product organisation

For a business which markets a variety of products, management will often be provided with a comprehensive report on the variances from plan in this important area, an example of which is shown in Fig. 60.

| SALES VARIANCE REPORT | | | | | | | |
|---|---|---|---|---|---|---|---|
| Quantities and values in '000s | | | | | | | |
| Product | Volume | | Revenue | | Margin variance | | |
|  | Actual | Budget | Actual | Budget | Total | Price | Volume |
| Washing machines | 420 | 460 | 78.1 | 88.7 | (6.5) | 1.1 | (7.6) |
| Dish washers | 260 | 240 | 61.2 | 58.0 | 2.2 | (1.4) | 3.6 |
| Refrigerators | 340 | 390 | 41.4 | 52.8 | (10.7) | 1.3 | (12.0) |
| TOTALS | 1,020 | 1,090 | 180.7 | 199.5 | (15.0) | 1.0 | (16.0) |

Fig. 60.—*Sales variance report.*

The report in Fig. 60 is a summary which could be supported by subsidiary statements analysing product groups by model and/or sub-analysing variances, as required.

For most management purposes, analysis of the sales price variance by cause (e.g. price concessions, quantity discounts) and analysis of the volume variance by type of customer or by geographical location is considered appropriate. In certain circumstances, however, it may be informative to assess the effect of deviating from the budgeted mixture of sales. Calculation of a mixture variance, however, is arbitrary and implies that sales of different products are inter-dependent.

A discussion of ways of calculating a mixture variance can be dispensed with at this stage but, to illustrate the possible relevance, Fig. 60 shows a total sales volume variance of £16,000 adverse which includes a favourable variance on dishwashers. It is unlikely that sales of the other two products were affected by increased sales of dishwashers but, if the three products were, say, different models of dishwasher then an increase in sales of one model could adversely affect sales of another. The models could have different margin rates and, although total units sold were as plan, total margin would differ because different proportions of each model were sold. Management may consider that, in such a situation, calculation of the effect on profit of deviating from the budgeted mixture of model sales is useful information.

## AN ILLUSTRATIVE EXAMPLE

It may be informative to summarise variance analysis by working through a simplified example, to show how the information is developed into an Operating Profit Statement.

*EXAMPLE*

Toadies Ltd. manufacture a single product, the Sniveller, which has a standard cost of:

| | | |
|---|---|---:|
| Direct materials: | 15 kg    at £1.20 per kg | £18 |
| Direct labour: | 5 hours at £2.40 per hour | 12 |
| Variable overhead: | 5 hours at £1.60 per hour | 8 |
| Fixed overhead: | 5 hours at £3.20 per hour | 16 |
| | | £54 |
| | Standard selling price | £66 |

The monthly budget for Toadies represents:

| | |
|---|---|
| Production and Sales | 2,500 units |
| Direct Labour | 12,500 hours |
| Fixed overhead | £40,000 |
| Variable overhead | £20,000 |

At the beginning of April, finished stock was 2,000 units. Work-in-progress is negligible and can be ignored. Actual data for April follows:

Sales: 2,400 units at £65 each. Production Output: 2,600 units
Direct materials used: 40,000 kg at £1.24 per kg
Direct wages: 13,200 hours at £2.34 per hour
Variable overhead: £22,000
Fixed overhead: £41,000

The accounting system for Toadies Ltd. includes a Work-in-Progress Account, a Finished Goods Account and a Total Variance Account. The Work-in-Progress Account is debited with actual costs and credited with completed production at standard. The Total Variance Account is analysed to prepare the Operating Profit Statement.

Prepare the ledger accounts and the Operating Profit Statement for April.

*Work-in-Progress Account*

| Direct materials: | | | Finished stock: | |
|---|---|---|---|---|
| 40,000 at £1.24 | £49,600 | | 2,600 at £54 | £140,400 |
| Direct wages: | | | Variance Account | |
| 13,200 at £2.34 | 30,888 | | (balance) | 3,088 |
| Variable overhead | 22,000 | | | |
| Fixed overhead | 41,000 | | | |
| | £143,488 | | | £143,488 |

*Finished Goods Account*

| Opening stock b/fwd: | | | Cost of sales: | |
|---|---|---|---|---|
| 2,000 at £54 | £108,000 | | 2,400 at £54 | £129,600 |
| Work-in-Progress | 140,400 | | Closing stock c/fwd | |
| | | | (balance) | 118,800 |
| | £248,400 | | | £248,400 |

The balance represents units in stock (Opening 2,000 + Production 2,600 − Sales 2,400) at standard cost per unit.

*Variance Account*

| Work-in-Progress | | | Profit and Loss (suitably | |
|---|---|---|---|---|
| | £3,088 | | analysed) | £3,088 |

*Analysis of Variances*

| | | |
|---|---|---|
| 1. Actual sales (2,400 at £65) | £156,000 | |
| Sales price variance (1 − 2) | 2,400(A) | |
| | | |
| 2. Actual units at standard selling price (2,400 × £66) | 158,400 | |
| 3. Actual units sold at standard cost (2,400 × £54) | 129,600 | |
| | | |
| 4. Standard margin on actual sales (2,400 × £12) | 28,800 | |
| Sales volume variance | 1,200(A) | |
| | | |
| 5. Budgeted margin (2,500 × £12) | £30,000 | |
| | | |
| 6. Actual cost of direct materials used | 49,600 | |
| Direct materials price variance (7 − 6) | 1,600(A) | |
| | | |
| 7. Actual materials used at std. price (40,000 × £1.20) | 48,000 | |
| Direct materials usage variance (8 − 7) | 1,200(A) | |
| | | |
| 8. Std. material cost of production (2,600 × 15 × £1.20) | £46,800 | |

| | | |
|---|---|---|
| 9. Actual direct wages cost | | 30,888 |
| *Direct wages rate variance* (10 − 9) | | 792 (F) |
| | | |
| 10. Actual hours at standard rate (13,200 × £2,40) | | 31,680 |
| *Direct labour efficiency variance* (11 − 10) | | 480 (A) |
| | | |
| 11. Std. wages cost of production (2,600 × 5 × £2.40) | | £31,200 |
| | | |
| 12. Actual variable overhead for April | | 22,000 |
| *Variable production overhead variance* (13 − 12) | | 1,200 (A) |
| | | |
| 13. Variable overhead absorbed (2,600 × £8) | | £20,800 |
| | | |
| 14. Actual fixed overhead for April | | 41,000 |
| *Fixed overhead expenditure variance* (15 − 14) | | 1,000 (A) |
| | | |
| 15. Budgeted fixed overhead for April | | 40,000 |
| *Capacity variance* (16 − 15) | | 2,240 (F) |
| | | |
| 16. Fixed overhead absorbed on hours worked (13,200 × £3.20) | | 42,240 |
| *Productivity variance* (17 − 16) | | 640 (A) |
| | | |
| 17. Fixed overhead absorbed in production (2,600 × £16) | | £41,600 |

NOTE:

(*i*) (A) = Adverse        (F) = Favourable.

(*ii*) Fixed overhead volume variance =

| | |
|---|---|
| Capacity | 2,240 (F) |
| Productivity | 640 (A) |
| | £1,600 (F) |

(*iii*) The sum of the cost variances (items 6 to 17) is £3,088 adverse, the balance on Total Variance Account.

### OPERATING PROFIT STATEMENT

| | |
|---|---|
| Budgeted sales: 2,500 units at £66 | £165,000 |
| *Less:* standard cost of budgeted sales: | |
| 2,500 units at £54 | 135,000 |
| | |
| Budgeted margin | 30,000 |
| Sales volume variance | 1,200 (A) |
| | |
| Standard margin on actual sales | 28,800 |

| Variances | Adv. | Fav. |
|---|---|---|
| Selling prices | £2,400 | |
| Material prices | 1,600 | |
| Wage rates | | £792 |
| Overhead expenditure: Fixed | 1,000 | |
| Variable | 1,200 | |
| Material usage | 1,200 | |
| Labour efficiency | 480 | |
| Fixed overhead volume | | 1,600 |
| | 7,880 | 2,392 |
| | | 5,488(A) |
| Actual margin | | £23,312 |

NOTE: Marketing and administration costs for the month would be deducted to arrive at Operating profit.

The Profit Statement discloses that margin for the month is about £6,700 less than planned, arising mainly from a reduction in selling price and increases in material and overhead costs. The situation would have been worse but for the fact that fixed overhead was absorbed on 200 units carried forward in stock and, as stocks cannot be increased indefinitely, the fixed overhead absorbed will be charged against profit in subsequent months when the stock is sold.

The Profit Statement will assist management by indicating the main areas which require attention; additional information will probably be requested so that the cause of and responsibility for specific variances can be identified. On the basis of such information, management will attempt to correct any undesirable trends and/or adjust future plans.

The introduction to the example indicated that the procedure was simplified and the student may find it useful to refer back to earlier examples to examine the effect of different treatment in the accounts and analysis.

## ADDITIONAL MATTERS RELATIVE TO VARIANCE ANALYSIS

It is hoped that the chapters on Budgetary Control, Standard Costing and Variance Analysis will have provided the reader with a general understanding of the principles, procedures and techniques involved in accounting for differences between actual and planned business activities. Before departing from the subject, however, a few additional points may merit brief explanation.

### Marketing and general administration costs

The illustrative example dealt with variances from planned margin and ended with Actual margin for the period. To arrive at Operating profit, Marketing and General administration costs are deducted.

In a variance accounting system, such costs are controlled against a budget and the difference between actual and budget for the period is disclosed in the Profit Statement in the following way:

| | | | | |
|---|---|---|---|---|
| Actual margin | | | | £23,312 |
| *Less:* | *Budget* | *Variance* | *Actual* | |
| Marketing | 4,000 | 350(A) | 4,350 | |
| General Admin. | 5,000 | 220(F) | 4,780 | |
| | | — — | | 9,130 |
| | Operating profit | | | £14,182 |

Analysis of the period variance usually takes the form of separate statements for each budget centre showing variances by cost item or by groups of associated costs.

In many businesses, marketing costs will include a significant amount of variable items, e.g. packing and transportation. Thus, a flexible budget can be assessed in relation to such items and the Marketing Cost Budget (and variance) separated into its fixed and variable constituents. The flexible budget is related to the actual volume of *sales* obtained.

## Analysis of material usage variance
In certain types of process industries, a finished product is obtained by blending a number of different input materials. The standard product cost will reflect the recommended proportion of each type of material necessary to produce a product of suitable quality at minimum cost but an adequate product could be obtained even though the standard mixture of materials is not adhered to. In such instances, the cost of deviating from standard can be calculated as useful information.

*EXAMPLE*
Washup is a soap solution made from two ingredients—Sope and Suds. The standard specification for 100 litres of Washup is:
> 60 litres of Sope at £3
> 40 litres of Suds at £6

In the month, 100 litres of Washup were made from 50 litres of Sope and 50 litres of Suds due to a shortage of Sope. The product was acceptable, being a much higher grade than normal production, and material prices were as standard.

A mix variance of £30 arises because of the increased usage of the expensive ingredient and decreased usage of the cheaper ingredient:
> Variance in usage of Sope $= (60 - 50) \times £3 = £30$ (F)
> Variance in usage of Suds $= (40 - 50) \times £6 = £60$ (A)

| | |
|---|---|
| Total variance | £30(A) |

It should be noted that the total input of material—100 litres—has not varied from standard. A mix variance arises with a change in the usage of a mixture of ingredients each of which has a different price. More importantly, a mix variance only arises when input ingredients are more or less interchangeable. When, for example, a door is constructed from a plank of wood, two hinges and a handle, the material usage variance represents the sum of the variances on the individual components, as a hinge could not be used in place of a handle.

In the standard mentioned in the example above, there was an assumption that no loss was expected. There are many instances, however, where a loss is anticipated, already explained in the section on normal losses in Chapter 8. If this is so, the output from a given input of material is termed a yield and may be expressed in the form of a percentage of the input. The first thing to note is that the standard cost of the product is increased.

*EXAMPLE*

In a canning process 8 one-litre cans of the product are obtained from 10 litres of the original liquid, owing to unavoidable spillage. The price of the liquid is £4 per litre.

If the loss of 2 litres is ignored the standard cost of the liquid in the can is £4. However, if, as is likely, the loss is included in the standard cost, it increases it to £5, i.e.

$$\frac{\text{Total standard cost}}{\text{Standard output}} = \frac{£4 \times 10}{8} = £5$$

If in the month the yield is 6 litres from every 10 litres of input, the adverse yield variance of 2 litres has cost $2 \times £5 = £10$.

It is important to note that the difference in yield is multiplied by the standard cost rate, not the original material price. The similarity of yield variances with abnormal gains or losses in process costing will be apparent.

## Budget revision variance

When a standard cost is revised during the currency of a budget period and the budget is not adjusted, a budget revision variance (the difference between the basic and the revised standard cost multiplied by the budgeted quantity for the period) is calculated so that the effect of the change in standard can be clearly disclosed when actual profit is compared with budgeted profit.

## Stock valuation revision variance

An inherent principle of variance accounting is that stock values are maintained at standard cost. When the standard cost is revised, a difference arises from the revaluation of stocks and work-in-progress at the commencement of a period.

Subsequent actual costs will be compared with the revised standard and, therefore, the stock valuation revision variance will be charged or credited to profit and loss in the period(s) during which the stock is sold.

## Variances on work-in-progress

In many businesses, work-in-progress is of significant value and subject to fluctuation and it is therefore inadequate to relate total costs to completed output only.

Work-in-progress may be capable of being expressed in terms of equivalent whole units of output, as examined in Chapter 8, or the standard value of work-in-progress assessed and the fluctuation between the opening and closing standard value added to or deducted from the standard cost of completed output.

## Standard marginal costing

So far, Variance Accounting has been considered in relation to Standard Absorption Costing. The application of marginal costing principles to variance accounting may be usefully left till the next chapter.

### SELF-STUDY TEST No. 9

*Analysis of Variances*

(*Refer to the Appendix on p. 362 for outline solutions.*)

1. The standard direct cost of product A is:

> Materials 2 kg at £1.25 per kg.
> Wages 10 mins. at £2.40 per hour.

Calculate the variances in materials price, materials usage, wages rate and labour efficiency in a period when: 420 units of A were produced; 860 kg of material were used at a cost of £1,030; and 72 hours of labour were worked at a cost of £180.

2. Name, and explain briefly, two possible causes of each of the four variances calculated in (1) above.

3. Give two examples of how the causes of one variance could have an effect on another variance.

4. In department X the following data is submitted for the week ended February 20:

| | |
|---|---|
| Standard output for 40-hour week | 1,400 units |
| Standard fixed overhead | £14,000 |
| Actual output | 1,200 units |
| Actual hours worked | 32 |
| Actual fixed overhead | £15,000 |

Calculate expenditure and volume variances and analyse the volume variance between capacity and productivity.

5. Name, and explain briefly, two possible causes of each variance calculated in (4), i.e. expenditure, capacity and productivity.

6. The sales budget of Stancost Ltd. for the month of October was as follows:

| Product | Quantity | Standard selling price, each | Standard sales | Standard margin on budgeted sales |
|---------|----------|------------------------------|----------------|-----------------------------------|
| A | 10,000 | £1.00 | £10,000 | £1,000 |
| B | 4,000 | 1.50 | 6,000 | 1,000 |
|   |        |       | £16,000 | £2,000 |

The actual sales in October were:

| Product | Quantity | Actual selling price | Actual sales |
|---------|----------|----------------------|--------------|
| A | 10,500 | £1.10 | £11,550 |
| B | 5,000 | £1.70 | 8,500 |
|   |        |       | £20,050 |

Reconcile Budgeted Margin with Actual Margin for the month, disclosing sales price and volume variances. Assume actual costs are as standard.

7. The following standard cost details apply to a manufactured product which has a standard selling price of £60 per unit:

| | |
|---|---|
| Raw materials 15 kg at £1.20 per kg | £18.00 |
| Direct wages 6 hours at £1.80 per hr | 10.80 |
| Fixed production overhead 6 hours at £2.70 per hr | 16.20 |
| | £45.00 |

Raw materials stock is maintained at standard price. Work-in-progress is charged at standard material prices, standard wage rates and budgeted overhead. Completed production is charged to finished goods account at standard cost.

The details which follow relate to the period under review:

| | |
|---|---|
| Opening Stock | |
| Materials | 18,000 kg |
| Finished product | 2,000 units |
| Work-in-progress | Nil |
| Budgeted sales and production output | 3,000 units |
| Budgeted overhead | £48,600 |
| Budgeted direct labour hours | 18,000 |
| Actual output of finished product (no closing W.I.P.) | 3,400 units |
| Actual sales | 4,500 units |

Purchases of raw materials: 60,000 kg at £1.22 per kg
Raw material usage: 54,000 kg
Direct wages: 20,550 hours at £1.84 per hour
Actual overhead. £49,560

You are required to:

(a) prepare journal entries for the transactions detailed above;
(b) show the ledger accounts for raw materials, work-in-progress and finished stock;
(c) prepare an Operating Profit Statement for the period.

8. Explain: (a) Revision variance; (b) Stock revaluation variance.

# CHAPTER 12

# Relevant Costs

## INTRODUCTION

Previous chapters have tended to emphasise the procedures involved in compiling and assembling cost information. It is now opportune to examine the ways in which cost information can be presented so that its relevance to the needs of management is recognised.

In this chapter we will mainly examine the principle of Marginal Costing and the technique of Differential Costing and discuss their usefulness in helping to solve business problems. The focal point, however, is the recognition of the way costs will behave in relation to changes in the form or volume of business activity.

## COST BEHAVIOUR

The problems which arise when an attempt is made to relate fixed costs to varying levels of production have been referred to in a previous chapter and it must be remembered that the term "fixed" is used to indicate that the expenses so classified are fixed only in relation to production; they are by no means fixed in relation to time and in fact they tend to vary in relation to the length of the period covered.

Before production can begin, an organisation of some kind must be set up. Premises must be purchased and a nucleus of supervisory and executive staff engaged, the cost of which will endure as long as the undertaking continues and which will tend to be constant, or fixed, whatever level of output is achieved. A fixed expense is one which varies, not in relation to production but in relation to the passage of time. For this reason they are sometimes referred to as period costs.

When production begins, other costs will arise: raw material must be purchased, power costs incurred and labour engaged. Those items (allowing for fluctuations in raw material stocks) will tend to vary in direct ratio to output and are termed "variable costs". Their amount is conditioned not by the size of the organisation but (within the limits of the factory) by the volume of production.

At this stage it may be useful to refer to the I.C.M.A. definitions of fixed cost, variable cost and marginal cost.

*Fixed cost.* A cost which accrues in relation to the passage of time and which, within certain output or turnover limits, tends to be unaffected by fluctuations in volume of output or turnover. Examples are rent, rates, insurance and executive salaries.

*Variable cost.* A cost which, in the aggregate, tends to vary in direct proportion to changes in the volume of output or turnover.

*Marginal cost.* The variable cost of one unit of a product or a service; i.e. a cost which would be avoided if the unit was not produced or provided.

NOTE: in this context a unit is usually either a single article or a standard measure such as the gallon (or litre), pound weight (or kilogram) etc., but may in certain circumstances be an operation, process or part of an organisation.

In most circumstances, marginal cost may be regarded as equivalent to total variable cost, as within the capacity of the organisation, an increase of production of one unit will cause an increase in the variable costs only, fixed costs remaining constant. For example, if variable costs per unit are £5 and fixed expenses are £1,000 per annum, an output of 500 articles per annum results in the following expenditure:

| | |
|---|---|
| Variable costs 500 × £5 | £2,500 |
| Fixed costs | 1,000 |
| Total costs | £3,500 |

If production is increased by one unit, i.e. to 501 articles per annum, the following expenditure is necessary:

| | |
|---|---|
| Variable costs 501 × £5 | £2,505 |
| Fixed costs | 1,000 |
| | 3,505 |
| *Less*: Total costs for output of 500 units | 3,500 |
| Marginal cost of one unit | £5 |

If the maximum capacity of the factory was 500 units per annum, the additional unit could only be produced by incurring additional fixed costs, say by purchasing additional machinery at a cost of £250. Accordingly the marginal cost of the additional unit would be £5 + £250 = £255. This example illustrates an important feature of the incidence of costs, which is that the variability of a cost depends upon whether it represents a commodity, or service, which can be purchased and used in small units. Most factors of production must be acquired in specific quantities, e.g. an employee providing 40 man-hours per week. If the employer can only provide regular weekly work for 30 hours then he incurs a fixed weekly labour cost which is not being fully utilised. Furthermore some factors of production are capable of a considerable range of work dependent upon the demands made on them. Thus the output from an employee depends among other things on the degree to which he is supervised and the efficiency of production administration.

The need to provide for expansion will sometimes mean that, in the short term, surplus capacity will be available and fixed costs will appear to be higher than is apparently justified by the present volume of the business.

Thus the majority of costs tend to increase in steps because they represent services, etc., which have a capacity range of two or more production units. With direct labour cost the steps are quite small and therefore it can be considered as a cost varying with production. Building costs, etc., will increase in larger steps, but less frequently, because they may remain unchanged whether the process is producing 100 or 10,000 units.

It is evident, therefore, that in order to make reasoned decisions and to plan effectively, management must be aware of the facets of cost behaviour which affect their particular business together with an assessment of the effect on costs and revenue of a particular course of action.

## MARGINAL COSTING

In the terminology published by the I.C.M.A., it is recommended that the term "marginal costing" is only applied where the routine system incorporates the marginal principle. The fundamental approach, therefore, is to relate only variable costs to cost units; fixed costs are considered to be attributable to the business in general. The Profit and Loss Statement produced from a marginal costing system will be based on valuing cost units at variable cost only and fixed costs will be written off in full in the period to which they are attributable.

Marginal costing assumes that the excess of selling price over variable cost provides a fund to meet the fixed costs and provide the undertaking's profit. Fixed overhead is therefore not allocated to cost units as the individual contributions of each are regarded as components of the total fund.

"Contribution" may be defined as the difference between sales value and the marginal cost of sales, and no net profit arises until total contribution equals fixed overhead. When this level of activity is achieved, the business is said to break even as neither profit nor loss occurs. Sales in excess of that necessary to break even will result in a profit equivalent to the excess units multiplied by the "contribution" per unit. Conversely, a loss is sustained if sales are less than that required to break even, amounting to the short-fall of units multiplied by the contribution.

Because of the practical difficulties involved and the dubious results obtained in absorbing fixed costs in production, it is contended that the marginal approach is superior as a basis for preparing routine operating reports. Reports prepared from an absorption costing system will reflect inconsistencies arising from the arbitrary nature of cost apportionment and absorption procedures; in addition, absorption costing neglects to recognise the fundamental difference between fixed and variable costs.

## The effect on profit of stock valuation bases

Under absorption costing, the unit cost at which stock is valued includes an amount for fixed costs obtained by dividing the total fixed costs for a period by the total production in the period. Thus, when production exceeds sales, part of the fixed costs will be carried forward to the next period. This procedure can result in unrealistic profits being reported when sales fluctuate and production is constant.

*EXAMPLE*

Product A sells at £8 each; variable costs are £6 per unit and fixed costs allocated to product A are £300 per month.

In month I, 300 units of A were produced and 200 units sold; in month II, 200 units were produced and 300 sold.

Using an absorption costing system, the monthly Profit and Loss Statement would appear as follows:

| | *Month I* | | | *Month II* | | |
|---|---|---|---|---|---|---|
| Sales: (200 × £8) | | £1,600 | | (300 × £8) | | £2,400 |
| Cost of sales: | | | | | | |
| Opening stock | — | | | | £700 | |
| Production cost | | | | | | |
| 300 × £6 | £1,800 | | | 200 × £6 | 1,200 | |
| Fixed | 300 | | | Fixed | 300 | |
| | | 2,100 | | | | 1,500 |
| Closing stock | | | | | | |
| 100 × $\frac{£2,100}{300}$ | (700) | | | | — | |
| | | | 1,400 | | | 2,200 |
| Profit | | | £200 | | | £200 |

The statements report the same profit for each month, even though sales volume has increased by 50 per cent in month II. This representation is obviously unrealistic and is caused by the fact that one-third of the fixed costs incurred in month I has been carried forward to month II in the stock valuation.

Using the marginal costing presentation, stock would be valued at variable cost only and the statements would give a more realistic view of the effect of increased sales volume:

| | Month I | | Month II | |
|---|---:|---:|---:|---:|
| Sales | | £1,600 | | £2,400 |
| Variable cost of sales: | | | | |
|   Opening stock | — | | £600 | |
|   Production | | | | |
|     (300 × £6) | £1,800 | | 1,200 | |
|   Closing stock | | | | |
|     (100 × £6) | (600) | | — | |
| | | 1,200 | | 1,800 |
| Contribution | | 400 | | 600 |
| Fixed costs | | 300 | | 300 |
| Profit | | £100 | | £300 |

The distortion can still arise if the absorption rate is predetermined or based on budgeted volume. If, in the above example, normal or budgeted output was 250 units, the fixed cost absorption rate would be £300 ÷ 250 = £1.20 per unit and the Profit Statements would show:

| | Month I | | Month II | |
|---|---:|---:|---:|---:|
| Sales | | £1,600 | | £2,400 |
| Opening stock | — | | £720 | |
| Production (300 | | | | |
|   × £7.20) | £2,160 | | 1,440 | |
| Closing stock (100 | | | | |
|   × £7.20) | (720) | | — | |
| | | 1,440 | | 2,160 |
| | | 160 | | 240 |
| Fixed cost over | | | | |
|   (under) absorbed | | 60 | | (60) |
| Profit | | £220 | | £180 |

The closing stock in month I includes £120 of fixed cost because it is valued at the predetermined rate so that effectively only £180 is charged against sales in month I. Using standard absorption costing, the over/under absorption would be termed a volume variance but the effect would be the same.

The above examples are extreme for illustration purposes but one can imagine that in a continuing period of low sales activity, stocks could be built up and profits overstated because fixed costs were being deferred as part of the stock valuation.

## Product comparison

When a business produces a variety of products in batches or by continuous process, an absorption costing system requires that fixed costs are allocated to products by means of procedures which involve subjective judgment and expediency, i.e.

1. The basis of assessing benefit derived by individual cost centres, e.g. number of employees, floor area occupied.

2. The level of output used to calculate the rate of absorption, e.g. normal volume, budget, maximum capacity.

3. The basis for measuring the use of resources represented by fixed costs, e.g. machine hours, percentage of direct labour cost.

Consequently, the unit product cost calculated is subject to major reservations concerning the relevance of the amount of fixed cost included. Furthermore, the fact that an amount of fixed cost can reasonably be attributed to a particular product does not really affect the profitability of that product. In the short term, the level of fixed costs is independent of the volume of products produced or sold and any change in the amount of fixed cost allotted to a product results from a change in accounting procedures rather than from alteration to the product's ability to earn profit.

## EXAMPLE

The cost accountant of a company which manufactures four products has prepared the following Budget Profit and Loss Statement for the coming year:

|  | Product W 2,000 | | Product X 2,000 | | Product Y 2,000 | | Product Z 2,000 | |
|---|---|---|---|---|---|---|---|---|
| Production units | Total | Unit | Total | Unit | Total | Unit | Total | Unit |
| Sales | £40,000 | £20 | £50,000 | £25 | £48,000 | £24 | £36,000 | £18 |
| Variable costs | 8,000 | 4 | 30,000 | 15 | 20,000 | 10 | 10,000 | 5 |
| Allocated fixed costs | 24,000 | 12 | 10,000 | 5 | 16,000 | 8 | 20,000 | 10 |
|  | 32,000 | 16 | 40,000 | 20 | 36,000 | 18 | 30,000 | 15 |
| Net profit | £8,000 | £4 | £10,000 | £5 | £12,000 | £6 | £6,000 | £3 |

The managing director considers that, as X and Y are more profitable, some production resources should be switched from products W and Z, and suggests that an additional 500 units each of X and Y be produced and 500 units less of W and Z. He estimated the following improvement in profit:

$$
\begin{array}{rcl}
W & -500 \times £4 = & -£2,000 \\
X & +500 \times £5 = & +£2,500 \\
Y & +500 \times £6 = & +£3,000 \\
Z & -500 \times £3 = & -£1,500 \\
\end{array}
$$

Net estimated improvement £2,000

The cost accountant revises the budget to accord with the wishes of the managing director and the result is as follows:

| | Product W | | Product X | | Product Y | | Product Z | |
|---|---|---|---|---|---|---|---|---|
| Production units | 1,500 | | 2,500 | | 2,500 | | 1,500 | |
| | Total | Unit | Total | Unit | Total | Unit | Total | Unit |
| Sales | £30,000 | £20 | £62,500 | £25 | £60,000 | £24 | £27,000 | £18 |
| Variable costs | 6,000 | 4 | 37,500 | 15 | 25,000 | 10 | 7,500 | 5 |
| Allocated fixed costs | 24,000 | 16 | 10,000 | 4 | 16,000 | 6.4 | 20,000 | 13.3 |
| | 30,000 | 20 | 47,500 | 19 | 41,000 | 16.4 | 27,500 | 18.3 |
| Net profit/Loss | — | — | £15,000 | £6 | £19,000 | £7.6 | £(500) | £(0.3) |

A comparison of the original and revised budgets reveals the following change in profit:

| Product | Original budget | Revised budget | Difference |
|---|---|---|---|
| W | £8,000 | — | −£8,000 |
| X | 10,000 | 15,000 | +5,000 |
| Y | 12,000 | 19,000 | +7,000 |
| Z | 6,000 | (500) | −6,500 |
| | £36,000 | £33,500 | −£2,500 |

The proposed change in production quantities will therefore cause total profit to fall by £2,500. This situation has arisen because the cost accountant has not explained that the net profit per unit depends upon the amount of fixed cost allocated to each product and the level of the production volume. If he had shown the contribution which each product yields, i.e. sales minus variable cost, his original budget would have been more meaningful:

EXTRACT FROM ORIGINAL BUDGET

| | Product W | | Product X | | Product Y | | Product Z | |
|---|---|---|---|---|---|---|---|---|
| | Total | Unit | Total | Unit | Total | Unit | Total | Unit |
| Contribution | £32,000 | £16 | £20,000 | £10 | £28,000 | £14 | £26,000 | £13 |

It is now apparent that products W and Y are the most profitable and if the mix of products is changed so that an additional 500 units of W and Y are produced, and a reduction of 500 units is made in the production of X and Z, the following will result:

Product W: $+500 \times £16 = +£8,000$
Product X: $-500 \times £10 = -£5,000$
Product Y: $+500 \times £14 = +£7,000$
Product Z: $-500 \times £13 = -£6,500$

Net profit improvement $+£3,500$

Assuming that fixed costs remain unchanged in total regardless of changes in the mix of work any alteration to the relative amounts allotted to products will not affect profit. If, in the above example, more floor space was given to W and Y at the expense of X and Z, profit would be unaltered. Each additional unit sold, however, will obtain the selling price and incur the variable cost per unit.

It is recommended, therefore, that when presenting statements which could be used for profitability comparison purposes, the marginal format should be adopted so that the recipient is not confused or misled by the inclusion of an arbitrary figure of fixed costs (and consequently profit) per unit.

## DIFFERENTIAL COSTING

From time to time, management is faced with decisions which involve evaluating the effect of various courses of action. Presentation of relevant information in a way which will assist management to arrive at the correct decision is a vital function of the cost accountant.

Relevant information must be considered in relation to the decision in hand but the broad technique used in such circumstances is known as Differential Costing, defined by the I.C.M.A. as:

*Differential costing.* A technique used in the preparation of *ad hoc* information in which only cost and income differences between alternative courses of action are taken into consideration.

The application of this technique may be best explained by examining some of the kinds of decision that occasionally confront management.

### Unprofitable activities

In businesses where all costs are apportioned to products there may be a temptation to discontinue the sale of products which consistently show net losses in the hope that the profit for the whole company will be improved. This would not necessarily be so, as a product may earn a useful contribution towards fixed overhead and profit, and to discontinue its sale would reduce the overall company profit.

### *EXAMPLE*

A manufacturer of packing cases makes three main types: Export, Home (Heavy) and Home (Light). Overhead is absorbed on the basis of labour hours. Estimates for the cases show the following:

|  | Export | Home (Heavy) | Home (Light) |
|---|---|---|---|
| Material | £5.00 | £4.00 | £3.00 |
| Wages | 3.00 | 1.50 | 1.00 |
| Overhead | 6.00 | 3.00 | 2.00 |
|  | 14.00 | 8.50 | 6.00 |
| Net profit/(loss) | (1.00) | 1.50 | (1.50) |
| Average selling price | £13.00 | £10.00 | £4.50 |
| Annual sales | 10,000 | 20,000 | 5,000 |

The manufacturer feels that he would be well advised to discontinue producing the Export and Home (Light) cases even though it would mean that some of the production facilities would remain unused. He cannot increase the sales of Home (Heavy) cases. You ascertain that 60 per cent of the overhead is fixed and are required to advise the manufacturer.

The total overhead absorbed is £60,000 on Export, £60,000 on Home (Heavy) and £10,000 on Home (Light). Fixed overhead represents 60 per cent or £78,000. The situation can therefore be presented as follows:

|  | Export | | Home (Heavy) | | Home (Light) | | Total | |
|---|---|---|---|---|---|---|---|---|
| Sales |  | £130,000 |  | £200,000 |  | £22,500 |  | £352,500 |
| Material | 50,000 |  | 80,000 |  | 15,000 |  | 145,000 |  |
| Wages | 30,000 |  | 30,000 |  | 5,000 |  | 65,000 |  |
| Variable overhead | 24,000 |  | 24,000 |  | 4,000 |  | 52,000 |  |
|  |  | 104,000 |  | 134,000 |  | 24,000 |  | 262,000 |
| Contribution |  | £26,000 |  | £66,000 |  | (£1,500) |  | £90,500 |
| Fixed overhead |  |  |  |  |  |  |  | 78,000 |
| Net profit |  |  |  |  |  |  |  | £12,500 |

The above figures show that the manufacturer is only justified in discontinuing the sale of Home (Light) cases as they are not providing a contribution. An alternative would be to increase prices or reduce production costs in order to make them profitable. The Export cases should continue to be sold because they provide a substantial contribution and the result of ceasing to sell them would be to change the profit to a loss of £12,000 (£12,500 + £1,500 from Home (Light) cases—£26,000). If in the long term the manufacturer is able to reduce his fixed overhead by discontinuing Export sales, he would be advised to do so only if the annual reduction exceeded £26,000, i.e. the amount of contribution forgone on Export cases.

SPECIFIC AND GENERAL FIXED COSTS

At this point it is necessary to probe further into fixed costs. They appear under two classifications:

1. Specific costs incurred for a particular production centre, e.g. supervisors' salaries and plant depreciation. Such costs may not change even though production fluctuates over a wide volume range but if the production centre were closed down, those costs could be eliminated.

2. General fixed costs, which are allocated to production centres on some arbitrary basis, e.g. production director's salary and the fixed costs of central services like the boiler house and maintenance gang. When a complete production centre is closed, it is likely that only a small reduction can be made in general fixed costs.

The accountant should, therefore, consider the above classification whn assembling statements.

## EXAMPLE

Assume the same basic data as in the previous example with the additional information that the fixed overhead of £78,000 should be analysed as follows:

| | |
|---|---|
| Specific fixed costs: Export | £30,000 |
| Home (Heavy) | £25,000 |
| Home (Light) | £5,000 |
| General fixed costs: | £18,000 |

The previous statement ought therefore to be revised on the following lines:

| | Export | | Home (Heavy) | | Home (Light) | | Total | |
|---|---|---|---|---|---|---|---|---|
| Sales | | £130,000 | | £200,000 | | £22,500 | | £352,500 |
| Material | £50,000 | | £80,000 | | £15,000 | | £145,000 | |
| Wages | 30,000 | | 30,000 | | 5,000 | | 65,000 | |
| Variable overhead | 24,000 | | 24,000 | | 4,000 | | 52,000 | |
| | | 104,000 | | 134,000 | | 24,000 | | 262,000 |
| Gross contribution | | 26,000 | | 66,000 | | 1,500 | | 90,500 |
| Specific fixed costs | | 30,000 | | 25,000 | | 5,000 | | 60,000 |
| Net contribution | | £4,000 | | £41,000 | | £6,500 | | 30,500 |
| General fixed costs | | | | | | | | 18,000 |
| Net profit | | | | | | | | £12,500 |

The decision changes slightly. Home (Light) cases should be discontinued but management must carefully review the market for Export cases. Although at the moment they show a negative contribution it may merely be due to insufficient volume. If the department producing the Export cases is operating at, say, 60 per cent of its capacity, it might be possible to increase existing production by 30 per cent without increasing the specific fixed costs. Then, provided the additional cases could be sold at the same prices, the gross contribution would be £33,800 ($\frac{130}{100} \times$ £26,000) and the net contribution £3,800. The overall profit would then change as follows:

| | |
|---|---|
| Existing net profit | £12,500 |
| Discontinuing Home (Light) | 6,500 |
| Increased sales of Export | 7,800 |
| | £26,800 |

## Scarce resources

Businesses are sometimes faced with circumstances in which certain factors of production are scarce and the company is unable to meet the full demand for its products. Plant may break down and be out of action for several weeks awaiting spare parts, material may be in short supply or skilled employees may leave and be difficult to replace. In such situations management must use resources as profitably as possible and will want to sell those products which yield the greatest profit per unit of the scarce resource (limiting factor). As we have seen, contribution is more meaningful than net profit when comparing profitability and, therefore, calculation of the amount of contribution earned per unit of the limiting factor used for each product will indicate the priority for production.

*EXAMPLE*

The Spongy Toy Company produces and sells three toy products which are made from a special rubber compound. Last month the sole supplier of the compound informed the company that because of a recent fire, supplies of the compound would be cut by one-third for the next twelve months. The following budget had previously been prepared for each month of the next year on information supplied by the sales and production managers. You are required to advise the company on the best mix of products to sell for the next year.

BUDGET FOR EACH 4-WEEKLY PERIOD OF 19...

|  | Toy rabbits | Toy cats | Toy bears | Total |
|---|---|---|---|---|
| Material | £2,000 | £750 | £1,000 | £3,750 |
| Wages | 500 | 2,000 | 2,000 | 4,500 |
| Variable overhead | 1,000 | 4,000 | 4,000 | 9,000 |
| Fixed overhead | 3,000 | 1,250 | 1,500 | 5,750 |
| Total cost | 6,500 | 8,000 | 8,500 | 23,000 |
| Net profit | 4,500 | 1,000 | 500 | 6,000 |
| Sales | £11,000 | £9,000 | £9,000 | £29,000 |
| Units sold | 4,000 | 1,500 | 1,000 | 6,500 |

From the above information the unit contributions can be calculated:

|  | Toy rabbits | Toy cats | Toy bears |
|---|---|---|---|
| Contribution (Profit and Fixed overhead) | £7,500 | £2,250 | £2,000 |
| Contribution per unit | £1.875 | £1.50 | £2.00 |

By dividing the contribution by the value of material, the contributions per unit of limiting factor are determined:

|  | Toy rabbits | Toy cats | Toy bears |
|---|---|---|---|
| Contribution per £1 of material: | $\frac{£7,500}{£2,000}$ | $\frac{£2,250}{£750}$ | $\frac{£2,00}{£1,000}$ |
|  | = £3.75 | = £3 | = £2 |
| Priority to produce | (1) | (2) | (3) |

Although the toy bears appeared to be most profitable in the original budget, they are the least profitable in terms of the rate at which they provide contribution for every £1 spent on material. It is therefore advisable for management to concentrate on production of the toy rabbits. Assuming that the sales budget represents maximum demand, priority should be given to production of the toy rabbits; 4,000 units are required which will use up £2,000 of the available material supply of £2,500 and the balance of £500 will enable two-thirds of the original budget for toy cats to be produced, i.e. 1,000 units. The revised budget would appear as follows:

REVISED 4-WEEKLY BUDGET (A) FOR 19...

|  | Toy rabbits | | Toy cats | | Total | |
|---|---|---|---|---|---|---|
| Sales |  | £11,000 |  | £6,000 |  | £17,000 |
| Material | £2,000 |  | £500 |  | £2,500 |  |
| Wages | 500 |  | 1,333 |  | 1,833 |  |
| Variable overhead | 1,000 |  | 2,667 |  | 3,667 |  |
|  |  | 3,500 |  | 4,500 |  | 8,000 |
| Contribution |  | £7,500 |  | £1,500 |  | 9,000 |
| Fixed overhead |  |  |  |  |  | 5,750 |
| Net profit |  |  |  |  |  | 3,250 |

If contribution per unit had been used to determine priority so that toy bears were given priority followed by toy rabbits and toy cats, the result would have been as follows:

REVISED 4-WEEKLY BUDGET (B) FOR 19...

|  | Toy rabbits | | Toy cats | | Toy bears | | Total | |
|---|---|---|---|---|---|---|---|---|
| Sales |  | £4,125 |  | £9,000 |  | £9,000 |  | £22,125 |
| Material | £750 |  | £750 |  | £1,000 |  | £2,500 |  |
| Wage | 187 |  | 2,000 |  | 2,000 |  | 4,187 |  |
| Variable overhead | 375 |  | 4,000 |  | 4,000 |  | 8,375 |  |
|  |  | 1,312 |  | 6,750 |  | 7,000 |  | 15,062 |
| Contribution |  | £2,813 |  | £2,250 |  | £2,000 |  | 7,063 |
| Fixed overhead |  |  |  |  |  |  |  | 5,750 |
| Net profit |  |  |  |  |  |  |  | £1,313 |

The example illustrates the importance of relating contribution to the limiting factor. However, the reader must realise the underlying assumptions in the example. It has been assumed that total fixed overhead is unaffected by changes in product mix and that wages and variable overhead will be reduced in direct proportion to the production level. In practice such assumptions may not be entirely true and the cost accountant must consider the effect of the decision on those costs.

In addition, the revised production plan will result in toy bears disappearing from the market for a year; even if there were no firm orders for that product, management would probably want to produce a nominal quantity at the expense of a small reduction in profit.

It may be informative to examine the differential costing approach to a problem of this type.

*EXAMPLE*

Using the same figures as in the previous example but assuming that demand for the product is virtually unlimited, available material supply will enable production of 5,000 rabbits or 5,000 cats or 2,500 bears; total material cost and total fixed overhead is the same whichever toy is produced and, therefore, relative contributions are as follows:

|  | Toy rabbits | | Toy cats | | Toy bears | |
|---|---|---|---|---|---|---|
| Sales units | 5,000 | | 5,000 | | 2,500 | |
| Sales value | | £13,750 | | £30,000 | | £22,500 |
| Wages | 625 | | 6,667 | | 5,000 | |
| Variable overhead | 1,250 | | 14,667 | | 10,000 | |
| | | 1,875 | | 21,334 | | 15,000 |
| Contribution | | £11,875 | | £8,666 | | £7,500 |

The calculation indicates that profit is maximised by concentrating production on toy rabbits. Note that each alternative uses the total material cost available and, therefore, material is not a cost difference.

## Make or buy decisions

Companies occasionally find that another manufacturer could supply a product or a component which they are currently making at a price below the company's own total cost. In the short term, the company will only benefit from purchasing outside if the outside purchase price is lower than the variable cost of manufacture. The assumption is that total fixed costs will not be reduced if the product is purchased and the amount currently being absorbed by this product will have to be absorbed by other company products.

*EXAMPLE*

The Jiffy-Tax Company manufactures a range of products and has just received a proposal from the Brown Machining Company that one of its products "Taxine", could be supplied to them advantageously. The cost accountant presents the following statement for consideration.

|  | *Taxine costs per unit* |
|---|---|
| Material | £1.50 |
| Process I | 1.50 |
| Process II | 0.50 |
| | £3.50 |
| Purchase price | £2.80 |

From further enquiries the following facts emerge:

1. Process I costs included an element of fixed overhead of approximately 40 per cent.
2. Process II is a joint process producing three products in addition to Taxine. The process costs would still be incurred if Taxine were not produced by the company.

A revised statement can therefore be produced:

*Taxine variable costs*
*per unit*

| | |
|---|---|
| Material | £1.50 |
| Process I: 60% | 0.90 |
| | £2.40 |

It is therefore advisable to continue manufacturing the product internally because the variable costs are less than the purchase price.

In the longer term, however, the company may be able to save more by reducing fixed costs than it pays in the excess cost of purchase.

*EXAMPLE*

Assume the facts in the previous example and that 1,000 units is the annual requirement for Taxine. In addition, it is estimated that, if production of Taxine was discontinued, annual plant costs in process I could be reduced by £300 and re-arranging operating facilities in the joint process would save £200 per annum.

A comparison of annual costs shows, therefore:

| | £ |
|---|---|
| Annual variable cost of producing Taxine (1,000 units at £2.40) | £2,400 |
| Specific fixed costs | 500 |
| | 2,900 |
| Purchase cost: 1,000 at £2.80 | 2,800 |
| Annual saving by outside purchase | £100 |

The above is obviously more easily expressed as excess purchase cost, $1,000 \times £(2.80 - 2.40) = £400$ versus savings in fixed costs of £500, giving a favourable cost difference by purchasing of £100.

In practice, management would probably consider that the annual saving would not justify making the company vulnerable to the whims of the outside supplier and other factors would have a significant influence on the decision, for example:

1. Future prospects for Taxine sales; if demand is likely to increase, the company may be forced to use the outside supplier to combat a shortage of production capacity.

2. Alternative use for manpower and facilities used to produce Taxine. If such resources could be used elsewhere to earn more than £400 profit (the annual excess of purchase cost) then purchasing outside could be a viable proposition.

3. Effect on labour relations (and compensation payments) if employees were dismissed.

Many companies are forced to consider using sub-contractors to produce articles which the company is unable to supply in the short term for a variety of reasons. There may be a bottleneck in manufacture because of a machine breakdown or because a customer wants his order urgently.

Various factors will influence the decision as to which of several products or components the sub-contractor is asked to supply, not all of them financial. However, as far as cost is concerned, the important consideration will be to make the most profitable use of the factor of production which is limiting the company's capacity to produce.

*EXAMPLE*

The Whistle Stop Company is experiencing problems in a section of its press shop owing to a recent influx of orders which must be made on a special type of press. The press makes three types of products: Squares, Rounds and Ovals. The company estimates that it will be short of forty-two hours of press time per week and another manufacturer is asked to quote prices for the three products. The following figures are assembled by the accountant for management's consideration.

|  | Squares | | Rounds | | Ovals | |
|---|---|---|---|---|---|---|
| Selling price | | £14.00 | | £16.00 | | £7.50 |
| Material | £2.00 | | £3.00 | | £1.00 | |
| Wages (at £2 per hour) | 6.00 | | 7.00 | | 3.00 | |
| Variable overhead | 3.00 | | 3.50 | | 1.50 | |
| | | 11.00 | | 13.50 | | 5.50 |
| Contribution | | £3.00 | | £2.50 | | £2.00 |
| Sub-contractor's price | | £13.40 | | £15.60 | | £7.00 |

The key to the situation is to calculate the difference in variable costs and relate this to the limiting factor, press time.

|  | Squares | Rounds | Ovals |
|---|---|---|---|
| Variable costs of manufacture | £11.00 | £13.50 | £5.50 |
| Sub-contractor's price | 13.40 | 15.60 | 7.00 |
| Excess cost of sub-contracting | £2.40 | £2.10 | £1.50 |
| Press time saved by sub-contracting | 3 hours | 3½ hours | 1½ hours |
| Excess cost per hour | £0.80 | £0.60 | £1.00 |

Although the least increase in cost per unit is on Ovals, the least increase per hour will be incurred on Rounds. Therefore it is the latter product which should be sub-contracted as every hour spent on manufacturing Rounds will save only 60p in excess purchase costs. If press time is still insufficient Squares would be considered next. The following statement should clarify the situation:

COMPARATIVE COSTS OF USING 42 HOURS OF PRESS TIME

|  | Squares | Rounds | Ovals |
|---|---|---|---|
|  | 14 products | 12 products | 28 products |
| Variable manufacturing costs | £154.00 | £162.00 | £154.00 |
| Sub-contractor's price | 187.60 | 187.20 | 196.00 |
| Excess costs per week | £33.60 | £25.20 | £42.00 |

Thus Ovals are the most expensive to sub-contract and therefore should be manufactured internally. Note that the selling prices are irrelevant information as they are not "differentials", i.e. they will remain the same whether or not products are purchased.

## Selling prices

Identification of fixed and variable costs is extremely useful when making a decision concerning the price at which a product should be sold. Frequently, a product may be sold in more than one market, e.g. in a luxury market, in which case the quantity sold may be small, or at a lower price through different trade channels, when a larger quantity may be anticipated.

*EXAMPLE*

A company is formed to produce and sell a patented article, the variable unit costs being estimated at £10. Market research shows that the following alternative outlets are possible:

(*a*) 1,000 articles per annum at a price of £20 each;
(*b*) 5,000 articles per annum at a price of £12.50 each.

If fixed costs are expected to be £6,000 per annum, the following estimates of profit can be prepared:

|  | (*a*) | (*b*) |
|---|---|---|
| Output per annum | 1,000 articles | 5,000 articles |
| Estimated sale price | £20 | £12.50 |
| Sales | £20,000 | £62,500 |
| Variable costs | 10,000 | 50,000 |
| Contribution | 10,000 | 12,500 |
| Less fixed costs | 6,000 | 6,000 |
| Estimated profit | £4,000 | £6,500 |

In spite of the considerably lower selling price which alternative (*b*) provides, the increased demand results in a greater contribution and as fixed expenses remain constant, net profit is increased by a like amount. Alternative (*b*) is therefore more attractive and the company may devote its energies to this market.

It is claimed that contribution is more relevant to management in tendering than are costs prepared with a loading for fixed expense. It is pointed out that the loading must, of necessity, vary with the level of output considered. This implies that when trade is bad and output small an attempt to recover all fixed overhead will result in an uncompetitive price. It is accordingly claimed that in practice many opportunities exist of obtaining a contract at a price which makes at least some contribution to fixed expenses, and that therefore a contract so obtained will result in a greater overall net profit (or smaller net loss) than if the contract were not obtained. There are of course dangers in this view and these are dealt with later. Subject to the dangers, there is little doubt that the approach is of value to businessmen, as it deals with the common business situation of a manufacturer desiring to maximise his profits (or minimise his losses) in the knowledge: (*a*) that he has an inescapable burden of fixed overhead, and (*b*) that he can attract or repel an order according to the price he quotes.

## EXAMPLE

The Estimating Department has prepared the following statement of cost for a tender:

| | |
|---|---:|
| Direct materials | £40,000 |
| Direct labour | 50,000 |
| Direct expenses | 10,000 |
| | |
| Prime cost | 100,000 |
| *Add* for overhead: 100% of direct labour | 50,000 |
| | |
| | £150,000 |

Of the charge for overhead, it is ascertained that £35,000 represents apportioned fixed expense, the balance being expenses which would not be incurred if the tender is unsuccessful. The contract is offered to the company at £125,000. Should it be accepted?

The marginal cost of the contract is:

| | |
|---|---:|
| Prime cost | £100,000 |
| *Add:* Variable expenses | 15,000 |
| | |
| Marginal cost | £115,000 |

A price of £125,000 will therefore result in a recoupment of £10,000 of the fixed expenses. If the contract is not obtained the whole £35,000 will be unrecouped. Accordingly the acceptance of the contract will, in ordinary circumstances, prove beneficial to the company.

In times of trade depression it may be wise to accept orders at a price lower than normal selling price and even under the figure of cost of sales if by so doing a proportion of the fixed overhead expenses, which would otherwise be unrecouped, can be recovered. A normal profit margin is not expected on orders accepted on such terms, but the loss for the business as a whole is reduced. It is apparent, however, that the lowest price which can be accepted must be not less than the expense which would be incurred in the execution of the order, i.e. the marginal cost.

If an article is sold at a price *below its marginal cost* a loss will result over and above the recouped fixed overhead; hence such sales if persisted in may well lead to insolvency. However, in certain circumstances, and for special reasons, sales at prices below marginal cost may be advantageous, for example:

1. Where, because labour is highly skilled and not easily replaceable, wages may be regarded at least temporarily as a fixed cost. If this view is taken, marginal cost would exclude some or all of the wages of productive employees, and sales at a price which does not fully recoup them may be considered. The course of action may in some circumstances be preferable to dispersing the labour force in a time of trade depression, but clearly it cannot be persisted in for a long period of time.

2. Where the materials to be used are in stock and are of a perishable nature, so that a loss will in any event occur if they are not used in the near future.

3. In a period of acute competition when losses may be deliberately sustained with the object of eliminating less powerful competitors from the market.

4. Where a new line is to be introduced to the public, and as a means of attracting sales the article is offered at a low price for a limited period.

It must be emphasised that the above reasons are only valid in the short term, and that there are obvious dangers in selling persistently at prices below marginal cost.

In certain businesses it may be worthwhile to sell one commodity consistently at a price less than the cost of sales if such a sale will induce the sale of other and more profitable products. The loss on the sale of the unprofitable product can be regarded as part of the cost of advertising the others.

In using marginal cost as a basis for tendering or for fixing selling prices the following must be borne in mind:

1. Economic selling prices cannot in the long run be set without regard for fixed expenses. Although in certain circumstances orders may be accepted at less than their total cost, such a course may result in a general reduction of selling prices due to intensified competition. The manufacturer may need to expand sales and activity generally in order to maintain his previous level of overall profit. Management must recognise that a new product which represents a small proportion of total sales at the moment, and which they may be prepared to sell at a figure below total cost but above the variable cost, will in time probably represent a substantial proportion of the total sales. In due course products which are currently bearing their full share of fixed overhead will be superseded by other products. Unless these other products also bear their share of fixed overhead, management may have to increase prices and sales volume to maintain profits. Such action could well prove disastrous.

2. The "time" costs are ignored and hence two jobs may have similar marginal cost but one may take twice as long as the other.

The fact that the job which takes the longer time thereby uses more of the business resources (represented by fixed costs) is not disclosed.

3. In reality, no cost is fixed in the long run, as demand artificially stimulated may result in an increase in fixed charges, e.g. owing to the necessity of increasing the size of the factory. Conversely a factory may be sublet or sold, and production discontinued.

4. Analysis of overhead into "fixed" and "variable" is frequently imprecise.

**Selling prices and scarce resources**

We have examined the importance of giving priority to those products which earn the greatest contribution per unit of limiting factor when a business is unable to fulfil demand for its products. The concept can be applied when management is considering the selling prices to be charged for customers' orders which have to be produced from a common limited production resource.

*EXAMPLE*

The Plastic Finishing Company coats customers' metal products with a special plastic substance. The company charges customers according to the estimated weight of plastic and the number of working hours required. Current charges are £5 per kg for plastic and £6 per processing hour. Results for the previous three months were as follows:

|  | Month 1 | Month 2 | Month 3 | Total |
|---|---|---|---|---|
| Material | £12,000 | £15,000 | £9,000 | £36,000 |
| Wages | 20,000 | 25,200 | 14,800 | 60,000 |
| Variable overhead | 10,000 | 12,000 | 8,000 | 30,000 |
|  | 42,000 | 52,200 | 31,800 | 126,000 |
| Fixed overhead | 10,500 | 10,500 | 9,000 | 30,000 |
| Total cost | 52,500 | 62,700 | 40,800 | 156,000 |
| Profit | 27,500 | 37,900 | 18,600 | 84,000 |
| Sales | £80,000 | £100,600 | £59,400 | £240,000 |

The plastic costs £3 per kg and the average wage-rate with bonuses and incidentals is £2 per hour. The sales manager obtains an order which will require 2,000 kg of material and 200 hours per month for four months. The purchasing manager had previously issued a report to the directors explaining that the company was likely to experience difficulty in obtaining supplies of the plastic coating substance and they may be restricted to 3,000 kg per month. You are asked to advise on the price to charge for the new order.

Analysis of the results yields the following:

Weight of plastic used $= \dfrac{\text{Material cost}}{\text{Cost per kg}} = \dfrac{£36,000}{3} = 12,000$ kg.

Hours worked $= \dfrac{\text{Wages}}{\text{Cost per hour}} = \dfrac{£60,000}{£2} = 30,000$ hours.

Therefore, a normal mix of work requires 5 hours for every 2 kg of material and the new order is substantially different. Since the supply of material is becoming restricted it will be important to ensure that profitability of the company is not adversely affected by accepting the new order and therefore the normal rate of contribution per kg of material used must be obtained from the new order:

|  | *Average costs* |
|---|---|
| Materials (2 kg) | £6 |
| Wages (5 hours) | 10 |
| Variable overhead | 5 |
|  | 21 |
| Contribution | 19 |
| Sales value | £40 (or 2 kg × £5, + 5 hours × £6) |

Contribution per kg of material $= \dfrac{£19}{2} = £9.50.$

The price of the new order should therefore be based on the variable cost plus the contribution as calculated above.

|  | *New order Costs per month* |
|---|---|
| Material (2,000 kg × £3) | £6,000 |
| Wages (200 hours) | 400 |
| Variable overhead | 200 |
|  | 6,600 |
| Contribution (2,000 kg × £9.50) | 19,000 |
| Sales value | £25,600 |

This contrasts with the sales value calculated under normal circumstances:

|  |  |
|---|---|
| Material (2,000 kg × £5) | £10,000 |
| Wages (200 hours × £6) | 1,200 |
| Sales value | £11,200 |

The company should therefore not accept the order unless the customer is prepared to pay £25,600 per month.

Similarly, if the company was faced with a labour shortage but could obtain unlimited supplies of material, the minimum price to charge for the order would be that which maintains the existing rate of contribution per labour hour, i.e. based on the last three months' figures:

$$\text{Contribution per labour hour} = \frac{\text{Profit} + \text{Fixed costs}}{\text{Labour hours}} = \frac{£84,000 + £30,000}{30,000 \text{ hrs}}$$
$$= £3.80 \text{ per hr}$$

The minimum price for the order is, therefore:

| | |
|---|---:|
| Variable costs as above | £6,600 |
| Contribution (200 hours at £3.80) | 760 |
| Sales value | £7,360 |

The reason behind the approach is that acceptance of the order would divert scarce labour from exisiting work which is earning £3.80 per hour. The fact that material supply is unlimited would mean that the order could be accepted at the above price even though it is lower than that fixed under normal circumstances.

**Opportunity costs**

The management of a business is frequently confronted with a choice between alternative courses of action and, in deciding which to adopt, it is desirable to ascertain which would yield the greatest profit. Examples of typical situations are as follows:

1. A semi-manufactured product may be either sold in its existing condition or processed further to yield a more valuable product.

2. When spare plant capacity is limited it may be necessary to decide which of a series of orders to accept, each order making different demands upon the available spare capacity.

3. Due to changing market conditions, it may appear desirable to cancel a contract for the construction of a piece of plant, perhaps under penalty. It would then be necessary to know the costs involved in thus cutting losses.

In making such decisions the company's prime concern is not with the *absolute* cost or profit of each alternative, but with their *relative* merits. It is therefore appropriate to use the concept of "opportunity cost", which is defined by the Institute of Cost and Management Accountants as:

The value of a benefit sacrificed in favour of an alternative course of action.

The opportunity cost may be described as the "alternative revenue forgone". Thus if a choice is being made between (*a*) selling a semi-finished material at £1 per kg and (*b*) introducing it into a further process to make a more refined and valuable product, then from the point of view of the choice the cost of the product to date is irrelevant. Course (*b*) would be selected as the more attractive only if it resulted, after paying the costs of the process, in a revenue in excess of £1 per kg, i.e. in excess of the *alternative revenue forgone*. To compute this profit it would be necessary to charge the process with the opportunity cost of £1 per kg irrespective of the historical cost of the material. The *additional* revenue which would result from the alternative is thus disclosed.

It must be emphasised that the opportunity cost of the semi-refined product would be used only where it is desired to make an estimate of the *additional* profit likely to accrue from one particular course of action, and the concept is therefore a valuable guide in making decisions between alternatives.

*EXAMPLE*

A company possesses a stock of 100 tonnes of material A, which cost £15 per tonne and which can be sold at an ex-works price of £25 per tonne. Alternatively, it may be further processed at a variable cost of £20 per tonne to yield 95 tonnes of material B with an ex-works sale price of £45 per tonne. Fixed costs of process B amount to £1,000. Which course of action should the company pursue in order to produce the maximum profit, assuming that if material A is sold, plant B would be: (*a*) fully occupied with other work; (*b*) idle?

If material A is further processed the result is:

| | |
|---|---:|
| Sales—95 tonnes of B at £45 per tonne | £4,275 |
| *Less:* Variable process cost of 100 tonnes at £20 per tonne | 2,000 |
| Additional revenue | £2,275 |
| *Less:* Opportunity cost of 100 tonnes of A at £25 per tonne | 2,500 |
| Adverse result of further processing | £225 |

It will be observed that the fixed costs of process B are ignored in the above calculation. If the plant can be fully occupied with other work no problem arises, for the £1,000 could properly be charged against this in the conventional process accounts. If, however, the sale of material A means that plant B will be idle, there will be no production against which the £1,000 can be charged and the overhead will remain unrecouped.

It might therefore be thought at first sight that the fixed costs should be deducted from the sales proceeds of material B in making the comparison with the additional revenue which further processing would produce. This is not so, however, because we are merely concerned with the problem of *which of two courses is the more profitable*. The fixed costs of process B will be incurred in any case; so in a statement of *comparative* profitability they must be ignored. This is not to say that whether plant B is operated or not is of no concern to the management for, clearly, additional profit could accrue from keeping the plant fully occupied. This, however, is not the point with which we are here concerned, the issue before us being the *relative* advantages of two alternative courses of action.

From the above statement therefore it appears that to sell material A is the more profitable course of action, as it will result in an additional surplus of £225, compared with the alternative.

## BREAK-EVEN ANALYSIS

Break-even analysis (otherwise known as cost-volume-profit analysis) is a general term for a number of techniques and procedures designed to assist planning and decision-making by clarifying the effect of changes in volume on business profitability.

The terminology is perhaps less important than the application so it may be advisable to examine its uses rather than confuse the reader with numerous definitions. At this stage, we may assume that separation of costs into fixed and variable constituents has been carried out; the procedures involved in such analysis will be described later.

### Contribution per unit

The following simple equations are fundamental:

$$\text{Sales value} - \text{Variable costs} = \text{Contribution}$$
$$\text{Contribution} - \text{Fixed costs} = \text{Net profit.}$$

In a limited period, and over a limited range of volumes of activity, we may assume that each additional unit sold achieves the same selling price and incurs the same unit variable cost. Thus, we can perceive that the contribution *per unit* will be a constant amount. Similarly, within the same limits, fixed costs can be assumed to remain the same *in total*. It follows, therefore, that the sales units required to attain a given amount of contribution represents the amount divided by the unit contribution.

At break-even point, net profit is nil, as contribution equals fixed costs. Therefore the sales volume required to generate a contribution sufficient to equal the fixed costs will be found as follows:

$$\frac{\text{Fixed costs}}{\text{Contribution per unit}} = \text{Break-even point.}$$

*EXAMPLE*

A product sells at £6 per unit. Variable costs per unit are £2 and annual fixed costs are £40,000. Calculate:

   (*a*) the break-even sales volume;
   (*b*) annual sales units required to achieve a profit of £20,000;
   (*c*) Annual sales units required to achieve a profit of £25,000 if selling price is increased by £1 and annual fixed costs increase by £10,000.

   (*a*) Break-even sales volume =

$$\frac{\text{Fixed costs}}{\text{Contribution per unit}} = \frac{£40,000}{£6-2} = \underline{10,000 \text{ units.}}$$

   (*b*) Contribution required =
   Fixed costs + Profit target = £40,000 + 20,000 = £60,000.

$$\text{Volume required} = \frac{\text{Contribution target}}{\text{Contribution per unit}} = \frac{£60,000}{£4} = \underline{15,000 \text{ units.}}$$

(c) Target = £25,000 + 40,000 + 10,000.

$$\text{Volume required} = \frac{£75,000}{£7 - 2} = \underline{15,000 \text{ units.}}$$

The above examples illustrate how the assumption of a continuing relationship between contribution and volume can be used to assess the effect or to predict the results of changes in prices, costs and activity.

It will be evident that the equation:

$$\text{Target volume} = \frac{\text{Contribution target}}{\text{Contribution per unit}}$$

can be used in various ways.

*EXAMPLE*

The UYJ Company is planning to launch a new product. Market research indicates that an annual volume of 10,000 units could be sold provided that the selling price is below £25. Variable costs are expected to be £15 per unit and annual fixed costs attributable to the product are £20,000. Management aims to achieve a 30 per cent profit margin on cost and requires that the new product will absorb £10,000 of general fixed overhead. Advise management.

| | | |
|---|---|---:|
| Total cost | = 10,000 units at £15 | £150,000 |
| | Specific fixed costs | 20,000 |
| | General fixed costs | 10,000 |
| | | 180,000 |
| Profit required | = 30% of £180,000 | 54,000 |
| | Sales value required | £234,000 |

The selling price which will achieve management's target, therefore, is £23.40 which is below the limit set of £25, and management would be advised to launch the product. Note how the calculation can be easily adjusted to reflect any changes in costs, objectives and volume estimates.

**Break-even charts**

The relationship between profit and volume of activity can be depicted in chart form by plotting sales value and total costs expected at various levels of activity. The horizontal axis represents activity and the vertical axis represents value; a straight line is drawn parallel to the horizontal axis at the level of fixed costs expected and total costs at each activity level plotted is obtained by adding the appropriate variable costs. The chart in Fig. 61 is derived from the following data:

*Accounting*
| *Period* | *Units sold* |
|:---:|:---:|
| 1 | 100 |
| 2 | 150 |
| 3 | 200 |

Variable costs per unit: £1
Fixed costs per period: £600
Selling price per unit: £6

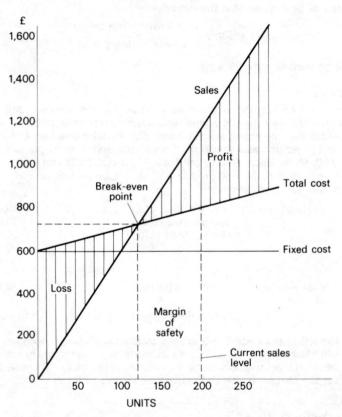

FIG. 61.—*Break-even chart.*

It is possible to use the break-even chart to predict the profit or loss to be obtained from a certain level of sales. The point at which sales equals total cost is known as the break-even point and the chart indicates that it is at 120 units or £720 sales value. The break-even point also indicates the reduction in sales that the business can suffer before it earns no profit. The difference between break-even and a given volume of sales (usually budget or normal volume) is known as the *margin of safety*, which can be derived from the chart as 80 units, i.e. the current sales level of 200 units less the break-even point at 120 units. The main application of the chart is to illustrate comparisons, e.g. actual *v.* plan, different products, different periods.

### The profit volume chart
The net profit to be earned at a particular level of sales is determined by the contribution per unit, the fixed costs and, of course, the actual sales level chosen. These three factors may be more clearly shown in the form of a profit volume chart illustrated in Fig. 62.

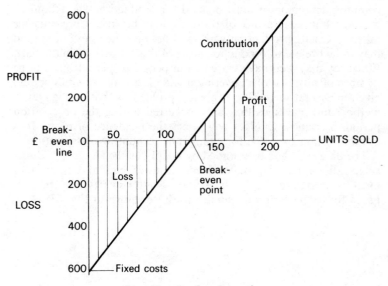

FIG. 62.—*Profit volume chart.*

The profit volume chart is prepared by plotting the fixed costs below the break-even line at nil sales and then for each unit of sales, reducing the loss by the contribution per unit.

There are many variations of the break-even chart designed to suit the needs of the recipient but at this stage the reader needs only to understand the basic principles of construction and application. One point worthy of mention, however, is that the measure of activity used for the horizontal axis is not confined to sales units. It could be expressed in terms of sales value or standard hours of production, for example.

### Analysing costs between fixed and variable

The methods used to discover the relationship between cost and activity fall into two main groups. The first is based upon past observations of costs and production levels. Costs may then be separated into fixed or variable classifications by judgment, or by statistical methods. The second method is to estimate the costs required to achieve various production levels—we may call this a *synthetic* approach—and this is used particularly when projecting costs into the future at production levels of which the business has, as yet, no experience.

Under the first method, a number of years' results needs to be obtained, preferably broken down into thirteen four-weekly periods. It is important to be able to isolate the effect of wage and price increases so that all cost data are at the same price level. A common denominator must be used for production, e.g. labour or machine hours, as a mix of products may be sold. Care must be taken to equate production with sales because the sales in a period may in fact relate to production costs of several periods in the past. Efficiency may well have varied from period to period but a large number of observations covering a wide range of activities should give representative results. A greater problem is that of changes in method and machines that have occurred during the observation period, as radical changes will affect the incidence of costs. It is also important to watch for changes in accounting classifications.

The data will then be grouped by major cost headings, e.g. direct wages, direct material, building costs, power, etc., and an attempt made to correlate cost with activity. Scatter charts may be prepared for each cost group similar to those shown in Fig. 63.

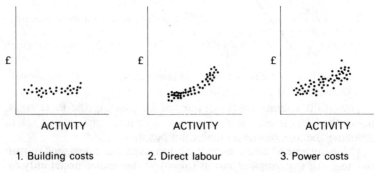

1. Building costs     2. Direct labour     3. Power costs

FIG. 63.—*Scatter charts.*

The first scatter chart for building costs shows a fixed cost and the high costs at some activity levels may merely be heavy repair costs which are not necessarily related to activity. The second chart indicates a variable cost although there is a small degree of change at low activity and a large degree of change at high activity. The third chart indicates a semi-fixed cost.

The separation of the fixed from the variable in the semi-fixed group of costs is a task that may be done graphically, i.e. in the above scatter chart a "line of best fit" could be drawn through the observations and extended to the value axis, thus indicating the fixed cost, i.e. a cost incurred at zero activity. It may also be done statistically by the method of least squares, but then we enter the realm of statistics, which is outside the scope of this book. It is necessary to point out that the semi-fixed cost can be shown in the form of a straight line or a curve, and interpretation of such factors may require a high degree of competence in statistical analysis.

The second, synthetic, approach is based on evaluating each level of production in terms of the requirements of direct labour, supervision, quality control, machines and equipment, working and storage space, etc. It clearly needs considerable experience in the type of manufacture being undertaken.

Situations often arise in which it is necessary to obtain an approximate idea of the relationship between cost and volume when limited information is available. The following example illustrates a simple method of analysing costs:

*EXAMPLE*
From the following information you are asked to predict overhead levels in steps of 1,000 products:

| Production (*units*) | Overhead cost |
|---|---|
| 4,000 | £1,000 |
| 7,000 | £1,600 |

The increase in production of 3,000 units required additional overhead of £600. Therefore this increase is assumed to be variable cost, i.e. it is incurred at the rate of £200 per 1,000 units. The cost levels would therefore be:

| Production: | 4,000 | 5,000 | 6,000 | 7,000 |
|---|---|---|---|---|
| Overhead: | £1,000 | £1,200 | £1,400 | £1,600 |

The fixed overhead can therefore be found by deducting the variable overhead at any particular level. At 4,000 units the variable overhead is £200 × 4 = £800 and therefore the fixed overhead is £200.

It does assume of course that all the increase from £1,000 to £1,600 is due to variable overhead whereas it could be due in part to an increase in fixed overhead.

**The contribution to sales (profit volume) ratio**
Readers should avoid the term "profit volume ratio". The ratio is not meant to describe *net* profit in terms of a given volume, but

to indicate the *rate at which profit is earned*. The ratio is normally expressed as a percentage, i.e.:

$$\frac{\text{Contribution} \times 100}{\text{Sales}}$$

and henceforth will be abbreviated to the "C/S ratio".

In the example used for break-even charts the ratio was $\frac{£5}{£6}$ = 83.3 per cent. The following example illustrates one of the areas where the C/S Ratio is useful.

*EXAMPLE*

Two small businesses Bones & Son and Drown Ltd. in the West Country approach you for additional funds. Your accountant prepares the following statement from the previous year's accounts of the business:

|  | Bones & Son | Drown Ltd. |
|---|---|---|
| Sales units | 1,000 | 2,000 |
| Sales value | £10,000 | £10,000 |
| Variable costs | 6,000 | 2,000 |
| Contribution | 4,000 | 8,000 |
| Fixed costs | 2,400 | 6,400 |
| Net profit | £1,600 | £1,600 |

The important feature of the above figures is that Bones & Son has a C/S ratio of 40 per cent and Drown Ltd. one of 80 per cent. Since the net profit is the same for both businesses at the present sales levels, it is important to know whether sales are likely to increase or decrease. If sales increase by half and both businesses have sufficient capacity to increase their activity without increasing the fixed costs the following will result:

|  | Bones & Son | Drown Ltd. |
|---|---|---|
| Sales | £15,000 | £15,000 |
| Variable cost | 9,000 | 3,000 |
| Contribution | 6,000 | 12,000 |
| Fixed cost | 2,400 | 6,400 |
| Net profit | £3,600 | £5,600 |

Owing to a high C/S ratio Drown Ltd. improves its results dramatically. However, if sales reduce by half the reverse will apply:

|              | *Bones & Son* | *Drown Ltd.* |
|--------------|---------------|--------------|
| Sales        | £5,000        | £5,000       |
| Variable cost | 3,000        | 1,000        |
| Contribution | 2,000         | 4,000        |
| Fixed cost   | 2,400         | 6,400        |
| Net profit (loss) | £(400)   | £(2,400)     |

Because of the high level of fixed costs in Drown Ltd. it suffers a greater loss when business declines. Comparison profit volume charts are shown in Fig. 64.

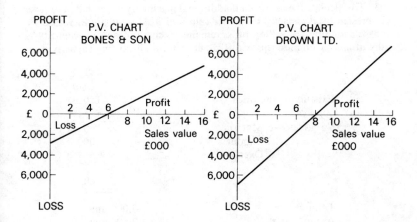

FIG. 64.—*Examples of profit volume charts.*

The C/S ratio can be used as a predictive tool in the same way as contribution per unit when results for a mixture of products are being considered or when a sales unit is an inappropriate measure, e.g. in a contracting business or jobbing manufacturer. The reader by now may have realised that the C/S ratio can be translated as contribution per £1 of sales value and that:

$$\text{Break-even point in sales value} = \frac{\text{Fixed costs}}{\text{C/S ratio}}$$

Thus, when the C/S ratio and total fixed costs are known, the sales value required to obtain a given amount of profit can be calculated.

### EXAMPLE

Referring back to the illustration used to prepare the break-even charts, the C/S ratio is 83.3 per cent and fixed costs are £600 per period.

Break-even sales value $= £600 \div 83.3\%$

$$= 600 \times \frac{6}{5} = £720 \text{ (or 120 units at £6 each)}$$

*EXAMPLE*

The managing director of a spring mattress manufacturing company anticipates that a wage increase of 10 per cent will take effect next year. No other cost changes are predicted. From the following data you are required:

1. To calculate the increase in selling price necessary to maintain the existing contribution/sales ratio.
2. To calculate the additional production required to maintain the same net profit if it is impossible to increase selling prices.
3. To calculate the net profit if additional machinery is purchased to raise the present total capacity by 20 per cent and fixed costs are increased by £5,000 assuming the selling price remains unchanged and all capacity is fully utilised. Compare this with the net profit if all existing capacity were utilised.

|  | *Per unit* |
|---|---|
| Existing selling price | £20 |
| | |
| Variable cost: Material | 7.50 |
| Labour | 3.00 |
| Overhead | 1.50 |
| | £12.00 |
| | |
| Total capacity | 3,000 units |
| Annual sales | 2,500 units |
| Fixed costs | £15,000 |

1.    Existing C/S ratio $= \dfrac{£(20 - 12)}{£20} = 40\%$

∴ Variable costs to sales $= 60\%$
Variable costs will increase by £0.30 per unit to £12.30
To maintain the C/S ratio, the selling price must be increased to

$$\frac{£12.3 \times 100}{60} = £20.50 \text{ per unit.}$$

Proof: C/S ratio $= \dfrac{£(20.50 - 12.30)}{£20.50} = 40\%$.

2.    Contribution per unit $= £(20 - 12) = £8$
Total contribution $= £8 \times 2,500 = £20,000$
Revised contribution $= £(20 - 12.30) = £7.70$

Sales volume required $= \dfrac{£20,000}{£7.70} = 2,597 \text{ units,}$

or an increase over existing sales of 4 per cent.

3.    Revised contribution £7.70
      Total capacity        = 3,600 units
      Total contribution    = 3,600 × £7.70 =     £27,720
      Total fixed costs     = £15,000 + £5,000 = £20,000

      Net profit            =                    £7,720

      Existing capacity     = 3,000
      Total contribution if all capacity
      is utilised and sold = 3,000 × £7.70 = £23,100
      Existing fixed costs                  = £15,000

      Net profit            =   £8,100

An expansion of sales to 3,000 units would increase the net profit by £7.70 × 500 = £3,850. A further increase to 3,600 units would increase contribution by a further £7.70 × 600 = £4,620, but this would be more than offset by the addition to fixed costs of £5,000. Therefore it is important to obtain more than a 20 per cent increase in sales from the additional machinery.

In the above examples, use of the C/S ratio merely expresses volume requirements in terms of sales value rather than in units. The C/S ratio is useful, however, for comparing different products when units are not appropriate measures, e.g. transistor radios versus batteries; or when comparing different companies. A further limitation is introduced when a C/S ratio for a mixture of products is used. Any predictions derived from such a ratio imply that the mixture proportions are constant or that the cost structure is similar for all the products.

*EXAMPLE*

| Period I | Product | Sales Value | Contribution |
|---|---|---|---|
| | A | £10,000 | £5,000 |
| | B | 10,000 | 4,000 |
| | C | 10,000 | 6,000 |
| | | £30,000 | £15,000 |
| C/S ratio | | 50 per cent | |
| *Period II* | A | 4,000 | 2,000 |
| | B | 20,000 | 8,000 |
| | C | 6,000 | 3,600 |
| | | £30,000 | £13,600 |
| C/S ratio | | 45 per cent | |

Note that total sales value and C/S ratio of individual products are unchanged in period II.

### Limitations of break-even analysis

The break-even chart, and profit volume analysis, assumes that simple straight lines can be drawn on a graph to represent sales revenue and costs at various levels of activity. While the concept is valid, one must recognise that there are basic weaknesses in presenting information in this form and any conclusions drawn need to be qualified by the following considerations:

1. The relationships are only true for an individual product or a specific mix of products. A change in mix may significantly change the results.

2. Selling prices are not constant at all levels of sales; a high level of sales may only be obtained by offering substantial discounts, depending, of course, on the degree of competition experienced.

3. Variable costs per unit will, in practice, fluctuate according to (*a*) the extent to which quantity discounts can be obtained on larger purchases of material, (*b*) overtime premiums to be paid to employees and (*c*) general operating efficiency at various levels.

4. Fixed costs are fixed only in respect of a given capacity and each fixed cost has its own "capacity". Factory rent will not increase while increased volume can be obtained from the same working-space, i.e. by working two or three shifts. Supervision, however, will probably increase with each additional shift found necessary.

5. The progression is only true at certain small steps in levels of activity and it is important to know whether an increase or decrease is being shown. When a business suffers a decline in sales it is unlikely to reduce its production employees in direct proportion to the reduction in activity. To do so would cause grave employee problems. It is only when it appears that the business has no hope in the short or medium term of recovering lost sales that it will lay off employees. The same will apply to fixed costs. They will not be incurred indefinitely if the business has considerable unutilised capacity, but the decision to reduce it may be delayed until there is clearly no prospect of obtaining extra business. Although a relationship may exist, or not exist, between activity and cost, the time lag involved in the relationship may obscure the relevance of any analysis.

Provided the above limitations are appreciated, the basic concepts can be usefully applied to business problems.

### The importance of capital employed

Profitability has so far been considered only in terms of a profit or a contribution earned by a product, and the input of factors of production like capital, labour, etc., has been overlooked. A full discussion of the various methods to measure the performance of management can be deferred, and it is assumed that the return on capital employed affords a sufficient practical indication of their efficiency in utilising the resources of the business. It is important to relate the contribution earned by a product to the capital involved in its production and distribution. This is often a difficult exercise, especially where products are processed in common production centres, as it involves an apportionment of common assets over all products. Products earning a small profit compared with the amount of capital invested for their production must be critically reviewed. Improvement may be found by increasing the volume, reducing costs or increasing prices, matters which have already been mentioned in some detail. However, another important aspect of profitability is the utilisation of capital, and some consideration must therefore be given to reducing the capital invested in such things as stocks of material, work-in-progress and finished goods, and also in debtors.

The relationship between profit and capital may be seen in the following equation:

$$\frac{\text{Net profit}}{\text{Sales}} \times \frac{\text{Sales}}{\text{Capital employed}} = \frac{\text{Net profit}}{\text{Capital employed}}.$$

In view of the nature of fixed costs, perhaps it would be more exact to re-write the equation thus:

$$\left(\frac{\text{Contribution}}{\text{Sales}} \times \frac{\text{Sales}}{\text{Capital employed}}\right) - \frac{\text{Fixed costs}}{\text{Capital employed}}$$

$$= \frac{\text{Net profit}}{\text{Capital employed}}$$

This equation shows the relationship between the four basic factors that govern the return on capital employed:

1. The contribution to sales ratio.
2. The volume of sales (Capital Turnover Rate—C.T.R.).
3. The level of fixed costs.
4. The level of capital employed.

*EXAMPLE*

A company manufactures a product which has a C/S ratio of 20 per cent. Annual fixed costs are £1,000 and the capital invested is £2,000. The company requires a return on capital of 10 per cent and wants to know the annual sales necessary to achieve that return.

From the above equation:

$$(20\% \times \text{C.T.R.}) - 50\% = 10\%$$
$$\therefore \text{C.T.R.} = 3$$

i.e. $\dfrac{\text{Sales}}{\text{Capital (£2,000)}} = 3.$

Annual sales $= 3 \times £2,000 = £6,000.$

Previously in this chapter it has been necessary to consider management decisions that are restricted to utilising existing resources as profitably as possible, i.e. the capital employed cannot be changed except in the long term.

## STANDARD MARGINAL COSTING

Chapters 9, 10 and 11 demonstrated the value of variance accounting in helping managers to control costs, as the system highlights variances between planned and actual results. Among the cost variances extracted the fixed overhead variance is analysed between expenditure and volume.

In the present chapter emphasis has been given to the importance of distinguishing fixed from variable overhead, and to the need to calculate the contribution which each product makes to its own fixed costs and to general fixed costs.

A logical extension of standard costing and marginal costing is a system which uses a standard based upon variable costs only. This is termed standard marginal costing.

### Accounting for standard marginal costs

Standard costs will be prepared in the manner described in Chapter 10, except that a fixed overhead absorption rate will not be calculated. A total standard variable cost will thus be obtained and, having set a standard selling price, the standard contribution is found. In preparing the master budget, therefore, budgeted sales units are multiplied by the contribution of each product to give a budgeted total contribution, and from this the budgeted fixed overhead is deducted to arrive at budgeted operating profit.

The costing procedure will follow the lines described in Chapters 10 and 11, and variable cost variances will be obtained in the normal way. Budgets are prepared for fixed overhead incurred specifically by each cost centre, and common fixed overhead, e.g. rent and rates, is budgeted separately without being apportioned to other cost centres. The actual fixed overhead is then allocated to appropriate cost centre accounts, the budgeted figure credited to those accounts and debited to Profit and Loss. Fixed overhead expenditure variances arising would be transferred to the Profit and Loss Account. As fixed overhead is not recovered in the standard cost of production, there is no need to evaluate or analyse volume variances.

### Advantages

Standard marginal costing allows the results of each separate trading period to be more usefully assessed. There is no danger that fixed overhead may be transferred from one accounting period to another, thus giving distorted results when production and sales fluctuate considerably from period to period. The importance of volume is highlighted, not by showing the combined effect on recovery of fixed overhead and on sales margin but by the sales volume variances alone, based upon the standard contribution.

## EXAMPLE

Kimonents Ltd. manufactures a product for the fashion industry and has forecast the annual demand at 40,000 units. Production is to be at an average rate of 10,000 units per three months but will be adjusted according to results of the previous three months. The standard variable cost is £5.00 and standard selling price is £12.00. The annual fixed overhead of the factory is £160,000. The units produced and sold per quarter were as follows:

|  | 1st quarter | 2nd quarter | 3rd quarter | 4th quarter | Total |
|---|---|---|---|---|---|
| Units produced | 10,000 | 9,000 | 10,000 | 11,000 | 40,000 |
| Units sold | 8,000 | 9,000 | 11,000 | 12,000 | 40,000 |

Assuming there were no expenditure or efficiency variances, present the results for each quarter under (a) standard costing and (b) marginal costing, showing in both cases a reconciliation of the budgeted profit with the actual profit.

(a) STANDARD COSTING

|  | 1st quarter £'000 | 2nd quarter £'000 | 3rd quarter £'000 | 4th quarter £'000 | Total £'000 |
|---|---|---|---|---|---|
| Sales | 96 | 108 | 132 | 144 | 480 |
| Standard cost of production | 90 | 81 | 90 | 99 | 360 |
| Stock transfer | (18) | — | 9 | 9 | — |
| Standard cost of sales | 72 | 81 | 99 | 108 | 360 |
| Standard profit | 24 | 27 | 33 | 36 | 120 |
| Fixed overhead volume variance | — | (4) | — | 4 | — |
| Actual net profit | 24 | 23 | 33 | 40 | 120 |

PROFIT RECONCILIATION:

|  | | | | | |
|---|---|---|---|---|---|
| Budgeted profit | 30 | 30 | 30 | 30 | 120 |
| Sales margin quantity variance | 6(A) | 3(A) | 3(F) | 6(F) | — |
| Fixed overhead volume variance | — | 4(A) | — | 4(F) | — |
| Actual profit | 24 | 23 | 33 | 40 | 120 |

(b) MARGINAL COSTING

| | | | | | |
|---|---|---|---|---|---|
| Sales | 96 | 108 | 132 | 144 | 480 |
| | | | | | |
| Variable cost of production | 50 | 45 | 50 | 55 | 200 |
| Stock transfer | (10) | — | 5 | 5 | |
| | | | | | |
| Variable cost of sales | 40 | 45 | 55 | 60 | 200 |
| | | | | | |
| Contribution | 56 | 63 | 77 | 84 | 280 |
| Fixed overhead | 40 | 40 | 40 | 40 | 160 |
| | | | | | |
| Net profit | 16 | 23 | 37 | 44 | 120 |
| | | | | | |
| PROFIT RECONCILIATION: | | | | | |
| Budgeted profit | 30 | 30 | 30 | 30 | 120 |
| Contribution quantity variance | 14(A) | 7(A) | 7(F) | 14(F) | — |
| | | | | | |
| Actual profit | 16 | 23 | 37 | 44 | 120 |

The most significant difference between methods (a) and (b) in the above example is seen in the results for the 1st quarter. It is due to the fact that £8,000 of fixed overhead has been carried forward to succeeding periods in the closing stock figures. When the stock was eventually sold in the 3rd and 4th quarters half of this fixed overhead was charged against the sales for each quarter in addition to the £40,000 which had already been incurred. Also under method (a) the results of the 2nd quarter look peculiar by comparison with the 1st quarter, due to the inclusion of fixed overhead in stock values. An increase of 1,000 units sold leads surprisingly to a decrease of £1,000 in net profit.

## SELF-STUDY TEST No. 10

### Relevant Costs

(Refer to the Appendix on p. 366 for outline solutions.)

1. The following information relates to one month's operations for a single product:

| | Actual | Standard or Budget |
|---|---|---|
| Production | 420 units | 400 units |
| Direct material | £4.30 per unit | £4 per unit |
| Direct wages | £6.20 per unit | £6 per unit |
| Fixed overhead | £3,360 | £3,200 |
| Sales volume | 380 units | 400 units |
| Sales value | £25 per unit | £25 per unit |
| Closing stock | 40 units | — |

Prepare Profit and Loss Statements from the above using (a) total absorption costing; (b) standard costing; and (c) actual marginal costing.

2. Osteopaths Ltd. produces three kinds of ski-suit, Bruise, Break and Crunch. Each type of suit uses the same kind of special material which has recently been introduced and is in short supply. Standard costs, based on monthly output budget of 200 units of each type, are as follows:

|  | Bruise | Break | Crunch |
|---|---|---|---|
| Direct materials | £8 | £16 | £24 |
| Direct labour | 6 | 10 | 20 |
| Overhead absorption | 12 | 20 | 40 |
|  | £26 | £46 | £84 |
| Selling price | £40 | £60 | £100 |

Supplies of raw materials are limited to £8,000 per month and management requires that a minimum of 100 of each, but no more than 200 of each, type of suit is produced each month.

You are required to state the production plan which will maximise monthly profit, subject to the restrictions noted, and calculate the budgeted profit based on your plan.

3. A manufacturing company produces three products, A, B and C. The processes by which they are produced are independent of one another and the sales of any one product are in no way affected by the prices or volume of sales of the other products.

The company's budgeted Profit and Loss Statement is as follows:

|  | Total | A | B | C |
|---|---|---|---|---|
| Sales | £200,000 | £30,000 | £20,000 | £150,000 |
| Variable production cost | £120,000 | £16,000 | £8,000 | £96,000 |
| Fixed production cost (apportioned to products) | 40,000 | 2,000 | 6,000 | 32,000 |
|  | 160,000 | 18,000 | 14,000 | 128,000 |
| Gross profit | £40,000 | £12,000 | £6,000 | £22,000 |
| Variable marketing cost | £16,000 | £5,400 | £5,200 | £5,400 |
| Fixed marketing cost (apportioned to products) | 4,000 | 1,400 | 1,400 | 1,200 |
|  | 20,000 | 6,800 | 6,600 | 6,600 |
| Net profit | £20,000 | £5,200 | — | £15,400 |
| Net loss | — | — | £600 | — |

You may assume that the bases of apportionment of fixed cost are acceptable.

In view of the loss shown by product B, the company proposes to eliminate that product from its range. You are required:

(a) to re-draft the budgeted profit and loss statement to show the profit that would result if product B were eliminated;

(b) to state whether or not you agree with the company's proposals. Give your reasons very briefly.

4. Management are often faced with the situation where a component which is manufactured by their own organisation has a cost, as disclosed by the cost accounts, in excess of that which would have to be paid if it were bought on the open market. However a decision to discontinue manufacture and buy in cannot be made simply by comparing internal costs with external buying prices. Discuss the other factors which management would have to consider distinguishing clearly between those of a financial and a non-financial nature.

5. The budgeted sales of three companies are as follows:

|  | Company 1 | Company 2 | Company 3 |
|---|---|---|---|
| Budgeted sales in units | 10,000 | 10,000 | 10,000 |
| Budgeted selling price per unit | £2.00 | £2.00 | £2.00 |
| Budgeted variable costs per unit | £1.50 | £1.25 | £1.00 |
| Budgeted fixed expenses total | £3,000 | £5,500 | £8,000 |
| Budgeted capacity | 80% | 80% | 80% |

From the above information you are required to compute the following for each company:

(a) the budgeted profit;

(b) the budgeted break-even point in unit sales;

(c) the budgeted margin between break-even point and budgeted sales expressed as a percentage of total capacity;

(d) the impact on profits of a ±10 per cent deviation in budgeted sales.

Comment briefly on the effect of changes in sales volume in relation to the distribution between the companies' fixed and variable expenses.

6. The following data relates to a manufacturing organisation:

| Total capacity | 75,000 units |
|---|---|
| Fixed expenses | £12,000 p.a. |
| Variable expenses | £0.75 per unit manufactured |
| Sales value: | |
| Up to 40,000 units | £1.50 per unit |
| and then at | £1.00 per unit |

Draft a break-even chart incorporating the above data.

7. Crown Manufacturing Co. Ltd., manufactures power tools. Maximum production from existing plant is 2,000 units per year. The production cost of each power tool is calculated as follows

| Direct material | £20 |
|---|---|
| Direct labour | 20 hours at £2 per hour |
| Variable overhead | £1.50 per hour |

Fixed overhead is estimated at £18,000 per annum. Selling price of the tool is £120. Next year sales are forecasted at 1,600 units.

You are required to do the following:

(a) To calculate: (i) break-even point; (ii) maximum profit; and (iii) profit at the forecast sales level of 1,600 units.

(b) An enquiry has been received regarding an export order for 400 power tools at a selling price of £110. If the order is accepted additional costs of £6,000 will be incurred.

Advise whether the order should be accepted giving reasons for your advice.

8. Under what circumstances can selling prices be advantageously set below total cost?

9. Rustnot Ltd. produces an anti-corrosion compound. The following budget has been prepared for next year

| | | |
|---|---|---|
| Raw material | 25,000 litres | £100,000 |
| Direct wages | 30,000 hours | 75,000 |
| Variable overhead | | 25,000 |
| | | |
| Variable costs | | 200,000 |
| Fixed costs | | 125,000 |
| | | |
| Total cost | | 325,000 |
| Profit | | 65,000 |
| | | |
| Sales | | £390,000 |

The company has received a bulk order for the compound but the managing director doubts the wisdom of acceptance because supplies of the raw material are scarce and the factory is already working at full capacity. The order would use 5,000 litres of material and 4,000 hours of labour.

Calculate the minimum price at which the company could accept the order, assuming that the price is based on:

(a) absorption costing principles with fixed overhead absorption on labour hours and profit based on total cost;
(b) raw material supplies are the limiting factor;
(c) direct labour is the limiting factor.

Add any comments you think relevant.

# CHAPTER 13

# The Double Entry Aspect of Cost Accounting

## INTRODUCTION

In previous chapters the desirability of combining financial and costing records has been emphasised, and the manner of making entries in the financial books based on data supplied by the cost department explained. It will perhaps be helpful if the records which the cost department maintains are summarised in this chapter so that the documents and procedures described throughout this book can be brought into focus and the manner in which they fit into the double-entry framework described.

The size of the business will probably determine the complexity of the cost records. Small businesses will doubtless keep simple records not linked to the financial accounts. Larger businesses will maintain a full set of cost accounts, which will provide the detail behind totals shown in the financial accounts. In some firms the cost accounts will be kept independently of the financial accounts and periodic reconciliations will be necessary. In others, the cost accounts form part of the formal accounting system and no reconciliation is necessary. The latter method is more satisfactory because it avoids duplication of effort and reconciliation problems. However, both are in use and the system which maintains a cost ledger separate from the financial ledger will be explained first.

## THE RECORDS

The cost accountant must use a great deal of the information which is also available to the financial accountant, e.g. purchases daybook, expenses daybook, payroll, main journal, sales daybook, etc. In addition, various abstracts and analyses are required: material requisitions/returns/transfers, time-sheets, purchase analysis, expense analysis, overhead distribution by cost centre, sales analysis, etc.

The structure of the cost accounts will be framed according to the complexity of the business and will often include accounts for: cost elements, cost centres (production, marketing and general administration), job costs (production, repairs, capital) and stock (raw material, component, finished goods).

Total accounts will be necessary for job costs and stocks, and small self-contained ledgers will be kept to facilitate control.

## THE COST LEDGER

It is now possible to illustrate the entries to be made in the cost ledger of a small business which is manufacturing to customers' specific orders. Such entries may be made at convenient intervals, depending on the frequency with which the accounts are prepared.

The cost ledger is the principal ledger in the cost accounting book-keeping system when the system is separated from the financial accounts. Generally, the cost ledger will contain

1. Control accounts for Stores, Work-in-progress, Finished goods and Overhead. Each control account will be supported by a subsidiary ledger to provide the necessary detail for accounting control and preparation of information.

2. Accounts for Wages, Sales, Cost of sales, together with any other account needed in the cost book-keeping system, e.g. Notional charges, Suspense accounts.

3. A Cost Ledger Contra Account. This account is needed to maintain the double-entry principle within the cost ledger and contains postings which affect accounts outside the costing system, e.g. Debtors, Creditors, Cash.

The focal point of the cost accounting system is the Work-in-progress ledger. In a specific order business, the ledger will contain a separate account for each job and will be debited with the cost of materials used, wages allocated and production overhead *absorbed*. The cost of completed jobs is debited to Finished goods ledger. When the job is delivered to the customer, Cost of sales will be debited with the Job cost and Sales credited with the selling price. Thus, a Costing Profit and Loss Statement can be prepared, analysed by job, and balances on the control accounts represent the cost value of Stores, Work-in-progress and Finished goods.

The entries are shown in diagrammatic form in Fig. 65.

*EXAMPLE*

The following data were extracted from the financial records for a month:

|  |  |
|---|---|
| Purchases | £21,296 |
| Gross pay | £8,640 |
| Direct expenses | £810 |
| Indirect expenses | £4,429 |
| Sales | £28,250 |

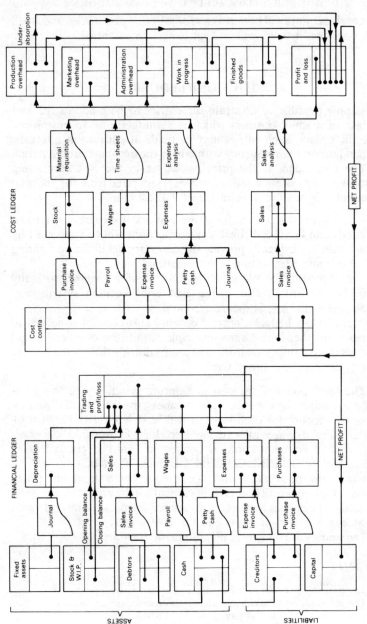

FIG. 65.—*Basic accounting entries in financial and cost ledgers.*

An analysis of sales invoices was prepared:

JOB NOS.

|  | 101 | 102 | 103 | 104 | Total |
|---|---|---|---|---|---|
| Sales value | £3,500 | £2,500 | £12,250 | £10,000 | £28,250 |

The cost department allocated direct costs to jobs for the month:

PRODUCTION JOB NOS.

|  | 101 | 102 | 103 | 104 | 105 | Total |
|---|---|---|---|---|---|---|
| Material | £1,839 | £998 | £6,205 | £5,264 | £940 | £15,246 |
| Transfers | 25 | — | — | (25) | — | — |
| Wages | 591 | 508 | 2,900 | 2,400 | 1,719 | 8,118 |
| Expenses | 50 | 280 | 217 | 245 | 18 | 810 |
|  | £2,505 | £1,786 | £9,322 | £7,884 | £2,677 | £24,174 |

The Overhead Distribution Summary provided the following analysis of expenses:

|  | Production overhead | Marketing overhead | Administration overhead |
|---|---|---|---|
| Fixed | £2,100 | £294 | £1,045 |
| Variable | 800 | 80 | 110 |
|  | £2,900 | £374 | £1,155 |

In addition, indirect materials amounting to £220 were issued from stock and the balance of gross pay represented indirect production labour.

A predetermined production overhead absorption rate had been set at the beginning of the year and overhead was debited to the job costs as follows:

PRODUCTION JOB NOS.

|  | 101 | 102 | 103 | 104 | 105 | Total |
|---|---|---|---|---|---|---|
| Production overhead | £289 | £205 | £1,062 | £906 | £693 | £3,155 |

Stock of raw materials at the beginning of the month was £2,465. There were no opening stocks of work in progress or finished goods.

The information would be posted to the cost ledger as follows:

### Cost Ledger Contra Account

| | | | |
|---|---|---|---|
| Sales | £28,250 | Balance b/f | £2,465 |
| Balance c/f | 11,665 | Purchases | 21,296 |
| | | Wages | 8,640 |
| | | Expenses | 5,239 |
| | | Profit and Loss Account: profit for month | 2,275 |
| | £39,915 | | £39,915 |

### Stores Control Account

| | | | |
|---|---|---|---|
| Balance b/f | £2,465 | Work-in-progress | £15,246 |
| Cost ledger contra | 21,296 | Production overhead | 220 |
| | | Balance c/fwd. | 8,295 |
| | £23,761 | | £23,761 |

### Wages Account

| | | | |
|---|---|---|---|
| Cost ledger contra | £8,640 | Work-in-progress | £8,118 |
| | | Production overhead | 522 |
| | £8,640 | | £8,640 |

### Expenses Account

| | | | |
|---|---|---|---|
| Cost ledger contra | £5,239 | Work-in-progress | £810 |
| | | Production overhead | 2,900 |
| | | Marketing overhead | 374 |
| | | Admin. overhead | 1,155 |
| | £5,239 | | £5,239 |

### Production Overhead Control Account

| | | | |
|---|---|---|---|
| Expenses | £2,900 | Work-in-progress (absorbed) | £3,155 |
| Stores | 220 | Profit and loss: under-absorbed | 487 |
| Wages | 522 | | |
| | £3,642 | | £3,642 |

### Work-in-progress Control Account

| | | | |
|---|---|---|---|
| Stores | £15,246 | Finished goods | £23,959 |
| Wages | 8,118 | Balance c/f | 3,370 |
| Expenses | 810 | | |
| Production overhead | 3,155 | | |
| | £27,329 | | £27,329 |

### Finished Goods Control Account

| | | | |
|---|---|---|---|
| Work-in-progress | £23,959 | Cost of Sales | £23,959 |

### Marketing Overhead Account

| | | | |
|---|---|---|---|
| Expenses | £374 | Profit and loss | £374 |

### Administration Overhead Account

| | | | |
|---|---|---|---|
| Expenses | £1,155 | Profit and loss | £1,155 |

### Cost of Sales Account

| | | | |
|---|---|---|---|
| Finished goods | £23,959 | Profit and loss | £23,959 |

### Sales Account

| | | | |
|---|---|---|---|
| Profit and loss | £28,250 | Cost ledger contra | £28,250 |

### Costing Profit and Loss Account
#### Job Nos.

| | 101 | 102 | 103 | 104 | Total |
|---|---|---|---|---|---|
| Sales | £3,500 | £2,500 | £12,250 | £10,000 | £28,250 |
| Prime cost | 2,505 | 1,786 | 9,322 | 7,884 | 21,497 |
| Overhead absorbed | 289 | 205 | 1,062 | 906 | 2,462 |
| | 2,794 | 1,991 | 10,384 | 8,790 | 23,959 |
| Gross margin | £706 | £509 | £1,866 | £1,210 | 4,291 |

| | |
|---|---:|
| Under-absorbed production overhead | £487 |
| Marketing overhead | 374 |
| Administration overhead | 1,155 |
| | 2,016 |
| Net profit to Cost Contra Account | £2,275 |

The balance on the Cost Contra Account can be agreed as follows:

| | |
|---|---:|
| Stores Control Account balance | £8,295 |
| Work-in-progress: Job 105 | 3,370 |
| Balance per Cost Contra Account | £11,665 |

NOTE:

(*i*) The term *"control"* account implies that a subsidiary ledger is kept. Entries to control accounts represent summary postings.

(*ii*) The Profit and Loss Account could be kept in double-entry form and re-arranged for the vertical presentation shown above.

(*iii*) In a small business of this kind, the Finished Goods Account may be dispensed with as completed jobs are generally despatched to the customer as soon as they are ready.

The reader will appreciate that the book-keeping system would need to be modified depending on the nature of the business and the requirements of management. The main modifications, however, would be to the subsidiary ledgers; for example, in a process type of business, the Work-in-Progress Ledger would be analysed by process and Finished Goods Ledger analysed by product. A standard costing system would require variance accounts to be incorporated as appropriate.

## RECONCILIATION OF COSTING AND FINANCIAL PROFIT

The profit disclosed by the Costing Profit and Loss Account may differ from that shown in the financial Profit and Loss Account and it is necessary to reconcile them. The difference may be due to the following matters:

1. APPROPRIATIONS OF PROFIT NOT DEALT WITH IN THE COST ACCOUNTS

(*a*) Corporation tax.

(*b*) Transfers to general reserve or any other fund of accumulated profits, e.g. dividend equalisation reserve.

(*c*) Charitable donations, where no direct benefit is derived therefrom by the company's employees.

(*d*) Dividends paid on the share capital of the company.

(*e*) Additional provisions for depreciation of buildings, plant, etc., and for bad debts.

(*f*) Amounts written off goodwill, preliminary expenses, underwriting commission, debenture discount, expenses of capital issues, etc.

(*g*) Appropriations to sinking funds for the purpose of providing for the repayment of loans or debentures.

2. PURELY FINANCIAL MATTERS, i.e. THOSE WHICH ARISE OUT OF POLITICAL DECISIONS AND WHICH ARE OUTSIDE THE SCOPE OF MANUFACTURE

(*a*) Interest *received* on bank deposits and investments.

(*b*) Rents receivable. If, however, rents are received from a portion of the business premises which has been sublet, the profit rental only should be excluded from the cost records. The proportion which represents recovery of rent paid will be deducted from total rent to ascertain the net cost of the premises to be included in the cost records.

(*c*) Profits or losses on sales of investments, buildings and other fixed assets; capital expenditure charged specifically to revenue.

(*d*) Interest on bank loans, mortgages, debentures and other borrowed money, if interest on capital is ignored in the cost records.

(*e*) Damages payable at law.

(*f*) Penalties payable for late completion of contracts.

(*g*) Losses due to scrapping machinery before the date estimated when depreciation and obsolescence were provided for.

3. ITEMS WHOSE COSTING TREATMENT DIFFERS FROM THAT ADOPTED IN THE FINANCIAL ACCOUNTS

(*a*) Under- and over-recoveries of overhead due to deliberate omission from the cost accounts, e.g. selling costs, or to approximation in the basis of recovery or to fluctuations in output.

(*b*) Differences in the valuation of stocks and work-in-progress. Stocks are frequently valued in the cost accounts at a figure which includes an appropriate allotment of overhead, which, from the point of view of ascertaining the profit on manufacture, is perfectly justifiable. It may be thought prudent when preparing the financial accounts to value stocks at prime costs only.

(*c*) Depreciation. It has been pointed out in Chapter 5 that depreciation in the cost accounts may in certain circumstances be charged on the basis of production units or hours, while in the financial accounts it is usually provided for in the form of a charge for the period, irrespective of the actual level of production output.

(*d*) Abnormal losses in production and storage, and abnormal idle time. In the financial accounts these losses will be "merged" in the appropriate accounts, i.e. the figure of sales will be *exclusive* of finished products wasted, and the debits for materials and wages will be *inclusive* of any abnormal losses of material or time. In the cost accounts such abnormal losses may be ignored as outside the scope of manufacturing costs.

## INTEGRAL ACCOUNTS

The reconciliation referred to in the previous section is frequently a task calling for considerable expenditure of time and effort, much of which can be avoided if the books are suitably designed and the concept of separate Profit and Loss Accounts for financial and costing purposes discarded in favour of a unified set of accounts which will serve both financial and management purposes. Such a system of accounting is referred to as "integrated" or "integral", and would be designed on the following principles:

1. The degree of integration must be determined. Some undertakings find it satisfactory merely to integrate up to the stage of prime cost, leaving overhead allotment to be dealt with in memorandum form only.

2. Dependent upon the degree of integration decided upon, the normal classification of expenditure by nature is discarded. In some systems a single control account is opened to which all expenditure and revenue which is the subject of costing treatment is posted. Such a control account operates in the same way as a debtors control account, i.e. it contains a summary of transactions posted to the cost ledger in detail. It is, however, more usual for separate control accounts to be opened in the formal records in the same way as control accounts were opened within the cost ledger for Stores, Work-in-progress, Overhead, etc., under a separate accounting system.

3. Full details of items posted to the control accounts are supplied to the cost department at convenient intervals, accompanied by prelists or registers of amounts to ensure completeness.

4. The information is then dealt with by the cost department in accordance with the system of costing in force and with the following objectives in mind:

(*a*) To provide the necessary costing data.

(*b*) To form the basis of journal entries so that the control accounts can be cleared to suitable revenue accounts, culminating in a profit and loss account.

5. The amount of detail which is recorded in the ledger itself depends upon circumstances but is usually kept to a minimum, full information regarding each department or process being contained in subsidiary ledgers (based of course upon exactly the same data). Postings to subsidiary ledgers are sometimes referred to as third

entries to emphasise that they are not part of the double entry of the accounting system.

Application of the above principles will facilitate preparation of operating statements in the form required from data which is subject to routine accounting control. The conventional analysis of expenditure required for statutory purposes and for external reporting can be accommodated by modifying the classification procedures within subsidiary ledgers.

## ACCOUNTS CLASSIFICATION AND CODES

In an organisation of any size, cost and financial data will be so numerous that details need to be summarised under suitable headings before it can be processed and assimilated by management. For example, many types of indirect material will be used in the factory and in reporting consumption typical headings under which it is summarised might be:

| | |
|---|---|
| Cleaning material. | Small tools. |
| Lubrication. | Packing material. |
| Fuel. | Foodstuffs. |
| Protective clothing. | Replacement parts. |
| Stationery. | Miscellaneous. |

By using such groups, the number of accounts can be reduced and the groups can also be used for budgeting purposes, etc. In order to assemble data under these headings, it is vital to use code numbers or letters and to prepare an accounts manual which contains, among other things, a list of all current codes with explanatory notes on their use. A good manual will be one which is comprehensive, unambiguous and well indexed, so that invoices, requisitions, time-sheets, etc., can be coded quickly and accurately.

The code structure adopted can be prepared in several ways but it is important that it follows a logical sequence, i.e. all common items are together, that it is flexible enough to accommodate additions and that it is arranged in a way that aids memory. If the system is so complex that a code in excess of 6 digits must be used then it is preferable to adopt a composite code suitably structured like 024–824–03 rather than in the form 2482403. A simple accounts code showing some of the accounts likely to be encountered is given below:

ASSETS

*Fixed Assets*

| | | | |
|---|---|---|---|
| 0000–0099 | Land | 0600–0699 | Handling equipment |
| 0100–0299 | Buildings | 0700–0799 | Heating plant |
| 0300–0399 | Machine tools | 0800–0899 | Tools and patterns |
| 0400–0499 | Containers and tanks | 0900–0999 | Miscellaneous fixed assets, patents and goodwill |
| 0500–0599 | Vehicles | | |

ASSETS—*cont.*

*Current Assets*

Raw stocks:

| | |
|---|---|
| 1000–1039 | gas |
| 1040–1079 | liquids |
| 1080–1129 | solids |
| 1130–1149 | miscellaneous |

Semi-finished
component stocks:

| | |
|---|---|
| 1150–1209 | unmachined |
| 1210–1279 | machined |
| 1280–1299 | miscellaneous |

Consumable stocks:

| | |
|---|---|
| 1300–1309 | cleaning |
| 1310–1319 | lubrication |
| 1320–1329 | fuel |
| 1330–1339 | protective clothing |
| 1340–1349 | stationery |
| 1350–1359 | small tools |
| 1360–1369 | packing material |
| 1370–1379 | foodstuffs |
| 1380–1389 | replacement parts |
| 1390–1399 | miscellaneous |

| | |
|---|---|
| 1400–1499 | Finished products |

Work-in-progress:

| | |
|---|---|
| 1500–1549 | stock orders |
| 1550–1599 | customer orders |
| 1600–1649 | asset orders |
| 1650–1699 | repair orders |
| 1700–1749 | miscellaneous orders |

| | |
|---|---|
| 1750–1799 | Debtors and pre-payments |
| 1800–1849 | Investments and loans to associated companies |
| 1850–1999 | Cash and bank accounts |

LIABILITIES

| | |
|---|---|
| 2000–2099 | Share capital |
| 2100–2199 | Loans, debentures and mortgages |

LIABILITIES—*cont.*

| | |
|---|---|
| 2200–2399 | Profit & Loss Account and Reserves |
| 2400–2499 | Taxation |
| 2500–2699 | Creditors and accrued charges |
| 2700–2999 | Miscellaneous liabilities |

COST CENTRES

*Manufacture*

| | |
|---|---|
| 3000–3009 | Foundries |
| 3010–3019 | Machine shops |
| 3020–3029 | Carpenters |
| 3030–3039 | Fabrication shops |
| 3040–3049 | Press shop |
| 3050–3059 | Electrical shops |
| 3060–3069 | Assembly shops |
| 3070–3079 | Finishing shops |
| 3080–3089 | Processes |

*Services*

| | |
|---|---|
| 3110 | Work study |
| 3120 | Stores and internal transport |
| 3130 | Production control |
| 3140 | Quality control |
| 3150 | Tool room |
| 3160 | Maintenance |
| 3170 | Power generation |
| 3180 | Factory management |

*Administration*

| | |
|---|---|
| 3210 | Correspondence and filing |
| 3220 | Accounts |
| 3230 | Costing and budgets |
| 3240 | Purchasing |
| 3250 | Computer department |
| 3260 | Corporate planning |
| 3270 | Secretarial |
| 3280 | Managing director |

*Research and Development*

| | |
|---|---|
| 3310 | Laboratory |
| 3320 | Product design |
| 3330 | Product testing |
| 3340 | Drawing office |

*Marketing*

| | |
|---|---|
| 3410 | Publicity |
| 3420 | Sales office |
| 3430 | Representatives |
| 3440 | Market research |
| 3510 | Garage |
| 3520 | Packing |
| 3530 | Despatch |
| 3540 | Warehouse |
| 3550 | Retailing |

INCOME

| | |
|---|---|
| 4000–4799 | Product sales |
| 4800–4899 | Investment income |
| 4900–4999 | Miscellaneous income |

EXPENDITURE
*Wages*

Direct employees:

| | |
|---|---|
| 5000–5099 | productive wages |
| 5100–5199 | non-productive wages |
| 5200–5299 | overtime and shift premiums |
| 5300–5349 | sick and holiday pay |
| 5350–5399 | miscellaneous wages |

Indirect employees:

| | |
|---|---|
| 5400–5499 | supervisory |
| 5500–5599 | clerical |
| 5600–5699 | technical |
| 5700–5799 | service |
| 5800–5899 | selling |
| 5900–5999 | miscellaneous |

*Expenses*

| | |
|---|---|
| 6000–6039 | Rent |
| 6040–6079 | Rates |
| 6080–6109 | Insurance |
| 6110–6149 | Depreciation |
| 6150–6189 | Outside cleaning |
| 6190–6229 | Professional fees |
| 6230–6269 | Carriage |
| 6270–6309 | Postage |
| 6310–6349 | Telephone |
| 6350–6389 | Travelling |
| 6390–6429 | Legal |
| 6430–6469 | Patents and royalties |
| 6470–6509 | Subscriptions |
| 6510–6549 | Donations |
| 6550–6589 | Advertising |
| 6590–6629 | Entertaining |
| 6630–6669 | Printing and sales literature |
| 6670–6709 | Pensions |
| 6710–6749 | Employer's N.H.I. |
| 6750–6789 | Training |
| 6790–6829 | Licences |
| 6830–6869 | Electricity |
| 6870–6909 | Water |
| 6910–6949 | Gas |
| 6950–6999 | Miscellaneous expenses |

MISCELLANEOUS ACCOUNTS

| | |
|---|---|
| 7000–7499 | Charges transferred from other cost centres |
| 7500–7999 | Repair costs charged to cost centres |
| 8000–8999 | Cost of sales and variance accounts |
| 9000–9999 | Non-costing items |

The block of codes allocated for work-in-progress would be used for product analysis. A serial number allocated in sequence would be given to each separate order. Similarly the block of codes for stock materials would relate to basic types and a more detailed code structure would be prepared so that each item of stock has its own code. This has already been illustrated in Chapter 3.

The section of expenditure codes 7000–7499 is used when, for example, service departments are charged to production departments. Similarly the section 7500–7999 is used when repair costs, collected in the work-in-progress section 1650–1699, are to be charged to departments for which the repairs are incurred.

The section 9000–9999 could be used for items of a confidential nature which are not to be charged in the cost accounts.

The working of the above accounts code is illustrated in the following example.

*EXAMPLE*

Production control issue a stock order for the production of 100 brass components by the light machine shop. The company employs standard costing.

The material requisition could be coded as follows:

Department using material        3012 (light machine shop)
Material identification code      1151–3987 (brass forging)
Stock order                       1510–1201 (serial job number)

The requisition could then be dealt with in the following way:

1. Perpetual Inventory Record 1151–3987 would be posted to update the stock balance and in the ledger, stock group account 1151 would be credited.

2. Work-in-Progress Account 1510 would be debited and the cost sheet for order 1510–1201 would be posted.

The time-sheet of the machinist would be similarly coded:

Department in which employed      3012
Wage classification               5012 (productive wages—lathe operator)
Stock order                       1510–1201

The entry for the above would be:

1. Credit Wages Control Account 5012.
2. Debit Work-in-Progress Account 1510 and enter the wages on the job cost sheet.

The overhead to be absorbed would then be calculated and the entries would be:

1. Credit Cost Centre Account 3012.
2. Debit Work-in-Progress Account 1510 and post the job cost sheet.

When the stock order has been completed and passed into stores a job completion note should be prepared which would be dealt with as follows:

1. Record the standard cost of the order.
2. Credit the Work-in-Progress Account at standard cost and close job cost sheet (computing the variance).
3. Debit the Stock Group Account 1215 (Brass components) and update the perpetual inventory record 1251–3987 with the receipt of 100 components.

## COST AUDIT

In any organisation the work of statutory auditors can be greatly assisted by the organisation itself maintaining full internal control. By this is meant the various steps taken to safeguard its assets and to secure the accuracy and reliability of its records. Mention has previously been made of the importance of internal check, i.e. a system of checks built in to daily routines whereby accounting work is so arranged that one person automatically checks the work of another. Internal check is but one aspect of internal control, the other being internal audit, which is an examination of the accounting records of the organisation to determine their accuracy and comprehensiveness. The cost audit is part of the work of the internal auditor and, as its name implies, is concerned with the audit of the cost accounts. The Institute of Cost and Management Accountants has defined cost audit as "the verification of cost records and accounts and a check on the adherence to the prescribed cost accounting procedures and the continuing relevance of such procedures."

The cost audit must be carried out systematically to a programme. The audit will cost money in terms of the auditor himself and of the time of employees spent in supplying information to the auditor. Audit work must be directed to those areas where weakness or errors are likely to be most serious in either fraud or false costing data. The auditor must be completely familiar with the manufacturing sequence and methods as well as with the accounting systems, but he must act virtually as an independent person and be allowed to operate as a statutory auditor. The scope for the cost audit will be in the following areas:

1. *Material.* The goods inwards procedure must be looked into to ascertain if materials are inspected when received and what detail is normally recorded of the goods received. The auditor should check that adequate payment control procedures exist for receipts of material.

Storekeeping arrangements would be scrutinised to assess security arrangements, storage methods, issuing methods and the degree of deterioration in stores.

Checks will be made to establish the adequacy of records for the movement of material including authorisation of requisitions and the record of stock balances, i.e. perpetual inventory records.

Pricing methods require careful scrutiny to determine, for example, the system for recording changes in stock prices and the accuracy of calculating, say, weighted average prices, if used. The system for checking stock regularly and/or at the accounting year end should be clarified, and the treatment of slow-moving and obsolete stock items.

The system employed to process the data to record material movements in the cost accounts must be tested to ensure that data cannot by-pass the accounts without it being reported and action taken.

2. *Wages.* All forms used in the preparation of the payroll must be checked, to ensure that the correct rate of pay is used and that the attendance hours on the clock cards agree with the hours recorded on the job cards, if any.

Authorisation and recording of wage-rate changes and overtime payments need to be checked.

Time recording methods should be looked into to ensure that job times represent time actually worked, and where bonus schemes are in operation enquiries should be made concerning the assessment of completed work in terms of quantity and quality.

The wages office procedures should be reviewed to ensure that a system of internal check is employed throughout.

3. *Overhead.* An approved system must be seen to operate for the authorisation for payment of expense invoices and petty cash disbursements.

Allocation and apportionment of overhead must be compared with the latest instructions given in the cost-accounting procedures manual.

The policy concerning the inclusion of overhead in stock, work-in-progress and internally manufactured assets must be compared with the current practice in the cost department.

Accounting entries for the under- or over-absorption of overhead must be checked to see if they agree with the organisation's policy. The adequacy of the absorption rates should be reviewed and the method of calculation and absorption in cost units.

4. *General.* Where standard costing is in use, the method of calculating new standards should be investigated and also the procedure for reviewing old standards.

As a general point, wherever master lists of accounting codes and instructions are kept, it should be seen that they are kept up to date, and that old instructions are properly withdrawn.

A possible extension of a cost audit would be to test the validity of fixed and variable classifications (if any) applied to overhead costs.

The cost auditor would use suitably worded questionnaires and should give a formal report to his superior (say, the chief internal auditor), who would then, where necessary, discuss these matters with the cost accountant.

## UNIFORM COSTING

The Institute of Cost and Management Accountants defines uniform costing as "the use by several undertakings of the same costing systems, i.e. the same basic costing methods and superimposed principles and techniques". It is not therefore a distinctive form of costing but refers to the cost system designed by, for example, a trade association for use by their members.

## Advantages

The advantages of uniform costing may be summarised as follows:

1. The smaller business probably feels that a full costing system is something of an expensive luxury, and tries to manage on rather scanty costing information. If the trade association, to which the business belongs, develops a system tailored to meet the specific requirements of the industry, the individual business will be able to adopt a useful system at reasonable cost. Help in implementing the system may well be given by experts working with the association.

2. It is always helpful for management to be able to compare the costs of its own business with the average costs in the industry. As the comparison will be derived from information prepared on the same principles, areas of inefficiency may be more clearly revealed.

3. Where selling prices are largely determined by the manufacturer's costs, there is a danger that a business may attract a high proportion of unprofitable work because its costing system is weak or unscientific and bears little resemblance to the systems adopted by most other firms. This situation will be rectified with a good uniform costing system. It will not destroy competition because prices will still be determined by the businesses themselves, but they will be based upon accurate cost data.

4. The adoption of uniform costing in an industry provides the means whereby relevant information can be obtained to help in negotiations with government departments, trade unions, etc.

The disadvantage of uniform costing is that some undertakings may find that because their circumstances are unlike those of the majority of members in the industry, the system does not really meet the needs of management and a compromise must be arrived at. A particular problem arises when a business manufactures a range of products and is a member of more than one trade association.

## Features

If the data assembled by a trade association from its members is to be useful, it must have been prepared according to specific instructions. The scheme must therefore instruct the members on the following matters.

1. The classification, coding and definition of account headings and cost centres. The principles used in distinguishing, for example,

between fixed and variable costs, direct and indirect costs, and sales overhead and distribution overhead, must be fully explained.

2. The cost units to be adopted, i.e. weight, volume or units.

3. The calculation of material prices. Material may form quite a high proportion of total costs and it is important therefore to give instructions as to the inclusion of items such as carriage, discounts, handling charges, duties and administration costs.

4. The method of pricing issues from stores, e.g. first in first out, weighted average, etc.

5. The treatment of items such as overtime and shift premiums, bonuses, idle time, etc.

6. The method of allotting overhead to cost centres. Some guidance should be given on the normal basis to be used, and the procedure for apportioning service department overhead to other cost centres.

7. The basis for absorbing overhead into cost units, e.g. machine hours, labour hours, etc., and the capacity to be used for calculating absorption rates.

8. The length of the costing period, e.g. a monthly or four-weekly period.

9. The treatment of joint costs (where applicable).

10. The treatment of scrap, stock losses, etc., including the proceeds of the sale of scrap.

11. The method of depreciation (e.g. straight line or reducing balance) and the treatment of deferred charges.

12. Recommendations on the inclusion of overhead in work-in-progress, and in internally manufactured assets, etc.

13. Method of presenting information. Normally standard forms will be designed where members are requested to report their results to the trade association.

14. Notional charges. Complications can arise where, for example, some firms own their own premises and others rent them, and notional items may be included to make the figures comparable with those of other members.

15. The treatment of under- and over-absorption of overhead.


## THE PREPARATION OF COST STATEMENTS

The information which a statement is designed to convey emerges with greater clarity, and is of more benefit to the reader, if it is prepared in accordance with certain principles, of which simplicity is one of the most important.

It must be borne in mind that the person to whom the cost statement is presented may not be trained in the rapid assimilation of figures, and indeed in many cases may be suspicious of, or even hostile to, them. The use of technical accountancy terms and the character-istic accountancy presentation in debit and credit form should usually be discarded. Most persons unversed in accountancy find the columnar presentation of figures easier to understand than the debit and credit method. Too many sub-totals and inset figures can also be confusing.

In preparing a cost statement its particular purpose should be borne in mind. Normally an exhaustive report on a whole series of transactions is not required. The main purpose is to direct attention to a particular circumstance or weakness in operation so that the recipient can take action either to remedy a state of affairs shown to be unsatisfactory or to expand those operations which appear to be sound and profitable.

It is therefore of assistance if the accountant, in preparing cost statements for the purpose of management, endeavours to place him-self in the position of the recipient, asking himself the question: What are the important matters, i.e. costs, losses, comparisons, etc., of which I should be informed so as to enable me to take the right decisions in controlling this particular set of operations?

The paramount necessity of simplicity in all cost statements has been emphasised. Clearly, over-simplification must be avoided, as the truth can be obscured as easily by too little information as by too much. But it is usually preferable to relegate detail to an appendix or supporting schedule so that it may be referred to when necessary, rather than to confuse the main statement with excessive data.

The variety of industrial activities and the consequent range of cost statements which the cost accountant may be called upon to prepare for control purposes make it impossible to do more than give the general principles which must be borne in mind in preparing them. It must be noted that within the same industry, and even within the same business, the form and layout of a cost statement will vary in accordance with the level of management for whom it is prepared and the information it is desired to show. Many control statements are prepared in quantities rather than in values and deal with such units as hours, tonnes and litres, though figures of cost may be tabulated side by side with physical units and a cost per unit cal-culated.

Examples of cost statements appear throughout this book and the reader will find it useful to appraise the statements with a critical eye to determine how the presentation could be improved and whether they communicate the vital information clearly.

## Basic rules

1. A suitable descriptive heading should be given, indicating the period covered.

2. The unit should be stated or, if both quantities and values are presented, each column should be clearly headed.

3. Columnar figures are preferable to those in debit and credit form. If comparable, figures of different departments should be set out side by side.

4. It is usually sufficient to work to the nearest pound of total figures.

5. Comparative figures should be suitably headed with the period to which they relate. They should be truly comparative, i.e. all figures should be prepared on the same basis.

6. The level of management for which the statement is prepared should be borne in mind and its scope designed accordingly. A departmental manager should receive details of the figures of his department only; his superior officer should receive details of all departments which he controls. Usually, subordinate levels of management will receive statements containing greater detail than will those in higher positions. The latter will receive statements which are wider in scope, to correspond with their wider responsibilities.

7. The date the statement is prepared, the title of the person preparing it, and the titles of the recipients should be stated.

8. The statement should not attempt to portray too much. To avoid confusion, subsidiary detail may usefully be relegated to supporting schedules. A series of simple statements is usually to be preferred to a single comprehensive one, which is of necessity so overloaded with detail that little information can be gleaned from it, and that with difficulty.


**The use of quantities**
Frequently, figures expressed in monetary terms alone are insufficient. It is necessary to amplify them with figures of the units to which they relate and possibly to compute a rate per unit. Per unit figures should be expressed as simply as possible, reflecting consistent application of principles and the degree of accuracy necessary. Insignificant decimals or fractions should be avoided. It is frequently more satisfactory to provide statements in which the unit is a real amount, e.g. an hour, a unit of electricity or a mile, rather than to convert into money cost. Comparisons, say, of usage, are not then confused by price changes. A statement prepared in such real terms should be clearly headed so that the reader is aware of the unit used.

Three examples of badly prepared statements of costing returns are given below, their faults described and the statements set out in a more satisfactory form. The first example is a badly prepared statement of sales.

## EXAMPLE

### Sales

| | Product 1 | | Product 2 | | Product 3 | | Product 4 | | Total | |
|---|---|---|---|---|---|---|---|---|---|---|
| North | 1,500 | 7,400 | 1,100 | 6,000 | 400 | 2,500 | 1,000 | 4,500 | 4,000 | 20,400 |
| Division | (1,450) | (7,000) | (1,200) | (7,000) | (800) | (3,100) | (900) | (4,800) | (4,350) | (21,900) |
| Branch M | 800 | 3,400 | 700 | 3,700 | 200 | 1,250 | 100 | 450 | 1,800 | 8,800 |
| | (650) | (3,500) | (900) | (5,000) | (600) | (2,250) | (200) | (1,000) | (2,350) | (11,750) |
| Branch N | 700 | 4,000 | 400 | 2,300 | 200 | 1,250 | 900 | 4,050 | 2,200 | 11,600 |
| | (800) | (3,500) | (300) | (2,000) | (300) | (850) | (700) | (3,800) | (2,000) | (10,150) |
| South | 150 | 740 | 110 | 600 | 40 | 250 | 100 | 450 | 400 | 2,040 |
| Divison | (145) | (700) | (120) | (700) | (80) | (310) | (90) | (480) | (435) | (2,190) |
| Branch Q | 80 | 400 | 55 | 300 | 25 | 150 | 90 | 405 | 250 | 1,255 |
| | (65) | (300) | (55) | (300) | (50) | (210) | (80) | (425) | (250) | (1,235) |
| Branch R | 70 | 340 | 55 | 300 | 15 | 100 | 10 | 45 | 150 | 785 |
| | (80) | (400) | (65) | (400) | (30) | (100) | (10) | (55) | (185) | (955) |
| London | 1,000 | 4,000 | 2,000 | 8,500 | 1,500 | 5,000 | 950 | 3,800 | 5,450 | 21,300 |
| | (900) | (3,600) | (2,200) | (9,100) | (1,700) | (6,000) | (900) | (3,600) | (5,700) | (22,300) |

The above statement has the following defects:

1. The heading is not specific; it does not disclose whether the figures relate to orders received or to sales actually delivered and invoiced.

2. The period covered is not disclosed.

3. The unit is not stated, it is not clear whether the figures are expressed in values or in some unit of quantity, nor what those in the right-hand columns relate to.

4. The figures in brackets are presumably inserted for comparison purposes. It is not clear whether they are budgeted figures or those of a past period, e.g. last year.

5. Neither the person preparing the report, the recipients nor the date of preparation are disclosed.

6. The statement embraces both divisional figures and their analysis over branches. It would be preferable to prepare separate statements of branch sales, as normally their information would be of value only to a lower grade of management than would the divisional figures.

7. The figures are so compressed as to be almost unreadable, and the amount of each increase or decrease is not plainly shown.

In order to present the same information in a form which is more readable and in which the data are confined to those appropriate to the particular level of management who receive the reports, the following series of statements is suggested:

1. Statements for the board of directors showing total sales analysed over: (a) products, and (b) branches. These statements are comprehensive and appropriate to the purview of the recipients, the details of branch sales being omitted.

(a)

A.B. Ltd.                                                           Products

*Statement of Sales Invoiced, Month of April, 19...*

| Product | This month | | Year to date | | Variances | | | |
|---------|-----------|--------|-----------|--------|----------|-----|--------------|-----|
|  | Budget | Actual | Budget | Actual | Month | % | Year to date | % |
| 1 | £2,495 | £2,650 | £11,300 | £12,140 | £155 | 6 | £840 | 7 |
| 2 | 3,520 | 3,210 | 16,800 | 15,100 | 310(A) | 9 | 1,700(A) | 10 |
| 3 | 2,580 | 1,940 | 9,410 | 7,750 | 640(A) | 25 | 1,660(A) | 18 |
| 4 | 1,890 | 2,050 | 8,880 | 8,750 | 160 | 8 | 130(A) | 1 |
|  | £10,485 | £9,850 | £46,390 | £43,740 | £635(A) | 6 | £2,650(A) | 6 |

(A) = Adverse Variance

Prepared by:....................        Date: May 5,....        Copies to: All Directors
                                                                          Secretary
                                                                          General Sales Manager

(b)

A.B. Ltd.                                                           Divisions

*Statement of Sales Invoiced, Month of April, 19...*

| Division | This month | | Year to date | | Variances | | | |
|----------|-----------|--------|-----------|--------|----------|-----|--------------|-----|
|  | Budget | Actual | Budget | Actual | Month | % | Year to date | % |
| North | £4,350 | £4,000 | £21,900 | £20,400 | £350(A) | 8 | £1,500(A) | 7 |
| South | 435 | 400 | 2,190 | 2,040 | 35(A) | 8 | 150(A) | 7 |
| London | 5,700 | 5,450 | 22,300 | 21,300 | 250(A) | 4 | 1,000(A) | 4 |
|  | £10,485 | £9,850 | £46,390 | £43,740 | £635(A) | 6 | £2,650(A) | 6 |

(A) = Adverse Variance.

Prepared by:....................        Date: May 5, 19...        Copies to: All Directors
                                                                           Secretary
                                                                           General Sales Manager

2. Statements of sales in respect of each of the three divisions, showing the analysis between products. Only the statement in respect of the North Division is illustrated, but similar statements would in practice be prepared for both the South and London divisions.

A.B. Ltd.                                                           North Division

*Sales Invoiced Month of April 19...*

| Product | This month | | Year to date | | Variances | | | |
|---------|-----------|--------|-----------|--------|----------|-----|--------------|-----|
|  | Budget | Actual | Budget | Actual | Month | % | Year to date | % |
| 1 | £1,450 | £1,500 | £7,000 | £7,400 | £50 | 3 | £400 | 6 |
| 2 | 1,200 | 1,100 | 7,000 | 6,000 | 100(A) | 8 | 1,000(A) | 14 |
| 3 | 800 | 400 | 3,100 | 2,500 | 400(A) | 50 | 600(A) | 19 |
| 4 | 900 | 1,000 | 4,800 | 4,500 | 100 | 11 | 300(A) | 6 |
|  | £4,350 | £4,000 | £21,900 | £20,400 | £350(A) | 8 | £1,500(A) | 7 |

(A) = Adverse Variance.

Prepared by:....................        Date: May 4, 19... Copies to: Managing Director
                                                                       General Sales Manager
                                                                       Divisional Sales Manager (North)

Subsidiary statements for each of the branches would be prepared, only that for Branch M being illustrated.

*A.B. Ltd.*          *North Division*

*Branch M—Sales Invoiced Month of April 19 . . .*

| Product | This month | | Year to date | | Variances | | | |
|---|---|---|---|---|---|---|---|---|
| | Budget | Actual | Budget | Actual | Month | % | Year to date | % |
| 1 | £650 | £800 | £3,500 | £3,400 | £150 | 23 | £100(A) | 3 |
| 2 | 900 | 700 | 5,000 | 3,700 | 200(A) | 22 | 1,300(A) | 26 |
| 3 | 600 | 200 | 2,250 | 1,250 | 400(A) | 67 | 1,000(A) | 44 |
| 4 | 200 | 100 | 1,000 | 450 | 100(A) | 50 | 550(A) | 55 |
| | £2,350 | £1,800 | £11,750 | £8,800 | £550(A) | 23 | £2,950(A) | 25 |

(A) = Adverse Variance.

*Prepared by:* . . . . . . . . . . . . . . . . . . .          *Date:* May 13, 19 . . .          *Copies to:* Divisional Manager (North)
Manager Branch M

Each of the above reports would in practice be supported by a report from the manager responsible, giving reasons for the variations and, no doubt, details of the remedial action taken or recommended.

## EXAMPLE

The following is a badly prepared cost statement:

*P.Q.R. Ltd.*
*Profit Statement 19 . . .*

| | | | |
|---|---|---|---|
| Stocks | £400 | Sales | £5,100 |
| Work-in-progress | 700 | Stocks | 450 |
| Purchases | 1,200 | Work-in-progress | 550 |
| Wages | 1,100 | | |
| Direct expenses | 200 | | |
| Depreciation: | | | |
| Plant | 100 | | |
| Vehicles | 150 | | |
| Factory expenses | 250 | | |
| Administration expenses | 400 | | |
| Selling expenses | 500 | | |
| Balance, net profit | 1,100 | | |
| | £6,100 | | £6,100 |

Its faults are as follows:

1. No comparative figures are shown.
2. There is no grouping of figures to give informative subdivisions of cost.
3. No figure of sales quantities are given and it is impossible to discover the costs per article.
4. No distinction is made between fixed and variable costs.
5. If there are separate departments or products, no relative analysis of sales and costs is provided.

Assuming figures where necessary, the statement should be amended as follows:

*P.Q.R. Ltd.*

*Operating Statement—Year Ended 31st December 19...*

| Comparative figures | | Dept. A | | Dept. B | |
|---|---|---|---|---|---|
| | Units | Per unit £ | 1,300 | Per unit £ | 2,500 |
| | Sales | 2.000 | £ 2,600 | 1.000 | £ 2,500 |
| | *Factory costs—variable:* | | | | |
| | Materials | | 600 | | 550 |
| | Wages | | 700 | | 400 |
| | Expenses | | 110 | | 90 |
| | | | 1,410 | | 1,040 |
| | *Add:* decrease in work-in-progress | | 100 | | 50 |
| | *Factory costs—fixed:* | 1.161 | 1,510 | 0.436 | 1,090 |
| | Depreciation—plant | 0.031 | 40 | 0.024 | 60 |
| | General | 0.077 | 100 | 0.060 | 150 |
| | Production cost | 1.269 | 1,650 | 0.520 | 1,300 |
| | Administration | 0.154 | 200 | 0.080 | 200 |
| | Marketing: | | | | |
| | General | 0.231 | 300 | 0.080 | 200 |
| | Depreciation of vehicles | 0.038 | 50 | 0.040 | 100 |
| | Cost of sales | 1.692 | 2,200 | 0.720 | 1,800 |
| | Net profit | 0.308 | 400 | 0.280 | 700 |
| | | £2.000 | £2,600 | £1.000 | £2,500 |

*Prepared by:*.............................................................  *Copies to:* Managing Director
*Date:*............  Secretary, etc.

NOTES: 1. Comparative figures would be those of the previous year and/or the budget for the year.

2. Work-in-progress should be analysed into its elements of cost. It would then be possible to show the figures per unit for each element of prime cost.

## EXAMPLE

The following statement of process costs is badly prepared:

*Process Y*

| | | | | |
|---|---|---|---|---|
| Stock (4,000 units) | £400 | Transfer— | | |
| Material (10,000 units) | 1,000 | Process Z (9,000 units) | £1,800 | |
| Labour | 700 | Abnormal waste (1,000 units) | 200 | |
| Expenses | 200 | Stock (3,000 units) | 300 | |
| | £2,300 | | £2,300 | |

*Process Z*

| | | | | |
|---|---|---|---|---|
| Stock (1,400 units) | £280 | Transfer— | | |
| From Process Y | 1,800 | Finished stock (8,360 units) | £2,508 | |
| Stores | 140 | Abnormal waste (440 units) | 132 | |
| Labour | 520 | Stock (1,500 units) | 300 | |
| Expenses | 200 | | | |
| | £2,940 | | £2,940 | |

Its faults are as follows:

1. The units handled are not properly tabulated and hence the normal process losses are not shown.

2. The costs of finished products per unit are not shown either in total or detail.

3. The debit and credit form of layout may be confusing to the recipient.

4. The period covered is not disclosed.

The accounts should be amended as follows:

*Process Cost Statements—June 19...*

|  | Process Y | | | Process Z | | |
|---|---|---|---|---|---|---|
|  | Units | Per unit |  | Units | Per unit |  |
|  |  | £ | £ |  | £ | £ |
| Stock at beginning of month | 4,000 | 0.10 | 400 | 1,400 | 0.20 | 280 |
| Material processed | 10,000 | 0.10 | 1,000 | 9,000 | 0.20 | 1,800 |
|  | 14,000 |  | 1,400 | 10,400 |  | 2,080 |
| *Less:* Stock at end of month | 3,000 | 0.10 | 300 | 1,500 | 0.20 | 300 |
|  | 11,000 | 0.10 | 1,100 | 8,900 | 0.20 | 1,780 |
| Stores | — |  | — | — | 0.016 | 140 |
| Labour |  | 0.063 | 700 |  | 0.058 | 520 |
| Expenses |  | 0.018 | 200 |  | 0.022 | 200 |
| Process loss—normal | 1,000 | 0.019 | — | 100 | 0.004 | — |
|  | 10,000 | 0.20 | 2,000 | 8,800 | 0.30 | 2,640 |
| *Less:* Abnormal process loss | 1,000 | 0.20 | 200 | 440 | 0.30 | 132 |
| To process Z | 9,000 | 0.20 | £1,800 |  |  |  |
| To Finished stock |  |  |  | 8,360 | 0.30 | £2,508 |

*Prepared by:*.................................................................................................... *Copies to:* Managing Director
*Date:*.................... Works Manager

## MANAGEMENT REPORTS

The cost accountant will be required not only to prepare statements giving regular information but also to give an opinion on specific matters. As part of the management team he must ensure that his contribution to solving problems is clearly expressed in order that decisions are made on the basis of all known facts and qualified advice. Important points to consider when preparing reports are as follows:

1. The report must be clearly addressed and, if copies are to be circulated, the recipients must be listed. It must be dated and signed by the person submitting it.

2. A brief title of the report indicating the subject-matter should be given.

3. It is important to keep the report as short as possible. Where reference is made to statements, these should be kept out of the body of the report and dealt with as appendices numbered for ease of reference. Where the report could contain a range of matters it is advisable to restrict these and make further reports

at a later stage. If the report is unavoidably long an index should be included, with a summary of the main conclusions and recommendations to enable senior management to grasp the whole picture without having to wade through all the report.

4. The report should be structured to make it easy to read. Subheadings should be used and each significant point made in a separate, numbered, paragraph. There should be a logical sequence beginning with the current position and scope of the report, then the results of investigation, etc., and concluding with recommendations giving reasons.

5. Care must be taken not to be ambiguous and to ensure that opinions are expressed as such and not confused with facts. Sentences should be short and the language simple and direct. Where technical expressions are used, explanations should be given.

SELF-STUDY TEST No. 11
*Double Entry Aspects*
(*Refer to the Appendix on p. 371 for suggested solutions.*)

1. The following trial balance results from entries in the cost ledger of a jobbing manufacturer.

|  | Dr | Cr |
|---|---|---|
| (a) Cost Ledger Contra Account |  | £11,590 |
| (b) Stores Ledger Account | £3,790 |  |
| (c) Work-in-Progress Account | 5,430 |  |
| (d) Finished Goods Account | 2,350 |  |
| (e) Factory Overhead Account | 50 |  |
| (f) Administration Cost Account |  | 30 |
|  | £11,620 | £11,620 |

Explain what each balance represents and the transactions out of which it has arisen.

2. (a) Explain how the results shown by the Cost Accounts and those shown by the Financial Accounts may be reconciled.

(b) According to the Cost Accounts profit for the year was £48,390.

The Financial Accounts disclosed the following position:

*Manufacturing Account*

| | | | | |
|---|---|---|---|---|
| Raw materials opening stock | £1,900 | Transfer to Finished Stock A/c | £111,400 |
| Purchases, *less:* returns | 54,900 | | |
| | 56,800 | | |
| *Less:* Closing stock | 1,800 | | |
| | | £55,000 | | |
| Direct labour | | 35,500 | | |
| Factory overhead | | 21,400 | | |
| | | 111,900 | | |
| Work-in-progress | | | | |
| Opening | 8,400 | | | |
| Closing | 8,900 | | | |
| | | 500 | | |
| Factory cost of production | | £111,400 | | £111,400 |

### Finished Stock Account

| | | | |
|---|---|---|---|
| Opening stock | £11,600 | Cost of sales transferred to Trading A/c | £110,700 |
| Transfer from Manufacturing A/c | 111,400 | Closing stock | 12,300 |
| | £123,000 | | £123,000 |

### Trading Account

| | | | |
|---|---|---|---|
| Factory cost of Sales transferred from Stock Account | £110,700 | Sales | £184,500 |
| Gross profit c/d | 73,800 | | |
| | £184,500 | | £184,500 |

### Profit and Loss Account

| | | | |
|---|---|---|---|
| Administration expenses | £15,600 | Gross profit b/d | £73,800 |
| Distribution expenses | 10,182 | Discounts received | 1,806 |
| Discounts allowed | 1,511 | Banks interest received | 37 |
| Debenture interest | 850 | Dividends received | 300 |
| Fines | 500 | | |
| Losses of a non-trading nature | 350 | | |
| Net profit | 46,950 | | |
| | £75,943 | | £75,943 |

Stock valuations in the Cost Accounts were as follows:

| | Opening balance | Closing balance |
|---|---|---|
| Raw materials | £1,969 | £1,850 |
| Work-in-progress | £8,280 | £8,730 |
| Finished stock | £11,396 | £12,810 |

Depreciation amounting to £6,146 was charged in the Cost Accounts, whereas Factory overhead in the Financial Accounts included £5,873 for this expense.

The profit shown in the Cost Accounts has been arrived at before charging Notional rent £1,500.

You are required to present a logical statement to reconcile the two profit figures.

3. The balances shown in the Cost Accounts at September 30th are as follows:

| | | |
|---|---|---|
| Cost Ledger Contra A/c | £34,800 | |
| Stores Ledger Control A/c | 1,848 | |
| Work-in-Progress A/c | 3,195 | |
| Wages Control A/c (accrued wages) | | £311 |
| Factory Overhead Control A/c (under-absorbed overhead) | 168 | |
| Finished Goods Stock A/c | 12,000 | |
| Cost of Sales A/c | 182,000 | |
| Administration Overhead Control A/c | 27,800 | |
| Marketing Overhead Control A/c | 18,500 | |
| Sales | | 280,000 |
| | £280,311 | £280,311 |

(a) You are required to open the accounts and record the following transactions for the month of October in so far as they affect the Cost Books (using the same accounts and any others you may deem necessary)

| | | |
|---|---|---:|
| Total invoices for materials (all stock) | | £15,122 |
| Gross wages payable (including employers' contributions £450) | | 8,900 |
| Factory direct wages | £6,000 | |
| Factory indirect wages | £2,900 | |
| | £8,900 | |

| | |
|---|---:|
| Accrued wages October 31st | 423 |
| P.A.Y.E. (I. Tax) deductions | 1,600 |
| Other deductions | 500 |
| Net wages cheque drawn | 6,350 |
| Materials issued to production | 14,185 |
| Wages allocated | |
|    Factory direct wages—£6,000 | |
|    Factory indirect wages—£3,012 | |
| Indirect materials issued to factory | 870 |
| Invoices for factory overhead expenses | 2,124 |
|    (N.B. factory overhead is absorbed at the rate of 100% on direct wages) | |
| Stores stock October 31st | 1,915 |
| Work-in-progress October 31st | 4,380 |
| Finished goods stock October 31st | 14,000 |
| Administration overhead incurred | 3,100 |
| Marketing overhead incurred | 2,050 |
| Sales | 32,000 |
| Interim dividend paid (net) | 8,000 |

(b) Extract the trial balance from the cost accounts as at October 31st.

4. What do you understand by the term "integrated accounting" and what advantages does it offer compared to separate systems of cost and financial accounting?

5. As cost accountant of a large engineering company, you are responsible for cost audit. You require certain of your staff to investigate the purchasing and stores routine of the company.

Prepare a brief schedule of instructions for issue to your staff setting out the functions to be investigated and stating the important points to be observed.

6. The growth in the volume of data handled together with technological advances in data processing equipment continues to emphasise the need for a satisfactory system of codification of accounts. In determining such a code, what principles should be observed.

7. You have been appointed as adviser to a trade association of toy manufacturers and are asked to prepare a report on implementing uniform costing systems.

List two aspects of overhead costing to be examined and explain how uniformity may be achieved in respect of each.

# Outline Solutions to Self-Study Tests

*Self-Study Test No. 1—The Role of Cost Accounting*

1. Accounting data assists management to:

   (*a*) plan future activities;
   (*b*) measure the efficiency of business activities; and
   (*c*) solve specific problems.

Examples of the kind of data provided are:

   (*a*) analysis of sales by product to indicate areas for concentration of sales effort (planning);
   (*b*) comparative statement of sales analysed by sales area (measure efficiency);
   (*c*) statement of comparative operating costs of different machines available for purchase (machine replacement problem).

2. Considerations when a costing system is introduced include the following:

   (*a*) Factory layout and production facilities, i.e. production and service departments, machines, operating sequence.
   (*b*) Organisation structure, i.e. managers, supervisors and relevant responsibility.
   (*c*) Administration controls, e.g. stores routine, payroll documents, production scheduling procedures.
   (*d*) Information requirements, e.g. degree of sales analysis required, pricing procedures, relative importance of cost items.
   (*e*) Principles and techniques, e.g. absorption or marginal principle, application of budgets and standards, basic costing method—job, batch, process.

3. "Cost unit": *see* p. 8 for definition. Examples include:

   thousand bricks—brickworks;
   contract—contractor;
   meal served—restaurant.

"Cost centre": *see* p. 8 for definition. Examples include:

   assembly department;
   wages office;
   fork-lift trucks.

4. The separation of direct and indirect costs is important because of the following:

(*a*) Cost accounting is directed to ascertaining, as accurately as is practicable, costs of products; costs that can be identified with a particular cost unit will not be subject to arbitrary allotment and absorption procedures which impair accuracy.

(*b*) Direct costs tend to fluctuate in relation to volume of production; indirect costs may be more affected by management action. Separation, therefore, will assist in determining why costs are incurred and how best to control them.

(*c*) Identification of indirect/direct cost-centre costs will assist in establishing responsibility.

5. (*a*) The major functions in a manufacturing organisation: Production; Marketing; General Administration; Research; Development.

| (*b*) | (*i*) Subjective (*nature*) | (*ii*) Objective (*centre*) |
|---|---|---|
| Production | Direct materials | Finishing Dept. |
| Marketing | Advertising | Eastern Sales Office |
| General Administration | Depreciation of office machinery | Personnel Dept. |
| Research | Analyst's fees | Laboratory |
| Development | Indirect materials | Quality Control Dept. |

6. Classification by behaviour:

Fixed; Variable; Semi-variable.

Examples include:

Fixed: rent, rates, factory manager's salary, depreciation of office machinery;
Variable: direct materials, piece-rate wages, power (unit rate);
Semi-variable: indirect materials, maintenance, power (sliding scale charge).

7. The basic costing methods:

Specific order costing: job, batch or contract.
Operation costing: process or service.

Examples:

Job—plumbing; motor repairs.
Batch—toy manufacture; quality shoes.
Contract—shipbuilding; petro-mechanical engineers.
Process—soap manufacture; motor-car manufacture.
Service—hotel; coach operators.

8. The essential elements of variance accounting would be as follows:

(*a*) Activities of the undertaking are clearly separated together with a clear definition of individual responsibility for activities.

(*b*) Planned activities are expressed in terms of functional budgets, departmental budgets, standard costs, standard selling prices and standard margins.

(*c*) Continuous comparison of actual results with plans by means of regular reports to all management levels.

(*d*) Formal control system which revolves on monitoring action taken as a result of variances disclosed.

(*e*) Information for reports derived from the routine accounting records and from the administrative systems which control the business operations.

### Self-Study Test No. 2—Materials

1. Documents used in the procedure for purchasing materials up to the stage of receipt into store would be:

(*a*) Purchase Requisition (stores);
(*b*) Purchase Order (purchasing);
(*c*) Goods Received Note (stores).

The Purchase Requisition, duly authorised, requests the purchasing manager to purchase specific materials to be delivered at a specific time and place.

The Purchase Order will be placed by the purchasing department with suppliers who will provide goods of the required quantity at competitive prices.

Goods Received Notes will verify that the goods delivered are in accordance with the purchase order and will serve as a posting medium for recording quantities received to the stock record.

2.

| MATERIAL REQUISITION | | | | | |
|---|---|---|---|---|---|
| Reqn. No.:................................ | | | | | |
| Date:................................ | | | | | |
| Deliver to:................................ ................................ Department | | | Charge:................................ ................................ | | |
| Quantity | Code number | Description | | Unit cost | Amount |
|  |  |  |  |  |  |
|  |  |  |  |  |  |
|  |  |  |  |  |  |
|  |  |  |  |  |  |
| Requisitioned by:................................ | | | Approved by:................................ | | |

3. (*a*) Re-order level may be defined as the level of stock at which a fresh order is placed. It is usually calculated by multiplying the maximum weekly consumption of a stock item by the maximum delivery period in weeks.

(*b*) The re-order level is set to allow for maximum consumption in the maximum delivery period. Under normal circumstances, therefore, stock should be at the minimum level when the fresh order is received, i.e. Minimum level = Re-order level − (Average consumption × Average delivery period); if average consumption occurs and average delivery periods obtain, therefore, the fact that replenishment is ordered when stock falls to the re-order level incorporates a safety factor.

(c) The factors to be considered in establishing re-order quantities and levels are:

(i) rate of consumption of the material;

(ii) time necessary to obtain new deliveries;

(iii) amount of capital necessary and available;

(iv) keeping qualities, e.g. risk of deterioration, evaporation, etc.;

(v) storage space available;

(vi) cost of storage;

(vii) extent to which price fluctuations may be important;

(viii) risk of changing specifications or obsolescence;

(ix) seasonal considerations as to both price and availability of supplies;

(x) incidence of quantity discounts and/or minimum order quantity accepted.

4. In the three months ended June 30th, issues of component PQ appear to be priced at the cost price of purchases during the previous month. This is an unusual and unscientific method as the quantity of an issue is totally unrelated to that purchased in the month upon which the issue price is based. Accordingly, the cost of a particular parcel purchased is not exhausted as in FIFO or LIFO, nor is an average cost price struck which can be used both for issues and closing stock valuation.

In periods of rising prices, such as the question implies, all issues are charged out at below replacement cost and some at below actual cost (e.g. 10,000 of the April 20th issue) and there are unidentified balances in the account which must be adjusted at balancing date. The stock at June 30th is presumably valued at the price of purchases in that month as, if valued at the May price (which consistency demands), the figure at which July issues are priced would be not that of the preceding month, but of the penultimate one.

The system provides no principle for pricing the stock shortage. If the shortage is ascertained at the end of June, presumably the May price would be used.

### Stores Account: Component PQ

| | Receipts | | | | Issues | | |
|---|---|---|---|---|---|---|---|
| | | Units | £ | | | Units | £ |
| April 1st | Stock | 10,000 (0.60) | 6,000 | April 20th | | 20,000 (0.60) | 12,000 |
| April 15th | Purchases | 12,000 (0.625) | 7,500 | May 16th | | 2,000 (0.625) | 1,250 |
| May 12th | Purchases | 3,000 (0.632) | 1,896 | May 22nd | | 400 (0.625) | 250 |
| June 18th | Purchases | 20,000 (0.65) | 13,000 | June 24th | | 15,600 0.632) | 9,859 |
| | | | | June 30th | | | |
| | | | | | Shortage | 300 (0.632) | 190 |
| | | | | | Stock c/d | 6,700 (0.65) | 4,355 |
| | | | | | Amount w/o | | 492 |
| | | 45,000 | £28,396 | | | 45,000 | £28,396 |

5. An outline procedure for stock differences arising from changes in unit of measurement would embody the following principles:

(*a*) Establish a conversion factor so that purchases can be recorded in both measurements.

(*b*) Establish a level of tolerable differences representing a percentage of quantity issued.

(*c*) Check, at frequent intervals, the quantity in stock using the unit of measure for issue quantities.

(*d*) If a difference between the physical stock and the book stock is disclosed which is more than the percentage of tolerable difference, based on the quantity issued since the last stock check, then further investigation is required.

In the cost accounts, unit prices will be maintained on the basis of the measurement used for issues. The issue price will be inflated to allow for the tolerable loss and any excess loss will be valued at the unit price and shown in a separate account.

6. *Control of obsolete materials.* The objective will be to minimise the loss arising when materials are found to be obsolete. Consequently, control should be directed at identifying materials where consumption has reduced in comparison to previous periods or to budget so that action can be taken to run down stocks before obsolescence actually occurs.

A periodic report should be prepared to list stock items which show a declining rate of usage. The report will be sent to a responsible executive in the technical function who can identify reasons for the decline in usage. Slow-moving items thus disclosed can be analysed into three main categories of remedial action to be taken:

(*a*) Items which will continue to be used but at a slower rate than before; maximum, minimum and re-order levels to be adjusted.

(*b*) Items which can be used for a different purpose; changes to product specifications required.

(*c*) Items which have become obsolete; disposal in the most lucrative way to be arranged.

The above report may be used as a basis for calculating a provision for loss on obsolete materials so that the prudence concept may be reflected in accounting for stocks.

7. *Imprest system of stores control.*

(*a*) *Procedure.* For each item in stock, a quantity will be determined which represents the number of articles that should be in stock at the beginning of any period. Consequently, at the end of the period the store-keeper will requisition for the number of items required to bring the physical stock up to the predetermined quantity.

(*b*) *Conditions.* An imprest system is most useful in a large factory where a number of different production departments use various standard articles continuously. A large factory implies that savings in handling arise by maintaining an imprest stock in each department.

(*c*) *Expected benefits.*

(*i*) Maintenance of essential stocks within the production centre should reduce the risk of production hold-up through non-availability of materials.

(*ii*) The need to requisition once only during a period should reduce administration and handling involved in more numerous replenishments.

(*iii*) Control and administration of sub-stores is simplified as stock in hand should represent the imprest stock less usage during the current period.

8. The advantages of main and departmental sub-stores are:

(*a*) the cost of internal transport is minimised, material being transported in bulk between the main and sub-stores;

(*b*) materials are stored in the department using them; thus materials are quickly available for issue, reducing delay and the danger that production will be brought to a standstill;

(*c*) losses of materials in the main store will not necessarily stop production;

(*d*) sub-stores provide facilities for the storage of finished production prior to transfer to other departments, or the finished stock warehouse;

(*e*) batching of materials or components for manufacture or assembly may be carried out in advance.

The disadvantages of main and departmental sub-stores are:

(*a*)  increased staffing and therefore an increase in indirect labour costs;

(*b*)  supervision of storekeepers is more difficult;

(*c*)  larger stocks may be carried entailing increased storage space and additional working capital;

(*d*)  a physical stock-take is more complex;

(*e*)  increased clerical and stationery costs; and

(*f*)  a greater risk of losses due to obsolescence.

9. (*a*) *Benefits of materials coding.* The benefits of using code numbers in a stores classification system are:

(*i*) reduction in clerical effort because writing out of precise descriptions becomes unnecessary;

(*ii*) ambiguity is avoided because everyone knows what material is being referred to;

(*iii*) it becomes easier to refer to items and to categorise them;

(*iv*) it is normally essential when handling material data in mechanical or electronic processing systems.

(*b*) *Example*

1st/2nd digits—major classification, e.g. raw materials, work-in-progress, consumable stores.

3rd/4th digits—material, e.g. steel, wood, aluminium.

5th/6th digits—type, e.g. tubing, planking, component parts.

7th/8th digits—measurement, e.g. metres, cubic metres, litres.

*Self-Study Test No. 3—Personnel and Labour Cost*

1. *Time-recording procedure.* The important point to bear in mind is that the procedure must be viewed from the view point of the cost accountant rather than the financial accountant. The cost accountant will be concerned to achieve the most efficient method of obtaining an analysis of wages costs. Accuracy of time recording is essential and it is advisable to use a time-recording clock. To record the time element between jobs, a combined time and job card can be used but then it will be necessary to use a recorder

that will allow a number of recordings to be made each day. A more suitable method, where workers are paid hourly, is to use subsidiary time cards. The employee will be required to punch these cards on commencing and finishing each job. At the end of the week the cards are collected by the wages office and the employee asked to complete a time sheet setting out the hours spent in each cost centre. When finished with by the wages office, the cards and time sheets are passed to the cost office for analysis. The totals of all allocations made to the cost centres through this analysis must agree with the total gross wages paid.

2. *Payroll documents.* Accuracy is a most important factor when considering the calculation of an employees pay. The following are documents that should be used if that accuracy is to be achieved and maintained:

(*a*) *Employee record card*—kept in the personnel department as a record of rates of pay, personal details, location, etc.

(*b*) *Clock card* (for attendance and time keeping only)—this should check with the total of individual bookings.

(*c*) *Time sheets* (daily or weekly)—prepared by direct and indirect workers. To analyse time spent.

(*d*) *Job cards* (for complete job or for operation)—usually prepared by production control as part of their work-scheduling function.

(*e*) *Piecework tickets*—for calculating gross wages under piecework for direct workers.

(*f*) *Payroll*—prepared by the wages office from clock cards, piecework tickets or job cards or time sheets. The payroll will also show deductions and the net wages payable.

(*g*) *Wages analysis sheets*—prepared in cost office from payroll. Direct wages will be posted to Work-in-Progress Accounts and Indirect wages posted to Overhead Accounts.

3. (*a*) *Proofing cost.*

| | May 23rd | | May 30th | |
|---|---|---|---|---|
| Units produced | 1,182 | | 1,384 | |
| Materials at 10p per unit | | £118.20 | | £138.40 |
| Labour: | | | | |
| Basic £1.20 per hr. | £420.00 | | £427.20 | |
| Bonus 16p per unit | 29.12 | | 32.00 | |
| 20p per unit | — | | 36.80 | |
| | | 449.12 | | 496.00 |
| Overhead: | | | | |
| Departmental | 600.00 | | 600.00 | |
| Supervisor's salary | 80.00 | | 80.00 | |
| Supervisor's bonus | 7.28 | | 17.20 | |
| Apportioned | 375.00 | | 375.00 | |
| | | 1,062.28 | | 1,072.20 |
| Total cost | | £1,629.60 | | £1,706.60 |
| *Cost per unit* | | £1.38 | | £1.23 |

NOTES:

(*i*) Labour bonus rate represents 80 per cent of unit rate, i.e. 20 per cent for supervisor.

(*ii*) Total labour hours worked are 350 and 356 for the two weeks but departmental overheads will be absorbed on the basis of normal departmental hours of 40.

(*iii*) Apportioned overhead = £18,750 ÷ 50 weeks.

(*b*) *Effective hourly rate of pay.*

| | | |
|---|---|---|
| £449.12 ÷ 350 | £1.28 | |
| £496.00 ÷ 356 | | £1.39 |

(*c*) *Comments.* Unit cost is lower in the second week because:

(*i*) more units produced per hour;

(*ii*) fixed costs unchanged in total but absorbed over more units in second week.

4.

*Job No. 873*

| | Halsey (50%) | Rowan |
|---|---|---|
| Basic: time taken and rate/hour<br>$4\frac{5}{12}$ hrs × 0.90 | £3.9750 | £3.975 |
| Bonus: 50% of *Time saved*<br>(50% × 1 hr 5 min) at 0.90 | 0.4875 | — |
| Bonus: $\dfrac{Time\ saved}{Standard\ time}$ × Basic<br>$\dfrac{1\ hr\ 5\ mins}{5\ hrs\ 30\ mins}$ × 3.975 | — | 0.783 |
| | £4.4625 | £4.758 |

5. *Labour turnover costs.* Labour turnover entails the cost of taking on, and in most cases the training of, new employees and such costs can be substantial. It is, therefore, necessary to record the facts and after considering the rate of turnover decide whether the position demands or is capable of improvement.

Labour turnover is the ratio of those leaving the company to the average number employed during a given period, and can be applied to departments or work-shops, or to categories of employees by sex or skill.

Costs affected by the rate of labour turnover include:

(*a*)   recruitment and advertising;

(*b*)   training;

(*c*)   personnel administration;

(*d*)   spoilt production and idle time incurred during periods when new employees are gaining experience.

A report on labour turnover prepared for management should include:

(*a*)   analysis of turnover rates according to types of employees, age groups, sex or any other suitable form of grading;

(*b*)   analysis of the reasons given for leaving;

(*c*)   how far research has been able to substantiate reasons given under (*b*) above;

(*d*) action taken to try and remedy any of the causes.

For purposes of analysis and subsequent action, labour turnover figures should be calculated under such headings as dismissal, voluntary termination, marriage, etc.

6. *Job grading* (or *job evaluation*) is concerned with determining a formal assessment of the relative importance or value of different jobs.

*Merit-rating* is supplementary to job evaluation and is concerned with rating individuals in relation to their capability for a particular job.

When deciding on the valuation of jobs, certain steps have to be taken and these can be summarised as:

(*a*) a study of the job;
(*b*) completion of a specification for each job;
(*c*) assessment of the jobs into order of importance.

When such a scheme is to be introduced, policy decisions have to be taken. It will be necessary, for instance, to decide on the persons who will do the evaluating (outside or internal); the way in which the evaluating will be done, i.e. ranking, points rating, factor comparison; and the way in which preliminary information must be collected and prepared.

Job evaluation attempts to deploy resources of ability more efficiently by matching the job with the worker and is used rather more for office conditions than for a factory.

The factors to be considered include mental requirement, skills, physical ability, job responsibility and working condition, volume of work, supervision required and promotional opportunities.

7. (*a*) Work measurement is one of the two main branches of work study and can be defined as a process of observing and recording the time required to carry out each separate element involved in an industrial operation, so that the actual time for performing a task can be ascertained at a specific level of performance.

(*b*) Four principal stages involved in work measurement are as follows:

(*i*) *Definition*—to ensure that the method measured is clearly defined. A given time is for a particular method and there must be no ambiguity over what is meant.

(*ii*) *Measurement*—a rated time study is made of each task to which a relaxation allowance is applied for personal needs and other relevant contingency allowances. Other methods may be used but direct observation using time study is the most accurate.

(*iii*) *Obtain work unit*—a work unit comprises an element of work and an element for recovery from fatigue. It permits comparison of different jobs using a standard unit.

(*iv*) *Establish*—this is the stage where a target is established for the method.

8. A workers' profit-sharing scheme is a collective scheme whereby an employer agrees that a predetermined share of the profits each year shall be paid to workers in addition to their wages. There are certain disadvantages in these schemes such as the following:

(*a*) Lazy or indifferent workers share equally with those who have worked hard and more efficiently.

(*b*) Additional earnings are usually comparatively small.

(*c*) Time lag between doing the work and receiving the additional payments is too long.

(*d*) Profits may be reduced by bad management.

(*e*) They are not favoured by trade unions.

An individual bonus scheme, in general, is an incentive offered to individual workers by means of financial payments or other benefits in addition to their annual wages. Financial incentive schemes can be based on merit-rating, measured day-work systems or piecework systems. One of the disadvantages of merit-rating schemes is the difficulty in measuring "effort" as the incentive payment must be extra pay for extra effort. The schemes are not liked by trade unions as they prefer more direct piecework schemes. A further disadvantage is that favouritism may arise. Similar disadvantages arise under measured day-work with the addition that it is difficult to discipline a worker who regularly fails to achieve the set standards; transferring or discharging him may cause a problem.

### Self-Study Test No. 4—Expenses and Overhead

1. (*a*) *Depreciation and obsolescence of machinery.* Details will be obtained from the plant register, which shows for each item of machinery:

   (*i*) date of purchase;
   (*ii*) cost;
   (*iii*) depreciation rate;
   (*iv*) location.

A cost journal voucher will be prepared to charge Overhead control in total and individual cost centres in detail with depreciation for the period. Additions or disposals should be recorded in the plant register as they occur so that they are reflected in subsequent depreciation calculations.

Obsolescence is the loss in value of an asset due to its being superseded at an earlier date than was foreseen (anticipated obsolescence should be reflected in the depreciation rate). Unforeseen obsolescence is usually excluded from the cost accounts.

(*b*) *Bad debts.* The cost of bad debts written off, plus/minus the adjustment to the provision for doubtful debts, will be charged to Marketing overhead. Abnormal items may, at management's discretion, be excluded from the cost accounts.

(*c*) *Rent, where premises are owned.* A notional amount, representing the amount the company would expect to pay for equivalent premises, may be charged to Overhead and credited to a memorandum account, so that product costs reflect, for comparison purposes, a realistic charge for rent. Alternatively, rent may be ignored in the accounts but the fact recognised when comparing costs with competitors.

(*d*) *Advertising.* Charged to Marketing overhead and allotted to products when such a procedure is informative for profitability comparisons.

2. Advantages to be gained from an efficiently operated plant and equipment record will include:

(a) number of hours operated by each machine readily available;
(b) effective life of each asset known;
(c) total, and analysed, depreciation charge easily ascertainable;
(d) good basis for keeping efficient maintenance records to establish a planned maintenance scheme;
(e) facilitates physical control of assets by providing documentary record of transfers, additions and disposals.

3. Production, marketing and administration are the major functions of business activity. Consequently, it is informative to analyse costs initially between major functions for broad comparison purposes and to facilitate cost control and budgeting procedures within each function.

Production overhead arises from goods or services produced during a period whereas Marketing overhead relates to goods sold and distributed. General administration Overhead arises from the provision of management and support services to all functions of the business.

NOTE: Students are advised to acquaint themselves with the types of overhead cost classified within each function.

4. *Pressings Ltd.—Machine Hour Rate*

|  | Per year | Per week | Per hour |
|---|---|---|---|
| Depreciation | £275 | | |
| Repairs and maintenance | 400 | | |
| Other factory overhead | 1,250 | | |
| | £1,925 | £38.50 | |
| Wages | | 32.00 | |
| | | £70.50 | £1.76 |
| Power | | | 1.50 |
| *Machine hour rate* | | | £3.26 |

5. *Allotment of overhead.*
   (a) *Readily identifiable expenditure.*

    (i) Indirect materials (dept. shown on requisition).
    (ii) Repairs.
    (iii) Metered power.

   (b) *Expenditure needing to be apportioned.*

    (i) Rent and rates.
    (ii) Canteen costs.
    (iii) Insurance of plant and machinery.

   (c) *Suggested bases.*

    (i) Depreciation of plant and machinery—capital values.
    (ii) Factory store keeping cost—requisitions (number or values).
    (iii) Lighting and heating—(a) number of electric lights or radiators; (b) floor area.
    (iv) Supervision—number of persons.

6. *Overhead to direct labour ratio.* Ratios could differ because:

(*a*) one business more mechanised;
(*b*) different grades of labour or rates of pay;
(*c*) differences in cost classification between direct and indirect, e.g. overtime premium, bonuses.

A higher ratio would imply a greater degree of mechanisation, which should lead to greater efficiency, but it may be a reflection of less effective control of overhead costs or lower wages paid.

7. (*a*) *Overhead classification*

| | | Production | | Marketing | Admin. and Finance |
| --- | --- | --- | --- | --- | --- |
| | | Machinery | Labour | | |
| Rent and rates | (*i*) | £44,800 | | | £11,200 |
| Repairs and maintenance | (*i*) | 4,200 | £1,480 | | 370 |
| Fuel, gas, water | | | 22,000 | | |
| Power | | 12,600 | | | |
| Maintenance | | 2,320 | | | |
| Interest on overdraft | | | | | 3,080 |
| Storekeeping | | | 5,890 | | |
| Production management | | | 7,600 | | |
| Depreciation | (*i*) | 80,100 | 4,000 | | 1,000 |
| Indirect wages | | | 10,200 | | |
| Carriage outwards | | | | £15,500 | |
| Commissions | | | | 13,000 | |
| Travelling expenses | | | | 13,400 | |
| Designing and estimating | | | 18,340 | | |
| General expenses | | | | | 17,160 |
| Management and secretarial | | | | | 23,000 |
| Advertising | | | | 32,700 | |
| General office | | | | | 9,830 |
| | | £144,020 | £69,510 | £74,600 | £65,640 |

NOTES: (*i*) Apportioned on area of buildings.

(*ii*) Raw materials. Direct wages, Carriage inwards and Sales are not overhead costs.

(*b*) Production overhead (Machines) will be recovered by using a machine hour rate calculated by dividing the total estimated amount, i.e. £144,020 by the budgeted machine hours (700,000) which gives a rate of £0.206 per machine hour. Production items (Labour) will be recovered by using a labour hour rate calculated by dividing the total estimated amount £69,510 by 800,000 hrs, i.e. a rate of £0.087 per labour hour. Marketing items are normally not absorbed but charged direct to Cost of Sales Account. Similarly, Administration and Financial Expenses are charged to Cost of Sales account or may be recovered by taking the total as a percentage of the cost of production.

(c)                    *Job No. 156*

| | |
|---|---|
| Materials | £70.00 |
| Wages | 165.00 |
| | 235.00 |

Production Overhead:

| | |
|---|---|
| Machinery | 10.30 ( 50 hrs at £0.206) |
| Labour | 13.06 (150 hrs at £0.087) |
| | £258.36 |

8. (a) *Production Overhead Schedule*

| | |
|---|---|
| Materials handling | £9,600 |
| Power* | 6,750 |
| Consumable stores* | 4,500 |
| Lighting and heating | 2,250 |
| Production control | 5,900 |
| Plant maintenance | 3,750 |
| Depreciation | 8,800 |
| Miscellaneous expenses | 4,200 |
| | £45,750 |

\* Direct labour hours without extra shift
  = 80 employees × 40 hrs × 50 weeks = 160,000 hrs.
Extra shift = 20 × 20 × 50 = 20,000 hrs,
  i.e. $12\frac{1}{2}$ per cent increase.

(b) (i) *Direct labour hour rate*
$$= \frac{£45,750}{180,000 \times 95\%} = 27\text{p per hr}$$

   (ii) *Percentage of direct labour cost*

Wages cost:

| | |
|---|---|
| 160,000 at £1.80 | £288,000 |
| 20,000 at £2.40 | 48,000 |
| | £336,000 |
| Production overhead | £45,750 |
| Absorption rate | 13.6 per cent |

9. *Apportioning service departments.* Overhead can only be recovered through production departments so that where service departments are included in apportionment of overheads, the totals must then be re-apportioned to the production departments. There are three main methods of carrying this out:

    (a) Ignoring the fact that service departments serve each other.
    (b) Continuous allotment (sometimes known as "repeated distribution").
    (c) Algebra.

Under method (*a*), each service department's total is apportioned to production departments only, using the most suitable basis. This is done with each service department in turn.

Under (*b*), each service department's total is apportioned to production departments and to other service departments until all the service departments' overheads have been absorbed into the production departments.

Under (*c*), algebra is used for apportioning the service departments but seldom practised in effect because the difference in accuracy between this method and the other two is so small that it is outweighed by the costs in time and energy involved.

*Self-Study Test No. 5—Specific Order Costing*

1. (*a*)                          Job No. 84

| | | |
|---|---:|---:|
| Direct materials | | £180.00 |
| Wages: | | |
| Dept. A | £31.50 | |
| Dept. B | 48.00 | |
| | | 79.50 |
| | | 259.50 |
| Variable overhead: | | |
| Dept. A | £9.00 | |
| Dept. B | 40.00 | |
| | | 49.00 |
| Fixed overhead: | | |
| $50 \text{ hrs} \times \dfrac{£28,600}{22,000}$ | | 65.00 |
| | | £373.50 |

(*b*) Profit percentage $= \dfrac{£126.50}{373.50} \times 100 = \underline{\underline{34 \text{ per cent}}}$ (approx.).

2.                          *Contracts Ledger*

| | *1* | *2* | *3* |
|---|---:|---:|---:|
| Expenditure totals | £105,000 | £96,600 | £24,400 |
| *Less:* | | | |
| Plant and materials c/f | 11,000 | 9,600 | 6,850 |
| | 94,000 | 87,000 | 17,550 |
| *Add:* | | | |
| Profit attributable | 4,500 | — | — |
| *Deduct:* | | | |
| Anticipated loss | | 5,000 | |
| W.I.P. c/f | £98,500 | £82,000 | £17,550 |

*Calculation of Attributable Profit*

|  |  |  |  |
|---|---|---|---|
| Work certified | £100,000 | £80,000 | £18,000 |
| Cost of work certified | 91,000 | 83,000 | 16,500 |
| Apparent profit/(loss) | £9,000 | (£3,000) | £1,500 |

Contract 1: Profit taken $= \frac{2}{3} \times £9,000 \times \frac{60}{80} = £4,500$

Contract 2: Apparent loss: £3,000

Anticipated loss $= £3,000 \times \frac{135}{80} = £(5,000)$ approx.

Contract 3: No profit taken as considered not far enough advanced.

*Balance Sheet Entries*

Current assets
    Contracts in progress at cost:

| | |
|---|---|
| (certified) | £190,500 |
| (uncertified) | 8,050 |
| | 198,550 |
| *Add:* Attributable profit | 4,500 |
| | 203,050 |
| *Deduct:* Anticipated losses | 5,000 |
| | 198,050 |
| *Less:* Progress payments | 148,500 |
| | £49,550 |

3. *Reconciliation*

|  | Financial Accounts | Cost Accounts |
|---|---|---|
| Materials: |  |  |
|   Opening stock (12,000 + 18,000) | £30,000 |  |
|   Purchases (102,600 − 4,200) | 98,400 |  |
|  | 128,400 |  |
|   Closing stock | 30,600 |  |
|     *Consumed* | £97,800 | £92,800 |
| Direct wages: |  |  |
|   Opening W.I.P.    6,000 |  |  |
|   Per Account    102,000 |  |  |
|    108,000 |  |  |
|   Indirect    24,400 |  |  |
|    83,600 |  |  |
| Closing W.I.P.    9,600 |  |  |
|  | £74,000 | £68,000 |

Overhead:

| | | | |
|---|---|---|---|
| Factory expenses | 40,000 | | |
| Indirect materials | 4,200 | | |
| Indirect wages | 24,400 | | |
| General office | 16,800 | | |
| Estimating/selling | 7,200 | | |
| | —— | £92,600 | £86,560 |
| Carriage | | £2,400 | £2,540 |

### Statement

| | | |
|---|---|---|
| Profit per Cost Accounts | | £44,100 |
| *Deduct:* | | |
| Materials under-charged | 5,000 | |
| Labour under-charged | 6,000 | |
| Overhead under-absorbed | 6,040 | 17,040 |
| | | 27,060 |
| *Add:* | | |
| Carriage over-recovered | | 140 |
| Profit per Financial Accounts | | £27,200 |

*Possible reasons for discrepancy*

(*a*) Materials issued but not covered by requisitions.
(*b*) Pricing of materials issued not based on cost.
(*c*) Direct labour time not booked to jobs.
(*d*) Indirect materials/wages treated as direct or vice versa.
(*e*) Overhead absorption rate leads to under-recovery due to lower volume and/or higher cost than estimated.

### Self-Study Test No. 6—Operation Costing

1. "Equivalent unit". A notional quantity of completed units substituted for an actual quantity of incomplete physical units in progress. The aggregate work content of the incomplete units is deemed to be equivalent to that of the substituted quantity.

The principle is used in process costing to facilitate apportionment of operating costs between work in progress and completed output.

2. (*a*)                    *Process Y Account*

| | Units | £ | | Units | £ |
|---|---|---|---|---|---|
| Materials | 1,000 | 3,000 | Process Z | 800 | 6,400 |
| Process costs | — | 4,800 | W.I.P. c/f | 200 | 1,400 |
| | 1,000 | £7,800 | | 1,000 | £7,800 |

*Workings*

|  | Materials | Process costs |
|---|---|---|
| Process Z | 800 | 800 |
| W.I.P. | 200 | 160 (80 per cent complete) |
| Units processed | 1,000 | 960 |
| Costs | £3,000 | £4,800 |
| Per unit | £3 | £5 |

*W.I.P. valuation*

| 200 units, materials at £3 | = | £600 |
|---|---|---|
| 160 equivalent units, process at £5 | = | 800 |
|  |  | £1,400 |

(b) (i)          *Process Y Account (FIFO Method)*

|  | Units | £ |  | Units | £ |
|---|---|---|---|---|---|
| W.I.P b/f | 200 | 1,400 | Process Z | 800 | 7,392 |
| Materials | 800 | 2,800 | W.I.P. c/f | 200 | 1,308 |
| Process costs | — | 4,500 |  | — | — |
|  | 1,000 | £8,700 |  | 1,000 | £8,700 |

*Workings*

(1) *Current month's cost per unit*

|  | Materials Units | Process costs Eq. Units |
|---|---|---|
| Process Z | 800 | 800 |
| Closing W.I.P. | 200 | 100  (50 per cent) |
| Opening W.I.P. | (200) | (160) (80 per cent) |
| Processing | 800 | 740 |
| Costs | £2,800 | £4,500 |
| Per unit | £3.50 | £6.08 |

(2) *Valuation of transfers to Process Z*

| Opening W.I.P. b/f (200 units) | £1,400 |
|---|---|
| Costs to complete (40 eq. units at £6.08) | 244 |
| Started and finished (600 units at £9.58) | 5,748 |
|  | £7,392 |

(3) *Valuation at closing W.I.P.*

| | |
|---|---:|
| 200 units of materials at £3.50 | £700 |
| 100 eq. units of process at £6.08 | 608 |
| | £1,308 |

(*ii*) *Weighted Average Method.*

| | | Materials | Process cost |
|---|---|---:|---:|
| Cost per unit will be: | | | |
| Opening value | | £600 | £800 |
| Current month | | 2,800 | 4,500 |
| | | £3,400 | £5,300 |
| Output units | | 1,000 | 900 |
| Per unit | | £3.40 | £5.89 |
| Values: | | | |
| Process Z | 800 at £9.29 | | £7,431 |
| W.I.P. | 200 at £3.40 | 680 | |
| | 100 at £5.89 | 589 | |
| | | | 1,269 |
| | | | £8,700 |

3. In a continuous process, or flowline production, a loss is expected due to scrap, waste, chemical change or evaporation. When a standard, or expected, level of loss is calculated and expressed as a percentage of input or output, the *normal* loss is that quantity which represents the expected percentage of actual input or output; the quantity lost in excess of expected represents the *abnormal* loss.

4. *Crackers Ltd.*

(*a*) *Normal spoilage.*

$$\text{Unit cost} = \frac{£323.75}{65} = £4.98$$

(*b*) *Abnormal spoilage.*

$$\text{Unit cost} = \frac{£323.75}{100} = £3.24$$

(Cost of 35 units charged to P/L)

(*c*) *10 per cent normal loss.*

| | Input cost | Normal output Units | Unit cost |
|---|---:|---:|---:|
| Process A | £30.00 | 90 | £0.33 |

|  | Input cost | Normal output units | Unit cost |
|---|---|---|---|
| Process B | | | |
| From A (95 @ 33p) | 31.35 | | |
|  | 142.50 | | |
|  | ——— | | |
|  | 173.85 | 86 | 2.02 |
| Process C | | | |
| From B (80 @ £2.02) | 160.16 | | |
|  | 90.00 | | |
|  | ——— | | |
|  | 250.16 | 72 | 3.47 |
| Process D | | | |
| From C (70 @ £3.47) | 242.90 | | |
|  | 61.25 | | |
|  | ——— | | |
|  | 304.15 | 63 | £4.83 |

Normal output represents good output plus/minus abnormal loss/gain. Value of abnormal losses/gains is charged/credited to P/L.

(d) *Scrap value 50p per unit.*

| Process A | £30.00 | | |
|---|---|---|---|
| Normal scrap | (5.00) | | |
|  | ——— | | |
|  | 25.00 | 90 | £0.28 |
| Process B 95 @ 28p | 26.60 | | |
|  | 142.50 | | |
| Normal scrap | (4.50) | | |
|  | ——— | | |
|  | 164.60 | 86 | 1.91 |
| Process C 80 @ £1.91 | 152.80 | | |
|  | 90.00 | | |
| Normal scrap | (4.00) | | |
|  | ——— | | |
|  | 238.80 | 72 | 3.32 |
| Process D 70 @ £3.32 | 232.40 | | |
|  | 61.25 | | |
| Normal scrap | (3.50) | | |
|  | ——— | | |
|  | 290.15 | 63 | £4.61 |

5. *Apportionment of joint costs.* Arbitrary apportionment of joint costs may be misleading if the unit costs so calculated are used as an indication of relative profitability or for assessing the effect of management decisions involving joint products.

It is essential, however, to calculate unit costs for stock valuation purposes and it would seem reasonable that stock values will relate to market value. The sales value basis would therefore be an equitable way of arriving at unit costs.

6. *Cost units.*
   (a) Hotel—guest/day.
   (b) Nursing home—patient/bed day.
   (c) Electrical wholesaler—£1 of sales value.
   (d) Travel agent—client/week.

7. *Motor vehicle costs.*

| | Class A | | Class B | | Class C | |
|---|---|---|---|---|---|---|
| Mileage<br>Tonnes carried | | | | | | |
| | £ | per tonne/km | £ | per tonne/km | £ | per tonne/km |
| Fixed charges<br>    Depreciation<br>    Tax<br>    Insurance<br>    Repairs<br>    Drivers' wages (basic) | | | | | | |
| Fluctuating charges<br>    Fuel<br>    Oil<br>    Maintenance<br>    Tyres<br>    Drivers overtime/bonus | | | | | | |
| TOTAL COST | | | | | | |

## *Self-Study Test No. 7—Budgetary Control*

1. *Advantages of Budgetary Control.*

(*a*) *Co-ordination*—master budget represents an integrated plan for the whole business; achievement of individual targets facilitates achievement of overall target.

(*b*) *Motivation*—budgets are agreed by individuals responsible for achievement.

(*c*) *Advance warning*—problems likely to arise can be identified while budgets are in preparation and action taken to prevent their occurrence.

(*d*) *Communication*—management's intentions, represented by budgets, are communicated unambiguously in terms of quantities or values.

(*e*) *Control*—action can be directed to weak points indicated by variances from budget.

2. *Fixed and flexible budgets.* The I.C.M.A. *Terminology* contains explanatory definitions (*see* p. 223).

3. *Master budget.* A budget which is prepared from, and summarises, the functional budgets (I.C.M.A.). The master budget is divided into separate functional budgets, each of which is the responsibility of a particular executive. Division into functional budgets facilitates delegation of responsibility and separates the administration and control activities into manageable parts.

4. (*a*) *Budget committee:*

    (*i*) defines the main objectives;

    (*ii*) communicates policy changes;

    (*iii*) resolves conflicts between functional heads;

    (*iv*) approves master budget.

(*b*) *Budget controller:*

    (*i*) prepares procedural instructions;

(*ii*) distributes information regarding budgets;
(*iii*) develops timetables for budget preparation;
(*iv*) Arranges, and performs secretarial function for, budget meetings.

5. *Budget manual contents.*

(*a*) Organisation chart showing responsibilities for functional budgets and budget centres.
(*b*) Procedures for guidance of staff involved in budget preparation.
(*c*) Programme and timetable for budget preparation.
(*d*) Format of budget reports and recipients.
(*e*) Coding structures for Accounts, Products, Materials, etc.

6. *Sales forecast—major factors.*

(*a*) Expected increase/decrease in total demand.
(*b*) Expected increase/decrease in market share.
(*c*) Impact of general economic, political or sociological trends, e.g. tax changes.
(*d*) Effect of changes in company policy, e.g. increased advertising, launching new products.
(*e*) Production capacity available.

7. *Marketing cost—budget centres.* The structure of a marketing budget will be appropriate to the particular arrangement of executive responsibilities but a typical structure (assuming three main product groups) would be:

Product Group A.
Product Group B.
Product Group C.
Sales Offices.
Showrooms.
Packaging.
Delivery Equipment.
Warehousing.
Distribution Management.
Publicity.

The above structure reflects a situation where selling costs are controlled within product divisions and distribution costs by activity.

8. *Cash budget.*

| | January | February | March |
|---|---|---|---|
| Receipts from sales | £62,000 | £50,000 | £47,000 |
| Payments: | | | |
| Purchases | 48,000 | 81,000 | 82,000 |
| Wages | 4,000 | 3,800 | 5,200 |
| | 52,000 | 84,800 | 87,200 |
| Surplus/(deficit) for month | 10,000 | (34,800) | (40,200) |
| Opening cash/(overdraft) | 8,600 | 18,600 | (16,200) |
| Cash balance/(overdraft required) | £18,600 | £(16,200) | £(56,400) |

9. (a) *Sales Budget—September/October.*

|  | Plain | Fancy | Total |
|---|---|---|---|
| Quantity: | | | |
| September | 8,400 | 8,800 | 17,200 |
| October | 14,700 | 26,400 | 41,100 |
| | 23,100 | 35,200 | 58,300 |
| Selling price | £1.50 | £1.00 | |
| Sales value | £34,650 | £35,200 | £69,850 |

(b) *Purchase Budget—September/October.*

|  | Nuts | Plain Packages | Fancy Packages |
|---|---|---|---|
| Sales budget: | | | |
| Plain | 11,550 kg | 23,100 | |
| Fancy | 8,800 | | 35,200 |
| | 20,350 kg | 23,100 | 35,200 |
| Budgeted closing stock | 400 | 600 | 800 |
| | 20,750 | 23,700 | 36,000 |
| Opening stock | 2,000 | 1,400 | 2,000 |
| Purchase qty. | 18,750 kg | 22,300 | 34,000 |
| Purchase price | 80p | 10p | 20p |
| Budget | £15,000 | £2,230 | £6,800 |
| Total purchases budget | | £24,030 | |

### Self-Study Test No. 8—Standard Costing

1. The benefits of a standard costing system include the following:

(a) Definition of optimum manufacturing methods.

(b) Target and measure of performance provided.

(c) Corrective action focused on weak points indicated by variances.

(d) Simplified stock valuation.

(e) Basis for pricing and decision-making.

2. An ideal standard is one which reflects the achievement of maximum possible efficiency; an attainable standard is one which is expected to be achieved under normal operating conditions.

Ideal standards are not considered to be satisfactory as measures of performance because:

(a) variances will include substantial amounts which are not really capable of being eliminated;

(b) consistent failure to achieve standard tends to have a de-motivating effect;

(c) such standards have to be adjusted before they can be used as a basis for stock valuation, pricing or cost analysis.

3. *Management by exception.* In a variance accounting system, management's intentions are expressed in the form of budgets, standard costs and standard profit margins. Consequently, the absence of a variance generally confirms that the intentions have been achieved and management can concentrate its attention and resources on the areas of activity where variances are occurring, i.e. the "exceptions".

Thus economy of management time is effected by immediate concentration on the weak points.

4. *Direct material standards—main factors.*

(a) Quantities required as defined in product specification; by type and quality specification.

(b) Levels of normal scrap expected; to be reflected in standard usage.

(c) Forecast changes in raw material price levels; will affect standard prices.

(d) Total quantities to be purchased; prices may be affected as a result of quantity discounts and/or need to obtain varying sources of supply.

(e) Confirmation of product specifications; changes in design or operating methods may lead to altered material specification.

5. *Capacity ratio*:

$$\frac{\text{Hours worked}}{\text{Budgeted standard hours}} = \frac{12,600}{12,000} = \underline{105 \text{ per cent}}$$

*Production volume ratio*:

$$\frac{\text{Standard hours produced}}{\text{Budgeted standard hours}} = \frac{(420 \times 10) + (360 \times 20)}{12,000} = \underline{95 \text{ per cent}}$$

*Productivity ratio*:

$$\frac{\text{Standard hrs produced}}{\text{Actual hrs worked}} = \frac{11,400}{12,600} = \underline{90.5 \text{ per cent}}$$

6. *Standard fixed overhead absorption rate.*

(a) Develop fixed overhead budget (annual) for each budget centre.

(b) Ascertain production budget (annual) for each centre, expressed in standard hours.

(c) Calculate standard absorption rate by dividing (a) by (b).

(d) Determine standard production time for working on the relevant product in each department; the standard time will include allowances for set-up and normal idle time.

(e) Accumulate standard overhead absorption by multiplying (c) by (d) for each department.

*Self-Study Test No. 9—Analysis of Variances*

1. *Product A.*

| | | |
|---|---|---:|
| (a) | Actual materials cost | £1,030 |
| | *Materials price variance $((b)-(a))$* | 45 (F) |
| (b) | Actual usage at standard prices $(860 \times £1.25)$ | 1,075 |
| | *Materials usage variance $((c)-(b))$* | 25 (A) |
| (c) | Standard material cost of production $(420 \text{ units} \times 2 \text{ kilos} \times £1.25)$ | £1,050 |
| (d) | Actual labour cost | £180 |
| | *Wages rate variance $((e)-(d))$* | 7 (A) |
| (e) | Actual hours at standard rate $(72 \times £2.40)$ | 173 |
| | *Labour efficiency variance $((f)-(e))$* | 5 (A) |
| (f) | Standard wages cost of production $(420 \text{ units} \times \frac{1}{6} \text{ hr} \times £2.40)$ | £168 |

2. Possible causes of variances in (1) above:

>    Materials price:
>       change of supplier;
>       additional quantity discount.
>    Materials usage:
>       higher scrap level;
>       inferior quality of material.
>    Wages rate:
>       higher than planned increase in rates of pay;
>       unplanned use of skilled labour.
>    Labour efficiency:
>       minor stoppage arising from faulty scheduling;
>       inexperienced operative used.

3. *Related variances.* As in (2) above, supply of inferior quality material could cause a favourable price variance but lead to an adverse usage variance because of difficulty in working.

Use of inexperienced labour could incur higher average hourly rate by needing highly-skilled operative for training purposes and also result in lower than standard efficiency while operatives are being trained.

4. *Department X.* Standard fixed overhead absorption rate

$$= \frac{£14,000}{1,400 \text{ units}} = £10 \text{ per unit}$$

or

$$\frac{£14,000}{40 \text{ hrs}} = £350 \text{ per hour}$$

(a) Actual fixed overhead                                          £15,000
      *Expenditure variance* ((b)−(a))                 1,000(A)

(b) Budgeted fixed overhead                                    14,000
      *Volume variance* ((c)−(b))                       2,000(A)

(c) Fixed overhead absorbed
    (1,200 units × £10)                                  £12,000

Budgeted fixed overhead                                      £14,000
Overhead absorbed on hours worked:
    (32 × £350)                                            11,200

    *Capacity variance*                                                £2,800(A)
Overhead absorbed on hours worked    11,200
Overhead absorbed in production         12,000

    *Productivity variance*                                            800(F)

Volume variance                                                        £2,000(A)

5. *Possible causes.*

   (a) *Expenditure variance*:
     (i) Higher charges for fixed overhead items, e.g. rent, rates.
     (ii) Unplanned use of resources, e.g. new machine (higher depreciation charge) additional supervisor.
   (b) *Capacity variance*:
     (i) Less production required due to shortfall in sales demand.
     (ii) Unplanned stoppages, e.g. power failure, shortage of materials.
   (c) *Productivity variance*:
     (i) Higher rate of output due to use of new machine.
     (ii) Less waiting time arising from improved scheduling.

6. *Stancost Ltd.*
Actual sales value                                                    £20,050
Standard cost of actual sales:
    A: 10,500 units at 90p                  9,450
    B: 5,000 units at £1.25                  6,250
                                     15,700

    Actual margin                                    4,350
    Budgeted margin                               2,000

Sales margin variance                                          £2,350(F)

Sales price variance:
    A: £11,550−(10,500×£1)                1,050
    B: £8,500−(5,000×£1.50)              1,000
                                     2,050

Sales volume variance:

| | | |
|---|---:|---:|
| A: 500 units at 10p | 50 | |
| B: 1,000 units at 25p | 250 | |
| | — | 300 |
| Sales margin variance | | £2,350 |

7. (a) *Journal entries.*

|  | Dr. | Cr. |
|---|---:|---:|
| (i) Raw materials (60,000 at £1.20) | £72,000 | |
| Materials price variance | 1,200 | |
| Cost ledger contra | | £73,200 |
| Purchases of raw materials for stock at standard price | | |

|  | | |
|---|---:|---:|
| (ii) Work in progress (54,000 at £1.20) | £64,800 | |
| Raw materials | | £64,800 |
| Issues of raw materials at standard prices | | |

|  | | |
|---|---:|---:|
| (iii) Work in progress (20,550 at £1.80) | £36,990 | |
| Wages rate variance | 822 | |
| Cost ledger contra | | £37,812 |
| Direct wages at standard rates | | |

|  | | |
|---|---:|---:|
| (iv) Work in progress (budget) | £48,600 | |
| Overhead expenditure variance | 960 | |
| Cost ledger contra | | £49,560 |
| Overhead distribution and variance | | |

|  | | |
|---|---:|---:|
| (v) Finished goods (3,400 units at £45) | £153,000 | |
| Material usage variance (3,000 kg) | 3,600 | |
| Labour efficiency variance (150 hrs) | 270 | |
| Overhead productivity variance (150 hrs) | 405 | |
| Overhead capacity variance (2,550 hrs) | | £6,885 |
| Work in progress | | 150,390 |
| Output of 3,400 units transferred to stock at standard cost | | |

|  | | |
|---|---:|---:|
| (vi) Cost of sales (4,500 units at £45) | £202,500 | |
| Finished goods | | 202,500 |
| Standard cost of 4,500 units sold | | |

|  | | |
|---|---:|---:|
| (vii) Cost ledger contra | £270,000 | |
| Sales (4,500 units at £60) | | £270,000 |
| Sales at standard selling price | | |

(b) *Ledger accounts.*

### Raw Materials Stock

| | | | |
|---|---|---|---|
| Balance b/f | £21,600 | W.I.P. (*ii*) | £64,800 |
| Purchases (*i*) | 72,000 | Balance c/f | 28,800 |
| | £93,600 | | £93,600 |

### Work in Progress

| | | | |
|---|---|---|---|
| Raw materials (*ii*) | £64,800 | Finished goods (*v*) | £153,000 |
| Direct wages (*iii*) | 36,990 | | |
| Overhead (*iv*) | 48,600 | | |
| Variances (*v*) | 2,610 | | |
| | £153,000 | | £153,000 |

### Finished Goods

| | | | |
|---|---|---|---|
| Balance b/f | £90,000 | Cost of sales (*vi*) | £202,500 |
| W.I.P. (*v*) | 153,000 | Balance c/f | 40,500 |
| | £243,000 | | £243,000 |

(c)          *Operating Profit Statement*

| | | | |
|---|---|---|---|
| Budgeted operating profit (3,000 units at £15) | | | £45,000 |
| *Add*: Sales margin variance (1,500 at £15) | | | 22,500 |
| Standard margin on actual sales | | | 67,500 |

| Variances | Adv. | Fav. | |
|---|---|---|---|
| Materials price | £1,200 | | |
| Wages rate | 822 | | |
| Overhead expenditure | 960 | | |
| Material usage | 3,600 | | |
| Labour efficiency | 270 | | |
| Overhead productivity | 405 | | |
| Overhead capacity | | 6,885 | |
| | £7,257 | £6,885 | 372(A) |
| Actual operating profit | | | £67,128 |

NOTE: Actual profit reconciles as follows:

| | | |
|---|---:|---:|
| Sales (4,500 units at standard) | | £270,000 |
| Actual costs for the period: | | |
| Materials | £73,200 | |
| Wages | 37,812 | |
| Overhead | 49,560 | |
| | 160,572 | |
| Finished goods stock reduction (at std.) | 49,500 | |
| Materials stock increased at std. | (7,200) | |
| | | 202,872 |
| | | £67,128 |

8. *Revision variance/stock revaluation variance*. The I.C.M.A. *Terminology* provides a description of these variances (*see* p. 269).

### Self-Study Test No. 10—Relevant Costs

1. (*a*) *Total absorption costing*.

| | | | |
|---|---:|---:|---:|
| Sales value (380 at £25) | | | £9,500 |
| Materials/Wages (420 at £10.50) | 4,410 | | |
| Fixed overhead | 3,360 | | |
| | | 7,770 | |
| Closing stock (£7,770 × $\frac{40}{420}$) | | 740 | |
| Cost of sales | | 7,030 | |
| *Profit* | | | £2,470 |

(*b*) *Standard costing*.

| | | | |
|---|---:|---:|---:|
| Sales | | | £9,500 |
| Production at standard cost (420 at £18) | 7,560 | | |
| Closing stock at standard cost (40 at £18) | 720 | | |
| | | 6,840 | |
| Standard margin | | 2,660 | |
| Variances: | | | |
| Material price | 126 (A) | | |
| Wages rate | 84 (A) | | |
| Overhead volume (20 at £8) | 160 (F) | | |
| Overhead expenditure | 160 (A) | 210 (A) | |
| *Profit* | | | £2,450 |

NOTE: Standard overhead absorption rate = £8 per unit (£3,200 ÷ 400) and a volume variance arises in respect of the 20 units produced in excess of budget.

(c) *Marginal costing.*

| | | |
|---|---:|---:|
| Sales | | £9,500 |
| Variable cost of Sales: | | |
| Production (420 at £10.50) | 4,410 | |
| Closing stock (40 at £10.50) | 420 | |
| | | 3,990 |
| Contribution | | 5,510 |
| Fixed overhead | | 3,360 |
| *Profit* | | £2,150 |

2. *Optimum production plan.*

| | Bruise | Break | Crunch |
|---|---:|---:|---:|
| Selling price | £40 | £60 | £100 |
| Variable costs per unit | 14 | 26 | 44 |
| Contribution per unit | £26 | £34 | £56 |
| Contribution per £1 material cost | £3.25 | £2.125 | £2.33 |
| Priority | (1) | (3) | (2) |

| Minimum production | Units | Material cost Per unit | Required |
|---|---:|---:|---:|
| Bruise | 100 | £8 | £800 |
| Break | 100 | 16 | 1,600 |
| Crunch | 100 | 24 | 2,400 |
| | | | 4,800 |

Balance to meet demand in priority indicated:

| | | | |
|---|---:|---:|---:|
| Bruise | 100 | £8 | 800 |
| Crunch | 100 | 24 | 2,400 |
| | | | £8,000 |

*Budgeted Profit.*

| | | | |
|---|---|---:|---:|
| Contribution: | | | |
| | Bruise  200 × £26 | £5,200 | |
| | Crunch 200 × £56 | 11,200 | |
| | Break   100 × £34 | 3,400 | |
| | | 19,800 | |
| Fixed overhead: | | | |
| | 200 × £(12 + 20 + 40) | 14,400 | |
| | | £5,400 | |

3. (a) *Redraft of Profit and Loss Statement.*

|  | Total | A | C |
|---|---|---|---|
| Sales | £180,000 | £30,000 | £150,000 |
| Variable costs: |  |  |  |
| Production | 112,000 | 16,000 | 96,000 |
| Marketing | 10,800 | 5,400 | 5,400 |
|  | 122,800 | 21,400 | 101,400 |
| Contribution | 57,200 | 8,600 | 48,600 |
| Fixed production and marketing costs | 44,000 |  |  |
| Net profit | £13,200 |  |  |

(b) *Comments.* Elimination of product B reduces profit by £6,800, which is the contribution made by that product to common fixed costs. It is unlikely that such costs could be reduced in total by that amount (about 16 per cent) if product B were eliminated and, therefore, management should not eliminate product B unless the resources could be used more profitably.

4. *Make or buy decision factors.*

(a) *Financial.*

(i) Apportioned fixed costs included in figures described by cost accounts.

(ii) Possible savings in specific or general fixed costs obtained by outside purchase; or cost of additional facilities required to continue manufacture.

(iii) Possible revenue or cost reduction obtained from alternative use of resources.

(iv) Penalty costs, e.g. redundancy payments.

(b) *Non-financial.*

(i) Loss of control over source of supply.

(ii) Impaired employee relations if staff are laid-off.

(iii) Effect of longer term forecasts of demand or changes in production requirements

5. (a) *Budgeted profit.*

|  | 1 | 2 | 3 |
|---|---|---|---|
| Sales | £20,000 | £20,000 | £20,000 |
| Variable costs | 15,000 | 12,500 | 10,000 |
| Contribution | 5,000 | 7,500 | 10,000 |
| Fixed costs | 3,000 | 5,500 | 8,000 |
| Profit | £2,000 | £2,000 | £2,000 |

(*b*) *Break-even point.*

$$\frac{\text{Fixed costs}}{\text{Unit contribution}} = \frac{\text{£3,000}}{\text{50p}} \quad \frac{\text{£5,500}}{\text{75p}} \quad \frac{\text{£8,000}}{\text{£1}}$$

$$= \quad \text{6,000 units} \quad \text{7,333 units} \quad \text{8,000 units}$$

(*c*) *Margin of safety.*

| | | | |
|---|---|---|---|
| Units (Budget—B/even) | 4,000 | 2,667 | 2,000 |
| Total capacity | 12,500 | 12,500 | 12,500 |
| Percentage | 32% | 21% | 16% |

(*d*) *Impact of 10 per cent deviation.*

| | | | |
|---|---|---|---|
| 1,000 units at contribution per unit | £500 | £750 | £1,000 |

*Comments.* Company 3 is particularly vulnerable to a reduction in sales volume because of the low margin of safety. It does have, however, the highest potential net profit, i.e. £4,500 at maximum capacity.

6. *Break-even chart.*

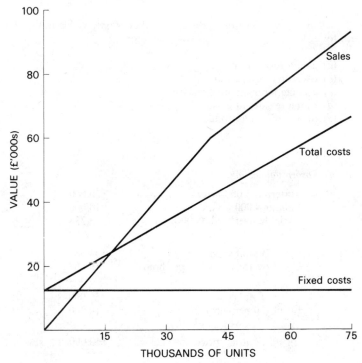

7. (a) Unit contribution = £120 − £(20 + 40 + 30) = £30

|     |     |     |     |     |
|-----|-----|-----|-----|-----|
| (i) | B/e point | £18,000 ÷ £30 | = | 600 units |
| (ii) | Maximum profit = (2,000 × £30) − £18,000 = | | | £42,000 |
| (iii) | Forecast profit = (1,600 × £30) − £18,000 = | | | £30,000 |

(b) Profit from order.

| | |
|---|---|
| Contribution: 400 units at £20 | £8,000 |
| Additional costs | 6,000 |
| Additional profit | £2,000 |

The order should be accepted provided that management is satisfied that:

(i) maximum production can be achieved; if production has to be diverted from the home market, the profit could soon be lost;
(ii) export sales at a lower price will not affect existing customer relationships.

8. *Selling prices below total cost.* Such policy is only viable in the short term to:

(a) gain a foothold in a new market;
(b) overcome competition;
(c) use temporary spare capacity;
(d) promote sales of a "tied" product;
(e) dispose of a by-product.

9. (a) *Absorption costing.*

| | |
|---|---|
| Materials 5,000 litres | £20,000 |
| Labour 4,000 hours | 10,000 |
| Variable overhead 4,000 hours | 3,333 |
| Variable cost | £33,333 |
| Fixed overhead £4.167 per hour | 16,667 |
| Total cost | 50,000 |
| Profit (20 per cent) | 10,000 |
| Contract price | £60,000 |

(b) *Material supply limited.*

| | |
|---|---:|
| Variable costs (as (a)) | £33,333 |
| Contribution: 5,000 litres at £7.60 | 38,000 |
| Contract price | £71,333 |

(c) *Labour limited.*

| | |
|---|---:|
| Variable costs | £33,333 |
| Contribution: 4,000 hours at £6.33 | 25,333 |
| Contract price | £58,666 |

If material supply is limited, the minimum contract price must maintain the budgeted contribution per unit of limiting factor, i.e.

$$\frac{£(125,000+65,000)}{25,000 \text{ litres}} = £7.60 \text{ per litre.}$$

Similarly, the budgeted contribution per labour hour is £190,000 ÷ 30,000 hours = £6.33.

### Self-Study Test No. 11—Double-Entry Aspects

1. *Cost ledger balances.*

(a) *Cost ledger contra*—the offset to balances on the cost accounts arising from entries which partly affect financial accounts, e.g. debtors, creditors.

(b) *Stores ledger*—the total cost value of raw materials in stock; arises from purchases less issues to production.

(c) *Work in progress*—the accumulated cost of uncompleted jobs; the account is debited with materials issued, allocated wages and overhead absorbed.

(d) *Finished goods*—the accumulated cost of jobs awaiting delivery to the customer; cost values are transferred from work-in-progress on completion.

(e) *Factory overhead*—under-absorbed overhead, i.e. the difference between factory overhead incurred for the period and the amount absorbed by means of a predetermined rate.

(f) *Administration cost*—similar to (f) but the balance represents the amount over-absorbed.

2. (a) *Reconciliation.* Cost and financial accounts will differ because of:
   (i) financial items not recorded in the cost accounts;
   (ii) costs or revenues treated differently;
   (iii) notional costs not reflected in the financial accounts.

Reconciliation is effected by adjusting one set of results for all known variations and by locating and correcting errors until the different results can be satisfactorily explained.

(b)

| | Add | Deduct | |
|---|---|---|---|
| Profit per Cost Accounts | | | £48,390 |
| Stock valuation: | | | |
| Raw materials | £19 | | |
| W.I.P. | 50 | | |
| Finished goods | | £714 | |
| Depreciation | 273 | | |
| | £342 | £714 | 372 |
| | | | £48,018 |

| | | | |
|---|---|---|---|
| Per Financial Accounts: | | | |
| Gross profit | | | £73,800 |
| *Less*: Administration | | 15,600 | |
| Distribution | | 10,182 | |
| | | | 25,782 |
| | | | £48,018 |

NOTE: All other items in the Profit and Loss Account would not appear in the Cost Accounts.

3. (a) *Journal entries.*

| | | |
|---|---|---|
| (1) Stores ledger control | £15,122 | |
| Cost ledger contra | | £15,122 |
| Invoices for materials | | |
| (2) Wages control | £8,900 | |
| Cost ledger contra | | £8,900 |
| Gross wages | | |
| (3) Work in progress | £14,185 | |
| Stores ledger control | | £14,185 |
| Materials issued | | |
| (4) Work in progress | £6,000 | |
| Factory overhead control | 3,012 | |
| Wages control | | £9,012 |
| Allocated wages | | |
| (5) Factory overhead control | £870 | |
| Stores ledger control | | £870 |
| Indirect materials issued | | |
| (6) Factory overhead control | £2,124 | |
| Cost ledger contra | | £2,124 |
| Overhead invoices | | |
| (7) Finished stock | £19,000 | |
| Work in progress | | £19,000 |
| Prime cost of goods completed (opening stock + materials/wages − closing stock) | | |

| (8) Finished stock | £6,000 | |
| Factory overhead | | £6,000 |

Absorbed overhead (100 per cent direct wages)

| (9) Cost of sales | £23,000 | |
| Finished stock | | £23,000 |

Factory cost of sales (opening stock +(7)+(8)− closing stock)

| (10) Administration overhead | £3,100 | |
| Marketing overhead | £2,050 | |
| Cost ledger contra | | £5,150 |

Overhead incurred

| (11) Cost ledger contra | £32,000 | |
| Sales | | £32,000 |

Sales

*(b) Trial Balance.*

| | | |
|---|---|---|
| Cost ledger contra | £35,504 | |
| Stores ledger control | 1,915 | |
| Work in progress | 4,380 | |
| Wages control | | £423 |
| Factory overhead control | 174 | |
| Finished goods stock | 14,000 | |
| Cost of sales | 205,000 | |
| Administration overhead control | 30,900 | |
| Marketing overhead control | 20,550 | |
| Sales | | 312,000 |
| | £312,423 | £312,423 |

4. *Integrated accounting.* A single set of accounts which provides both financial and management accounting information.

*Benefits.*

(*a*) Obviates need for reconciliation.

(*b*) More reliance can be placed on cost information as subject to formal control procedures.

(*c*) Facilities development of integrated systems, e.g. stock control, payroll, which incorporate accounting records.

5. *Cost audit—Purchasing and Stores.*

(*a*) Functions:

    (*i*) Requisitioning.
    (*ii*) Purchasing.
    (*iii*) Receiving.
    (*iv*) Storekeeping.
    (*v*) Stock control.
    (*vi*) Issuing.

(*vii*) Payment of suppliers.

(*b*) *Important points:*

(*i*) Authority to request purchase clearly defined.

(*ii*) Comprehensive records of suppliers available.

(*iii*) Adequate inspection procedures laid down and tolerances specified.

(*iv*) Detailed instructions available for protecting materials.

(*v*) Maximum, minimum and re-order stock levels specified and regularly reviewed.

(*vi*) Schedule of employees authorised to requisition materials available.

(*vii*) Adequate supporting information for processing payments.

6. *Principles of coding.*

(*a*) *Simplicity*—the structure should be consistent in terms of number of digits and arrangement of sub-codes.

(*b*) *Flexibility*—capable of being adjusted to meet changes in requirements.

(*c*) *Unambiguity*—assigned codes should be such that duplication is prevented.

(*d*) *Controllability*—the coding structure should be properly documented and responsibility for creating new codes defined.

7. *Uniform costing—overhead costs.*

(*a*) *Functional classification*—a schedule showing the types of cost considered appropriate to each function.

(*b*) *Item classification*—a schedule indicating the recommended grouping and/or sub-analysis of cost items.

(*c*) *Direct/indirect*—recommendations concerning treatment of items where complex apportionment procedures are impractical and where alternative treatment is possible, e.g. overtime premium, estimating costs.

(*d*) *Bases of apportionment*—suggested bases for apportioning to cost centres and for apportioning service departments to production.

(*e*) *Absorption methods*—recommended bases for typical cost centres, recommended treatment of administrative/marketing overhead and guidelines concerning overhead included in work in progress and finished stock.

# Index

Details of some other Macdonald & Evans publications on related subjects can be found on the following pages.

For a full list of titles and prices write for the FREE Macdonald & Evans Business Studies catalogue and/or complete M & E Handbook list, available from Department BP1, Macdonald & Evans Ltd., Estover Road, Plymouth PL6 7PZ

## Advanced Cost Accountancy
### J. BATTY

This book, intended as a companion volume to the author's *Management Accountancy*, attempts to present the latest ideas concerning cost accountancy. A detailed treatment of process costing is given, and a comparison between marginal and absorption costing; the term "responsibility costing" has been coined to describe the costing approach combining the best features of both techniques. Personnel aspects are also discussed in some detail.

*Illustrated*


## Advanced Economics
### G. L. THIRKETTLE

This HANDBOOK, is intended as the successor to the author's *Basic Economics*. Students preparing for the final examinations of professional bodies will find that it deals in considerable detail with theoretical aspects of economics and also covers most of the ground of the theory of first-degree courses. Every chapter is extensively illustrated with graphs and diagrams.

*Illustrated*


## Applied Economics
### E. SEDDON & J.D.S. APPLETON

This HANDBOOK is intended for a very wide range of students, from those taking G.C.E. "A" Level to those preparing for papers in Applied Economics in the examinations of academic and professional bodies. It analyses the main problems which confront the British economy today and tests the validity of theoretical solutions to these problems against the results that have been achieved.

*Illustrated*

## British Tax Law
### MERVYN LEWIS

For law and accountancy students of taxation and for professional practitioners, this book states the main principles of tax law in relation to the major direct taxes and explains them in considerable depth, illustrating the practical application of various statutory rules with numerous examples of a computational nature.


## Business Administration
### L. HALL

This HANDBOOK, specially written for students preparing for A.C.A., I.C.M.A. and I.C.S.A. examinations in business administration and office management, describes the general principles of management, including the most up-to-date techniques, and sets out the organisation and control of office procedure in some detail. Personnel management, channels of communication, marketing and sales are also covered.


## Business and Financial Management
### B. K. R. WATTS

This HANDBOOK is intended primarily for students preparing for I.C.A. and A.C.A. examinations or for any other intermediate or final professional examinations where a knowledge of industrial structure, investment and financial management is required. "This book is a most competent and concise summary on a wide range of financial matters. If you do not know much about — let us say — the sources of export finance, this book will tell you where to start." *The Director*
*Illustrated*

## Business Mathematics
### L. W. T. STAFFORD
This HANDBOOK is designed for the business student taking the examinations of the professional bodies, universities and technical colleges, which increasingly require a knowledge of mathematics. Also for those already in business who feel they have an insufficient grasp of the newer mathematical techniques and their applications in the fields of finance, operational research and mathematical statistics.
*Illustrated*

## Commercial and Industrial Law
### A. R. RUFF
This new HANDBOOK aims to take account of the considerable body of industrial and commercial legislation, especially that enacted in recent years. In addition, more detail is given to the law of contract than is usually possible in a book of this nature. This book will be invaluable to students, personnel officers, and to others concerned with the administration of factories and offices.

## Corporate Planning and Control
### R. G. ANDERSON
The prime purpose of this HANDBOOK is to provide a framework for systematically planning and controlling the operations of a business. The interrelationships of related functions and systems are studied in detail, as are the uses of management information in providing a firm foundation on which to build an effective business structure. It has proved invaluable to students taking the various professional examinations in the subject.
*Illustrated*

## Data Processing and Management Information Systems
### R. G. ANDERSON
This HANDBOOK, winner of the Annual Textbook Award of the S.C.C.A., provides a comprehensive study of the field of data processing, embracing manual, electro-mechanical and electronic systems and covering such topics as data transmission, systems analysis and computer programming. It is designed to fill the needs of students preparing for examinations in data processing and computer applications and "will also be valuable to those no longer concerned with examinations who require an understanding of the method and techniques available for the processing of data for management". *The Commercial Accountant*
*Illustrated*

## A Dictionary of Economics and Commerce
### J. L. HANSON
Most of the entries in this dictionary refer to principles of economic theory and applied economics. They enable the reader quickly to find an explanation – not merely a definition – of some matter of economic interest without having to search through a number of books for it.
*Illustrated*

## Economic Theory and Organisation
### ALFRED G. McARTHUR & JOHN W. LOVERIDGE
This textbook has been written with a view to the requirements of the Economics syllabuses of the B.I.M., I.W.M., I.B., H.N.C./D. in Business Studies, I.C.S.A., I.C.M.A. and A.C.A. ". . . a high quality product . . . deserves a good share of the market which is its concern". *Times Higher Education Supplement*
*Illustrated*

## Economics for Professional Studies
### HENRY TOCH
This HANDBOOK draws on the author's experience over fifteen years of teaching economics to professional students, and uses topical situations and examples to illustrate a detailed survey of economic theory and practice.
*Illustrated*

## English for Professional Examinations
### J. R. L. McINTYRE
This HANDBOOK — previously entitled *Intermediate English* — has been retitled to reflect the wide range of readers for whom the new edition caters. Students of professional intermediate examinations and those taking "O" and "A" Level English will find guidance on how to approach the most recent style of questions, many of which are included.

## Framework of Accountancy
### C. C. MAGEE
Presenting the essentials of accounting theory in the context of financial and economic activity, this book will be of value to first-year students of accountancy who propose to carry their studies into a second or third year. The conceptual approach to the subject has been followed throughout, and emphasis has been placed on the significance of the information that appears in accounting reports.

## Income Tax
### HENRY TOCH
Intended for students in accountancy, law, secretarial practice and business studies, this HANDBOOK explains in concise form the basic principles of income-tax law and pratice. Regularly updated

## Industrial Administration and Management
### J. BATTY, *assisted by specialist contributors*
This book gives concise coverage of the subject of industrial administration, emphasising the latest ideas such as ergonomics, value analysis, work study, marginal costing, budgetary control, the seven-point plan and job evaluation. Its practical slant should make the book very useful to working managers, although its scope was determined by the syllabuses of the various examining bodies.
*Illustrated*

## Managerial Standard Costing
### J. BATTY
A companion volume to the highly successful *Standard Costing,* this is a comprehensive study of, and comparison between, the principles and practice of the managerial aspects of standard costing. The author provides completely new information about the role of standard costing as a tool of management which will be invaluable for furthering the working harmony between accountant and manager.
*Illustrated*

## Model Business Letters
### L. GARTSIDE
Over 500 specimen letters, indexed for quick reference, deal with almost any business situation likely to arise, with a commentary outlining the commercial and legal relationships each one creates. Other features are the glossaries of terms and classified lists of expressions useful when composing letters. This edition incorporates some additions to the explanatory text providing more detailed information on certain types of transactions.